Yale Russian and East European Studies, 11

FENYO, Mario D. Hitler, Horthy, and Hungary; German-Hungarian relations, 1941–1944. Yale, 1972. 279p tab bibl 72-75189. 10.00.   ISBN 0-300-01468-6
Polemical writing by Central Europeans about Hungary's role in World War II, as the author points out, is mainly of two sorts. On the one hand, the apologetic accounts of Hungarian conservative exiles exaggerate Horthy's resistance to Hitler; on the other, the Hungarian Communist as well as German non-Communist interpretations exaggerate Hungary's eagerness to collaborate with Hitler. Fenyo strikes a judicious balance between these biases. His book particularly well supplements C. A. Macartney's *A history of Hungary, 1929–1945* (2v., 1957), which was published as *October fifteenth* in Great Britain, so far the principal Western scholarly work in the field. Fenyo makes good use of German and Hungarian documents which, in the 1950s, when Macartney wrote his monograph, were either unprocessed or unavailable. In addition to being a good scholar, Fenyo writes well (he dedicates his book to the memory of his father, a distinguished man of modern Hungarian letters). His book should be welcomed both by scholars and by the general public interested in Central Europe.

CHOICE   *MAY '73*

History, Geography &

Travel

Europe

HITLER, HORTHY, and HUNGARY

German-Hungarian Relations, 1941–1944

by Mario D. Fenyo

New Haven and London, Yale University Press

1972

Published with assistance from the foundation
established in memory of Philip Hamilton McMillan
of the Class of 1894, Yale College.

Library of Congress catalog card number: 72-75189
International standard book number: 0-300-01468-6

Designed by John O. C. McCrillis
and set in Baskerville type.
Printed in the United States of America by
The Vail-Ballou Press, Inc., Binghamton, N.Y.

Published in Great Britain, Europe, and Africa by
Yale University Press, Ltd., London.
Distributed in Canada by McGill-Queen's University
Press, Montreal; in Latin America by Kaiman & Polon,
Inc., New York City; in Australasia and Southeast
Asia by John Wiley & Sons Australasia Pty. Ltd.,
Sydney; in India by UBS Publishers' Distributors Pvt.,
Ltd., Delhi; in Japan by John Weatherhill, Inc., Tokyo.

To Max Fenyo, † 1972

Contents

Preface

The history of Hungary and of Hungarian-German relations during World War II has become the subject of controversy. There are less than a dozen monographs covering aspects of Hungarian history in the 1930s and early 1940s in detail; but there are scores of articles debating some of the key issues in this period—the Hungarian declaration of war on the Soviet Union in June 1941, the German occupation of Hungary, the coup d'état of October 15, 1944, and the persecution of the Jews. Most of these monographs and articles are the work of historians or other social scientists writing in good faith; yet what diversity of interpretations, how much variation even in the relation of facts and events! How promising a field for the student of history wishing to exercise his critical faculties!

My study is based to a large extent on German documents. While the Hungarian authorities were kind enough to allow me a free examination of pertinent materials in the Hungarian National Archives, these materials proved to be incomplete, the most important documents having been destroyed by order of the Hungarian prime minister about March 19, 1944, when the German troops occupied his country.[1] The records of the Hungarian Foreign Ministry suffered damage once again, at the time of the uprising of 1956; most of the documents I have handled seemed to have been retrieved from pools of water. Some of these documents already have been included in the documentary series published by the Hungarian Academy of Sciences. The documents on Hungarian foreign policy, selected for publication in the series from among the limited number that have survived, have been edited with competence and scientific purpose.

The German documents used in this study include the documents of the German Foreign Office, of the armed forces (OKW) and the Army High Command (OKH), of German army units down to the division level, and of other ministries and organs of the Reich government. These documents were captured by the western Allied forces as they occupied much of German territory. A few of the documents were used or merely collected in connection with the Nurem-

1. Prime Minister Miklós Kállay wrote in his memoirs: "I ordered the burning of the secret archives of the ministries of foreign affairs, the interior, the defense, and others, of the more important offices, and of course, most of my own ministry" (*Hungarian Premier*, p. 425, also p. xxxii).

berg trials, but most of them were removed from the country and taken to Whaddon Hall in England or to Alexandria, Virginia, where great quantities of them were microfilmed. With few exceptions, the documents have by now been returned to the German Federal Republic; in most cases I have resorted to the microfilm copies in the custody of the National Archives of the United States.

My reliance on the German documentation has certain implications. These documents reveal the arguments of the National Socialist leaders, and sometimes even their methods and long-range objectives. These methods often involved pressure in one form or another, and the facts of Hungarian history in this period may indicate to what extent these pressures were effective. The German documents cannot show to what extent these pressures were actually necessary and to what extent the Hungarian government may have been prepared to meet the German requests of its own accord.

My reliance on German documentation resulted, I hope, in a balanced interpretation. I have considered German-Hungarian relations mainly from a Hungarian point of view. It was, I believe, logical to do so. Even during the war when the business of the Reich Foreign Office must have been sharply curtailed because Germany maintained relations with only a score of countries, Hungary was not of paramount interest to National Socialist Germany; notwithstanding, I will attempt to show that because of certain resources in Hungary and because of the contracting sphere of German influence in the last stages of the war, Hungary came to acquire very nearly a paramount position. "Hitler rather disliked Hungarians and, in any case, he regarded them as unimportant," writes Professor Macartney.[2] Perhaps Ambassador Paul Schmidt was also correct in maintaining that Hitler despised the Magyars.[3] On the other hand, Hitler had not always spoken unkindly of them; there is some indication he admired their martial virtues until he became convinced these were imaginary or strictly a matter of the past. More relevant is what the Hungarian leaders thought of Hitler, and what were Hungary's relations with National Socialist Germany. To Hungary, relations with Germany and Italy were of paramount importance, and the influence of Germany in Hungarian affairs grew as that of Italy declined to the point where Hungary herself became one of the occupied territories. I

2. Carlyle Aylmer Macartney, "Hungary's Declaration of War on the U.S.S.R. in 1941," p. 155.

3. Paul Schmidt, *Hitler's Interpreter,* p. 206.

have hoped to compensate for approaching the problem of German-Hungarian relations from a Hungarian point of view by relying heavily on German documentation.

Certain problems I have purposefully omitted. I have not dealt with the important problem of the German ethnic groups in Hungary, the "Souabians" in Hungary proper, and the "Saxons" of Transylvania. Their fate was of greatest concern to the leaders of the Reich, and this concern may explain the recurrent antagonism of many of these leaders toward Hungarians whom they tended to regard as chauvinists.[4] Perhaps the main reason I have neglected to deal with this issue was lack of interest on my part, but another reason is that the volume of this study might have had to be doubled. Furthermore, an excellent study on the subject has been written by Professor Géza Paikert; it is titled *The Danube Swabians: German Populations in Hungary, Rumania, Yugoslavia, and Hitler's Impact on Their Patterns* (The Hague: Martinus Nijhoff, 1967). As for strictly military matters, I have touched on these only occasionally: I understand a group of former Hungarian officers living in the United States and Great Britain is preparing a study, or a series of studies, on that subject.

I have also omitted the introduction. It is true that Hungarian foreign policy was determined by geographic, geopolitic, economic, psychological, and a number of other factors. Rather than write an introduction containing this essential background information I preferred to begin in medias res and to mix in the background information with several of the chapters. I have discussed Hungary's economic relations with Germany in the between-the-wars period along with Hungary's economic relations during the war. I have given indications of Hungary's geographic and geopolitical predicament as flashbacks in the course of the first chapter. Here and there I made references to those emotional and psychological factors which accounted to a large extent for an atmosphere of anti-Semitism and for a considerable degree of Hungarian sympathy toward the cause of National Socialist Germany.

I feel the style of my study requires an explanation. The study of history is my chosen field because I find historical research exciting. I want to share some of my excitement with the reader. Rather

---

4. Hitler's off-the-cuff remark: "Die Ungarn sind die durchkochtesten Nationalisten, die es gibt" (Henry Picker, ed., *Hitlers Tischgespräche im Führerhauptquartier, 1941–1942*, p. 183).

than attempt to camouflage the research process, rather than pretend I had proceeded in a systematic and infallible way to discover the truth regarding Hungarian-German relations, I have preferred to let the reader perceive the groping, fumbling nature of my investigations. I am aware of the drawback: my study appears rough, unfinished. On the other hand, I am convinced the process of investigation itself is interesting, perhaps as interesting as the topics or materials under investigation. At least I will have earned a reputation of honesty in my endeavor.

Within these limitations I have attempted a study that is factual and easy to interpret. If I have been at all successful it is thanks to my former professors at the American University in Washington, D.C., who have spent days or perhaps weeks on the weary dissection of my original draft, improving both my method of approach and my style: Carl G. Anthon, Jean Joughin, Béla Maday, and Ivan Rudnytsky. I am particularly grateful to Professor István Deák, Director of the Institute on East Central Europe at Columbia University, not only for the many suggestions for improvement, all of them warranted, but also for the encouragement he gave to finish my task. Professor Robert L. Zangrando, both as editor and as historian, has given me much valuable help. So has Mrs. Barbara Palmer, who is to be credited with a thorough job of editing. I wish to thank Dr. Elek Karsai, who not only helped me find some pertinent materials in the Hungarian National Archives but combed through my manuscript and found a number of errors. I am indebted to Professor George Barany whose conscientiousness in scholarship prompts others to be likewise. Nor could I have written this study without the assistance of Mr. Robert Wolfe of the National Archives in Washington, who imparts his expert knowledge of German documents and of recent German history readily and graciously. I must also thank the management of the National Archives for making these documents or microfilms available to me and for encouraging me in my research.

M. D. F.

Universidad Católica de Puerto Rico
August 1971

1. How Hungary Came to Declare War against the Soviet Union

Sunday, June 22, 1941, the German armies in the East, supported by Romanian and Finnish forces, attacked the Soviet Union; four days later, on June 26, some military aircraft appeared over the city of Kassa (Košice), then in northeastern Hungary,[1] circled over the city, and dropped bombs, causing casualties and damaging property. The headlines in the daily newspapers, based on the reports of the Hungarian Wire Service (MTI), uniformly read: "Soviet aircraft carried out attacks against Hungarian sovereign territory Thursday!" Furthermore, "Kassa was bombed: five dead, several wounded, a few buildings damaged. . . . A second bombing of Kassa and the penetration of the Budapest air space by the Soviet aircraft were prevented by the Hungarian antiaircraft defense."[2] In somewhat greater detail, the reports of the wire service explained that the attack was carried out by three Soviet aircraft "provided with misleading markings" and that they dropped about eight bombs. A few days later the attack was magnified. The June 29 issues of the *Magyar Nemzet* [Hungarian nation] stated that twenty-seven people were killed in the air raid.

In vain did the editorial of the politically independent *Magyar Nemzet* point out, on June 27, that the "situation created by the German operations [on the Soviet front] was so favorable that any further aid would be superfluous." About an hour and a half after the raid, the Hungarian cabinet met and the ministers were told Soviet aircraft had bombed Kassa, whereupon it was resolved that war would be declared on the Soviet Union. This was done on June 27. Such were the circumstances of the Hungarian declaration of war as known at the time.

Practically all other circumstances surrounding the event are controversial; but perhaps the least controversial in this category is the surmise that the aircraft which dropped bombs on and around

1. Kassa, a city with a population of about 58,000 in 1940, was reannexed to Hungary as a result of the first Vienna Award, on November 2, 1938.

2. The June 26, 1941, issue of the afternoon paper, the *Kis Ujság* [Little newspaper], and the June 27, 1941, issues of the *Nemzeti Ujság* [National daily] and of the *Magyar Nemzet* [Hungarian nation].

Kassa were not really units of the Soviet air force. The official Hungarian version of the event, that the city of Kassa had been the victim of an unprovoked Soviet attack, was probably not believed even at the time. I know of only one author who has held to this official version in retrospect: Maj. Ferenc Adonyi, in his history of the Hungarian army in World War II, seems to be oblivious of the consensus, asserting without hesitation that the bombers were indeed Russian and that they caused considerable havoc, killing 35, seriously wounding 63, and inflicting light wounds on 220 persons.[3] The Hungarian public, at least that part of the public which followed the reports of political events with some degree of critical evaluation, seems to have felt that the bombers were not disguised or undisguised Soviet planes but rather German planes. Some Hungarian historians feel that not only the public but Regent Horthy also suspected trickery, although the regent has claimed, in his *Memoirs,* that he was not properly informed until 1944.[4] "But if we assume, nevertheless, that [Horthy] did not know," writes József Kun, "this would only show his unbelievable lack of political insight and acumen." [5]

True enough, it did not seem reasonable that the Soviet government should deliberately provoke Hungary at a time when the Soviet Union was sorely pressed by the German attack. The Soviet minister of foreign affairs Vyacheslav Molotov and his aides saw the Hungarian minister in Moscow, József Kristóffy, on June 22 and again on June 23, when Hungary broke diplomatic relations with the Soviet Union.[6] At first Molotov wanted to know what Hungary's intentions were; [7] he even seems to have intimated that if Hungary remained on the sidelines she could count on Soviet diplomatic sup-

---

3. *A magyar katona a második világháborúban, 1941/1945* [The Hungarian soldier in World War II], p. 27. For a recent account of the Kassa bombing, basically in agreement with that of Adonyi, I have read an unpublished manuscript by Professor Nándor Dreissiger.

4. Horthy wrote, "The Moscow denial [of the raid], however, was true enough and the message from our Chief of the General Staff was not in accordance with the facts. I find myself forced to this bitter conclusion by information given me in 1944 by the Prime Minister's parliamentary secretary, Bárczy, who revealed to me the details of a plot I could not have believed possible" (*Memoirs,* p. 191).

5. József Kun, "Magyarország második világháborúba való belépésének katonapolitikai vonatkozásai" [Hungary's entry into World War II and her military policy], p. 34.

6. Kristóffy left Moscow only after July 1, 1941 (János Komlós, *Elárult ország* [A country betrayed].

7. Mihály Korom, *A fasizmus bukása Magyarországon* [The fall of fascism in Hungary], p. 45.

port in regaining the part of Transylvania still in Romanian posses-sion.[8] After the Kassa incident Molotov again called Kristóffy to tell him Soviet planes were not involved. Nor did the Hungarian min-ister, to whom special cabling facilities were made available, fail to report on any of these interviews. But László Bárdossy, the Hun-garian prime minister, did not seem to have made much of Kristóffy's messages. To be sure, the southern part of Transylvania was not a major objective of Hungarian foreign policy: after all, Hungarian irredentist claims had been better vindicated in the last few years than the most sanguine irredentists had dared to hope. It seems as if Bárdossy had been simply determined to bring Hungary in on the side of Germany, being confident in a German victory and fearful of being outdone and outshone in Hitler's esteem by Ion Antonescu, the Romanian leader.

Again, historians disagree as to whether the regent was informed of Molotov's message regarding the bombing of Kassa. After his ar-rest in Bavaria in 1945, Bárdossy told his interrogator that he had shown Regent Horthy the telegram from Kristóffy asserting Soviet innocence of the bombing.[9] Another author, writing in the United States, believes that Horthy knew about all the telegrams from Mos-cow.[10] In that case, Horthy either dismissed the information because he had already made up his mind about joining the fray or simply considered Molotov a liar under the circumstances.

It does not appear impossible, of course, that Kassa, situated only a short distance from what was then the eastern front, may have been bombed by mistake; navigational errors accounted for the loss of many innocent lives in World War II. But the evidence tends to

---

8. Antal Ullein-Reviczky, *Guerre allemande, paix russe*, p. 101. See also Elek Karsai, *A budai Sándor palotában történt* [It happened in the Sándor palace in Buda], p. 472. Hungary had regained about half of Transylvania as a result of the second Vienna Award which, like the first, was an almost unilateral decision taken by Ribbentrop and Ciano (August 30, 1940). While the territory returned to Hungary was inhabited by a majority of Hungarians, it is clear that the decision could only have alienated Romania and the Romanians from the Axis. Nevertheless, even in Romania, the award had repercussions that proved a boon to the Axis cause: King Carol abdicated, and Marshal Antonescu took over. A German historian specializing in the Balkans com-ments: "Welche Motive Hitler letzlich veranlassten, die Grenze so und nicht anders zu ziehen ist schwer zu bestimmen, da er sowohl in der Zeit vorher als auch besonders später Rumänien stets den Vorzug gab Ungarn gegenüber, den er seit der Sudetenkrise misstraute" (Andreas Hillgruber, *Hitler, König Carol und Marschall Antonescu*, p. 91).

9. Márton Himler, *Igy néztek ki a magyar nemzet sirásói* [The faces of the grave-diggers of the Hungarian nation], pp. 48–50.

10. Dezsö Sulyok, *A magyar tragédia* [The Hungarian tragedy], p. 381.

indicate that Kassa was not bombed in error. An officer at the airfield, Col. Ádám Krudy, claims to have taken off during the bombard-
ment and noted that despite Russian markings the aircraft bore yellow stripes on the fuselage that were a characteristic and common
marking of the Axis air forces. Moreover, he noted, the planes flew
in a foursome formation also characteristic of the German air force
at the time.[11] The commander duly reported his findings, and his
telegram was handed to Bárdossy in the afternoon of June 26. Bárdossy chose to ignore its contents as he had ignored the contents of
Kristóffy's messages. Only a few minutes after the bombing, Antal
Ullein-Reviczky, Bárdossy's right-hand man and chief of the Press
Section, received a call from Bárdossy informing him that Soviet
planes had dropped bombs in certain areas of northeastern Hungary, causing insignificant damage and wounding one person. Bárdossy then enjoined Ullein-Reviczky to suppress the news.[12] Within
an hour and a half Bárdossy had already changed his mind. Even
though he had not yet received Colonel Krudy's report, it seems
likely he had already begun to suspect German trickery. It is also
quite possible that this very suspicion was the cause of Bárdossy's new
determination: if the bombs were indeed dropped by disguised German aircraft, that would be proof enough that Germany definitely
wanted Hungary to participate in the war.[13]

Instead of exercising leadership, Bárdossy seemed to accept the
fatality of events. There had been no way out other than war, Bárdossy told Ullein-Reviczky after the cabinet meeting in which he
had advocated the war declaration. Had he resigned, it would have
been worse, for his successor would undoubtedly have been appointed by the Germans. Besides, argued Bárdossy, if the Hungarian
General Staff was conspiring with the Germans, what was there to be
done?[14]

Bárdossy's logic with regard to German intentions need not surprise us; for proof that the German government definitely expected

---

11. J. Kun, "Magyarország második világháborúba," p. 33.
12. *Guerre allemande,* p. 106. Censorship in the Hungarian state was introduced
by statute number 8140 of 1939. See *Tanulmányok a Horthy-korszak államáról és
jogáról* [Studies on the constitution and law of the state during the Horthy era], p. 58.
13. See also Mario Fenyo, "The Allies Axis Armies at Stalingrad," p. 59. György
Ránki, *Emlékiratok és valóság Magyarország második világháborús szerepéről* [Memoirs
and facts regarding Hungary's role in World War II], p. 149.
14. Ullein-Reviczky, *Guerre allemande,* p. 108.

active Hungarian participation in the campaign—that is, military contributions—was rather wanting until the Kassa incident. Not only did Bárdossy not possess such proof but, indeed, no unequivocal evidence to that effect seems to have turned up among the archives that were captured by the Allies in Germany. For a long time after Hitler first mentioned his concept of an attack on the Soviet Union in August 1940, Hungary was not counted in as a possible military ally. At a "Führer conference" on December 5, 1940, while discussing the attack on the Soviet Union with his generals, Hitler indicated that the Finns and the Romanians must cooperate with Germany, because their future depended on a German victory.[15] The Hungarians were not mentioned then; mention of Hungary in this connection seems to have occurred a few days later, around December 13. On that day Franz Halder, chief of the German General Staff, held a "conference" with a Hungarian official (probably with the military attaché in Berlin, Maj. Sándor Homlok) and noted, in his diary, that Hungary was an Axis partner who seemed willing to collaborate with Germany but was beset with "internal difficulties."[16] The famous directive for Operation Barbarossa, dated December 18, again contemplated only the participation of Romania and Finland. During subsequent meetings of the German General Staff, Operation Barbarossa was a frequent topic, and Finland and Romania were often mentioned, but for a while Hungary seems to have been consistently omitted from the discussions. As late as mid-June, during his visit to Hungary, Freiherr Ernst von Weizsäcker told Bárdossy that "if anyone said that a German-Soviet conflict was imminent, he knew more than the Führer."[17] In fact, Weizsäcker may indeed have been uninformed.[18] Hungary, however, was mentioned at a General Staff meeting on April 30, 1941, when a "confrontation of Russian and the Reich forces" was sketched; Halder simply noted in his diary: "Possibility to make use of Hungarian forces." Hitler had said that the Finns, the Romanians, *and* the Hungarians must be spoken to as follows: "It is necessary to protect ourselves in the East. Russia has treated us in an unfriendly manner a few times, so we must assure ourselves against surprises, foreseeably by May 23."[19] German

15. Franz Halder, *Kriegstagebuch*, 2 : 213 (hereafter cited as Halder, *KTB*).
16. "*Ungarn*. Ein Angriff unsererseits ruft Russland auf den Plan. Achsenpartner—folgt willig—innere Schwierigkeiten" (ibid., 2 : 227).
17. Macartney, "Hungary's Declaration of War," pp. 157–58.
18. *Memoirs of Ernst von Weizsäcker*, pp. 254–55.
19. Halder, *KTB*, 2 : 387.

intervention in Yugoslavia and Greece, "to secure the flanks," obliged the planners to delay Operation Barbarossa for another month. At any rate, Hungarian participation, while not positively advocated, was not a priori rejected.

The reasons for German hesitation with regard to Hungary may not be difficult to understand. Hitler counted on Finnish and Romanian cooperation because both countries had recently lost territory to the Soviet Union. Moreover, Hitler had been less than satisfied with the Hungarian contributions to the Axis cause. When Germany occupied the Sudetenland, the part of Czechoslovakia inhabited mainly by Germans, the Hungarian army made no move to recover the long coveted Magyar-inhabited areas of Czechoslovakia.[20] On January 16, 1939, Hitler had told Count István Csáky, the Hungarian foreign minister who was then a guest at Berchtesgaden, that it was because of Hungary that he had had to sit down and negotiate with Prime Minister Neville Chamberlain, instead of attacking Czechoslovakia outright.[21] It is true that the Hungarians did have a hand in the liquidation of the remainder of Czechoslovakia: Ribbentrop and Ciano met in Vienna on November 2, 1938, and in the name of the Four Powers (Great Britain, France, Germany, and Italy), awarded to Hungary parts of Slovakia inhabited predominantly by Hungarians. In March 1939, when Germany absorbed the remainder of Bohemia and Moravia, Hungarian

20. In August 1938, during Horthy's visit to Germany, one of the topics of conversation was, of course, Czechoslovakia. In response to a German invitation to participate in an attack on that country, the Hungarian minister of defense stated: "Hungary, for her own ends, has decided to take action against Czechoslovakia; she cannot, however, determine a schedule. The Fall of this year would not be suitable, because our preparations have not reached an advanced stage." The German officials explained that they had no intention of forcing the Hungarian government to take action, but they nevertheless pointed to the possibility of regaining Hungarian territory. Hitler: "If you want to share in the meal, you must help in the kitchen" (Minutes of conversations between Germany and Hungarian officials, 22 Aug. 1938, Hungarian Collection, National Archives Record Group 242, 2 : 4. No doubt the Hungarian attitude reflected in part the thought of certain military leaders in Germany, in particular Ludwig Beck and Walther von Brauchitsch, who felt that, should Germany attack Czechoslovakia, France would not stand by idly and a worldwide conflagration would ensue. After consultation between Regent Horthy and Kálmán Kánya, the Hungarian officials modified their position. Kánya told Ribbentrop on August 25, 1938, that the Hungarians might be ready as early as October of that year (Horthy, *Memoirs*, p. 162). Nevertheless, the Hungarian army made no move when the Germans occupied the Sudetenland on October 1, 1938.

21. Hitler added, irritatedly, that the "mistaken utterances" of the Hungarian press should cease or else "he might correct them some day" (Memorandum by Hewel, *Documents on German Foreign Policy, 1918–1945*, series D, 5 : 362–63 [hereafter cited as *DGFP*]).

troops marched into the "Carpatho-Ukraine" (sometimes called Ruthenia), the easternmost section of former Czechoslovakia. Yet this clearly aggressive move was not in line with German foreign policy: [22] one avowed aim of the Hungarian government was to establish a common frontier with Poland.[23] The Polish leader, Col. József Beck, and even certain British diplomats, regarded the Hungarian move as a step toward the establishment of a bloc of east European states, a bloc that might even be capable of resisting German aggression. When Germany attacked Poland, in September 1939, setting off World War II, Hungary again proved less cooperative than the Reich Foreign Office seems to have expected: a request to allow transit rights for German troops was refused outright in the name of the tradition of Polish-Hungarian amity.[24] The German request came on September 9, when Germany seemed to be having little trouble winning the war. The request may have been merely an attempt to compromise the Hungarians vis-à-vis world opinion and themselves. Six months later, on April 4, 1940, Halder took cryptic notes of a Führer conference in his diary: "Hungary has made no sacrifices at all to date . . . (England and Hungary, one heart and one soul . . . The Führer has not yet forgiven the Hungarians for not letting him in the Polish campaign use the Kassa railroad, which they owe him.)" [25] Even before the outbreak of hostilities, Count Csáky had indicated to Ribbentrop that Hungary would remain

22. Contemporary historians in Hungary often seem dedicated to the task of compiling information derogatory to the regime that was in power prior to 1945, that is, the Horthy regime. Nevertheless, a prominent historian writing about these events in present-day Hungary saw fit to discuss Hungarian efforts to dodge German influence and pressure in the 1930s: ". . . la politique hongroise de temporisation," he writes, "ne fit que provoquer le mécontentement, voire la colère, de l'Allemagne. A cela vinrent s'ajouter les négociations engagées avec la Petite Entente et la déclaration de Bled d'août 1938; des explications eurent lieu à l'occasion du voyage de Horthy en Allemagne au cours de cette même année en compagnie du premier ministre Imrédy, et du ministre des affaires étrangères Kánya. Si les pourparlers se terminèrent mieux que l'on ne s'y attendait, grâce surtout à l'intervention de Horthy, le gouvernment hongrois continuait de se montrer réservé vis-à-vis de l'Allemagne" (László Zsigmond, "La politique extérieure de la Hongrie de 1933 à 1939," p. 15).

23. Stephen D. Kertesz, *Diplomacy in a Whirlpool*, p. 44. Kertesz notes that Great Britain rather favored the Hungarian move and comments that the British were "20 years late in trying to form a bloc of states capable of resisting the eastwards expansion of Germany."

24. Erdmannsdorf to Ribbentrop, Sept. 10, 1939, *DGFP*, series D, 8 : 42.

25. Polycopied translation, National Archives Record Group 242. A similar complaint is recorded by Erich Kordt, *Wahn und Wirklichkeit*, p. 308: "Bekanntlich zeigte Hitler nie besondere Vorliebe für Ungarn. Er hatte Ungarn sein 'schleppe Haltung' 1938 und die Verweigerung des Durchtransportes von Truppen während des polnischen Feldzuges schwer verübelt."

neutral in the case of a German-Polish conflict but would side with the Axis in the case of a more general conflict.[26]

The second Vienna Award, on August 30, 1940, again engineered by Ciano and Ribbentrop, resulted in another substantial territorial increase for Hungary; Romania was compelled to return about half of Transylvania. The territory returned to Hungary was inhabited by a majority of Hungarians but also by about one million Romanians; on the other hand, a Hungarian minority in the southern part of Transylvania remained under Romanian jurisdiction. Some Hungarians felt the second Vienna Award was of little profit to Hungary,[27] but most Hungarians were probably inwardly surprised at the size of the award at the expense of Romania, Germany's main supplier of oil. Hitler felt his source of oil in Romania endangered by the anti-German feelings the award itself had provoked there.[28] Hitler was not aware that he had unduly favored the Hungarians, and he told the Hungarian minister in Berlin that if the Axis lost the war, "which was out of the question to be sure," these territorial revisions would become void.[29] Hence some Hungarian patriots were emotionally commited to support the German cause, either to increase the chances of an Axis victory or simply as a manifestation of national gratitude; others saw the return of these territories with misgivings.

In the next few months Hungary went far to redeem the sins of its past; and there came a time, in December 1940, when Hitler found cause to praise the attitude of the Hungarian government in a long letter to Mussolini:

> Without doubt it is Hungary and Romania who in this conflict have adopted the most clear-cut attitude. . . .
> 6. The attitude of the Hungarians is no less loyal. Since December 13, German troops have been continually in transit in the direction of Romania. Hungary and Romania have put

26. Abwehr report, Sept. 11, 1939, National Archives Microcopy T-77, roll 1026 (National Archives hereafter cited as NA).

27. Statement by Gen. Imre Ruszkiczay-Rüdiger, former deputy minister of Defense in Hungary at the Nuremberg trials, *Trial of the Major War Criminals before the International Military Tribunal*, 7 : 321–24.

28. Testimony of Keitel, *Trial of the Major War Criminals*, 10 :524.

29. "The Führer stated . . . it had not been easy to induce the Romanians to surrender so large a territory. They had told the Führer at a conference that they could at best return a territory of 14 square kilometers. The Government was too weak to survive greater sacrifices." (Record of the reception by the Führer of Count [*sic*] Sztójay, Sept. 10, 1940, *DGFP*, series D, 11 : 49–50.)

at my disposition their railway network so that German divisions can be rapidly moved to the points of pressure. I cannot say any more yet of the operation which we are planning or which may become necessary, for these plans are being drawn up at this very moment. The strength of our forces will in any case be such that any threat of lateral counter-measures will be excluded.[30]

Toward the end of March 1941, after the military coup in Belgrade displaced the Cvetković government which had just adhered to the Tripartite Pact, the Hungarian government agreed to cooperate with Germany in an armed attack on Yugoslavia.[31] After years of courting the Yugoslav governments, Hungary had signed a treaty of "eternal" friendship with that country only a few months earlier! But solemn promises are forgotten, eternity shrinks to a moment as the chances of conquest or reconquest become bright (yet how many of those Hungarians who were willing to forget the treaty with Yugoslavia came to insist that Hungary remain "faithful" to Germany to the end, for the sake of her honor!). The details of the joint offensive were worked out during the visit of Gen. Friedrich von Paulus to Budapest on March 30. There seemed no reluctance on Hungary's part to allow the deployment of German troops on Hungarian territory; in fact, the Hungarian government agreed to attack Yugoslavia with its own troops.[32] But the Hungarian plans were marred, if not wrecked, by the suicide of Count Pál Teleki, the Hungarian prime minister.[33] The note Count Teleki sent to Regent Horthy to explain his action on April 2 was published many years after the war ended:

> Your Serene Highness!
>
> We betrayed our words—out of cowardice—the words in our treaty of eternal peace that was based on your speech of Mohács. The nation is aware of it, and we disregarded her honor.
>
> We have sided with the scoundrels; indeed, not a word of the so-called atrocities is true! No atrocities have been comitted,

30. Quoted in Sir Winston Churchill, *The Grand Alliance* (Boston: Houghton Mifflin, 1950), p. 13.

31. On March 28, 1941, Horthy telegraphed to Hitler that he was looking forward to the proposed "contacts" between the German and Hungarian army commands (*DGFP*, series D, 12 : 401).

32. *Trial of the Major War Criminals*, 7 : 257.

33. Fenyo, "The Allied Axis Armies at Stalingrad," p. 58.

either against Hungarians or against Germans! We will become despoilers of corpses—the lowliest of nations!

I am guilty.

Pál Teleki.[34]

Horthy was willing to pursue the course initially set, Teleki's suicide notwithstanding, but only after Croatia would declare its independence. An independent Croatia signified the dissolution of the Yugoslav state and provided the Hungarian government with an excuse for disregarding the treaty of eternal peace. On April 3 Horthy wrote to Hitler to explain, and perhaps apologize for, the suicide of Count Teleki. Yet Hungary must save face, wrote Horthy;[35] and on April 4 an official of the Reich Foreign Office noted that Horthy requested "to be released in some generally comprehensible manner from the moral obligation contained in the Hungarian-Yugoslav Pact." [36]

Marshal Eugen Kvaternik declared Croatia independent on April 10, and the Hungarian troops crossed the Yugoslav border early on April 11, five days after the Germans. The Hungarian units reached the Danube on April 13 and 14 without encountering serious re-

34. *Horthy Miklós titkos iratai* [Confidential papers of Nicholas Horthy], p. 292.

35. In part, the letter ran as follows: "Minister-President Count Teleki shot himself last night. He was the symbol of exaggerated correctness, of purity, of devotion to duty; a highly educated, talented statesman and scholar who, as a result of overwork and under the burden of weighty events no longer knew any other way out.

"He left me a letter, in which he wrote that he felt conscience-stricken because at the Council of Ministers over which I presided night before last and at which the Chief of the General Staff was present he did not sufficiently protest against the fact that, although obligated to Yugoslavia by the Friendship Pact recently concluded we were nevertheless taking advantage of the present opportunity to become despoilers of corpses. . . .

"At this meeting, I myself was of the opinion, in view of the pact of friendship recently concluded, we had to try to save face. In the end, however, we were of the same opinion that, after the entry of the German troops, Croatia would probably secede from the Yugoslav body politic and that thereby the treaty partner, the kingdom of Yugoslavia, would cease to exist as such.

"Count Teleki fell the victim of a conflict of conscience which is felt also by the entire nation.

"I do not doubt that Your Excellency will understand that this tragic case, unique in recent history, has deeply shaken me and with me the entire nation.

"In accordance with my letter of March 28, we have already taken military measures. But the conflict of conscience confronting us, to the magnitude of which nothing attests more clearly than the suicide of the Prime-Minister, compels us to request that the German Army Command assign to our troops only such tasks as are reconcilable with our conscience" (*DGFP*, series D, 12 : 447).

36. Memorandum by Weizsäcker, Apr. 4, *DGFP*, series D, 12 : 450.

sistance. On April 13 Hitler turned to Horthy once more asking that the Hungarian motorized unit continue its advance beyond the Danube; [37] while elements of this corps may indeed have crossed the Danube and the Drava,[38] the Yugoslav surrender on April 14 rendered further operations unnecessary.

Despite the less than honorable role Hungary played in the attack on Yugoslavia, the evidence presented suffices to show that Hungary was in many ways a reluctant satellite of Germany.[39] The full extent of Hungarian reluctance becomes apparent if we consider that it was thanks to Hitler, as much as to Mussolini, that Hungary had at least partly achieved her aspirations of the last twenty years, the recapture of some of the territories she had lost in 1920 as a result of the Treaty of Trianon, the territories inhabited by a Magyar population in particular. It had been Count Galeazzo Ciano and Ribbentrop who determined the first Vienna Award, on November 2, 1938, by which portions of southern and eastern Slovakia with a population of 1,081,247 were returned to Hungarian jurisdiction. It was again Ciano and Ribbentrop (or perhaps one should write Mussolini and Hitler) who, by the second Vienna Award on August 30, 1940, allocated about half of Transylvania with a population of 2,577,291, under Romanian rule since 1919, back to Hungary.[40] On September 2, 1940, having heard of the decision reached at Vienna, Horthy wrote to Hitler: "If at all possible, the second Vienna Award has strengthened Hungary still further in her conviction that the National Socialistic Reich and Fascist Italy, conscious of the true interests of the European community, are prepared, through resolute and unselfish action, to demonstrate their determination to pacify and reorganize the Continent." [41] Hitler told Döme Sztójay, the Hungarian minister in Berlin who delivered Horthy's letter, that "it was Hungary's great good luck that, as a former Austrian, he was well acquainted with the conditions down there, for otherwise Hungary would never have got Cluj." [42] The Hungarians were

37. Hitler to Horthy, *DGFP*, series D, 12 : 538.

38. According to Major Kun, the motorized corps was advancing toward Sarajevo ("Magyarország második világháborúba," p. 16).

39. See John F. Montgomery, *Hungary, the Unwilling Satellite.*

40. *Recollections of Tibor Eckhardt: Regicide at Marseilles* (New York: American Hungarian Library, 1964), p. 241. See also Jenő Horváth, *Az országgyarapitás története, 1920–1941* [The history of the country's increase], *passim.*

41. *DGFP*, series D, 11 : 7–8.

42. Record of reception by the Führer of Sztójay, Sept. 10, 1940, *DGFP*, series D, 11 : 53.

pleased with the size of the award, which would have been considerable even had Cluj (Kolozsvár) been left in the hands of Romania. Indeed, it is difficult to understand why Hitler, who unlike Mussolini was no friend of the Hungarians, should have gone to these limits to please the Hungarians on this occasion, at the expense of Romania, whose friendship was probably more important to Germany. Could this have been the whim of a man who delighted in redrawing the map of Europe? Or are there more cogent reasons, yet unrevealed, which explain Hitler's partiality? Hitler was also responsible for the return of the Bácska and of the triangular tip of Baranya (Voivodina) to Hungary after the campaign against Yugoslavia; although it should be noted that the Bánát, which Hitler had also promised to Hungary, was never delivered. The policy makers of the Reich used the Bánát, as they had used Transylvania, to compel Hungary and Romania to outbid one another in currying Germany's favors.

Hungary seemed an unreliable, even ungrateful ally. Nor did Germany insist on a formal alliance; nevertheless, certain pressures were, indeed, exerted to persuade Hungary to join the attack on the Soviet Union. It also appears the Hungarian government, or various elements thereof, was given clews regarding German intentions. It is true that the Hungarian government was not officially informed about the attack until a few days before it was launched; but then the Romanian and Finnish governments were not informed either, even though their active cooperation was taken for granted.[43]

The following episodes indicate that consideration of Hungary as an ally or partner against the Soviet Union was not excluded. One of the witnesses at the Nuremberg trials, Colonel István Ujszászy, testified that in November 1940 a letter was delivered by Col. Günther Kappe of the German General Staff; the letter was written by General Halder and addressed to Gen. Henrik Werth, the Hungarian chief of the General Staff. Halder informed Werth that Hungary would have to participate "if only in her own interests" in a preventive war, possibly against Yugoslavia but definitely against the Soviet Union.[44] I have been unable to locate this letter to check up on the accuracy of Colonel Ujszászy's statement; after

---

43. Marshal Antonescu was informed about Operation Barbarossa in Munich on June 11, 1941 (Hillgruber, *Hitler, König Carol und Marschall Antonescu*, p. 132).

44. *Trial of the Major War Criminals before the International Military Tribunal*, 7 : 329–36.

all he was reporting on an event that had happened five years earlier, and so much had happened in those five years. Gen. Ernst Alexander Paulus writes that the Armed Forces High Command (OKW) had forbidden any reference to Operation Barbarossa, during discussions centered on Yugoslavia; [45] it is possible, however, that this ban was imposed only at the moment of crisis, early in April. On November 29, 1940, when Hungary acceded to the Tripartite Pact,[46] Hitler warned Count Teleki that although Germany had treaties with the Soviet Union he relied more on instruments of power; "in the spring the Germany Army will have 230 divisions . . ." Hitler remarked.[47] According to General Warlimont, Hitler did consider using Hungarian forces as early as November 12, 1940, in his directive number 18: "I propose," quotes Warlimont, "to keep the overall direction of this campaign in my own hands, including the allotment of objectives for the Italian and Hungarian forces within the framework of the operation as a whole." [48] We have seen that Gen. Franz Halder probably gave similar hints to the Hungarian military attaché in Berlin, Major Homlok, around December 13, 1940.[49] At the same time there were conversations between Wilhelm Keitel and the Hungarian minister of defense Károly Bartha and also between Admiral Canaris and Colonel Ujszászy, the two intelligence chiefs; again campaigns against Yugoslavia and the Soviet Union were discussed: "for the war against Russia, Hungary must make available 15 operational units (including three mobilized, cavalry, and Panzer units) . . . As a political compensation for her participation, Hungary will receive territory in Yugoslavia and in Soviet Russia (the ancient principality of Halicz) and the land at the foot of the Carpathian Mountains, up to the River Dniester." [50]

45. Ernst Alexander Paulus, *Ich stehe hier auf Befehl!*, p. 131.

46. Hungary insisted on being the first of the small countries to join the pact. Romania signed the pact on November 23 and Slovakia on November 24.

47. Record of conversation between Hitler and Teleki, Vienna, Nov. 20, 1940, *DGFP*, series D, 11 : 633. This same record indicates that "Count Teleki brought up the Jewish question and said that when peace was concluded the Jews would have to be moved out of Europe" (p. 635).

48. Walter Warlimont, *Inside Hitler's Headquarters, 1939–1945*, pp. 128–29.

49. Halder, *KTB*, 2 : 227; also Kordt, *Wahn und Wirklichkeit*, p. 307. But on June 28, 1941, a day after Hungary declared war on the Soviet Union, Colonel Homlok complained to Kramarz, an official of the German Foreign Office, that the Hungarian army had not been informed of the attack on the Soviet Union (NA Microcopy T-120, roll 91, 103760).

50. *Trial of the Major War Criminals*, 7 : 332; Wilhelm Keitel, *The Memoirs of Field-Marshal Keitel*, p. 129; also J. Kun, "Magyarország másodìk világháborúba," p. 21.

It is possible that these propositions had not been cleared by Hitler, for, as we shall see, Hitler was unwilling to even consider "political compensation" for Hungary in the Soviet Union. In a conversation with Halder concerning Operation Barbarossa, in February 1941, Hitler did not positively rule out Hungarian participation. The relevant passage in the minutes of this conference reads as follows:

> Hungary's position. If Hungary is not to be included, we must nevertheless use Hungary as a detraining area. The objective of the expedition will be ostensibly Romania and at the last moment the pressure will be applied against the Russian border. Hungary will allow everything if given specific political assurances. Conversation can be carried on with all the participating countries as late as the very last moments—except for Romania. For Romania cooperation with us is a matter of life or death. . . . To approach Hungary concerning transit rights at the beginning of April . . .[51]

A questionnaire dated March 24, 1941, and entitled "Preparations for Barbarossa," described Hungary as simply a transit zone (*Durchmarschgebiet*); but a corrected version of this questionnaire, dated April 23, stated that Hungary was to be regarded not simply as a zone of transit but in the same sense as Finland.[52] The meaning of this is not made clear, and it is not impossible the suggestions contained in this questionnaire were, in any case, rejected by the high command. On May 1, when the final date for the attack (June 22) was set, it appears that Hitler thought the Hungarians would be willing to protect their borders but would not allow a German attack from Hungarian soil.[53] According to an entry in Halder's diary in March, it was decided to let the Hungarians know of the German plans, simply because "they cannot be lied to much longer." [54] Hitler still thought Hungary could not be trusted, "due to her close connections with countries hostile to Germany." [55]

51. Microcopy T-77, roll 792, 5521109.

52. "Entgegen der Ziffer 6. der Bezugsverfügung sind auch Vorbereitungen für *Ungarn in demselben Umfang wie für Finland* (Ziffer 1), der Bezugsverfügung erforderlich geworden. Die im Verteiler genannten Dienststellen werden um Übersendung von entsprechenden Unterlagen und Anmeldung ihrer Forderungen bis 28. 4. 41. gebeten" (NA Microcopy T-77, roll 792, 5521175).

53. Memorandum of May 1, 1941, NA Microcopy T-77, roll 792, 5521212.

54. Halder, *KTB*, 2 : 317.

55. *Trial of the Major War Criminals*, 7 : 256–58; also Paulus, *Ich stehe hier auf Befehl!*, p. 129. Paulus also insists that, despite the complications, Hitler counted on Hungarian participation in the war (p. 131).

By May and especially early June of 1941, clews to the German design were certainly not lacking. During his visit to Mussolini in Rome on June 5, 1941, Bárdossy was informed by Mussolini that war with the Soviet Union appeared likely; this information, incidentally, was returned with some surprise to the German Foreign Office by the German minister in Budapest, Erdmannsdorf.[56] General Keresztes-Fischer was informed of the same likelihood during his visit in Berlin on June 10.[57] The first truly official warning, from Ribbentrop, seems to have reached Budapest only on June 15. Ribbentrop's telegram, bearing the highest classification mark (*Geheimvermerk für geheime Reichssache*), stated: "In view of the heavy concentration of Russian troops along the eastern German border the Führer will probably be compelled, by the beginning of July at the latest, to clarify German-Russian relations unequivocally, and in this connection to make certain demands." What was expected of Hungary? "Since it is impossible to foretell the outcome of these negotiations, the German government considers it necessary for Hungary, too, to take steps to secure its frontiers."[58] Similar instructions were given by Weizsäcker to Sztójay in Berlin on June 16; Weizsäcker added, however, that Hungary should undertake nothing "alarming," as this may disturb German plans.[59] The chief of the Hungarian General Staff, Gen. Henrik Werth, submitted several memoranda to the Hungarian cabinet urging that, should it come to blows between Germany and the Soviet Union, Hungary enter the war on the side of Germany;[60] but the Hungarian government merely carried out the requested precautionary measures along the country's northeastern border. Then, on June 22, a few hours after the beginning of the German attack, Horthy received Hitler's letter of the day before giving reasons for the attack on the Soviet Union:

56. Telegram from Erdmannsdorf to German Foreign Office, June 10, 1941, NA Microcopy T-120, roll 91, 103698.

57. Dispatch of the Hungarian military attaché, Colonel Homlok, dated June 13, 1941, *Magyarország és a második világháború* [Hungary and World War II], ed. Magda Ádám, Gyula Juhász, and Lajos Kerekes. This documentary publication also gives the text of further warnings from the Hungarian representatives in Berlin, as well as the text of one of General Werth's memoranda, dated June 14, advising Hungarian participation in an eventual conflict (pp. 357 ff.).

58. Ribbentrop to Erdmannsdorf, *DGFP*, series D, 12 : 1030.

59. ". . . wünsche die Ungarische Regierung mit militärischen Sicherheitsmassnahmen nicht zu spät zu kommen, andererseits wolle sie auch nichts Alarmierendes unternehmen, was die deutschen Absichten störe" (notes on conversation with Sztójay, NA Microcopy T-120, roll 91, 103718).

60. Ránki, *Emlékiratok és valóság*, pp. 134–35; also, by the same author, "Magyarország belépése a második világháborúba" [Hungary's entry into World War II], p. 41.

the presence of 160 Soviet divisions along Germany's border, the
repeated border incidents.[61] Hitler concluded his letter by thanking
Horthy for the defensive measures already adopted by the Hun-
garian army. The letter does not hint at, let alone request, active
Hungarian military participation in this campaign.[62] Although
Horthy's reply to Hitler's letter has not been found, the German
Army High Command claimed that in his message of June 22
Horthy "sincerely regretted not having been called upon to take his
share in Germany's struggle against Communism." [63]

Assuming that the bombing of Kassa was indeed carried out by
disguised or undisguised German aircraft, a change must have occurred in the German attitude toward Hungarian participation;
perhaps not a radical change because, as I had attempted to show,
Hitler and the German General Staff had never definitely excluded
the possibility of participation, but at least a change in emphasis.
This change took place sometime between June 21 and June 26,
1941. What occasioned it? Was it perhaps the rather unexpected
difficulties encountered by some of the German armies from the
very beginning of the campaign? Or was it rather the result of
Horthy's enthusiastic reception of the news of the attack, and Prime
Minister Bárdossy's obvious eagerness to receive specific instructions
from Berlin? On June 22 the German minister in Budapest, Erdmannsdorf, reported to the German Foreign Office concerning his
audience with the regent in the following words: "At 10:30 a.m. I
handed the Regent the Führer's letter. The Regent thanked me
very much for transmitting this communication, which he called
wonderful. For 22 years he had longed for this day, and now was
delighted . . ." [64] As for Bárdossy's attitude? On June 23 Bárdossy

61. This seems fantasy, as Soviet officers were instructed to avoid border incidents
at almost any cost. The Soviet commanding officer at Lvov (Lemberg) did not return
the German fire on June 22, as he was under the delusion that the Germans were
merely target practicing and missing the target. Similar instances are recorded in Harrison Salisbury, *The 900 Days* (New York: Harper and Row, 1969).

62. "As far as the attitude of Hungary is concerned, Your Highness, I am convinced that in her national consciousness she will appreciate my attitude. I should
like at this point to thank Your Highness for the understanding measures of the
Hungarian armed forces, which by the mere fact of having strengthened their
frontier defense will prevent Russian flank attacks and tie down Russian forces"
(*DGFP*, series D, 12 : 1071).

63. Macartney, "Hungary's Declaration of War," p. 160.

64. *DGFP*, series D, 12 : 1077. Horthy had ridden to power on his white charger in
the wake of the Hungarian Commune. The ensuing "White Terror," although not
organized by Horthy, was not suppressed until Count Bethlen became prime minis-

broke diplomatic relations with the Soviet Union.[65] When informed of this measure, Erdmannsdorf told Bárdossy that this was the least Hungary could do under the circumstances.[66] Perhaps Bárdossy meant to go no further; Ullein-Reviczky portrays Bárdossy as a leader who firmly resisted German pressure, until the bombing incident. On June 24, writes Ullein-Reviczky, upon reading another memorandum by General Werth advocating Hungarian participation, Bárdossy banged the table with his fist and declared: "this war is none of our business." [67]

On June 22 Halder noted in his diary that Germany was not making demands on Hungary; if the soldiers wanted to cooperate, "let them persuade their politicians." [68] This may have been the message Alfred Jodl gave General Kurt Himer, the German liaison officer in Budapest, during a telephone conversation late on June 22.[69] Jodl added, however, that Germany would welcome any Hungarian assistance, provided this did not hamper communications with Ro-

---

ter in 1920. Hungary, writes Horthy rather proudly in his *Memoirs*, was one of the last countries to extend diplomatic recognition to the Soviet Union—in 1934, a year after the United States had done so. Nor did Horthy think it superfluous to warn Hitler of the dangers of bolshevism and to predict that sooner or later "there will be a settling of accounts between Germany and Russia" (*Horthy Miklós titkos iratai*, p. 222). In another letter, addressed to Hitler and conceived some time in the second half of April 1941, Horthy wrote: "In my belief there can be no happiness, peace and order as long as a Soviet and that immense Russia exist, which can be governed only by terror—be it by the tsar or by the Communists" ("Horthy's Secret Correspondence with Hitler", p. 190). One of the agents of the SS in the Balkans, Dr. Wilhelm Hoettl, even believed that Horthy strengthened Hitler's determination to attack the Soviet Union: "Man darf den Einfluss, den Horthy in dieser Frage auf Hitler ausübte, nicht unterschatzen; zweifellos hat er Hitler in seiner Absicht, die Sowjetunion anzugreifen, zumindest bestarkt. Hitler had diese Rolle Horthys im verschiedenen Gesprächen durchblicken lassen, mit dem Hinzufügen, wenn Ungarn auf deutsche Seite gegen Russland marschiere, musse er bestimmt keinen Verrat befürchten. . . . So sehr der englandfreundliche Horthy Gegner eines Krieges mit der Westmächten war, so begeistert vertrat er den Gedanken eines Präventivkrieges gegen die Sowjetunion" (Walter Hagen [Wilhelm Hoettl], *Die geheime Front*, p. 341).

65. Telegram from Erdmannsdorf to Berlin, NA Microcopy T-120, roll 91, 103734. Hungary did, indeed, break relations with the Soviet Union right away, although the assistant foreign Minister, Jenő Ghyczy, told Erdmannsdorf that Hungary was waiting to hear whether the German Foreign Office had any objections to a break in relations (NA Microcopy T-120, roll 91, 103735-36).

66. Ullein-Reviczky, *Guerre allemande*, p. 102.

67. Ibid., p. 103.

68. Halder, *KTB*, 3 : 6.

69. Elek Karsai, *A budai vártól a gyepüig, 1941–1945* [From the castle in Buda to the western frontier of Hungary], p. 6.

mania.[70] General Himer reported in a telegram that he tried to carry out Jodl's instructions but was unable to reach Hungarian officials that Sunday: the chief of the General Staff was unavailable, the minister of defense went fishing, and the regent was watching a polo game on Saint Margaret Island. The only person at his desk on this critical day was the "tireless" Col. Dezső László. Colonel László communicated Himer's message to General Werth in the course of the evening (still on the twenty-second). It was only the following day, in the early afternoon, that General Werth was able to receive General Himer on a personal call. Himer repeated to Werth that, according to the German Army High Command and Gen. Franz Halder, Germany would be grateful for any Hungarian contribution. In his telegraphic report to the German General Staff, however, Himer was careful to note that no demand was made of the Hungarians: "Eine Forderung wurde jedoch nicht gestellt werden [sic]." Himer also mentioned to General Werth that the German lines of communications with Romania must remain undisturbed. General Werth told Himer that if Hitler's letter to Horthy contained no specific requests it would prove difficult to persuade the politicians to take action. The politicians should have received hints four weeks earlier. With the necessary diplomatic and political groundwork, the army would be prepared and ready to cross the borders of the Soviet Union. Ten days earlier, "political queries" had been made in Germany, but it appeared that the Führer did not want Hungary to participate. In fact General Halder had indicated that Hungary should do nothing to alarm the Russians. According to General Werth, it was too late to do anything about it now. Himer answered that it was still "shortly before the hour of noon" and there was time for Hungary to participate in the crusade against Bolshevism "along an uninterrupted front." On the whole, Himer was less than enchanted with General Werth's attitude: "In the course of the conversation I had the impression that General Werth did not live up to the greatness of the moment." [71] General Werth had the no doubt well-deserved reputation of being pro-German, a characteristic which many Hungarian authors explain by noting that he was of ethnic German descent, as was a large proportion of the Hungarian General Staff; but on this occasion

70. Halder, *KTB*, 3 : 8.
71. Also printed in *DGFP,* series D, 13 : 64; see also Karsai, *A budai vártól,* p. 6.

General Werth hesitated to commit himself and Hungary entirely to the cause of the Reich. General Werth reported his conversation with General Himer to the minister of defense and the prime minister, and the latter two felt these developments were significant enough to disturb the regent who was resting at his estate at Kenderes.[72] General Werth also submitted another memorandum to the Hungarian cabinet, and this time what Werth seems to have told Bárdossy was rather different from the purport of Jodl's message to Himer: "the Germans desired Hungarian participation," or words to that effect. Bárdossy in turn summoned Erdmannsdorf on June 24 to ask for clarification. Bárdossy explained that in recent weeks time and again the Hungarian government had attempted to find out about German intentions, only to be told, until lately, that there was no "Russian problem." Finally, on June 19 General Halder had told the chief of the Hungarian General Staff that perhaps the Hungarian troops should have been reinforced to a greater degree along the border.

> Yesterday—continued Bárdossy—the German General with the High Command of the Hungarian Armed Forces had informed the Chief of the Hungarian General Staff that the participation of Hungarian troops in the advance into the Soviet Union was desired. He, the Minister President, considered this to be primarily a political question, and therefore, asked for clarification whether there was actually a German wish to this effect and if so to what extent Hungarian participation was desired.[73]

Obviously the content of Halder's message to the Hungarian government had been considerably distorted by this time. Perhaps Bárdossy's query even indicated a willingness to participate; and there is little doubt the German Foreign Office interpreted his query as such an indication. Besides cabling to the Foreign Office, Erdmannsdorf called General Himer that same day to find out just what had been said. General Himer explained that he had simply left a note on the desk of the chief of the Mobilization Section of the General Staff to the effect: "Every Hungarian assistance will be accepted at any time. We do not wish to *demand* anything, but everything that is offered voluntarily will be gratefully accepted.

---

72. Karsai, *A budai vártól*, p. 6.
73. Telegram from Erdmannsdorf to Berlin, June 24, 1941, *DGFP*, series D, 13 : 13–14.

There is no question of our not wanting participation by Hungary." [74] General Himer also told Erdmannsdorf that he had spoken in the same sense to General Werth but that it was possible that General Werth had passed on his statement in a stronger form to Bárdossy in order to exert pressure on him.[75] General Himer, it appears, was being less than frank, for he himself had strongly urged the Hungarian chief of staff to push for Hungarian participation in the war.

On June 25 Slovakia declared war on the Soviet Union, and this may have also influenced Hungarian views regarding participation. Romania and Slovakia, it was felt by elements of the Hungarian government, would earn Hitler's gratitude by their eagerness to assist; who knew whether Hitler might not find some way to reward them at Hungary's expense? Martin Himler, the official of the Office of Strategic Services who interrogated Bárdossy before the latter's extradition to Hungary in 1945, asked Bárdossy whether the Germans had requested Hungary's participation. "They didn't," answered Bárdossy. "That was precisely why we felt it necessary to take part in the war, in order not to lose the regained northern part of Hungary and Carpatho-Ruthenia should the German campaign be victorious. In fact, our honor also demanded that we fight on the side of our ally." [76] Indeed, the Romanian and Slovak governments entertained similar considerations and, like the Hungarian government, vied for Hitler's favors.

On the morning of June 26, having received no reply from Berlin, Bárdossy repeated his query regarding Hungarian participation to Erdmannsdorf.[77] But the German Foreign Office was dilatory. On the morning of June 26, that is, two full days after Erdmannsdorf had cabled Bárdossy's query from Budapest, Weizsäcker told Sztójay in Berlin that the question had been relayed to Ambassador Karl Ritter, assigned to work with Ribbentrop directly at the Führer headquarters.[78] The Reich Foreign Office probably suspected that if Hungary were requested to participate the Hungarian

74. Telegram from Erdmannsdorf to Berlin, June 24, 1941, *DGFP*, series D, 13 : 16; Ránki, *Emlékiratok és valóság*, p. 142; see also Mario Fenyo, "Allied Axis Armies at Stalingrad," p. 59.

75. Telegram from Erdmannsdorf to Berlin, *DGFP*, series D, 13 : 16.

76. Himler, *Így néztek ki a magyar nemzet sírásói*, p. 48.

77. Telegram from Erdmannsdorf to Berlin, June 26, 1941, *DGFP*, series D, 13 : 24; see also Ránki, *Emlékiratok és valóság*, p. 146.

78. Telegram from Sztójay to Bárdossy, June 26, 1941, *Magyarország és a második világháború*, pp. 367–68.

government would not hesitate long. But Hitler still preferred to make no requests. On June 25 Halder noted in his diary: "Hungary's collaboration would be desirable. Hungary, however, wants to be asked officially. The Führer will not do that, for political reasons." [79]

It was the next day that the Kassa incident took place. Hungarian military intervention seemed desirable from the German point of view. Hitler did not want to turn to the Hungarians with a request, but a little trickery might achieve the objective. The manner of the trickery may have been suggested by a recent episode. The casus belli for Hungary's participation in the war against Yugoslavia, earlier in April 1941, had been sporadic raids over Hungarian territory by presumably Yugoslav aircraft. These air raids took place on April 7 and 8, but there is some debate as to whether these were carried out by the Yugoslav air force.[80] The American chargé d'affaires reported, on April 7, that during Count Teleki's funeral air raid alarms sounded over Budapest; and later László Bárdossy, the new prime minister, informed the chargé that the "Hungarian air corps shot down six planes (some of which were British) when they bombed Pécs, Szeged, Villány, and Siklós where he states there were no German troops." [81] The Department of State disagreed. It accepted the notion that the bombs had been dropped by Yugoslav aircraft (and not German aircraft), but it pointed out to the Hungarian government that the raids were directed not against Hungary but against German troops stationed on Hungarian territory.[82] The

79. Halder, *KTB*, 3 : 15.
80. John A. Lukacs, for one, believes the bombings were perpetrated by Germans: "On April 7 and April 8 'Yugoslav' planes dropped half-a-dozen light bombs on villages in southern Hungary; this was arranged between the Hungarian and German General Staffs" (*The Great Powers and Eastern Europe*, p. 376). The report of the chief of the General Staff (signed by Colonel Kúthy) stated that Yugoslav airplanes penetrated on April 7 into the Villány and Pécs areas, where they dropped two bombs. At about the same time, further Yugoslav airplanes flew over the city of Szeged, dropping a bomb on the railroad station. Six (!) British aircraft were shot down by the Hungarian defense. The Hungarian ministers in London and Washington were immediately informed that the bombing was an unprovoked attack against Hungary, as there were no German troops stationed at Szeged. Political Section, Ministry of Foreign Affairs, Hungarian National Archives, K63, bundle 15 (1941–44), tétel 2.
81. *Foreign Relations of the United States 1941,* 1 : 303 (hereafter cited as *FRUS*). Bárdossy added that "Hungary has no intention of aiding Germany unless Yugoslavia commits further acts against Hungary and denied general mobilization is under way or contemplated."
82. Telegram from Erdmannsdorf to the German Foreign Office, Apr. 9, 1941, *DGFP*, series D, 11 : 495.

Hungarian government denied there were German troops stationed at Szeged, one of the bombed cities (see above, note 69). The Hungarian press was instructed by the press office to play up the incidents.[83] The attacks were described as provocative; in 1945, at Nuremberg, Horthy still thought of them as the grounds for the Hungarian attack on Yugoslavia.[84] This incident may well have been the one from which the plotters of the Kassa air raid, if plotters there were, derived their inspiration.

I have found no documents indicating that the Kassa incident was devised by Germans, or anyone else. Most Hungarian authors assume the Reich government was involved but believe the bombing was not a strictly German affair; that it was arranged with the connivance of certain elements on the Hungarian General Staff; more precisely, that the plot was hatched by the German air attaché in Budapest, Col. Kuno Heribert Fütterer, and by Colonel László, the chief of the mobilization section of the Hungarian General Staff.[85] There is, of course, the eyewitness report of Col. Ádám Krudy, who never wavered from his conviction that the aircraft were German. Additional circumstantial evidence in support of Krudy's conviction is presented by Dániel Csatári in his monograph on Hungarian-Romanian relations.[86] At least one Hungarian ex-official with whom I have discussed the incident is convinced that the trick was devised by Hungarian officers, with some German help.[87] There are other, less commonly held hypotheses, including the ones advanced by prominent scholars in the field such as Professor Hillgruber and Professor C. A. Macartney of Oxford. The former seems to hold the view that the bombings at Kassa were perpetrated by disgruntled Slovak aviators, whereas the latter thinks the least unlikely hypothesis is that Kassa was bombed by Czech

83. Ránki, "Magyarország belépése a második világháborúba," p. 37.

84. Horthy interrogations, NA Record Group 238, World War II War Crimes Records.

85. See, for instance, Komlós, *Elárult ország*, p. 39. A German diplomat, Erich Kordt, wrote on this subject: "Ein unwürdiges und verbrecherisches Spiel würde von einigen [deutschen] Generalstablern in Szene gesetzt, indem Kaschau angeblich von Sowjetfliegern, in Wirklichkeit aber von eigenen Flugzeugen bombardiert wurde. Ob der ungarische Generalstabschef, von Werth, mit im Spiele war, steht nicht fest. Vermutlich startete die Fliegergruppe vom slowakischen Truppenübungsplatz Malacky" (*Wahn und Wirklichkeit*, p. 308, note).

86. *Forgószélben* [In the whirlwind], pp. 90–93.

87. István de Szent-Miklósy to author.

pilots on their way to seek refuge in the Soviet Union! [88] In support of his hypothesis, Macartney quotes an article which appeared in a Hungarian newspaper in 1942. According to this article a Czech-born officer of the Russian air force by the name of Andrej Andele, taken prisoner by the Axis forces, confessed to having bombed Kassa.[89] With all due respect to Macartney, he has simply failed to exercise his critical faculties with regard to the source of this information; it was certainly impossible for a Hungarian newspaper to publish an article in 1942 to the effect that the Kassa bombings were carried out by disguised (or undisguised) German aircraft. More important, perhaps, was the implication, made in the midst of the war, that Hungary had entered into the war and was jeopardizing its very existence as a nation as a result of an error, a matter of mistaken identity! Yet I must admit I have found no direct evidence to substantiate the assumption that the air raid on Kassa was a matter of German or Hungarian trickery. One must assume that even if the incident had been plotted by the German air attaché in Budapest, the orders must have come from Hitler and Halder; yet I have found no trace of such authorization. (See note on p. 26.)

88. Andreas Hillgruber, "Der Einbau der verbündeten Armeen in die deutsche Ostfront 1941–1944," p. 666. "The question, whether indeed Soviet bombs were involved and not, as it was asserted at the Nürnberg trials, German bombs, has been decided on the basis of authentic notes in the war diary of the 'Deutschen General beim Oberkommando der Kgl. Ungarischen Wehrmacht.' But the further questions, whether a conscious provocation on the part of Soviet authorities was involved, or whether it was an initiative of vengeful Slovakian flyers—and there is much to support the latter view—has not yet been authoritatively studied." It should be pointed out, however, that Hillgruber presents no evidence to support his point of view, nor is the reader told where such evidence may be found. As to the bombs, Hillgruber does not explain why he believes the Slovakians could procure bombs manufactured in the Soviet Union more easily than the Germans. There is evidence, however, indicating that in the fall of 1940 the Slovak government had ordered the construction of an airport near Vranov in eastern Slovakia and that this project was kept secret from the Germans (Yeshayahu Jelinek to author, Dec. 14, 1970). For further discussion, see Mario Fenyo, "Allied Axis Armies at Stalingrad," pp. 58–59. The evidence presented by C. A. Macartney is less than convincing. One of the bombs, writes Macartney, "which by miraculous good fortune failed to explode," was dug out and shown to have been manufactured at the Putilov works in Leningrad (*October Fifteenth*, 2 : 32). One must note, however, that bombs that fail to explode are not a miracle or even a rarity and that it is not overly difficult to reconstitute a bomb even if it does explode. Furthermore, it does not strike me as unlikely or difficult for the Germans to have procured bombs of Soviet make—no more difficult or complicated than to disguise an aircraft. Macartney himself admits this possibility in his essay "Hungary's Declaration of War," p. 164.

89. Macartney, "Hungary's Declaration of War," p. 165.

The following morning, on June 27, Bárdossy appeared in the
Hungarian House of Parliament and declared:

> Honored House! I wish now only to make a brief report. The
> Presid̦ent [of the House] has branded with telling words the
> illegal and despicable attack by the Soviet Union. The Royal
> Hungarian Government concludes that in consequence of these
> attacks a state of war has come into being between Hungary
> and the Soviet Union.

After the applause subsided, Bárdossy added: "Only one more sentence. The Hungarian Air Force will take the appropriate measures
of reprisal." [90]

Was Bárdossy's declaration of war unconstitutional? [91] Macartney
states that Bárdossy "drove a cart and a horse" through the Hungarian constitution.[92] Similar comments are made by other authors
on the subject.[93] These comments are based on paragraph 13 of
Law 1 of 1920 which defined the constitution of the Hungarian
state, a constitution which remained in effect, with some changes
and amendments, until 1945: according to this law the previous
consent of Parliament was necessary for a declaration of war or for
the use of the army beyond the country's borders. In that same year,
in 1920, the powers of the regent, already considerable, were extended; thus Law 17 of 1920 stated, among other stipulations, that
the regent may use the army outside the borders of the country,
although the cabinet is responsible and the Parliament must give
its ulterior approval.[94] Bárdossy asked, and obtained, the Parlia-

90. Macartney, *October Fifteenth*, 2 : 29. In the same context, Macartney added:
"[Bárdossy's] proud and sensitive spirit felt that it was not only cheaper but also more
dignified to volunteer than to take orders, thus preserving at least the outward forms
of independence and sovereignty" (ibid., 2 : 27).

91. A Hungarian author wrote, around 1946, a book whose title may be translated
"Mitigating circumstances in the judicial trial of Hungary." This work appears to
have been written with a view to the forthcoming Paris peace conferences where, incidentally, the punishment meted out to Hungary was no less than at the Treaty of
Trianon twenty-seven years earlier. The Hungarian delegation to the peace conference
needed arguments in Hungary's defense. With regard to the declaration of war on the
Soviet Union, the author of the above-mentioned work, Andor Kun, wrote: "It is no
excuse, but nevertheless it must be mentioned" that Bárdossy declared war unconstitu-
tionally, since that privilege belonged to the Parliament (*Enyhítő körülmények Magyarország bűnperében*, p. 18).

92. *October Fifteenth*, 2 : 30.

93. See, for instance, Sulyok, *A magyar tragédia*, p. 381; and Kun, "Magyarország
második világháborúba," p. 35.

94. *Tanulmányok*, pp. 46, 47.

ment's ulterior sanction of the declaration of war on the Soviet Union on July 24, about a month after he announced the state of war. Thus it appears that Bárdossy's action were not unconstitutional; but whatever the merits of the argument, the point is relatively unimportant and academic. The fact remains that not only Bárdossy but Horthy, the cabinet, and the parliament favored war against the Soviet Union. The minutes of the cabinet meeting at which the decision was taken, although they appear to have been tampered with, indicated that the minister of the interior, Ferenc Keresztes-Fisher, objected to the declaration of war. István Bárczy, who took these minutes, asserted after the war that three other ministers present at the meeting also raised various objections.[95] It is clear, however, that the conviction of those who favored belligerent action was strong enough to prevail.

With regard to the attitude of the regent, most sources, except his own *Memoirs,* seem to agree that he favored a declaration of war. The regent may have allowed himself to be persuaded by Gen. Henrik Werth, the chief of the General Staff, Károly Bartha, the minister of defense, or Bárdossy, all of whom called on Horthy on June 26 shortly after the news of the air raid was received by them.[96] It is possible that the regent wanted "reprisals" and Bárdossy took this to mean war.[97] But Horthy does not seem to have disapproved of the course taken by Bárdossy at the time: Horthy's enthusiastic reception of the news of the German attack, on June 22, was probably sincere. Some authors claim the "crusade against bolshevism" was really Horthy's idea in the first place. Many of Horthy's friends and followers who are alive today make no attempt to conceal their conviction that Horthy was eager to participate in an anti-Soviet crusade and that, furthermore, events of the last twenty-five years have proved him right! [98] In any case, important evidence may have

95. Macartney, *October Fifteenth,* 2 : 27; see also Ránki, *Emlékiratok és valóság,* p. 148, note 238.

96. Ránki, *Emlékiratok és valóság,* pp. 146–47. Macartney, *October Fifteenth,* 2 : 25–26.

97. Macartney, "Hungary's Declaration of War," p. 162.

98. In the introduction to the English-language version of Horthy's *Memoirs,* Nicholas Roosevelt wrote: "The last time I saw this staunch old admiral was when I paid my farewell visit to him before returning to the United States in 1933. He spoke with passionate earnestness about his conviction that Russia was the greatest threat, not only to Hungary but to the western world. . . . Events have proved that his fears were justified. . . . The Hungarian Regent in this case had foreseen correctly, but he was unable to convince either British or American leaders that communist

been withheld from Horthy. Since the end of the war, Horthy has repeatedly declared that Kristóffy's telegrams concerning Molotov's intervention were never shown to him.[99] In his *Memoirs* Horthy repeats that the telegram from Colonel Krudy in Kassa was never shown to him and that Bárdossy had attempted to suppress that evidence.[100] Scholars may disagree; but it is clear that, at least at the time he was writing his *Memoirs*, Horthy felt the declaration of war had been a grave mistake.

Russia was even more rapacious and greedy than Czarist Russia, and that it was folly to believe that if Russia was treated as a friendly ally, that country would respond in kind" (Horthy, *Memoirs*, p. 10).

99. Macartney, *October Fifteenth*, 2 : 26.

100. Horthy, *Memoirs*, p. 191. Dezső Sulyok testifies that István Bárczy told him he had personal knowledge of the fact that not only Bárdossy but also Horthy knew about the telegrams from both Kristóffy and Krudy (*A Magyar tragédia*, p. 381).

Note added in proof, for p. 23, above: The latest contribution to the debate is that of Juliányi Borsányi (published in *Uj látóhatár*, volumes 5 and 6). His investigations began the day after the raid, in his capacity as an official of the Ministry of Defense, and have continued ever since. He argues, convincingly enough, that Col. Ádám Krudy could not have taken off during the raid, and that the raid was carried out by two aircraft rather than three or four. His conclusions, that the raid was carried out neither by Hungarians, nor by Germans, nor by Soviet pilots, rest on assumptions that are somewhat less than completely convincing.

2. The Role of the Hungarian Military in the Campaign against the Soviet Union until the Eve of Stalingrad

On March 5, 1938, as the clouds of war were gathering over Europe, the Hungarian prime minister Kálmán Darányi delivered a speech in Győr, an industrial town in northwestern Hungary, announcing a five-year plan for rearmament; the main objective of the plan, actually attained in about two years, was to equal and surpass the existing strength of the Romanian army.[1] Until that time the specifications and restrictions imposed on the armed forces by the Treaty of Trianon had been observed. By the fall of 1938 Hungary had seven army corps; with the return of parts of Slovakia and Transylvania the number of corps rose to nine.[2] These army corps consisted altogether of twenty-seven infantry brigades (dandár) of two regiments each (the equivalent of twenty-seven light divisions), plus two cavalry and two motorized brigades.[3]

Yet in 1941, when the world war overtook Hungary, the Hungarian army was still unprepared for a major campaign. Although it may have been the latest one organized, it was antiquated from the beginning. The air force was small, the armored vehicles few and light, the bulk of the army unmotorized.[4] In December 1940, according to the table of weapons and equipment of the Hungarian armed forces, the air force consisted of 302 military aircraft. As a result of an inspection conducted in March 1941, however, it turned out that 53 of these aircraft were just not there, and 60 more were not operational. The remaining 209 operational aircraft were obsolete.[5] According to a different source, however, the Hungarian air force had 363 planes by 1941, but there is no information regarding

1. Sándor Tóth, "A Horthy-hadsereg helyzete a Szovjetunió elleni háborúba lépés idején" [The condition of the Horthy army at the time of the entry into the war against the Soviet Union], pp. 500, 525.

2. Ibid., pp. 501–2.

3. Jenő Czebe and Tibor Pethö, *Hungary in World War II*, p. 16. The effectives of a Hungarian infantry regiment were a little less than 4,000. Miklós Horváth, *A. 2. magyar hadsereg megsemmisülése a Donnál* [The annihilation of the Second Hungarian Army at the Don], p. 17.

4. Tóth, "A Horthy-hadsereg helyzete," p. 503.

5. Ibid., p. 519.

their condition.[6] The tanks were almost exclusively Italian-made (by the Ansaldo firm), light, two person armored vehicles. The Hungarians began to build their own tanks (Toldi) in 1938, but the designs were not up-to-date.[7] Later on, various Hungarian firms began to manufacture tanks designated as Turan I, II, and III, 440 of which were actually produced by 1944; but at the time Hungary entered the war only 190 tanks of the older type had been commissioned.[8] As a result of the rearmament program in 1938, the government ordered 1,400 trucks that year and a further 1,400 in 1941. According to the table of weapons and equipment of December 1, 1940, the Hungarian army had 866 small motor vehicles and 2,835 trucks.[9] These numbers may have sufficed for the two motorized brigades, but that would have meant the bulk of the Hungarian army remained inadequately motorized, even after a requisition of private vehicles.[10] As late as 1943, when the Hungarian army was better motorized than it had been in 1941, only one-third of the number of trucks needed was actually available. While the foreign policy of the Hungarian governments in the between-the-wars period consistently pursued the revision of the Treaty of Trianon, and especially the reoccupation of certain territories awarded to neighboring countries, the state of the Hungarian army would not have allowed military measures. Hungarian revisionism could be aggressive only in tone. Even after March 1938, when it was decided to expand the Army in disregard of the treaty, Hungary was unprepared, and unwilling, to take unilateral military actions against Czechoslovakia, Romania, or Yugoslavia; proof of this was the Hungarian leaders' refusal to take action against Czechoslovakia when Hitler made suggestions to that effect in August 1938. Militarily speaking, Hungary was even less prepared to launch an attack on the Soviet Union. It is clear that the Hungarian attack had not been premeditated.

The deplorable condition of the Hungarian air force soon became evident as a result of a "retaliatory" raid carried out against some Soviet towns on June 26, before the actual declaration of war

6. Iván Berend and György Ránki, "Hadianyaggyártás Magyarországon a második világháború alatt" [Manufacture of war materials in Hungary during World War II], p. 708.

7. Tóth, "A Horthy-hadsereg helyzete," p. 503.

8. Berend and Ránki, "Hadianyaggyártás," pp. 707–8.

9. Karsai, *A budai vártól*, p. 12.

10. Tóth, "A Horthy-hadsereg helyzete," p. 514.

against the Soviet Union. According to the historian Elek Karsai, most of the Hungarian aircraft participating in the raid—nineteen bombers and one fighter—did not reach their targets, which were only a short distance from the Hungarian-Soviet border; furthermore, two planes were damaged during takeoff, two effected forced landings, and two more were shot down.[11]

The ground units sent against the Soviet Union consisted of the two motorized brigades, one cavalry brigade—composing the mobile army corps—and ten battalions of alpine troops,[12] all under the command of Gen. Ferenc Szombathelyi, Hungary's next chief of the General Staff. Szombathelyi and the Hungarian units were subordinated to the Seventeenth German Army and later to the First Armored Group.[13] The actual advance of the Hungarian units began on July 1. The mobile corps seems to have fared well in the campaign—a fact which one military observer ascribes to the continual "tactical" retreat of the Soviet forces.[14] Whatever the case may be, the Hungarian units, only inadequately motorized, reached the Dniester and the Donets rivers, advancing a distance of about a thousand miles in the course of the campaign. All went well; an incident in which the Soviet forces captured German orders to the effect that German units should beat the Hungarians to the oil areas in Galicia seems to have passed unnoticed, despite Soviet attempts to capitalize on the seized document by broadcasting its contents in Hungarian.[15] The document was most likely genuine; General Paulus testified at Nuremberg that Hitler had not disclosed his designs on the Soviet Union to the Hungarians because he was unwilling to give them a chance of seizing the oil fields in the Russian oil district of Drogobitch.[16]

Hungarian losses were moderate. Between June 27 and August 3 the mobile corps lost 59 officers and 918 troops[17] These sacrifices

11. Karsai, *A budai vártól*, p. 8.
12. Czebe and Pethö, *Hungary in World War II*, p. 18.
13. Karsai, *A budai vártól*, p. 29.
14. Vilmos Nagy, *Végzetes esztendők, 1938–1945* [Fateful years], p. 69.
15. "Die Ungarn werden voraussichtlich am 3. 7. mit ihren vordersten Kräften über die Karpathen in Richtung Stanislaw-Kolomea antreten. Die Besetzung des Ölgebietes muss so durchgeführt werden, dass es auf keinen Fall vorher von den Ungarn erreicht werden kann . . ." (telegram from Ritter to Erdmannsdorf, July 9, 1944, NA Microcopy T-120, roll 91, 103792).
16. *Trial of the Major War Criminals*, 7 : 256–58, 329–30.
17. Karsai, *A budai vártól*, p. 12. Karsai does not indicate whether these are total casualty figures or the number of killed.

of the Hungarian forces seem to have made no particular impression on the chief of the German General Staff: between June 26 and September 9, 1941, Halder's diary contains practically no mention of the Hungarians, with one exception which will be discussed below.[18]

On August 19 General Werth had submitted to the Hungarian cabinet a memorandum advocating increased Hungarian participation in the war effort; in response Bárdossy asked the regent to choose between General Werth and himself, accusing Werth of interference in political matters. If the Germans asked the Hungarians to contribute more, Bárdossy wrote the regent, then this request ought to be considered, but it would certainly not be to the country's advantage to volunteer to contribute more.[19] Werth was asked to resign, and his resignation took place just a few days before Horthy's scheduled visit to the Führer headquarters.[20] This change in personnel was accompanied by a change in policy. Not only were Horthy, Bárdossy, and the Hungarian government now reluctant to contribute more to the war effort, but they became determined to recall the bulk of the Hungarian forces fighting in the Soviet Union. Perhaps Horthy had already regretted his hasty decision to declare war on the Soviet Union. For one thing, he was always inclined to believe the British navy would win the war; also, the warnings of the American representatives in Hungary were occasionally heeded. Furthermore, Hungary had already obtained all the territory her leaders felt justified to claim. Yet the causes of this reversal of policy remain one of the mysteries of Hungary's role in World War II; I have found no documents and only incomplete testimony bearing upon them.

The German military attaché in Budapest was approached with

18. An article in the Sept. 9, 1941, issue of the *Deutsche Allgemeine Zeitung* commented favorably on Hungarian military accomplishments: "It must be recognized," wrote the author of the article, "that the leadership of the Hungarian mobile corps remained mobile even in militarily difficult situations. This leadership mastered all situations in a manner which meets with German principles. The Hungarian mobile corps advanced from the border to Nikolajev, fighting incessantly, a thousand miles" (quoted by Karsai, *A budai vártól*, pp. 38–39). Such articles, however, were usually "fed" to the National Socialist press.

19. Gyula Juhász, *Magyarország külpolitikája, 1919–1945* [Hungary's foreign policy], pp. 244–45.

20. Ibid., p. 32; see also telegram from Major Toussaint to OKW Berlin, Aug. 5, 1941, NA Microcopy T-120, roll 91, 103912. Bárdossy's long-winded memorandum, date Aug. 26, concerning General Werth's unwarranted interference in the affairs of the state is printed in *Horthy Miklós titkos iratai*, pp. 300–07.

a request for the recall of the Hungarian mobile corps on September 3. Although General Halder dismissed the speculation that political motives underlay this request, he noted that the Hungarian units were in no worse condition than the German ones and decided to oppose the Hungarian request.[21] After all, he argued, there were sixteen Romanian divisions fighting on the eastern front, and the Romanian government had already complained about the paltry Hungarian participation in the war.[22] The Hungarian prime minister was reported to have stated in an interview that Hungary had nothing against the Russian people but was only fighting bolshevism. It seems, argued the Romanian minister in Berlin, that the Hungarians are saving their troops for a different objective.[23]

On September 1, 1941, Ernst von Jagow, the new German minister in Budapest, was instructed by Ribbentrop to invite Horthy to the headquarters of the Führer. Horthy accepted the invitation.[24] In a further telegram Ribbentrop suggested a date for the visit and added that the composition of the Hungarian delegation would be entirely up to the regent: "Regarding the military members of the delegation," continued Ribbentrop, "Hitler would be most pleased if the chief of the General Staff, General Werth, and the chief of the Operations Section, General László, were included." [25] Both generals, however, had been replaced that very day, on September 2. Two telegrams from Jagow provided the Reich Foreign Office with a list of the members of the Hungarian delegation.[26] A further telegram, on September 5, announced that General Szombathelyi, the newly appointed chief of the General Staff, would accompany Horthy instead of Werth.[27] If Werth's dismissal may have seemed a direct affront to Germany, especially after Hitler practically appointed him a member of the Hungarian delegation, the next telegrams of Jagow must have reassured the Reich Foreign Office and Hitler's entourage: Szombathelyi's former name was Knaus, which indi-

21. Halder, *KTB*, 3 : 212.

22. Hillgruber, *Hitler, König Carol und Marschall Antonescu*, p. 138.

23. Memorandum by Weizsäcker, July 18, 1941, NA Microcopy T-120, roll 91, 103823.

24. Telegram from Ribbentrop to Jagow, Sept. 1, 1941, NA Microcopy T-120, roll 91, 104001; telegram from Jagow to Berlin, Sept. 2, 1941, NA Microcopy T-120, roll 91, 104002.

25. NA Microcopy T-120, roll 91, 104027.

26. Jagow to Berlin, Sept. 3, 1941, NA Microcopy T-120, roll 91, 104030; Jagow to Berlin, Sept. 4, 1941, NA Microcopy T-120, roll 91, 104037-38.

27. Telegram from Jagow to Berlin, Sept. 5, 1941, NA Microcopy T-120, roll 91, 104043.

cated that Szombathelyi, like Werth, was a member of the German
ethnic minority in Hungary. As this argument may not have sufficed to clinch a favorable bias, Jagow added that Szombathelyi was
"einwandrei deutsch orientiert"—clearly pro-German.[28]

I have found no detailed description of what happened at the
Führer headquarters on September 7; a succinct account of the
Hitler-Horthy meeting is given by General Halder, who described
the confrontation as rather impassioned at certain moments:

> The arguments concerning the further participation of the
> Hungarian mobile corps in operations were at times somewhat
> heated. The new chief of the General Staff presented the selfish
> point of view that Hungary's forces must be preserved in view
> of their tasks in the Balkans. . . . Finally it was agreed that
> the mobile corps may remain until the end of the operations,
> and in case of a later recall, replacement was suggested.[29]

According to a memorandum of a conversation between Ribbentrop
and Bárdossy on September 7, the former suggested the Hungarian
mobile unit be withdrawn and reequipped and replaced by some
rear-echelon troops.[30]

Since Germany was making steady progress on the eastern front,
no serious objections were raised to the Hungarian design for partial
withdrawal; the objections General Halder had raised in September
seem to have been overcome. As late as November 23, Halder noted
in his diary that Russian military power was no longer a threat to
the "reconstruction of Europe." [31] On October 3 General Halder
had discussed the withdrawal of the Hungarian mobile corps with
Col. Adolf Heusinger.[32] The mobile corps was actually withdrawn
from the eastern front in the course of October, November, and December 1941. On November 27, during Bárdossy's visit to Germany,
Hitler told Bárdossy "that the Hungarian unit had fought really
splendidly on the Eastern Front" and deserved to have a period of
rest for recovery.[33] Hitler sent Horthy the large gold cross of the

28. Telegram from Jagow to Berlin, Sept. 5, 1941, NA Microcopy T-120, roll 91,
104044; and Jagow to Berlin, same date, NA Microcopy T-120, roll 91, 104045. In fact,
a good indication of the oversimplification of German foreign policy during the
war is the mania German diplomats had of describing the politicians of their allies
as either "pro-German" or bad and unreliable.

29. Halder, *KTB*, 3 : 217–18.

30. Karsai, *A budai vártól*, pp. 41–42; see also Macartney, *October Fifteenth*, 2 : 55.

31. Halder, *KTB*, 3 : 306.

32. Ibid., p. 266.

33. Memorandum by Hewel, Nov. 28, 1941, *DGFP*, series D, 13 : 857.

Order of Holler as a token of his gratitude.[34] Yet a day after November 27 Hitler might have spoken differently: that day Marshal von Kleist was forced to withdraw his German units from Rostov—the first German defeat of the war. Hitler's praise of the Hungarian feats was also about his last occasion to praise them. While at one time Hitler may have thought of the Hungarians as fierce barbarians (thanks, perhaps, to certain references in Wagner's *Lohengrin*), his admiration for their martial virtues began to diminish in 1942.[35]

There remained on Soviet territory a fairly large contingent of lightly armed Hungarian troops whose task it was to maintain order in the rear, which increasingly meant to fight the partisans. The German military authorities felt the Hungarians were suited for this task. If the complimentary remarks in the German war diary of the Army High Command are any indication, the Hungarian units carried out their antipartisan operations with success and zeal,[36] perhaps more zeal than the Hungarian commanders liked to acknowledge a year or two later. In his speech of November 6, 1641, Stalin listed the Hungarians among the enemies of the Soviet Union. During their conversations on December 16–22, 1941, Stalin gave Anthony Eden the impression he felt "great antagonism towards Hungary." But when Eden related this impression to Sumner Welles, in March of 1943, it may already have been out of date.[37] By the end of December most Hungarian troops had been withdrawn from Soviet territory, and in a speech on February 23, 1942, Stalin listed

34. Telegram from Horthy to Hitler, Apr. 15, 1942, Political Section, Ministry of Foreign Affairs, Hungarian National Archives, K63, bundles 187–88, tétel 21.

35. On the night of Jan. 4–5, 1942, Hitler is reported to have remarked: "The Hungarians are good auxiliaries for us. With proper stiffening we find them very useful. As for Rumania, she has only one man, Antonescu" (*Hitler's Secret Conversations, 1941–1944,* ed. Hugh Trevor-Roper, p. 148). By August 1942, Hitler had reversed his estimates: "If the Hungarians go to war with the Rumanians, then, unless I am much mistaken, Antonescu will knock hell out of them" (ibid., p. 505). It may also be noted that, disregarding historical evidence, Hitler was wont to consider the Hungarians as the descendants of the Huns. Comparing Vienna, Linz, and Budapest, Hitler remarked at table (on Apr. 26, 1942): "Ausserdem sei es ja auch—geschichtlich gesehen—eine unverzeihlich Parodie, wenn die Haupstadt der Nachfahren Etzels [Attila] und seiner Hunnen die schönste Stadt [Budapest] am Nibelungstrom [Danube] wäre" (Picker, *Hitlers Tischgespräche,* p. 299).

36. *Kriegstagebuch des Oberkommandos der Wehrmacht, 1940–1945,* 2 : 374, 376, 387, 395, 401 (hereafter cited as *KTB, OKW*).

37. "Mr. Eden said that he had encountered upon his last visit to Moscow great antagonism towards Hungary. I asked Mr. Eden if he could tell me specifically what Stalin might have stated with regard to Hungary and Mr. Eden replied that he thought all that was said was that Stalin demanded that 'Hungary be punished'" (memorandum of conversations between Eden, Lord Halifax, and Sumner Welles in Washington, Mar. 16, 1943, *FRUS 1943,* 3 : 23).

only the Italians, Romanians, and Finns as supporting the Germans.[38]

If Hungary's omission in his speech was an indication that Stalin no longer considered Hungary directly involved in the hostilities, he was soon disabused. In late November and December 1941, it had become obvious even to the German High Command that the war was not over; the German advance had been checked—in fact, the German armies were at times forced to give ground. To remedy the situation the Reich government approached the Axis partners, through political and military channels, requesting all-out participation. It was nearly successful in obtaining such participation.

Even before the crisis had set in, the Hungarian government was under the impression the Reich government had requested additional troops. A telegram from Special Ambassador Karl Ritter to Jagow, October 25, 1941, found among the records of the German Foreign Office, explained that some time earlier Szombathelyi had spoken to the German military attaché in Budapest. Szombathelyi had said that clearly Hungary would gradually have to commit all her forces on the side of Germany, and to be prepared he would like to know in advance what military support Germany expected from Hungary during the coming year.[39] Ritter, however, repeated the argument we have already encountered several times, that one must avoid giving the impression that Germany had any requests to make from the Hungarians: "We attach importance to explaining to the Hungarian government that the conversation between the general staffs was initiated by the Hungarians, and that our proposition becomes inoperative if the Hungarians attach political, military or economic counterterms to our agreement." [40]

Bárdossy replied to Jagow that the German Army High Command must have misunderstood something, the Hungarian government had made no offer.[41] Nevertheless, on November 11, 1941, Jagow presented Bárdossy with some specific German wishes: two more brigades for occupation purposes and certain specialized units. Bárdossy was now prepared to grant the wish but hoped for an "adjust-

---

38. On the latter date Stalin simply said: "The German Fascist army has the direct support at the front of Italian, Rumanian, and Finnish troops" (Joseph Stalin, *On the Great Patriotic War of the Soviet Union*, pp. 23, 43).

39. NA Microcopy T-120, roll 92, 104314.

40. NA Microcopy T-120, roll 92, 104315–16.

41. Telegram from Jagow to Ritter, Oct. 27, 1941, NA Microcopy T-120, roll 92, 104321; see also Karsai, *A budai vártól*, pp. 53–55.

ment" of the northeastern border of Hungary in exchange.[42] Such counterterms were precisely what the German Foreign Office had wanted to avoid. More significantly, this territorial claim, small as it was, invalidated the moral or historical justification for the revision of the peace treaty, which had been the cardinal point of Hungarian foreign policy between the wars. Up to this point Hungarian claims for land within the Carpathian basin could be justified by historical considerations or even by the principle of self-determination; no such considerations or principles could be invoked with regard to territories lying in Galicia, beyond the Carpathian range.[43]

In the course of the next months the Reich Foreign Office and the German Army High Command sacrificed one of the fine points of their foreign policy—the pretense that Germany was making no requests from its Hungarian ally was dropped. On December 20, 1941, Hitler outlined the military tasks for the coming year to the General Staff: these tasks included obtaining substantial additional forces from Italy, Romania, and Hungary, to be transported to the eastern front before the snow melted, to avoid the mud.[44] Accordingly, Hitler addressed a letter to Horthy on December 29. This letter explained the general military situation, in particular the situation on the eastern front. It explained that only the bad weather which plagued the German army (but apparently not the Soviet army) for three months out of six had prevented the occupation of even larger territories. It explained that the Soviet Union still disposed of large masses of men, in part without any weapons, who were being hurled against the German lines with a typically Asiatic disregard for the value of human life. Then came the main point of the letter:

> My candid wish, Your Excellency, is that Hungarian units may participate in the decisive fight once again in the coming year. In the long run this war is, after all, a confrontation which will decide the existence or nonexistence of us all. If Your Excellency decides, as I earnestly hope, to take part in these opera-

42. Telegram from Ritter to Jagow, Nov. 9, 1941, NA Microcopy T-120, roll 92, 104365; telegram from Jagow to Berlin, Nov 12, 1941, NA Microcopy T-120, roll 92, 104379; see also Karsai, *A budai vártól*, p. 57.

43. This Hungarian claim is discussed in a report by Jagow, Dec. 2, 1941, NA Microcopy T-120, roll 92, 104405.

44. Halder, *KTB*, 3 : 361. A further entry in the Halder diary indicates that between June 22 and Dec. 31, 1941, the German army lost 25.96% of its personnel, or 830,903 soldiers, including 173,722 killed (ibid., 3 : 374).

tions again during the coming year with Hungarian units, then I would like to make the one request that these units be sent out to the place designated for the start of the offensive before the snow begins to melt, as the melting snow delays any movement for a matter of many weeks.[45]

The letter concluded by pointing out that Germany was prepared to equip the Hungarian units, if at all possible.[46]

The next step was a visit by Ribbentrop. This visit, January 5–9, 1942, was billed as a courtesy call in response to a long-standing invitation and featured a hunting party at which Horthy was host.[47] But the surviving documents make it clear that Ribbentrop's visit had primarily a political purpose. On January 4 Field Marshal Keitel had prepared a memorandum for Ribbentrop's use. This memorandum summarized the contributions Hungary had hitherto made to the campaign in the East and outlined what could be expected of Hungary in the future. Keitel was more specific than Hitler had been: the memorandum states that, in addition to the mobile corps which the Hungarians had withdrawn and which was being re-equipped, Hungary was expected to contribute the major part of her army to the "great common cause." Keitel's memorandum explained, moreover, that the German military attaché in Budapest would keep the regent au courant of military events, especially in the southern sector of the eastern front, on a day-to-day basis. This briefing would be carried out in such a manner as "to prepare the Hungarian chief of state for the necessity of greater participation of the Hungarian army in the Russian campaign of 1942." [48]

Although Ribbentrop seems to have made no specific demands, the tenor of the political conversations centered around the desirability of total Hungarian participation in the war; [49] no doubt Rib-

45. NA Microcopy T-120, roll 610 (Loesch Collection), F50283–82.

46. Ibid., F50279–78. This letter, incidentally, is not printed in *Horthy Miklós titkos iratai.*

47. Horthy's invitation to Ribbentrop was probably sent in November 1941. This invitation is printed in *Horthy Miklós titkos iratai,* p. 312, without a date. The visit had originally been scheduled as simply a hunting party back in September 1940. Note by Aladár Szegedy-Maszák, Nov. 30, 1941, Political Section, Ministry of Foreign Affairs, Hungarian National Archives, K63, bundles 187–88, tétel 21.

48. "Beitrag OKW zur Besprechung des Reichsaussenministers mit Reichsverweser von Horthy," Jan. 4, 1942, NA Microcopy T-120, roll 610 (Loesch Collection), F50303–301.

49. A pencil mark at the bottom of the aforecited "contribution" reads "6 Korps a 3 mobile Brigaden," possibly a notation by Ribbentrop himself (ibid., F50301).

bentrop figured, as would any businessman, that by asking for everything he would receive more. According to a brief memorandum by
an official of the German Foreign Office, Ribbentrop emphasized in
the course of conversations with both Horthy and Bárdossy the
urgency of "wiping out bolshevism once and for all, in the coming
year!" Along this line of thought the Reich foreign minister made
the request that Hungary place its whole army at the disposal of
the campaign this year, in order to take part in attaining the given
objective." [50]

After talks with other members of the Hungarian government,
Horthy and Bárdossy told Ribbentrop, on the last day of his visit,
that Hungary could not offer her military forces "one hundred percent" for the eastern campaign but was prepared to contribute *bis
zur äussersten Grenze des Möglichen*—"to the absolute limit of the
possible." Ribbentrop was satisfied. The details were not discussed,
as it was agreed that these could be settled during the coming visit
of Field Marshal Keitel himself.[51]

A Hungarian Foreign Ministry report described Ribbentrop's visit
in most unfavorable terms. He used, according to this report, "the
well-known method of promises and threats" to persuade the Hungarian leaders to participate more actively in the war. The promises
consisted in establishing a connection between the extent of Hungarian military participation and Hungarian territorial claims (for
instance, in the Bánát). Ribbentrop is also reported to have declared at one point that if Hungary should refuse to contribute her
entire military force such a decision may have an unforeseeable
effect on Hitler's "just but passionate nature." [52] Is it possible, then,
that the thought of invading Hungary had already occurred to Hitler in early 1942?

On January 10, the day Ribbentrop left Budapest, Horthy sat
down to write Hitler a long letter. In this letter Horthy pointed out
the dangers threatening Hungary and Germany from the direction
of the Balkans including, of course, from Romania. Various groups
of partisans were already active in Yugoslavia, and it is possible that
Horthy seriously believed in the possibility of an attack from that
quarter (this was also the time of the Hungarian mass reprisals in

50. Memorandum by Weber, Jan. 17, 1942, NA Microscopy T-120, roll 92, 104502 ff.;
same report reproduced on NA Microcopy T-120, roll 2415, 221632 ff.
51. Ibid.
52. Karsai, *A budai vártól*, p. 96.

the Bácska). But the implication of the argument, never clearly stated, was readily apparent: Hungary could not send all her armed forces to the eastern front, as some of these were needed for defensive purposes.[53]

On January 15, 1942, between the calls made by Ribbentrop and by Keitel, Count Ciano paid a visit to the Hungarian capital. The Hungarians were exasperated with the Germans, wrote Ciano in his diary: "It is not possible to remain alone with a Hungarian without him starting to say bad things about Germany. All of them: from the regent on down to the last jerk on the street." [54] Horthy, wrote Ciano, admired the Germans but found them insupportable, tactless, "villainous." Count István Bethlen, who had been prime minister of Hungary through the 1920s, was more measured in his condemnation of German interference, but Ciano nevertheless felt the "tremendous restraint" the man had to exercise in the course of their conversation.[55] It was fortunate that Ciano had no inclination to tell on the Hungarians; and perhaps he secretly rejoiced at all the anti-German feeling he detected in Hungary. In fact, he told Jagow only that Count Bethlen had assured him he was not anglophile.[56]

A few days later, in a telegram to Jagow, Ribbentrop explained he had talked to Keitel regarding the Hungarian commitments, namely, that the Hungarians had promised to collaborate fully: "I have understood this to mean" continued Ribbentrop, "that one may count on a participation at any rate of perhaps two-thirds of the Hungarian army in the eastern campaign; and this will be a guide line for Field Marshal Keitel's conversations as well." [57]

53. *Horthy Miklós titkos iratai*, pp. 313–18. When the Romanian minister in Berlin complained to an official of the Reich Foreign Office that the Hungarians were not contributing enough to the common cause but were still hedging, the official dismissed the complaint by saying that one could not quarrel with the Hungarians' promise to give to "the limit of the possible."

54. Galeazzo Ciano, *Diario, 1939–1943*, 2 : 124. This impression was later confirmed by the Italian ambassador in Budapest, Filippo Anfuso, who, unlike Ciano, was a good Fascist and was not anti-German—"Chaque fois que je vis Horthy, il se déchaîna contre les Allemands" (*Du Palais de Venise au lac de Garde*, p. 225).

55. Ciano, *Diario*. Horthy's description of the German "national character" as reported by Ciano is almost identical with the description Horthy had given to Minister Pell (see below, p. 49).

56. Telegram from Jagow to Berlin, Jan. 19, 1942, NA Microcopy T-120, roll 92, 104512.

57. Telegram from Ribbentrop to Jagow, Jan. 19, 1942, NA Microcopy T-120, roll 92, 104513–14.

Keitel arrived in Budapest the next day, on January 20. About a month earlier Hitler had relieved Field Marshals Brauchitsch, Rundstedt, and Bock of their far-reaching responsibilities and had in fact taken over the command of the German army. Field Marshal Keitel was now uncontestably his right-hand man, a matter the Hungarian officials could not have ignored. At first General Szombethelyi seemed prepared to fully satisfy the German requests; in a memorandum to the cabinet he had suggested that the number of units to be contributed for the eastern campaign should not be made an issue, as Hungary might find herself at a disadvantage vis-à-vis Romania at the peace conference (a prophecy which proved correct in 1946 but for different reasons). Instead of numbers, continued Szombathelyi in his memorandum, the equipment of the Hungarian forces should be made the subject of the discussions. But Szombathelyi's views were not accepted, and Keitel's demands, regarded as excessive, were rejected. Keitel asked for three army corps of three divisions each, the mobile corps, an alpine brigade, and the five occupation divisions, twenty-one divisions all told.[58] According to Macartney, the initial German request was even more considerable; fifteen divisions, the mobile corps, and seven occupation divisions,[59] or twenty-five divisions all told, which was more than the Hungarians actually had, for seven of the twenty-eight divisions listed in the order of battle existed mostly on paper; [60] and it is not clear whether the five light divisions already in the Soviet Union as occupation forces were or were not to be included in the twenty-five. It is true Keitel did not insist that Horthy be briefed, from day to day, in such a manner as to see "the necessity of greater participation," perhaps because the regent had seen that "necessity" already. The Hungarian government, after "not very simple" conversations, did agree to furnish a force not incommensurate with the one Keitel had requested: three army corps of three divisions each, a strong mobile unit, and somewhat later yet another light division, in addition to the five light divisions already in the East.[61] There was one catch, however: the Hungarian units, whether referred to as brigades or divisions, were all light.[62] In subsequent documents of the Ger-

58. Karsai, *A budai vártól*, pp. 103, 104–5, 108.

59. Macartney, *October Fifteenth*, 2 : 67.

60. Karsai, *A budai vártól*, p. 105.

61. Telegram from Jagow to Berlin, Jan. 22, 1942, NA Microcopy T-120, roll 92, 104519–20.

62. Karsai, *A budai vártól*, p. 106.

man Army High Command the Hungarian units are, as a matter
of fact, almost invariably referred to as "light divisions." The military experts may draw their own conclusions from a transportation
schedule prepared by the German Army High Command on February 28, 1942. According to this schedule, on April 1 of that year the
Hungarian Third Army Corps was to be transported to Russia in
215 to 225 trains: this army corps consisted mainly of the Sixth,
Seventh, and Eighth Light Divisions. On May 1 it would be the
turn of the First Armored Division,[63] and the Fourth Army Corps
in 315 to 325 trains; the Fourth Army Corps consisted of the Tenth,
Twelfth, and Thirteenth Light Divisions. Finally, on June 15, the remainder of the Hungarian Second Army was scheduled to be transported: the Seventh Army Corps, consisting of the Nineteenth,
Twentieth, and Twenty-third Light Divisions.[64] These forces
amounted altogether to about 250,000 men including the personnel
of the forced labor battalions.[65]

Although Romanian participation had been considerable at the
onset of the campaign, the Romanian high command had also withdrawn most of its units from the front in the winter of 1941–42,
as a result of serious losses suffered especially during the siege of
Odessa. In January 1942, Field Marshal Keitel also visited Romania,
and Field Marshal Antonescu promised him practically all the forces
at his disposal.[66] During Antonescu's visit to Hitler on February 11,
1942, it seemed, however, that Antonescu would be reluctant to
carry out this commitment unless reassured on the score of the Hungarians. Romania, declared Antonescu, had mustered 700,000 men
during the campaign of the previous year and lost 25 percent of
the officer corps and 23 percent of the troops.[67] Antonescu then complained about the lack of sacrifices on the part of Hungary and her
anti-Romanian stance. Hitler explained that Ribbentrop's and
Keitel's journeys had served to persuade Hungary to bring about

63. The Hungarians had requested material for three armored divisions in November 1941; the Germans were able to supply material for one (Halder, *KTB*, 3 : 314).

64. This schedule was marked "Chefsache" and "geheime Kommandosache" (NA
Microcopy T-77, roll 786, 5514836–41).

65. Czebe and Pethö, *Hungary in World War II*, p. 22.

66. Hillgruber, *Hitler, König Carol und Marschall Antonescu*, pp. 138, 145. General
Jacobici, the chief of the Romanian General Staff, resigned in protest against the commitments made by Antonescu.

67. Notes by Schmidt on meeting between Hitler and Antonescu, NA Microcopy
T-120, roll 59, 47652. In numbers the casualties amounted to about 5,400 officers and
130,000 men. Later Antonescu explained that there had been 40,000 dead (ibid., 47658).

greater sacrifices of blood.[68] Indeed, added Hitler, it would not be
proper for one country to spare herself while the others were making
all the sacrifices.[69] Antonescu's fears were not unjustified; nor were
his complaints simply a manifestation of the desire to see Hungary undergo sufferings similar to those of Romania. Romanian-Hungarian
tension, elicited in large part by the second Vienna Award, which was
supposed to have an assuaging effect, was not pacified by a joint Italo-
German commission that had been active in Transylvania for over
three months. The majority of the dispatches sent by the German ministers from Budapest and Bucharest in this period pertain to the continuing tension between the two countries and the incidents deriving
from it. Hungarians and Romanians engaged in virulent verbal abuse
of each other, and the Hungarians in particular massed troops along
the new border with Romania to defend Hungary against the "Romanian threat." While Romanian threats appeared daily in Romanian
newspapers, these were not supported by Romanian armed might, the
bulk of which was being bled in the Ukraine. At times the Romanian threat was merely an excuse for the Hungarian leaders to
maintain troops in Hungary and thus minimize contributions to
the campaign in the East. At times the threat was taken seriously,
and Hungarian officials were really preparing to defend the country
against a Romanian attack (however imaginary). At all times Romania was a very important factor in Hungarian foreign and military policy, perhaps the most important. Miklós Kállay, the prime
minister who followed Bárdossy in the spring of 1942, makes no
bones about it in his memoirs: "Practically the sole reason," he
wrote, "why we entered the war and sent an army against the Russians was the Rumanians were already taking part with full force
against the Russians, whereas we were not, and thus we risked losing
German favor and Transylvania." [70]

Whether reassured by Hitler's words or not, Marshal Antonescu
was persuaded to commit almost the entire Romanian army to the
campaign in the East. On September 1, 1942, the allied Axis armies

68. NA Microcopy T-120, roll 59, 47657.

69. *KTB, OKW*, 2 : 29.

70. Kállay, *Hungarian Premier*, p. 61. To the newly appointed Defense Minister
Nagy, preparing to pay his courtesy call on Hitler in October 1942, Kállay explained:
"We must keep a free hand with regard to the Romanian situation. We have to point
out that there is no enthusiasm in Hungary for the present war. Our true war
threatens us from the direction of the Balkans, for Antonescu keeps inciting against
Hungary" (Nagy, *Végzetes esztendők*, p. 87).

on the eastern front comprised ten Hungarian divisions (plus occupation forces), eleven Italian divisions, twenty-four Romanian divisions, and twenty-four Finnish brigades—not to mention volunteer
units such as the Spanish "Blue Division." [71]

The Hungarian troops, under the command of Gen. Gusztáv Jány,
arrived in the Ukraine on schedule.[72] They participated in the operations of the "von Weichs group" beginning on June 28. On July 19
some Hungarian units reached the Don River.[73] Again, the references found in Halder's diary, as in the diary of the Army High
Command, are strictly uncomplimentary.[74] August 6, 1942: "The
Hungarians are allowing the Russians to come back across the Don!"
August 8: "South of Voronesh the Hungarians are running." August 10: "The Hungarians are making no progress in cleaning up
the west bank of the Don. They stop trying and take up defensive
positions." August 11: "The situation in the Hungarian sector is
becoming less and less reassuring: The Hungarians weaken under
every enemy attack." The losses of the Hungarian Second Army,
from the beginning of the offensive on June 28 to September 15
amounted to 911 officers and 20,710 men.[75]

The explanation for Halder's deprecating comments, which may
be exaggerated, rests first of all in the inadequate weapons and
equipment provided for the Hungarian units. The Hungarian armored division, for instance, soon became aware of the fact that its
tanks were obsolete in comparison with German tanks and nearly
defenseless when facing Soviet tanks and antitank artillery. A Hungarian politician, who fought as a colonel in the war, noted that the
equipment and clothing were of poor quality and the supply system
disorganized; the rifles would not fire more than three or four times,
the mosquito nets were distributed in November.[76] Quite apart from

---

71. Halder, *KTB*, 3 : 515.

72. The Hungarian Second Army was transported to the eastern front between
Apr. 11 and July 27, 1942, in 882 trains (Adonyi, *A magyar katona a második
világháborúban*, p. 43). General Jány reported to the Führer headquarters on May 16,
1942 (*KTB, OKW*, 2 : 360). Vilmos Nagy, who became Hungary's minister of defense
in the fall of 1942, wrote of General Jány: "Although he was of German origin from
his father's side he was not beloved by the Germans because he often opposed Hitler's
exaggerated demands and fought to have the Germans bring about conditions which
would allow the Hungarians to carry out their defensive assignments along the Don"
(*Végzetes esztendők*, p. 70).

73. *KTB, OKW*, 2 : 458, 509. Parts of the Hungarian Third Army Corps may have
reached the Don as early as July 8 (Karsai, *A budai vártól*, p. 158).

74. See Halder, *KTB*, 3 : 500-503, for the entries quoted.

75. Karsai, *A budai vártól*, pp. 159, 188.

76. Sulyok, *A magyar tragédia*, pp. 386 ff.

the political situation on the home front, which we shall consider in a subsequent chapter, the inadequacy of weapons and equipment were sufficient to instill in the troops a sense of inferiority.[77] These, then, were the circumstances which will account, in large part, for the rout of the Hungarian army at Voronezh in January 1943.

77. Károly Gindert, "Az 1. páncélos hadosztály harcai a 2. magyar hadsereg doni hidfő csatáiban, 1942, július-október" [The operations of the First Armored Division of the Second Hungarian Army at the Don bridgehead] p. 478.

3. Hungary at War with Both Great Britain and the United States

It was actually Great Britain that broke diplomatic relations with Hungary, rather than the other way around. The British Foreign Office was not convinced Hungary was a reluctant satellite. Anthony Eden—regarded by some Hungarians as an "anti-Hungarian"—states in his memoirs that the Polish foreign minister Col. József Beck professed in April of 1939 that Hungary was still not entirely subservient to the Axis.[1] Colonel Beck's opinion was vindicated in September of that year, when the Hungarian government refused transit rights to units of the German army lining up during the attack on Poland. But Hungary seemingly suffered no ill consequences of this boldness; and the British Foreign Office may have concluded that Hungary had freedom of action, that she had little to fear from Germany. Hence, when the Yugoslav crisis occurred, Great Britain condemned the Hungarian attitude. Sir Arthur O'Malley, the British minister in Budapest, objected to Hungarian participation in the attack as a "dastardly action." He pointed out the situation in which Hungary would find herself after an Anglo-American victory and suggested that the regent's "sole means of protest" at the moment would be to leave the country.[2] At the same time the Foreign Office warned György Barcza, the Hungarian minister in London, that should Hungary take part in the German move against Yugoslavia she must expect a declaration of war from Great Britain.[3] Barcza's telegram from London may have been the instrument which

1. "In reply to the question about Roumania, M. Beck maintained that if Poland, Britain and France were to enter into an arrangement with Roumania now it could have the effect of finally driving Hungary into the arms of Germany. M. Beck professed to have some hopes that Hungary was not yet entirely subservient to the Axis. He laid emphasis on Hungarian national pride and pleaded that the moment was not yet ripe for such an arrangement with Roumania though he admitted that the occasion might subsequently arise" (*The Reckoning: The Memoirs of Anthony Eden*, p. 58). Ann M. Cienciala likewise states that Beck resisted the British request for a guarantee to Romania "on the grounds that he wished to avoid throwing the Hungarians into the arms of Germany" (*Poland and the Western Powers 1938–1939* [London: Routledge and Kegan Paul, 1968], p. 232).

2. Telegram from Howard Travers to secretary of state, Apr. 3, 1941, *FRUS 1941*, 1 : 299.

3. Churchill, *The Grand Alliance*, p. 166.

brought Count Teleki to the realization that he had been too weak, and the regent ill advised, in allowing the German attack from Hungarian soil, nay, in planning to participate in that attack. Count Teleki committed suicide.[4] Churchill was impressed. He commented on Teleki's suicide in a speech in Parliament. In his history of World War II he wrote: "His suicide was a sacrifice to absolve himself and his people from guilt in the German attack upon Yugoslavia. It clears his name before history. It could not stop the march of the German armies nor the consequences." [5] Indeed, Teleki's suicide accomplished little. The German units did not withdraw from Hungarian soil. The Hungarian government itself, momentarily stunned, went ahead with its plan of military operations. Around April 5 Sir Alexander Cadogan of the British Foreign Office seems to have repeated to Barcza that the British legation would leave Budapest if Hungary permitted the passage of German troops; if Hungary herself should take action against Yugoslavia, continued Cadogan, Great Britain would declare war and drop bombs on Hungarian territory.[6]

On April 7, a few days before Hungarian troops began operations against Yugoslavia, Great Britain broke diplomatic relations with Hungary.[7] In a note to the Hungarian Foreign Ministry the British minister stated that he had been instructed to withdraw his mission from Budapest because of Germany's "manifest breaches" of Hungarian neutrality.[8] While there may be some injustice in punishing Hungary for a "breach" committed by Germany, the British action received its justification a few days later when the Hungarian military forces attacked remnants of the Yugoslav army; however, Great

4. According to Ullein-Reviczky, the British ultimatum may even have been the cause of Teleki's dejection. Ullein-Reviczky visited Teleki at 9:00 P.M. on Apr. 3, shortly before his suicide, and was present when Teleki read Barcza's telegram. Teleki simply said: "I have done all I can; I can no more" (*Guerre allemande*, p. 93).

5. *The Grand Alliance*, p. 167. In Parliament Churchill had added that at the coming peace conference "a chair shall be reserved" for Teleki (*Recollections of Tibor Eckhardt*, p. 246). This promise, as we know, was forgotten.

6. Telegram from Erdmannsdorf to German Foreign Office, Apr. 6, 1941, *DGFP*, series D, 11 : 483–84.

7. Macartney, *October Fifteenth*, 2 : 8.

8. "Recently the German army has established itself upon Hungarian territory near the borders of Yugoslavia, and has simultaneously launched an attack upon Yugoslavia. The conclusion is inescapable that these two events are parts of a single plan; and His Majesty's Government are therefore now obliged to take a graver view than heretofore of manifest breaches of Hungarian neutrality . . ." (note from British legation, Apr. 7, 17941, Political Section, Ministry of Foreign Affairs, Hungarian National Archives, K 63, bundle 15, tétel 2).

Britain did not go so far as to declare war on Hungary right away. From that time until December 1941, British interests in Hungary were represented by the American legation in Budapest. The United States took over British espionage activities in Hungary, as Ribbentrop put it.[9]

The declaration of war was also a British initiative, prompted by Stalin's urgent requests. Churchill and the British Foreign Office must have realized that Hungary had lost much of its independence of action in the previous few months. "These countries," said Churchill about Finland, Romania, and Hungary in a message to Stalin on November 4, 1941, "are full of our friends . . . A British declaration of war would only freeze them all and make it look like Hitler were the head of a grand European alliance solid against us . . ." [10] But he was willing to make sacrifices, continued Churchill, in response to Stalin's "pressing appeal." [11] It may be noted, however, that the wording in Churchill's memoirs is not altogether clear. Stalin insisted only on a declaration of war against Finland. With regard to Hungary and Romania Stalin seemed to have more patience: in a letter transcribed in Churchill's memoirs Stalin had written, "we can perhaps wait a little while." [12] But the British government decided not to wait and, accordingly, an ultimatum was sent to all three East European countries. The ultimatum, delivered on November 29 to the Hungarian Foreign Ministry by the American minister and the first secretary of the American legation, stipulated that Hungary was to withdraw from all participation in the war against the Soviet Union by December 5.[13] The American minister must have delivered the message regretfully; he had warned the Department of State, hoping the department would transmit his warning to London, that a British declaration of war against Hungary would only result in strengthening the "war party" in Hungary, hitherto in a minority.[14] Churchill seems to have believed that this ultimatum might indeed have some effect, at least on Finland. The ultimatum had no effect, and Great Britain declared war on Finland,

9. Memorandum by Rintelen, of a conversation between Bárdossy and Ribbentrop, Nov. 27, 1941, *DGFP*, series D, 13 : 839.

10. Churchill, *The Grand Alliance*, p. 528; also, *The Reckoning*, p. 325.

11. Churchill, *The Grand Alliance*, pp. 528, 533.

12. Ibid., p. 532.

13. Macartney, *October Fifteenth*, 2 : 60; see also Karsai, *A budai vártól*, p. 63.

14. Telegram from Pell to Department of State, Nov. 7, 1941, Papers of Herbert Pell, Franklin D. Roosevelt Library, Hyde Park, N. Y.

Romania, and Hungary on December 7.[15] It may be noted, however, that the bulk of the Hungarian troops, including all front-line units, had been withdrawn from the eastern front by December 1941; it is true that this was not a measure the Hungarian government wished to publicize at the time, and the British intelligence may not have known, or cared. In any case, the British ultimatum was scorned. On December 4 Sztójay explained to Ernst Woermann of the Reich Foreign Office that Bárdossy had told the American minister that the Hungarian government had taken cognizance of the British ultimatum but that there would be no reply, as Hungary was not inclined to gear its behavior to the decisions of the British government. Bárdossy also said that the entire Hungarian nation might feel that Great Britain was giving aid and comfort to the Soviets by "terrorizing" and attempting to sacrifice Hungary.[16] Such, at least, was the report the Hungarian government gave of the incident to the German government.

At his trial in 1945 Bárdossy declared he had actually told the American minister at the time that no Hungarian forces were engaged against the Soviet Union, that these forces had been withdrawn two weeks earlier, and that Hungary had no intention of taking further direct part in the military action. Minister Herbert Pell had answered that he had tried but failed to dissuade the British government from submitting this ultimatum.[17] I have been unable to find, among the records of the Department of State, the dispatch which might corroborate Bárdossy's account of his interview with Pell.

The British declaration of war was delivered by Pell around midnight between December 6 and 7.[18] The following day the United States became involved in World War II.

Relations between American diplomats and Hungarian officials had almost always been cordial in the between-the-wars period. American diplomats in Hungary, John F. Montgomery, Herbert Pell, and Howard Travers (first secretary of the legation), were at pains to point out to the Department of State that, despite appearances, Hungarians in general and Horthy in particular were not pro-German but rather pro-British and pro-American. "The Regent

15. Churchill, *The Grand Alliance*, pp. 533–35.
16. NA Microcopy T-120, roll 92, 104415–16.
17. See Karsai, *A budai vártól*, pp. 63–64.
18. Macartney, *October Fifteenth*, 2 : 61.

is firmly determined, he informed me," wrote Montgomery back in November 1940, "to refrain from taking any step in his relations with Germany, such as granting of military or air bases, which would involve a loss of sovereignty. I hope, however, that the matter will not be put to the test." [19] Just after the suicide of Count Teleki, the American chargé d'affaires Howard Travers reported that his feeling was that Hungary would do all in its power not to participate in the war against Yugoslavia. "However," he continued in his dispatch, "it is doubtful whether any such efforts could prove successful against strong German pressure." [20]

Herbert Pell, who as a close friend of the Roosevelts can be assumed to have had the ear of the president, took it for granted that Germany had forced Hungary into the wars against Yugoslavia and the Soviet Union and that the German legation in Budapest was making "increasing demands of all sorts (some of them described by officials as fantastic) upon the Hungarian Government which apparently offers as much opposition in its own defense as possible." [21] On August 22 Pell had an hour-long interview with Horthy at his mansion in Gödöllő, in the course of which Horthy talked partly "in English and French but mostly in German." It should be noted, perhaps, that at this time National Socialist power in Europe was about to reach its apogee, and the Soviet Union seemed near defeat.

> He (Horthy) spoke at great length about Germany. According-
> ing to him the German higher officers are an extraordinary class

19. Montgomery to Department of State, Nov. 23, 1940, NA Record Group 59, General Records of the Department of State, 740.0011 E.W. 1939/7284.

20. Telegram from Howard Travers to secretary of state, Apr. 7, 1941 *FRUS 1941*, 1 : 303.

21. Herbert Pell to Department of State, Nov. 22, 1941, NA Record Group 59, 762.64/312. One Hungarian author has claimed that the Hungarian attitude was not only "understood" in the United States but appreciated as well. The United States government continued to treat Hungarian subjects in the country in a friendly manner. The last Hungarian minister, György Ghyka, was encouraged to remain in the United States by President Roosevelt. Sometimes the conversations with Hungarian diplomats even had conspiratorial overtones. Cordell Hull is supposed to have expressed his satisfaction at Hungary's anti-Bolshevist stand (Dezső Nemes, *Magyarország felszabadulása* [The liberation of Hungary], p. 13). Another official of the Department of State, A. A. Berle, told an unidentified Hungarian in Washington that the Hungarian army must remain intact in order to hold up an eventual Russian invasion (report from Washington, May 6, 1942, Political Section, Ministry of Foreign Affairs, Hungarian National Archives, K 64, bundle 86). Was Berle sincere and outspoken? Or was he merely using an argument he felt might have some weight with the Hungarian politicians? With regard to the last point it may be noted that both Regent Horthy and Prime Minister Kállay professed to believe, in early 1944, that the Hungarian

of hereditary soldiers, which has developed from father to son an almost exclusive military outlook. The German faculty for organization, he said, was even superior to that of America. He seemed to have been particularly impressed by their method of instructing reserve submarine crews, so that when they suddenly increased their fleet of U-boats trained crews were ready to take them right out.

He said that the Hungarians had sent very few soldiers to the war with Russia; that in his opinion the Soviets were practically beaten. Their resistance, according to the Regent, had cost them nearly five million men—the German losses being well over a million. The Germans, he said, had not sent their best troops to this campaign or their best officers.

He hoped to see peace resumed by some process or arrangement as Germany now had access to adequate raw materials and was practically unbeatable. He seemed to attribute a great deal of English weakness to the disproportionate losses suffered by the better classes in the last war.

This dispatch by the American minister combines a summary of Horthy's political views, fixed ideas, and subjective estimates of the Allies and of Germany with clues to his personality, which I have reason to believe are accurate. Though his regime cannot truly be described as a dictatorship and though his personality was less than strong, Horthy's ideas and attitudes profoundly affected the course of Hungarian history. The reader will excuse me if I quote further from this hitherto unpublished dispatch:

> He described the Germans as "taktlos und humorlos" and as totally unfit to dominate the world. Hitler, he said, was an intelligent man when not discussing his enthusiasms, and was blessed with a remarkable memory. He said that he had frequently urged Hitler not to attack the British world dominion. Altogether he thought that a rapid and fair solution of the present mess would be difficult to reach, because of the terrific force of hatred both in England and in Germany. . . .
>
> Reverting to the subject of Germany he said that the Germans could not, because of their arrogance and lack of sympathy, control a civilian Europe for a long time. He referred

army might be able to hold up the Red Army at the line of the Carpathians unassisted (Horthy, *Memoirs*, p. 210).

sympathetically to Poland and bitterly to the Gestapo which he described as the same as the Ogpu—a Hungarian could say nothing worse.

As I left he expressed, as usual, his wish to visit America and his hearty admiration of the President. That he gave me an interview during his vacation the day after it was asked and talked to me over an hour suggest that he appreciates the need of an anchor to windward.[22]

Several incidents suggested reasonably close relations between Hungarian and American officials; one of these is the portrait Mrs. Pell was allowed to paint of the regent and his wife, and for which both actually sat.[23] This episode is related by Antal Ullein-Reviczky in his wartime memoirs.[24] What Ullein-Reviczky does not mention in his memoirs is that the artistic endeavor of the wife of the American minister did not remain a secret from the German authorities, and that during his trip to Germany as chief of the Press Section of the prime minister's office, in November 1941, he felt obliged to assert in the presence of German officials that no such portrait was ever painted.[25] Bárdossy also received complaints from German officials to the effect that the activities of American diplomats in Budapest were not adequately controlled; on November 26, in Berlin, Ribbentrop reproached Bárdossy for allowing Americans to take over British espionage activities in Hungary.[26] Bárdossy replied with something to the effect that indeed there was an old American

22. Herbert Pell to Department of State, Aug. 22, 1941, NA Record Group 59, 864.00/1025. On Oct. 2, 1941, an official of the Division of European Affairs in the State Department analyzed the Hungarian situation as follows: "1. As a result of Horthy's policy, and without any risks or military losses, Hungary got back a large part of Transylvania, most of the territories of the South, and parts of Slovakia; 2. On one pretext or another, Hungary has been able to abstain from giving any major help to the Germans in the Russian war; 3. The Hungarian army is therefore still more or less intact, while the Yugoslavs are broken, and the Rumanian army has been decimated in the Russian campaign; 4. If the war is to continue until Hitler is defeated, Hungary will suffer, but if a negotiated peace could be arranged, she would have obtained maximum advantages at minimum cost, and still have her army to hold the spoils" (NA Record Group 59, typewritten note, no decimal file number).

23. Mrs. Pell informs me she still has this portrait in her apartment (letter of May 10, 1967).

24. Ullein-Reviczky, *Guerre allemande*, p. 122.

25. Note by Erdmannsdorf, Nov. 20, 1941, NA Microcopy T-120, roll 92, 104388.

26. Memorandum by Rintelen, Nov. 27, 1941, *DGFP*, series D, 13:839; see also minutes of conversation between Ribbentrop and Bárdossy, Nov. 26, 1941, NA Microcopy T-120, roll 614, F90157.

gentleman (*bácsi*) in Budapest, but they never saw each other.[27] It may be noted here that—as the American minister well knew—the telephones of the legation were tapped.[28]

Nevertheless, after the German declaration of war against the United States, on December 11, Bárdossy told Pell he was obliged to sever diplomatic relations with the United States "but not (repeat not) with intention of declaring war"; such, at least, was the language used by Herbert Pell in his "triple priority" telegram to the Department of State.[29] Bárdossy may have felt compelled to take this measure to forestall a request, or a demand, on the part of the Reich Foreign Office for more drastic measures. If that was the case, he failed. The next day Karl Werkmeister, the first secretary of the German legation, and Count Giuseppe Talamo of the Italian embassy called on Bárdossy regarding the Hungarian attitude toward the United States. Bárdossy told these representatives that Hungary had spontaneously and most rapidly—meaning before Germany's other allies—taken the steps warranted by Article 3 of the Tripartite Pact: Hungary was obliged to support Germany, Italy, and Japan with every political, economic, and military means at her disposal.[30] Hungary had done this politically by breaking relations with the United States, economically she had been giving the Axis full support ever since the beginning of the war, but militarily there was nothing she could do directly. She had expressed her strongest support by declaring her solidarity with the Axis powers. Bárdossy felt that he would put himself in the ridiculous position of a "Panama and Costa Rica," who had declared war on Japan despite the disproportion involved, if he now declared war on the United States. Werkmeister, uncon-

27. Karsai, *A budai vártól*, pp. 61–62.

28. Montgomery to Department of State, Nov. 23, 1940, NA Record Group 59, 740.0011 E.W. 1939/7284. A list of lines tapped by the Hungarian counterintelligence service is given in an SD report transmitted by Schellenberg to Luther, Oct. 20, 1942, NA Microcopy T-120, roll 1096, 452311–14.

29. Herbert Pell to Department of State, Dec. 11, 1941. NA Record Group 59, 125.0040/79. The version printed in *FRUS 1941*, 1 : 591, is slightly different: the phrase "repeat not" is omitted.

30. Article 3 of the Tripartite Pact, signed on Sept. 27, 1940, reads as follows: "Germany, Italy and Japan agree to cooperate, in the course of their efforts, along the lines stated. Furthermore, they assume an obligation to support each other with all political, economic and military means, if one of the contracting parties is attacked by a power which is not, at the moment, participating in the European conflict or in the Sino-Japanese war." Hungary joined the Tripartite Pact on Nov. 29, 1940. A text of both agreements is printed in *Magyarország és a második világháború*, pp. 308–10.

vinced, replied simply that he did not think the Hungarian initiative sufficient.[31]

Once again Bárdossy eventually adopted the German point of view. The following day, on December 13 at 5:30 in the afternoon, he informed Pell that Hungary considered a state of war to exist between Hungary and the United States:

> The Royal Hungarian Government, under the terms of the so-called "Three-power Pact" of September 27, 1940, and under the provisions of Hungary's adherence thereto on November 20, 1940, respectively, further, in accordance with the declaration of the principle of solidarity of December 11 of this year, considers the state of war, which exists between the United States of America, on the one hand, and the German Empire, Italy and Japan, on the other hand, to be existing also with respect to Hungary.   Budapest, December 12, 1941.[32]

The explanation of this turnabout may be that Romania and Bulgaria had already declared war, or their intent to do so, and the German government was pressing Hungary, through the obliging Hungarian minister in Berlin, to do the same.[33] To his pro-Anglo-American friends Bárdossy explained that he had not really declared war but had simply noted that a state of war existed between the two countries as a consequence of the stipulations of the Tripartite Pact.[34] It is not Bárdossy's fault that this subtlety was not appreciated, or even noticed, by the American Department of State. On the contrary, the Hungarian declaration of war—for it was taken as such by everyone concerned—was received with appropriate con-

31. NA Microcopy T-120, roll 92, 104441–2; see also Ullein-Reviczky, *Guerre allemande*, pp. 115 ff. In his diary Count Ciano relates a pertinent anecdote: "Il disagio ungherese è espresso da questa storiella che circola a Budapest. Il Ministro d'Ungheria dichiara la guerra agli Stati Uniti, ma il funzionario che riceve la comunicazione non e molto forte nelle questioni europee e fa quindi alcune domande. Chiede: 'L'Ungheria è una repubblica?' 'No, è un regno!' 'Allora avete un Re?' 'No, abbiamo un Ammiraglio.' 'Allora avete un flotta?' 'No, non abbiamo mare.' Allora avete delle rivendicazioni?' 'Si.' 'Contro l'America?' 'No.' 'Contro l'Inghilterra?' 'No.' 'Contro la Russia?' 'No.' 'Ma contro chi dunque avete queste rivendicazioni?' 'Contro la Rumania.' 'Allora dichiarerete la guerra alla Rumania?' 'Nossignore, siamo alleati.' " (Entry for May 11, 1942, *Diario*, 2 : 176.) Same anecdote was quoted by *Time* magazine and by Paul Nadanyi, *Hungary at the Crossroads of Invasions*, pp. 8–9.

32. Herbert Pell to Department of State, Dec. 13, 1941, NA Record Group 59, 740.0011, E.W. 1939/17497; see also letter to U.S. embassy, Dec. 12, 1941, Political Section, Ministry of Foreign Affairs, Hungarian National Archives, K 64, bundle 86.

33. Macartney, *October Fifteenth*, 2 : 63.

34. Ibid., p. 64; see also Karsai, *A budai vártól*, p. 68.

tempt. Cordell Hull states in his memoirs that "at least for the time being, we would not ask Congress for declarations of war against these satellites. We realized that their Governments were puppets of Hitler and had merely jumped when the strings were pulled." [35]

Thus the difference between British and American policies with regard to Hungary becomes clear. Generally speaking, the British held the Hungarians responsible for their own actions; the Americans did not. During the German attack on Yugoslavia, for instance, the British minister to Budapest told an American diplomat he expected the Americans to protest Hungarian participation in the same terms; [36] the American diplomats, however, felt Hungary was subjected to tremendous pressures by Germany and could not be expected to act altogether independently. For several years thereafter the American attitude, or rather the attitude of the Department of State, continued to be more lenient to Hungary than the British. [37]

In the spring of 1942, however, the president and the United States Congress decided to declare war on Hungary, Romania, and Bulgaria despite new evidence of some opposition to German demands. Hungary had just undergone a change of cabinet. Ray Atherton, an official of the Division of European Affairs in the Department of State, noted that the "New Hungarian Premier is so notoriously anti-German that his appointment, following closely on the flouting of German ideas in the matter of vice-regency, must be taken to mean that Hungary no longer feels that Germany is now in a position to exact complete subservience." [38] It was also about this time, on March 17, that the daily newspaper of the extreme right-wing Arrow-Cross party was banned for good by the Hungarian Ministry of Interior. [39] Nevertheless, a few days later, on March 24,

35. *The Memoirs of Cordell Hull*, p. 1114. President Roosevelt's note addressed to Hull on Dec. 12, 1941, on the same subject, observed: "It is my present thought that the U.S. should pay no attention to any of the declarations of war against us by puppet governments" (Ibid., p. 1175).

36. Telegram from Howard Travers to Secretary of State, Apr. 3, 1941, *FRUS 1941*, 1 : 300.

37. The American attitude was not lenient enough nor the British line tough enough to satisfy all critics. Thus Count Mihály Károlyi, who lived in London, deplored the "soft line" adopted by the British Broadcasting Corporation toward Hungary and notes that when this line became tougher it was "already too late" (*Faith without Illusions*, p. 301).

38. Memorandum by Atherton to Sumner Welles, Mar. 17, 1942, *FRUS 1942*, 2 : 837.

39. Miklós Lackó, *Nyilasok, nemzetiszocialisták, 1935–1944* [Arrow-Cross men, National Socialists] (Budapest: Kossuth, 1966), p. 297.

1942, the United States legation in Bern received the following instructions from the Department of State:

> This Government has viewed with increasing concern the aid given by Rumania, Hungary, and Bulgaria to the enemies of the United States and is constrained to assume that agreement has been given by them to the continuance of this participation in the war against the United States and the other United Nations. This Government has, therefore, the intention of declaring a state of war between the United States and the governments of Rumania, Hungary, and Bulgaria, respectively, unless in some definite form these governments severally give prompt evidence that they will not engage in military aid or operations of assistance to the Axis powers.[40]

The Hungarian government received this note on April 7, 1942. On April 17 it replied that Hungary had been forced into the war by the Soviet attack on Kassa "causing enormous losses in lives and property. Accordingly Hungary considers that she is carrying on a defensive war against the Union of Soviet Socialist Republics." [41] Ernst Woermann, the official of the Reich Foreign Office to whom this exchange of notes was reported by Sztójay on April 18, remarked:

> I told Mr. Sztójay we have been right well surprised that we had heard immediately from Bucharest and Sofia regarding these measures, but not from Budapest. Because of this we had charged our representative in Budapest to make inquiries and at the same time to point out that the Bulgarian government intended to leave the note unanswered.[42]

I found no evidence, among the records of the Department of State, that the varying responses to the American ultimatum by Bulgaria, Romania, and Hungary were noted.[43] Cordell Hull notes only that

40. Sumner Welles to American minister in Bern, *FRUS 1942*, 2 : 838–40; see also *Memoirs of Cordell Hull*, pp. 1175–76. The same instructions had been sent to the American minister in Turkey on Feb. 28, but the Turkish government was not interested in relaying the message to the Hungarian government (*FRUS 1942*, 2 : 835–36).

41. Telegram from Harrison (in Switzerland) to Secretary of State, Apr. 22, 1942, *FRUS 1942*, 2 : 840; see also memorandum of May 8, 1942, NA Record Group 59, 764.1111/1.

42. Note by Woermann, Apr. 18, 1942, NA Microcopy T-120, roll 92, 104872.

43. Romania likewise did not answer the American note. It is possible that Woermann did not give Romania as an example to the Hungarian minister out of

the three governments continued to extend their military activities, and while the war declarations were held in abeyance for a few more weeks, they were finally signed by President Roosevelt on June 5, 1942.[44] During the visit of Vyacheslav Molotov to Washington at the end of May 1942, President Franklin D. Roosevelt "casually mentioned" to Molotov that the United States had never gotten around to declaring war on Romania (the other countries were not even mentioned) "as it seemed something of a waste of effort." Molotov, however, thought it would not be a waste of effort, whereupon Roosevelt indicated war would be declared on Romania, Hungary, and Bulgaria the following week.[45] It is clear, however, that what Molotov may have understood to be a spontaneous favor was, in fact, a matter that had been decided upon well before his visit.

Thus Hungary found herself at war with three of the greatest military powers on earth. It is true that if Hungary had not declared war on the Soviet Union and the United States (the case of Great Britain is different) she would probably have been forced to do so sooner or later by Germany. Certainly the government had not been subjected to internal pressures. The Arrow-Cross party and other smaller groups of native National Socialists, that is, those elements who might have been in favor of Hungary's total commitment to the war, had lost considerable electoral support since their good showing in 1939. In June 1941 the Hungarian government had adopted part of their program: war on bolshevism. In September 1941 there was a further split in the party as a result of German intervention in party affairs. While Ferenc Szálasi, still the leader of the Arrow-Cross party, insisted that his movement was not intellectual but for the masses, it is clear the masses were no longer for him.[46] Hence the popularity of the Bárdossy government was not at stake. Bárdossy had not really considered Hungarian public opinion. The critics of the Bárdossy government were justified in arguing Hungary had

---

délicatesse, as Hungary would not, generally speaking, want to follow Romania's example.

44. *FRUS 1942,* 2 : 841; also *Memoirs of Cordell Hull,* p. 1176.

45. Memorandum of a conversation between Roosevelt, Molotov, Litvinov, Hull, etc., May 29, 1942. Papers of Cordell Hull, Correspondence (container 50), Library of Congress, Washington, D.C.

46. Lackó *Nyilasok, nemzetiszocialisták,* pp. 266–72; see also Nicholas M. Nagy-Talavera, *The Green Shirts and the Others.*

complied with German wishes too readily.[47] Perhaps Bárdossy's attitude becomes clarified when in 1944, two years after his demise from
power, he is found among the ranks of the extreme right.

47. Yet Bárdossy told Filippo Anfuso, the new Italian minister to Budapest, early in
1942: "Dieu nous a mis en face d'Hitler. Lorsque les Allemands me demandent
quelquechose, je donne toujours le quart de ce qu'ils me demandent. Si je refuse de
façon catégorique, ils prennent tout, ce qui est pire" (Anfuso, *Du Palais de Venise,*
p. 221).

4. The Political Aspect of German-Hungarian Relations in 1942

The initial enthusiasm of the Hungarian government for the "crusade against bolshevism" subsided soon after the declaration of war. We have seen that the Hungarian government retrieved most of its units from the eastern front in the fall and winter of 1941–42. A Hungarian field army was sent to the East in the summer of 1942, but this Hungarian contribution was far less spontaneous than the one of the preceding year. Both the composition and the policies of the Hungarian government changed in 1942.

A test of the friendly relations between Germany and Hungary was the replacement of Prime Minister Bárdossy early in 1942. Despite occasional hesitations, Bárdossy had served the Germans well. The German government suspected that Bárdossy's friendly, or perhaps overfriendly, attitude was precisely the reason for his removal. But while this attitude was doubtless a factor that explained his removal, it was probably not the only one; another factor may have been Bárdossy's failure to give full support to István Horthy, the regent's elder son, in his candidacy for the newly established office of vice-regent. While this aspiration of the young Horthy, and of the regent, was an internal matter and thus not of our concern, the personality of István Horthy and his political stand may well be. It is conceivable that Bárdossy's hesitation in this regard—and one can speak only of a relative reluctance, because practically no political element in Hungary saw fit to object openly to the young Horthy's candidacy—was due to István Horthy's rather well-known sympathies for the Anglo-American powers. It seems, indeed, that István Horthy was one of the few people in Hungary who felt all along that Germany would not win the war. His father practically admitted as much: during an interrogation by the DeWitt C. Poole Mission in Germany, late in the summer of 1945, Regent Horthy declared that, unlike István, in June 1942 he did not think the Germans had lost the war.[1]

1. "When Germany attacked the Soviet Union, Horthy's son had expressed extreme skepticism as to the victorious outcome of the war, but Horthy thought that it was not really lost at that time" (interrogation of Miklós Horthy, Sept. 1, 1945 [at

57

It does not seem that the young Horthy had concealed these sympathies well enough; his "pro-Anglo-Saxon" feelings did not remain undetected by German agents and the leaders of National Socialist Germany.[2] An agent of the German *Sicherheitsdienst* in Hungary devoted an entire paragraph, in a report on the Hungarian political situation, to informing his superiors that István Horthy had visited a nightclub named "Országház Grill," which was owned by Jews and where the customers, also mostly Jewish, greeted the young Horthy with applause.[3] Somewhat later Joseph Goebbels noted in his diary:

> Horthy's son is a pronounced Jew-lover, an Anglophile to the bones, a man without any profound education and without broad political comprehension; in short, a personality with whom, if he were Regent of Hungary, we would have some difficulties to iron out. But this isn't the time to bother about such delicate questions. When in need the devil will eat flies, and in wartime we will stand even an objectionable deputy regent of Hungary.[4]

These remarks must be tallied as so many compliments for the young Horthy.

Perhaps a brief account of the remaining events of the young Horthy's life is not out of order. István Horthy was proclaimed vice-regent by the Hungarian House of Parliament on February 19, 1942; only the Hungarian National Socialist party—not by any means the strongest right-wing extremist group—objected openly.[5]

Wiesbaden], NA Record Group 59, DeWitt C. Poole Interrogations). A Hungarian author notes that after the rapid German victory over France there were very few individuals left in Hungary who continued to doubt the possibility of a final German victory (Imre Csécsy, *Ha Hitler győzött volna* [Had Hitler won], p. 5).

2. Despite the report the American minister to Hungary had sent from Lisbon, a stopover on his return to the United States: "Mr. Horthy is a patriotic intelligent man in his late thirties. His chief earlier activities were in support of Hungarian aviation and of polo. . . . He is undoubtedly pro-Anglo-Saxon, but he has a high sense of tact and a reticence which shields his feelings" (Herbert Pell to Department of State, Feb. 26, 1942, NA Record Group 59, 864.00/1037).

3. SD report on Hungary, Mar. 3, 1941, NA Microcopy T-120, roll 4199, K204478–84.

4. Entry for Feb. 20, 1942, *The Goebbels Diaries, 1942–1943*, ed. Louis P. Lochner, p. 95. Jagow gives a similar if more dignified estimate of the young Horthy in a telegram to the Reich Foreign Office, Feb. 19, 1942: "Es besteht kein Zweifel daran, dass er [István Horthy] ausgesprochen englandfreundlich war und dass er den National-sozialismus innerlich ablehnt" (NA Microcopy T-120, roll 92, 104586).

5. Karsai, *A budai vártól*, pp. 125 ff.

The Arrow-Cross party did not campaign against the nomination in the open, and its undercover campaign served only to further alienate the regent. Some leaders of the Arrow-Cross, including Gyula Suttő, a member of the Parliament, were imprisoned.[6] The representatives of the German ethnic group in the Hungarian Parliament were instructed by the German Foreign Office, "unter der Hand" (underhandedly), to handle the issue in such a way as not to clash with the government party, of which they were members; in other words, not to raise open objections to the young Horthy's candidacy.[7]

Shortly thereafter István Horthy went to the front as a pilot, in which capacity he had already performed noteworthy feats. The regent, however, decided to have him recalled, because of the dangers to which the vice-regent exposed himself. István Horthy was ordered to return on August 21, the day after the Hungarian national holiday of Saint Stephen, which was, by the same token, István Horthy's name day, an occasion for twofold celebrations. István Horthy took off the morning after, and shortly after takeoff his Italian-made aircraft (Caproni) crashed to the ground and its pilot was killed.[8] Despite investigation by a special commission, the circumstances of the crash were never clearly explained, and some Hungarians suspected foul play on the part of the Germans.[9] Such suspicions are excusable, but I have found no evidence to support

6. Lackó, *Nyilasok, nemzetiszocialisták,* p. 277.

7. Draft instructions prepared by Woermann and Luther, Feb. 12, 1942, NA Microcopy T-120, roll 1, 10572.

8. A report on the accident compiled on Aug. 29, 1942, by the SS leader Schellenberg reads as follows: "Ohne Nachtschlaf und im alkoholisierten Zustand bestieg Stefan v. Horthy um 5 Uhr seine schwer gepanzerte Caproni, die infolge ihres grossen Gewichtes sich an und für sich schwer von Boden abhob und durch unvorsichtige Bedienung in der Kurve aus etwa 200 m. Höhe abstürzte. Gerade diese Art des Unglücks machte es der ungarischen militärischen Führung schwer, mit einer Bericht über den Hergang des Unfalles vor die Öffentlichkeit zu treten" (NA Microcopy T-120, roll 1096, 452388–89). The regent referred to such an interpretation as "slanderous rumours" (*Memoirs,* p. 200).

9. See Horthy, *Memoirs,* pp. 199–200, and Kállay, *Hungarian Premier,* p. 105. In a conversation with me, Miklós Horthy, Jr., the regent's younger son, expressed his conviction that foul play by the National Socialists was involved. A remark Hitler is reported to have made on Aug. 28, 1942, seems to provide the Reich government with a convincing alibi: "Taking a wholly dispassionate view," said Hitler, "I think it is a great pity that Horthy's son has been killed. The internal stability of the country would have been much more strongly assured had he survived. The old man himself is animated by a fanatical desire to conserve his own health. He's a bull of a man, and was, without doubt, the bravest man in the Austrian Navy. The Hungarian aristoc-

the view that the young Horthy's death was anything but an unfortunate accident.

Bárdossy may have irked the regent by not promoting István Horthy's candidacy. C. A. Macartney gives about equal weight to the two factors involved in Bárdossy's forced resignation: his refusal to fully endorse the young Horthy's candidacy, and his consistent playing into the German hands.[10] Kállay saw the principal cause of his predecessor's demise in his excessively pro-German attitude, the many faits accomplis with which he confronted the regent (one assumes this refers to the declarations of war against the Soviet Union and the United States), and his plan to rid the cabinet of Keresztes-Fischer, Dániel Bánffy, and József Varga, three outspokenly anti-Nazi ministers.[11]

Whatever the reason, Bárdossy ceased to be prime minister on March 7, 1942; the publicized explanation was prolonged illness.[12] Horthy's decision did not come on the spur of the moment. Horthy had hinted to Ciano during the latter's visit to Budapest, January 15–18, that Bárdossy's ill health might necessitate his replacement. Horthy seems to have toyed with the idea of appointing Count Bethlen prime minister once again, which may also explain why the count was at such pains to point out to visiting Axis dignitaries that he was not an anglophile.[13] But the plan for the appointment of Count Bethlen was dropped (possibly at his own request), and the plan for Bárdossy's dismissal was kept secret, at least from the Germans. Bárdossy's forced resignation and Kállay's appointment seem to have occurred too suddenly for a timely German intervention. The Reich Foreign Office seemingly accepted the explanation regarding Bárdossy's illness at its face value. In his memoirs Kállay wrote that Germany betrayed no reaction whatever, but this assertion is contradicted in the next sentence, wherein he explains he received not a single telegram of congratulations from Germany or her "satellites." [14]

racy has predominantly German blood in its veins . . ." (Trevor-Roper, *Hitler's Secret Conversations*, p. 542). Hitler's estimate of the regent, however, will have changed within two years.

10. *October Fifteenth*, 2 : 80 ff.

11. Kállay, *Hungarian Premier*, p. 8.

12. According to Dezső Sulyok, Bárdossy attempted to commit suicide on that day, but the attempt was not reported in the press (*A magyar tragédia*, p. 472).

13. Bethlen had been prime minister from 1921 to 1931 (Ciano's minutes of conversations with Hungarian leaders, Jan. 15–18, 1942, Lisbon Papers, NA Microcopy T-816, roll 2196).

14. Kállay, *Hungarian Premier*, pp. 23–24.

Kállay formed his cabinet on March 10, 1942.[15] Jagow's telegram of that day indicates a wait-and-see attitude toward the new prime minister: "Kállay is basically an apolitical person and has not been active, in the last few years, either in internal or foreign affairs. National Socialism to him is an 'alien concept' and he bears no inner sympathy to it. Nevertheless he will no doubt continue the same relations to Germany as his predecessor."[16] The Reich government's main concern was not the new prime minister, already designated, but rather the vacant post of minister of foreign affairs, not filled when the list of new ministers was announced. The person the Reich government did not want to see fill that post was the chief of the press office, Antal Ullein-Reviczky. On March 7, a few days before the new cabinet was formed, Jagow had reported that Ullein-Reviczky was a likely prospect for that post.[17] On March 9 a Swedish newspaper reported the same conjecture, with the comment that this represented a trend away from collaboration with Germany: but it appears that this item was planted in the Swedish press on instructions from the Reich Foreign Office, with the purpose of frightening the Hungarian government away from such a choice.[18] Just in case this subtle hint might not have the desired result, Ribbentrop instructed one of his subordinates, on March 13, to tell Sztójay, "even more clearly than before," that Ullein-Reviczky could not be tolerated as Hungarian minister of foreign affairs and that he, Ribbentrop, would refuse to have intercourse with such a minister. On the other hand, the return of Bárdossy to the post of minister of foreign affairs should be described as Ribbentrop's "urgent wish." The entire shakeup of the cabinet, complained Ribbentrop, was difficult to understand. Bárdossy had been the only man who

15. The new cabinet, not very different from the old, was composed as follows: prime minister, Miklós Kállay; minister of the interior, Ferenc Keresztes-Fischer; minister of justice, László Radocsay; minister of trade and communications and minister of industry, József Varga; minister of finance, Lajos Reményi-Schneller; minister of defense, Károly Bartha; minister of cults and education, Bálint Hóman; minister of supply, Sándor Györffy-Bengyel; minister of agriculture, Baron Dániel Bánffy; minister of propaganda, István Antal. Among these Kállay could count on the loyal support of only four: Keresztes-Fischer, Radocsay, Varga, and Bánffy (Kállay, *Hungarian Premier,* p. 20).

16. NA Microcopy T-120, roll 92, 104680.

17. Telegram from Jagow to Berlin, Mar. 8, 1942, NA Microcopy T-120, roll 92, 104668.

18. "Die Nachricht ist von Bulls Presstjänst mit unserer Hilfe nach Schweden gelangt" (note from Schmidt to Weizsäcker, Mar. 9, 1942, NA Microcopy T-120, roll 92, 104672.

fitted logically in the pattern of Hungarian foreign policy.[19] The same note gave the reason for Ribbentrop's outspoken dislike of Ullein-Reviczky: he had heard from a reliable source in Ankara that the British, Americans, and Russians had been receiving "surprisingly" accurate information from a Hungarian source. After the departure of the American minister from Budapest, accurate information continued to reach Turkey and the Allies by way of the Turkish minister in Budapest. Ribbentrop suspected the source of some of this information to be Ullein-Reviczky or his wife, the daughter of a former British consul in Istanbul.[20] In mid-March the Hungarian minister in Berlin, Sztójay, flew home to Budapest; according to Secretary Weizsäcker, Sztójay's objective was once again to dissuade Kállay from appointing Ullein-Reviczky and to advocate the reappointment of Bárdossy.[21] Ribbentrop even wrote Bárdossy a personal letter encouraging him to continue as the minister of foreign affairs.[22]

The German demarches seem to have taken extraordinary proportions, especially if we consider that there was little evidence Ullein-Reviczky was ever a serious candidate for the post of minister of foreign affairs.[23] Neither Kállay's memoirs (*Hungarian Premier*) nor those of Ullein-Reviczky (*Guerre allemande, paix russe*) mention that possibility. The incident would not be particularly significant, did it not provide an indication of the extent to which the Reich Foreign Office sought to influence Hungarian politics and the degree of success it enjoyed in these endeavors. The fact that Bárdossy was never reappointed minister of foreign affairs may serve to indicate that the diplomatic pressure exercised by the Reich Foreign Office had limited success. Perhaps these limitations are a result of Ribbentrop's own shortcomings as minister of foreign affairs, shortcomings which will become even more obvious at the time of the German occupation of Hungary. A more able diplomat would have,

19. Unsigned note of Mar. 13, 1942, NA Microcopy T-120, roll 92, 104695–96.

20. NA Microcopy T-120, roll 92, 104695–96.

21. Note from Weizsäcker to Ribbentrop, Mar. 18, 1942, NA Microcopy, T-120, roll 92, 104717.

22. Ribbentrop to Bárdossy, Mar. 17, 1942, NA Microcopy, T-120, roll 92, 104711.

23. The alleged candidacy of Ullein-Reviczky is also discussed in a lengthy report of the Sicherheitsdienst, signed by Reinhard Heydrich, as late as May 29, 1942. According to this report, Ullein-Reviczky made protestations of his pro-German orientation in the course of a conversation with Heydrich, because his ambition was to become minister of foreign affairs and he feared the Germans might object (NA Microcopy T-120, roll 1096, 452330–35).

in this case, either exerted more outright pressure on the Hungarians, and may well have succeeded in effecting Bárdossy's reappointment, or would have refrained from exercising any pressure whatever and saved himself the humiliation of seeing his protégé disregarded. Goebbels may have had a clearer image of the situation when he wrote, on March 11, 1942: "For the present we have no possibility whatever of exerting any influence upon the formation of the Hungarian Cabinet, since we must ask a great deal of the Hungarians during the next weeks and months and therefore keep them in good humor. But we can later catch up with what we are neglecting today." [24]

Kállay kept the Reich officials guessing until May 22, when he took charge of the Ministry of Foreign Affairs himself, explaining that this was a temporary recourse.[25] In the meantime the Reich leaders continued to exert pressure on Kállay by repeated postponements of the by-then traditional invitation to visit the Führer. Whenever a new leader appeared in the allied or satellite countries, a visit to Hitler was in order. In fact this ritual had become so entrenched that the new official could hardly consider himself "consecrated" or confirmed in his office until he had received Hitler's invitation. The invitation to Kállay was delayed for over two months after his appointment by the regent. The Reich Foreign Office had

24. *Goebbels Diaries,* p. 120. On the same grounds, the principle of noninterference in internal matters, the undersecretary of the Foreign Office, Weizsäcker, as well as Hitler, refused to receive the Hungarian Archduke Albrecht, who peddled intrigues in order to bring about a pro-National Socialist government in Hungary under his guidance (NA Microcopy T-120, roll 92, 104802). Ribbentrop explained Hitler's decision regarding the archduke to a go-between: Hitler bears a friendship for Horthy, is loyal to the Hungarian state, and does not wish to appear to interfere in Hungarian affairs (Ribbentrop to Jagow, Jan. 17, 1942, NA Microcopy T-120, roll 92, 104498).

25. Telegram from Jagow to Berlin, May 22, 1942, NA Microcopy T-120, roll 92, 105002. In August of 1942 Kállay seems to have had another minister of foreign affairs in mind, the Hungarian minister to the Vatican, Baron Gábor Apor. Baron Clemens von Waldbott, whose estate neighbored that of Kállay and who must have been a personal friend, was sent to Berlin to sound out the Reich Foreign Office. Upon inquiry, Bergen, the first secretary of the German embassy in Rome, reported that Baron Gábor Apor did not sympathize with the National Socialists. Erdmannsdorf, who had met Baron Apor in the course of their diplomatic careers back in 1937, also described Apor's attitude as reserved vis-à-vis National Socialist Germany and Apor himself as "not quite reliable" (memorandum by Weizsäcker, Aug. 7, 1942, and note from Erdmannsdorf to Weizsäcker of the same date, NA Microcopy T-120, roll 93, 105646–54). Hence, the matter was dropped by the Hungarian government, and Baron Apor remains unaware of it to this day.

even suggested that Kállay visit Italy first; Kállay insisted that Germany come first as she was the greater power and, in the contrary case, world opinion might be "misled."[26] On April 20 Sztójay was asked to tell his government Kállay must wait yet a little longer because the Führer was "still very busy with military matters."[27] Finally, on May 27, Kállay received an invitation to visit Hitler on June 6.[28] The invitation came five days after Kállay had assumed the title of minister of foreign affairs; it seems, then, that the German leaders had waited long enough to make sure Ullein-Reviczky would not be appointed to that post.

Even prior to his visit Kállay had gone out of his way to reassure the German leaders regarding his feelings toward Germany. Within a month and a half after Kállay took over, left-wing elements, including some Social Democrats, were arrested by the hundreds and either detained in prisons or sent to the front as members of forced labor battalions. Kállay's first speeches emphasized the continuity of Hungarian foreign policy. On March 19, in his first parliamentary speech, he went so far as to declare the war was "our war"; Hungary was fighting in her own interests.[29] Kállay also pointed out, in his public utterances, that the Jewish problem must be solved by the deportation of all Hungarian Jews after the war.[30] These declarations had the desired results. Just before Kállay's visit to Hitler, Jagow dispatched a favorable characterization of Kállay: a man who saw his main role as supporting Germany in her struggle against bolshevism. "Furthermore," added Jagow, "he has taken a firmer anti-Jewish stand than any of his predecessors."[31]

It is often said that the pro-German and sometimes pro-National

26. Note by Weizsäcker on conversation with Jagow, Apr. 14, 1942, NA Microcopy T-120, roll 92, 104845.

27. Weizsäcker to Sztójay, Apr. 20, 1942, NA Microcopy T-120, roll 92, 104876.

28. Telegram from Ribbentrop to Jagow, May 27, 1942, NA Microcopy T-120, roll 92, 105021–22.

29. Macartney, *October Fifteenth*, 2 : 91. In his memoirs Kállay wrote: "Should anyone pick out my pro-Axis and similar statements exclusively, he would make out a successful charge-sheet against me. But such a winnowing would be both stupid and dishonest. . . . I was the only one among the leaders of the countries wriggling in Germany's clutches who occasionally dared to differ with German views" (Kállay, *Hungarian Premier*, p. 72).

30. Speech of Apr. 20, 1942; see Kállay, *Hungarian Premier*, and Karsai, *A budai vártól*, p. 148.

31. Telegram from Jagow to Berlin, June 2, 1942, NA Microcopy T-120, roll 92, 105168. Baron Alexander von Dörnberg, the German chief of protocol, also reported favorably on Kállay as a result of an interview in April (report by Dörnberg to Ribbentrop, Apr. 20, 1942, NA Microcopy T-120, roll 92, 104884–85).

Socialist attitude assumed by Kállay was a manifestation of his so-called *hintapolitika,* or policy of the swing. His policies swung to the left and to the right in an attempt to extricate Hungary from her orbit as Germany's satellite without arousing the leaders of the Reich and provoking a German occupation. Kállay describes his own program as follows: "To defend and to preserve the independence that Hungary still possessed in domestic affairs, and to work for the restoration of the independence that had been lost." [32] This program did not necessarily mean to extricate Hungary from the war. Dezső Sulyok, a Hungarian politician who had been a member of the liberal opposition, averred that Kállay did not even practice a "policy of the swing"; it was only at the time of Stalingrad that Kállay finally realized Germany would lose the war and attempted to carry out an about-face of Hungarian foreign and military policy.[33] But even the program of limited independence Kállay seems to have pursued in 1942 could not be pursued openly. The program could be carried out only by deceit, by deceiving the leaders of the Reich as well as Hungarian political leaders, a majority of whom favored even closer collaboration with the Reich.[34] Whether Hungary was actually a "satellite" of Germany can be a matter of argument; but, whatever Hungary's status in relationship with Germany, it changed little between the beginning and the end of the year 1942. Perhaps Kállay's program was doomed to failure; perhaps Kállay's attempt to carry it out was halfhearted or too measured.

Though the German leaders may have continued to disapprove of Kállay, despite his protestations of loyalty, Hitler raised no specific objections to either Kállay or the policies of the Hungarian government during the latter's visit on June 6.[35] The atmosphere of the meeting seems to have been rather cordial. Surprisingly enough,

32. Kállay, *Hungarian Premier,* p. 12.

33. "It was only after the breakthrough at Voronezh and General Paulus' catastrophe at Stalingrad that Kállay really changed his evaluation of the war. From then on he tried to save what could be saved by committing all his personal energies to this cause. He was a well-meaning and honorable man from the start and wanted to do good for his country. When he preached a pro-German policy he was deeply convinced that policy was the right one" (*A magyar tragédia,* p. 477).

34. Kállay, *Hungarian Premier,* p. 70.

35. Kállay was accompanied by Andor Szentmiklósy, and Aladár Szegedy-Maszák of the Foreign Ministry, by Gen. János Vörös, as well as by one of his own sons (Jagow to Berlin, June 1, 1942, NA Microcopy, T-120, roll 93, 105163). Kállay himself states, in his memoirs, that the visit took place on Apr. 15, 1942 (*Hungarian Premier,* p. 90). This error is repeated in some subsequent works on this period of Hungarian history, for instance by Karsai.

Hitler did not monopolize the conversation during Kállay's visit as was his custom.[36] And when Kállay brought up the subject of the "Jewish question" Hitler merely declared that "he would not, of course, intervene in Hungary's internal affairs . . ."[37] On the basis of Jagow's reports, Hitler had no cause to complain of Kállay's approach to this question.

Hitler had a concrete reason to be satisfied with the meeting.[38] It appears that Kállay and Gen. János Vörös—the future chief of the Hungarian General Staff who accompanied Kállay on his visit as chief of the Operations Division—promised the Reich leaders two more Hungarian occupation or light divisions for the eastern front. Future negotiations on this score indicate, however, that the Hungarian government forgot this commitment until reminded by the Germans.[39] Jagow called on Kállay during September and was told the Hungarians would be prepared to send 20,000 men as replacements to the eastern front, a number somewhat in excess of the actual casualties suffered by the Hungarian Second Army up to that time.[40] On October 9 an official of the German embassy in Budapest reported that the Hungarian Crown Council had agreed to send two more divisions to the Soviet Union for occupation purposes.[41] It was the disaster which overtook the Hungarian Second Army at Voronezh that ultimately prevented the fulfillment of this Hungarian commitment.

One episode seems to have jarred, if not marred, the pleasantness of the meeting at the Führer headquarters; Kállay requested, according to the German report, that Hitler "turn a benevolent blind eye if the Hungarians started a fight with the Rumanians."[42] No men-

36. "I had always understood," write Kállay, "that one of Hitler's by no means pleasing customs was to pour out a flood of words from the start without allowing his guest to open his mouth. Just the contrary took place. We sat down, and he turned and asked me to inform him on the Hungarian situation" (*Hungarian Premier*, p. 90).

37. Ibid., p. 92.

38. Hitler expressed his gratitude to Kállay by sending Mrs. Kállay an airplane for the transport of the wounded (Political Section, Hungarian Foreign Ministry, Hungarian National Archives, K63, bundles 187–88, tétel 21).

39. Telegram from Jagow to Berlin, July 18, 1942, NA Microcopy T-120, roll 93, 105377. The telegram from Ritter to Jagow, Sept. 22, 1942, notes that the Hungarians seem to have forgotten their promise (NA Microcopy T-120, roll 93, 105724–25).

40. Telegram from Jagow to Berlin, Sept. 1942, NA Microcopy T-120, roll 92, 105726.

41. Telegram from Werkmeister to Foreign Office, NA Microcopy T-120, roll 93, 105782.

42. Trevor-Roper, *Hitler's Secret Conversations*, p. 418.

tion is made of the incident in Kállay's memoirs, and it is possible, as we have seen, that the Hungarian-Romanian conflict was, in part, dust in the eyes of National Socialist Germany.

The friendly spirit of the June meeting dissolved rapidly, because Kállay's deeds did not measure up to his words. The measure of pro-German sentiment and of statesmanship, in the eyes of the National Socialist leaders of Germany, was the degree of anti-Semitism exhibited by the leaders of the allied and satellite countries. While Kállay had professed to be an anti-Semite (and in his memoirs, published in 1954, he still examined the "Jewish question" in all earnest), professions of this kind did not suffice; action was necessary. In Finland and Italy, where the number of Jews was small, liberal policies prevailed. But anti-Semitic measures adopted in Hungary lagged behind those adopted in other "independent" countries of eastern Europe. In other words, the situation in Hungary compared favorably, in this respect, with the situation in Romania, Croatia, and Slovakia, where the anti-Jewish measures had already resulted or were about to result in the extermination of all or part of the resident Jews and Jewish nationals.

It cannot be said, however, that anti-Semitism was not strong in Hungary. Occasionally some Hungarian politician boasted that Hungary had invented anti-Semitism. Indeed Hungary had been the first country to introduce the principle of *numerus clausus* at Hungarian universities after World War I, in 1920: the number of Jewish students admitted was theoretically set at 6 percent, or slightly above the actual proportion of Jews in Hungary.[43] According to the census of 1930 there were 444,567 Jews in Hungary constituting 5.1 percent of the total population. Hungary thus may have had the largest concentration of Jews in the world next to Poland, although some statisticians claim the proportion of Jews was also higher in Lithuania and Romania.[44] With the return of territories in 1939

43. It appears that the *numerus clausus* principle was not fully enforced, but it was enough to encourage the emigration of promising young Hungarian Jews (one need only mention the names of Edward Teller, Leo Szilard, John von Neumann, George Lukacs, Tódor Kálmán) to German and other universities.

44. Sulyok, *A magyar tragédia*, p. 512; also Béla Vihar, ed. *Sárga könyv: adatok a magyar zsidóság háborús szenvedéseiből, 1941–1945* [Yellow book: data on the sufferings of the Hungarian Jewry during the war], pp. 208–9. A report by Werkmeister of the German legation, dated July 26, 1937, indicated that both Lithuania (with 6.55%) and Romania (with 5.54%) had a higher percentage of Jews than Hungary. The same report divided the Hungarian Jews into the following classes: 24% belonged to the lower class (*Proletariat*), 40% to the lower middle class (*Kleinbürgertum*), 28% to the upper middle class (*Mittelstand*), whereas there were twenty-five Jewish families

and 1940, the total number and even the proportion of Jews in Hungary increased.[45] While a number of Jews converted to Christianity between the wars and during World War II, thus confusing the statistics, the number of persons of Jewish faith increased further during the years from 1939 to 1943 because of an influx of refugees from Poland, Slovakia, and Romania.

After the law of 1920 no further discriminatory measures were taken against the Jews in Hungary until the eve of World War II. The so-called First Jewish Law was passed in 1938, limiting Jewish participation in the country's economic life to 20 percent.[46] That same year a Second Jewish Law, entitled "Law to restrict Jewish penetration in the public affairs and economic Life of the country," was passed—[47] thanks, in part, to the sponsorship of Count Pál Teleki, the man who committed suicide when Hungary became involved in the German campaign against Yugoslavia. Law 15 of 1941, passed on August 8, defined a Jew much in the same terms as the "Nuremberg laws" had done and prohibited miscegenation. Finally, Law 12 of 1942 resulted in the confiscation of all landed property owned by Jews.[48] The upper house of the Hungarian Parliament, which included Jews, passed these laws after some debate. The lower house passed them without protracted debate. It would be safe to say this house was, by and large, not only right wing but also anti-Semitic. During the period 1939 to 1944, when no new elections took place, the house included 5 Social Democrats (3 of whom seem to have cooperated with the police in keeping an eye on the other two),[49] 7 independent members, and 14 members of the Smallholders party, whereas the remainder of the 296 delegates, including the 178 members of the government party, can safely be

---

among the aristocracy (the missing 8% is not accounted for). Furthermore, 34.4% of the doctors in Hungary were Jews and 16% of the medical students, despite the *numerus clausus* law. 49.2% of the lawyers were Jewish and 30.4% of the musicians. "Astonishingly," added the report, "the Jewish influence is considerable even in the field of sports." These statistics were based on Hungarian estimates. (Werkmeister to Berlin, July 26, 1937, NA Microcopy T-120, roll 1058, 424522 ff., or roll 4357, 424519 ff.; see also "Überblick über Staat and Wirtschaft Ungarns," Apr. 22, 1940, NA Microcopy T-84, roll 135, 1437945.)

45. Altogether 724,306 Jews were registered by the census of 1941, and 585,265 of them declared themselves Hungarian (E. R. Kutas, "Judaism, Zionism, and Anti-Semitism in Hungary," p. 379).

46. Jenő Lévai, *Black Book on the Martyrdom of the Hungarian Jewry,* p. 379.

47. The law was presented to the House on Dec. 23, 1938 (ibid., p. 14).

48. Ibid., pp. 25, 28.

49. Sulyok, *A magyar tragédia,* p. 403.

described as right wing and pro-German, sometimes even National Socialist.[50]

The cumulative effect of the laws discriminating against Jews was severe economic hardship. Jews were not allowed to hold or own land. Jewish participation in the professions and in commerce was limited to 6 to 12 percent. Furthermore, the Jews were eliminated from the Hungarian civil and military services; drafted Jews were herded into special units called labor service battalions and were not allowed to bear arms. The death rate in these forced labor battalions was far higher than in other military units. Taken cumulatively, these laws caused a large number of Jews to lose their livelihood and sometimes their lives.[51] Had they been carried out to the letter, no doubt the misery inflicted would have been even more considerable.

Although these imperfectly applied laws amounted to severe discrimination, they did not amount to terror. Generally speaking, the Hungarian Jew did not have to fear for his life, except in two notorious incidents.

The first of these incidents was the fate of the so-called Galician Jews in Hungary, most of whom had fled the areas occupied by German armies, especially Poland. The internment of all Jews in Hungary unable to show proof of citizenship was ordered in 1941. During negotiations conducted by the Hungarian general József Heszlényi with German military authorities concerning economic matters and the administration of occupied territories, the issue of the deportation of 12,000 Jews from Hungary was raised.[52] The Reich government, which had hitherto refused to allow deportations into territories occupied by the German armies, finally granted General Heszlényi's request in January 1942. About 14,700 Jews were seized and deported to Galicia, regardless of whether they originally came from that province or not.[53] It is unnecessary to describe the fate of

50. *Tanulmányok,* p. 53. There had been no universal suffrage in Hungary between the wars. Voting rights depended on ten years of citizenship, two years of residence in one place, and the completion of four grades of schooling for men, six grades for women; women under thirty were disenfranchized by the electoral law of 1922. The number of voters in the country was reduced to 2,382,000. The electoral law of 1938 raised the residency requirement to six years. (*Tanulmányok,* pp. 50–52.)

51. Lévai, *Black Book,* pp. 12–14. According to Lévai's computations elsewhere in this book, 272,668 Jews lost their livelihood as a result of these laws (p. 36). See also François Honti, *Le drame hongrois,* p. 34.

52. Memorandum of conversation between Heszlényi and Becker, Jan. 13, 1942, NA Microcopy T-120, roll 2563, 312575.

53. Dezső Saly, *Szigorúan bizalmas* [Strictly confidential], p. 380. Lévai, however, writes that there may have been as many as 20,000 deportees (*Black Book,* p. 25).

the deported Jews; nor can it be said that the Hungarian authorities who ordered and executed these deportations were not acting *en connaissance de cause*. And it was again the German authorities who finally requested the Hungarian government to halt these deportations.[54] In all fairness to the Hungarians, however, I have found several documents referring to incidents in which the reputedly anti-Semitic officers of the Hungarian army of occupation irked the German authorities by measures that can only be characterized as pro-Semitic or anti-Nazi. An SS officer's report from Galicia, dated September 18, 1942, mentioned that Hungarian commanders of certain labor service battalions had ordered the exhumation of mass graves harboring the bodies of Jews shot by the Sipo (Sicherheitspolizei) and the SD (Sicherheitsdienst) "during their attempt to cross the Hungarian border"; and photographs were taken which could naturally be used for "atrocity propaganda" purposes. Furthermore, Jewish refugees were greeted with open arms by the Hungarians on the Hungarian side of the Ukrainian or Galician border.[55]

The second atrocity I must mention was the massacre at Ujvidék (Novi Sad). Ujvidék is a town on the Danube in the province of Bácska which Hungary had regained as a result of her participation in the attack on Yugoslavia. A few months after the Hungarian army had occupied the province, manifestations of partisan activity occurred. According to a Hungarian report dated January 8, 1942, the Hungarian casualties included seventeen dead whereas the "Četnic" (Serbian nationalist) casualties amounted to several hundred dead. Some Hungarian officers in command of units in the area ordered mass reprisals, thus adding to the number of the victims. Gen. József Bajnóczy, the area commander, reported that "we now have the opportunity to rid ourselves of all undesirable elements and to give the population a frightening example."[56]

Several hundred inhabitants of Serbian villages were summarily shot. Among the records of the Hungarian Foreign Ministry I found

54. On Sept. 25, 1942, Eichmann wrote to Karl Klingenfuss (both of the SS) that it would require too much effort to deport Jewish refugees from Hungary; it would be best to solve the whole Hungarian Jewish problem at one blow (NA Microcopy T-120, roll 2561, 310841–42).

55. NA Microcopy T-175, roll 21, 2526491. A similar report, dated Nov. 23, 1943, is reproduced in NA Microcopy T-120, roll 688, 311982–84.

56. Report by Gen. József Bajnóczy about the events at Csurog and Zsablya, Political Section, Ministry of Foreign Affairs, Hungarian National Archives, K63, bundles 187–88, tétel 21.

signed "confessions" in the Hungarian language, made entirely "free of physical or moral pressure"; yet most of those who "confessed" stated they knew no Hungarian.[57] Finally the massacres spread to the town of Ujvidék, where some of the victims, mostly Serbs and Jews, were marched to the swimming pool on the Danube River and disposed of through holes carved in the ice.[58] Authors disagree on the exact number of victims, but the number revealed in the course of the subsequent hearings, 3,309 for all the shootings in the period January 17–22, does not seem to be an underestimate.[59] The prime minister (Bárdossy) and the chief of the General Staff (Szombathelyi) were slow to order the cessation of the *razzia* (raid): Szombathelyi's order to desist was dated January 30, by which time the razzias had already ceased anyway.[60] The local commander, Gen. Ferenc Feketehalmi-Czeydner, was slow to obey that order.[61] It was because of this atrocity that the Yugoslav courts of law condemned Generals Feketehalmi-Czeydner and Szombathelyi, who ordered the razzia, to death, although the degree of responsibility of the latter could not have been clearly determined. In this connection, the postwar Yugoslav government also requested from the Allies the extradition of Regent Horthy. The request was denied; yet it had been the regent who, in August 1942, on the motion of General Szombathelyi, dismissed the charges brought against the officers responsible for the massacres.[62]

Kállay may be credited for reopening the proceedings against the officers involved in the mass shootings, on October 11, 1943, although the initial impetus came from the Smallholder member of the Parliament, Endre Bajcsy-Zsilinszky, certainly (with Károly Rassay) the most courageous member of the opposition.[63] The officers

57. Ibid.

58. Hungarian authors are quick to point out that the three leaders of the massacres, Gen. Ferenc Feketehalmy-Czeydner, Col. József Grassy, and Márton Zöldi were all of "German descent"; see, for instance, Kállay, *Hungarian Premier*, p. 110.

59. According to the official hearings, 869 persons were shot at Zsablya, 168 at Obecse, 195 at Mozsor, and 879 at Ujvidék proper. There were 147 children among the victims. Karsai, *A budai vártól*, p. 164.

60. Political Section, Ministry of Foreign Affairs, Hungarian National Archives, K63, bundles 187–88, tétel 21.

61. Karsai, *A budai vártól*, p. 113.

62. Ibid., p. 165.

63. Bajcsy-Zsilinszky's parliamentary interpellation on the subject was delivered on Dec. 2, 1942 (Karsai, *A budai vártól*, pp. 214 ff., 278). He had, however, addressed a memorandum on the subject to Horthy soon after the event, on Feb. 2, 1942 (Jenő Buzási, *Az ujvidéki razzia* [The *razzia* at Novi Sad], p. 58). In a speech on July 15,

responsible were sentenced to prison terms ranging up to fifteen years, but the four main accused escaped to Germany, where they were admitted as "guests of the Reichsführer of the SS." [64] After his arrest by the American forces in 1945, General Feketehalmy-Czeydner claimed he had escaped with the understanding of Regent Horthy.[65] I know of no witness or document to support this contention; but it is certain Regent Horthy was so firmly convinced of the honorability of the Hungarian officer corps that it may have been difficult for him to believe that Feketehalmy-Czeydner and his companions had perpetrated acts which did not redound to the honor of Hungarian arms.

The German leaders had become disenchanted with Kállay as early as the fall of 1942, mainly because of Kállay's inactivity in the war against the Jews. The Wannsee conference, where the "final solution" of the Jewish problem was definitely adopted, had taken place on January 20, 1942, and it was in the Reichstag speech of April 6, 1942, that Hitler announced his decision to solve the "Jewish problem" immediately and radically; but for reasons that are not clear to me, the National Socialist leaders waited till the fall of 1942 to advocate their solution to all their allies. On September 24, Martin Luther of the Reich Foreign Office received a telephone call from his chief, Ribbentrop, instructing him to emphasize the necessity of evacuating the Jews from all countries in Europe. After Ribbentrop described the deportations taking place in Slovakia, Croatia, Romania, and the occupied territories, he instructed Luther to request that similar procedures be instituted in Bulgaria, Denmark, and Hungary.[66] Accordingly, on October 2 Luther gave Sztójay detailed suggestions regarding the handling of the "Jewish question." These included (a) "progressive" laws to exclude the Jews from the cultural and economic life of the country, (b) compulsory identification marks for all Jews, and (c) deportation of the Jews to

---

1942, Kállay still asserted that the killings at Ujvidék had been in self-defense, partisans having infiltrated the town and attacked the gendarmes with hand grenades (ibid., pp. 4–5).

64. István Deák to author; also, telegrams of Jan. 16 and 17, 1944, NA Microcopy T-120, roll 99, 109708–9, 109716.

65. Himler, *Igy néztek ki a magyar nemzet sírásói*, p. 181. Feketehalmy-Czeydner returned to Hungary with the German troops of occupation; he became assistant minister of defense after Oct. 15, 1944.

66. NA Microcopy T-120, roll 2561, 310856.

the East, in collaboration with German authorities.[67] Luther noted that Sztójay gave him the following reply:

From former conversations with the prime minister he knows that Kállay is especially interested in knowing whether after their deportation to the East the Jews are provided with means of livelihood. There are many rumors in this regard which he, Sztójay, does not believe, of course, but which nevertheless worry the prime minister . . . I answered that all deported Jews, including, of course, the Hungarian Jews, will be employed in building roads in the East and later will be brought together in a reservation. This answer calmed him visibly, and he observed that such information will have a specifically calming and encouraging effect on the prime minister.[68]

The sentence concerning the employment of Jews in road construction work and the creation of reservations was underlined in pencil by Ribbentrop himself. The euphemism "road construction," however, was not an original contribution of Martin Luther; the Romanian government, for one, had used the same terminology during the roundups of Jews in that country in August 1941.[69]

Apart from Sztójay's report to the Hungarian government, the Reich Foreign Office also instructed Jagow to make a demarche. Luther explained to Jagow that while the measures already taken by the Hungarian government were appreciated they fell far short of the anti-Jewish measures adopted in Germany and in other European countries "that are willing to renew themselves."[70] Jagow reported, on October 17, that he had handed Luther's communication regarding the Jewish question to Jenő Ghyczy, the undersecretary for foreign affairs. At first Ghyczy would not accept the note.[71]

67. Memorandum by Luther on conversation with Sztójay, Oct. 2 and Oct. 6, 1942, NA Microcopy T-120, roll 2561, 310813 ff. A partial translation of the memorandum of Oct. 6 is printed in *Trials of War Criminals before the Nuernberg Military Tribunals*, 13 : 259–61.

68. Ibid.

69. See, for instance, telegram from Neubacher to Berlin, Aug. 6, 1941, *DGFP*, series D, 13 : 287–88.

70. Telegram from Luther to Jagow, Oct. 14, 1942, NA Microcopy T-120, roll 2561, 310805–7.

71. Telegram from Jagow to Berlin, Oct. 17, 1942. (NA Microcopy T-120, roll 2561, 310792). Among the exhibits printed in vol. 13 of *Trials of War Criminals before the Nuernberg Military Tribunals*, there is a telegram from Luther to Jagow dated Oct.

Finally Ghyczy took the note and Jagow was later received by Kállay, but Kállay pointed out that the Jewish question was an internal affair of Hungary.[72] He also pointed out that the question was an extraordinarily difficult one. Because of their lack of international influence, the Hungarian Jews were far less dangerous than the French, Swiss, or American Jews. Moreover, continued Kállay, the Hungarian peasant was absolutely not anti-Semitic, and the number of baptized Jews was only 40,000. "It should be noted," reads the report prepared for Ribbentrop on the basis of Jagow's dispatches, "that Kállay remarked that if he had to eliminate the Jews completely he would have to make up for that by increased assimilation of the German ethnic group." [73] This remark was calculated to worry the Reich officials who were intent on seeing the *Volksdeutsche* of Hungary preserve their ethnic identity.[74]

While the evidence above is culled from German diplomatic records, it serves to corroborate the pertinent observation in Kállay's memoirs.[75] The evidence presented by Kállay seems based, apart from his own memory, on documents presented by Jenő Lévai in his works on the vicissitudes of the Hungarian Jews. These documents show that while Kállay's attitude toward the Jews was not always free of unfavorable bias,[76] he definitely rejected the National Socialist brand of anti-Semitism, both in theory and in application.

16, summarizing a conference between Ernst von Weizsäcker and Sztójay regarding the deportation of Hungarian Jews (p. 263).

72. Telegram from Jagow to Berlin, Oct. 27, 1942, NA Microcopy T-120, roll 93, 105840–41.

73. Memorandum prepared for Ribbentrop, Dec. 3, 1942, NA Microcopy T-120, roll 2561, 310778.

74. Hitler is quoted as having remarked in 1942: "The Hungarians are wildly nationalist. They assimilate the Germans at extraordinary speed, and they know how to select the best for posts of command. We shan't succeed in preserving the German minorities in Hungary except by taking over control of the State—or else we shall have to withdraw our minorities from Hungary" (Trevor-Roper, *Hitler's Secret Conversations*, p. 275).

75. Kállay relates the German demands as follows "1) The Jews to wear a yellow star. 2) A ghetto in every town, segregation of the Jews in ghettos. 3) 300,000 able-bodied Jewish men and women to be placed at Germany's disposal, in connection with the rehabilitation of the industry and agriculture of the Ukraine" (*Hungarian Premier*, p. 113). This request, writes Kállay, was repeated three times (p. 358).

76. In this regard Kállay wrote in 1954: "I was determined that Jews were not to be discriminated against for racial reasons—this was inhumanity—but that they were to be judged and acted towards strictly in relation to their role in economic and social conditions in Hungary. In such, of course, were the roots of the whole question" (ibid., p. 15).

The German officials were not so easily discouraged; they continued to harp on the alleged danger represented by the presence of almost one million Jews "in the middle of Europe." Sztójay was asked to relay the displeasure of the Reich government when, on January 1, 1943, it was learned that the agency of the Hungarian government in charge of finding a solution to the Jewish question had been disbanded. "We cannot remain inactive in the face of such danger . . . ," Luther told Sztójay, "we can only hope our persistent pressures will yet lead to results." [77] Late in 1942 the German authorities proceeded to deport foreign Jews from various western countries but preferred to consult with the interested governments first. Many governments expressed no interest, but the Hungarian government insisted on recalling the Hungarian Jews from Belgium, Holland, France, and Germany. The Jews listed by the Hungarian government were allowed to leave by the German authorities.[78] On March 12, 1943, when the leader of the government party, Béla Lukács, paid a visit to Germany, Martin Bormann, chief of the Reich Chancellery, discussed with him the necessity of ridding Hungary of Jews. Bormann explained to Lukács that because of his cleverness (*Geschicklichkeit*) every Jew was about the equivalent of a secret service agent who, moreover, had the advantage of being cloaked by his citizenship and of having "unlimited funds" at his disposal. The solution proposed by Bormann did not differ from the one suggested by Ribbentrop and Luther in October 1942: the immediate and indiscriminate elimination of Jews from the cultural and economic life of Hungary, the immediate marking of Jews to facilitate the application of government regulations against them and to enable the people to keep the Jews at a distance, and consent to immediate deportations to the East by the responsible German

77. Note by Luther on conversation with Sztójay, Jan. 16, 1943, NA Microcopy T-120, roll 4357, K215078. It is clear, however, that the German suggestions regarding the solution of the Jewish problem in Hungary did not emanate from Martin Luther. The following month, in February 1943, Luther found himself in a concentration camp.

78. "The Hungarian Government finally took steps to repatriate the Hungarian Jewish families threatened after the constantly repeated claims of the Nazi Government became more insistent still and the date fixed for the proposed measures against them expired after already having been extended several times. In the first group, 21 Jewish families were repatriated from Brussels. On January 16, 17 Jewish families of Amsterdam, in June, 1943, 57 Jewish families of Paris and 70 Jewish families of Berlin were repatriated by the Hungarian Government. . . . More than 400 families were resettled in Hungary, among them many who had lost their Hungarian nationality and were only included on the lists for purely humanitarian reasons" (Lévai, *Black Book*, p. 31).

organization.[79] The repeated use of the word *immediate* may indicate that the National Socialist leaders were losing patience.

There were other indications that the Hungarian government was not inclined to adopt stricter measures vis-à-vis the Jews. Jagow pointed out, in a dispatch dated April 15, 1943, that two Jewish members of the upper house had been elected to serve on the Committee for Foreign Affairs, whereas the Committee on Finances was wholly in the hands of Jews. "These elections," wrote Jagow, "show clearly that the Hungarian government has no intention of adopting a policy course with regard to the Jews that would be in line with ours." [80]

German criticisms were not directed at Kállay alone; aside from the fact that the regent was responsible for the appointment of his prime minister, Horthy's views on the Jewish question were likewise inadequate from the National Socialist point of view. An unsigned report of an interview with Regent Horthy—transmitted to Heinrich Himmler's office in July 1943—stated that Horthy seemed willing to rid the country of the "little Jews, who originally came from Galicia, but that all those Jews who had made contributions in the fields of science, industry, or finance must be regarded as patriots and must remain unharmed." Even as far as the destitute "little Jews" were concerned, declared Horthy, these should not be removed to the Ukraine but much rather set to do useful work in Hungary proper.[81]

Another official of the Hungarian government who aroused the antagonism of the National Socialists was the new minister of defense, Vilmos Nagy; Bartha, who had consistently gone far to meet the German requests for troops and reinforcements, was asked to resign on September 24, 1942. At first the new minister's appointment was greeted with relative satisfaction by the National Socialist leaders, because Nagy was believed to be a member of the circle of Béla Imrédy, the right-wing politician and former Hungarian prime

79. Memorandum from Bergmann to Bormann, Mar. 9, 1943, NA Microcopy T-120, roll 2561, 310707–11.

80. NA Microcopy T-120, roll 4357, K215079. The two members of the Foreign Affairs Committee referred to by Jagow were Ferenc Chorin and Aurél Egry. The members of the Committee on Finances were Ferenc Chorin, Aurél Egry, Baron Móricz Kornfeld, Jenő Vida, and Baron György Ullman. Most of these men were Christians of Jewish parentage.

81. NA Microcopy T-120, roll 1096, 452386–87. A similar report is given by a German agent (*Gewährmann*) in late 1942 or early 1943 (NA Microcopy T-120, roll 2561, 310757 ff.).

minister. Nagy was not actually claimed by the Imrédy circle as a member, noted Jagow, but only because he had a Jewish sister-in-law.[82] Indeed, the sister-in-law proved an ill omen. In a matter of weeks Nagy intervened to ease the sufferings of the Jewish men who had been drafted into the forced labor battalions. Thousands of young Jews had perished in the service because of the often officially condoned sadistic treatment accorded them; indeed, such treatment was at times even encouraged by Hungarian officers.[83]

But in trying to eliminate abuses Nagy inevitably encountered not only the opposition of Axis officials but also the enmity of the majority of the Hungarian Parliament, of the military establishment, and of some officials within the Ministry of Defense. Kállay rejected Nagy's resignation on two separate occasions, but Nagy was finally asked to resign, on the prompting of the Italian minister who in turn had been prompted by the German. Jagow, who was not on speaking terms with Kállay during much of 1943, asked the Italian minister, Filippo Anfuso, to secure the dismissal of Nagy. Kállay agreed: "I will try to dismiss him in about a month to give you pleasure." To which Anfuso, ever a faithful Fascist, replied: "You are giving me no pleasure at all. I am speaking in the interest of us all. We must win the war." [84] Nagy's resignation was accepted on June 8, 1943.[85] The pendulum had swung to the right.

Thus already in 1942 German-Hungarian relations had become strained. It is true that the Hungarian government continued to contribute to the German war effort economically and especially

82. Telegram from Jagow to Berlin, Sept. 25, 1942, NA Microcopy T-120, roll 92, 1057030.

83. These atrocities are described by Nagy himself. He cites a case where sick Jews, concentrated in a barn which caught (or was set on) fire, were shot down as they jumped out the windows, in order to "prevent the spread of fire." Of the perhaps 50,000 labor-service men (not exclusively Jews but including some young Marxists and other politically "undesirable" elements), only about five to six thousand returned after the battle of the Don River. This meant that the rate of casualties in the forced labor battalions was far higher than in the combat infantry itself (Nagy, *Végzetes esztendők* pp. 82–84, 106–7). Extensive documentation on the forced labor battalions can be found in Elek Karsai, ed., *"Fegyvertelen álltak az aknamezőkön . . . ,"* [They stood in the minefields defenseless . . .]. An interesting work on the non-Jewish labor-service man is István Kossa's *Dunától a Donig* [From the Danube to the Don].

84. Anfuso, *Du Palais de Venise*, pp. 241–42.

85. Although Nagy writes with sympathy of the policies adopted by Kállay, he comments on his own resignation with bitter words, because Kállay did not explain to him frankly that it was his humanitarian undertaking and Hungary's condition of servitude vis-à-vis Germany that led to the request for his resignation (*Végzetes esztendők,* pp. 140 ff.).

militarily; but the handling of the Jewish question, which remained "unsolved" in Hungary, was the true barometer of the sentiments of the Hungarian government and overshadowed the "positive" factors in the relations between the two countries. If, nevertheless, a breakout was avoided, it was partly because of the continued success of German arms and partly because of the hesitations of the Kállay government. There is no doubt that Kállay preferred to solve the Jewish problem in a humane manner. It is rather more doubtful that Kállay would have liked to denounce the agreements Hungary had reached with the German leadership, even if this could have been done without risking retaliation on the part of Germany.

5. The Economic Side of German-Hungarian Relations

The memoirs of Miklós Kállay, while a valuable source for the history of Hungary in this period, are concerned, as are the memoirs of most statesmen, with the good reputation and historical image of their author; and perhaps to an equal degree they are a patriotic account presenting Hungary's role in World War II in as favorable a light as the unfortunate and undeniable facts will permit. Hence, these memoirs stress the extent of German pressure on Hungary and the extent of Hungarian resistance to it. Of the various forms this resistance took, asserts Kállay, the economic one was the most successful.[1] Hungary contributed less than half of what she might have contributed to the German armament program;[2] and the actual Hungarian contributions were only a portion of those pledged. But does the documentary evidence support these contentions?[3]

While the polemical argument that Nationalist Socialist Germany had territorial ambitions in southeast Europe, and with regard to

1. Kállay, *Hungarian Premier*, p. 283. Stephen D. Kertesz also writes that "the most important results of the Hungarian resistance were attained in economic matters" (*Diplomacy in a Whirlpool*, p. 62).

2. Kállay, *Hungarian Premier*, p. 207. Kállay's data concerning Hungarian "economic resistance" seem to be taken, in good part, from a work by Lajos Jócsik, *German Economic Influences in the Danube Valley*, which contains some inexactitudes. The latter seems to have been written with the coming Paris peace conference in mind.

3. An example of the diverging views on Hungary's economic contributions to the German cause is provided by the case of Hungarian oceangoing vessels. Both Lajos Jócsik and Kállay point out, in their respective works, that Hungary placed her merchant fleet, including oil tankers, at the disposal of the Allies (Jócsik, *German Economic Influences*, p. 30). I have found no German records regarding this claim; Hungarian shipyards seem to have contributed to the Allied navies only before September 1939. On the other hand, I found a telegram by Carl Clodius, the chief of the Economic Section of the German Foreign Office, to the effect that Hungary had six oceangoing vessels, all of which were at the disposal of Germany. Two had been chartered by the German air force, and the Germany navy needed the other four as supply vessels on the Black Sea. Hungary was prepared to loan the vessels for two months, "despite the risk involved and despite the difficulties this might cause to Hungarian economy" (telegram from Clodius to Berlin, July 12, 1941, NA Microcopy T-120, roll 2563, 312245).

Hungarian territory in particular, rests on skimpy evidence,[4] German economic imperialism in this same area is undeniable. The expansion of German trade was, of course, neither reprehensible per se nor strictly National Socialist; but it was during the National Socialist period rather than, say, the Weimar Republic, that this expansion took forms which might be characterized as imperialist. These forms are discussed in some detail and with great competence by Antonín Basch in *The Danube Basin and the German Economic Sphere.*

The Treaty of Trianon in 1920 brought about conditions which made Hungary an easy prey to German economic, hence also political, influence. The old kingdom of Hungary, which would be an anachronism in our era of nation-states, was nevertheless a geographic and economic whole. While Hungary was, and remained, a predominantly agricultural country, industrialization had set in before World War I, as it had in most parts of east Europe. The industrial plants were concentrated around the city of Budapest; many raw materials, especially minerals, came from the Carpathian Mountains. On the other hand, the inhabitants of the mountainous regions had to rely for some of their supplies on the produce of the fertile Hungarian plains. This exchange resulted in a large degree of economic autarchy. The Treaty of Trianon severed the mountains from the plains, and Hungary ceased to be autarchic. The new borders also intersected the railroad lines converging toward Budapest. While the treaty did not, of course, forbid trade between Hungary and the "successor states," it brought about political conditions which set obstacles to such trade.[5] The Allied and associated powers

4. The Volksdeutsche Mittelstelle under the Reichsführer SS worked out a plan, in 1939, for the deportation of Hungarians from Transdanubia and the settlement of the area by Volksdeutsche. There was also a plan to settle both banks of the Danube south of Mohács with Volksdeutsche. The Reichstelle für Raumordnung elaborated a plan for the extension of Germany as far as Lake Balaton and the city of Győr, Hungary to be compensated in the East. Dr. Hugo Jury, the gauleiter for the "Lower Danube," submitted several memoranda regarding the incorporation of Sopron into the Reich (Wolfdieter Bihl, "Zur nationalsozialistischen Ungarnpolitik 1940–41," pp. 21–26). Some of these projects came to the attention of the Hungarian government late in 1943, but Ribbentrop boldly denied their authenticity. See telegram from Ribbentrop to Jagow, Jan 7, 1944, NA Microcopy T-120, roll 99, 109696–97; also Franz von Papen, *Memoirs* (London: André Deutsch, 1953), pp. 508–9.

5. "The treaties of St. Germain (Art. 222) and of Trianon (Art. 205) contained provisions for preferential tariff agreements between Czechoslovakia, Austria, and Hungary, which were limited to five years after they came into force. It is clear today (1944) that these provisions should have been made compulsory, and should have extended to all succession states" (Antonín Basch, *The Danube Basin and The German Economic Sphere*, p. 32).

punished Hungary, as they did Germany and the other Central Powers, for the crime of bringing about World War I and then losing it. But Hungary was punished more severely than Germany; she was dismembered, retaining less than one-third of the territories formerly constituting the kingdom of Hungary. Hungary lost all territories not inhabited by Magyars, and in case of doubt the successor states reaped the benefit. About three million Magyars, a fourth of Hungary's population, were left outside the borders of the new rump Hungary. Although Hungary signed it, the Treaty of Trianon was not accepted by the Hungarian governments in the between-the-wars period; despite the limited franchise in Hungary, it may have been politically unwise to do so. On the other hand, it may have been politically expedient to blame all the ills of the country on the unsatisfactory settlement of Trianon. Revision of the Treaty of Trianon became a principle of Hungarian foreign policy. This revisionist policy in turn led to the formation of the Little Entente—eventually comprising Hungary's neighbors, Czechoslovakia, Romania, and Yugoslavia—the principle aim of which was protection from a Hungarian attack.[6] Given the military limitations imposed on Hungary at Trianon (armed forces not to exceed 30,000 men), the possibility of such an attack was distant indeed; it was only too late that the countries of the Little Entente awoke to a more serious danger, that of an attack from Germany. The continued political tension between the successor states and Hungary hampered economic intercourse. It may be noted, furthermore, that Trianon had deprived Hungary of her only outlet to the sea, the port of Fiume (Rijeka), the Danube River, although navigable, being blocked by Romania, for relations between Romania and Hungary were most unfriendly. Hence, if Hungary was to pay reparations and war debts, or merely survive, she had to rely on commerce with her former partner and relatively friendly neighbor, Austria,[7] and the other defeated or discontented powers, Germany and Italy. The so-called Rome Protocols, signed on March 17, 1935, by Italy,

6. Ibid., p. 152.

7. Relations between Austria and Hungary were not invariably friendly in this period, because the framers of the Treaty of Trianon threw a "bone of contention" between the two countries by awarding a strip along the western border of Hungary, the Burgenland, to Austria. Hungarian exacerbation with the "successor states" only increased when Hungary regained a part of the Burgenland as a result of a plebiscite held in that specific part. This was the only plebiscite held in former Hungarian territories, and it was often interpreted, in Hungary, as indicating that the lost populations would always have voted for Hungary, no matter what their ethnic background, if only given a chance.

Austria, and Hungary, provided for an increase in trade between these countries and the marketing of Hungarian wheat in particular. The price Italy and Austria agreed to pay for Hungarian wheat was at least double the world-market price.[8]

The German economic offensive known as the New Plan began in September of 1934; the emphasis with regard to southeast Europe was shifted from export to import. In fact, Germany took increased interest in southeast Europe, partly because the countries in that area could be reached by land in time of war and partly because being relatively unindustrialized they complemented German economy well: they could become a source of raw materials and of agricultural products, and at the same time, these countries remained a market for German machinery and finished products. In 1936 Hungary obtained 70 percent of her total machine imports from Germany while she was able to meet Germany's demand for additional supplies of meat, cattle, lard, and poultry. Between 1929 and 1937 Hungarian exports to Germany rose from 20 to 26.2 percent.[9] France, Great Britain, and the United States expressed only limited interest in trade with the countries of southeast Europe, even under the improved economic conditions of 1937.[10] While American, British, and French capital investment declined somewhat between 1937 and 1938, falling from 49 to 46 percent, German investments in Hungary increased from 10 to 17 percent within the same year.[11] By 1939, the percentages of imports from and exports to Germany both exceeded 50 percent.[12] From that time through 1943 these

8. Basch, *Danube Basin*, pp. 158–59.

9. Ibid., pp. 169, 170 ff., 179–87, 188. "When it is realized," continues Basch, "that, in 1937, 54% of Hungary's exports went to Germany, Austria and Italy, all of them paying higher prices than were available elsewhere, the enormous influence of German purchases upon the whole of Hungarian economy becomes apparent. Throughout this period the free-exchange countries took only 20–25% of Hungary's exports, the largest share, about 8%, being that of Great Britain. A shift to Germany as a source of imports was only the logical consequence of this development." The statistics cited by Basch are matched by the figures given by Iván Berend and György Ránki in the case of exports. There is a slight discrepancy in the case of imports from Germany: 25.9% as opposed to the 26.2% quoted by Basch (*Magyarország a fasiszta Németország életterében 1933–1939* [Hungary in the *Lebensraum* of Fascist Germany], p. 175). The figures cited by Jócsik are entirely different. In the year 1937 imports from Germany would have amounted to 43.9% and exports to Germany to 40.8%. Apparently Jócsik included Austria in these figures, even though the Anschluss was not to take place until the following year (*German Economic Influence*, p. 25).

10. Basch, *Danube Basin*, p. 198.

11. Jócsik, *German Economic Influence*, p. 4.

12. It was 52.2% in the case of exports, and 52.5% in the case of imports (Berend and Ránki, *Magyarország a fasiszta Németország életterében*, p. 189). The figures

figures seem to have increased but little.[13] It may be worth noting that German economic penetration of Hungary, either before or after the outbreak of the war, was not significantly greater than her penetration of the other countries of southeast Europe; hence, Hungarian trade with Germany is insufficient, by itself, to explain the pro-German orientation of Hungarian foreign policy.

In this study we are primarily interested in Hungarian contributions to the German cause, hence in exports to Germany. These exports consisted mainly of agricultural products and certain minerals. A top secret (*geheime Reichssache*) German report compiled on July 19, 1944, when the German authorities had access not only to their own but also to Hungarian statistics, however confidential, explained that in 1943 Hungarian exports constituted 4.5 percent of Germany's imports. The most important products imported from Hungary were listed: livestock (40,040 head of cattle and 44,391 pigs), about 105,000 tons of wheat and wheat flour, about 42,000 tons of corn, and a large variety of other produce in small quantities. Among raw materials imported from Hungary were about 7,300 tons of flax, 885,000 tons of bauxite, 27,000 tons of manganese ore, 300,000 tons of oil, and 25,225 tons of charcoal.[14] Other significant items were ammunition and aircraft, both of which were manufactured or built in large part by the Manfréd Weiss concern or one of its subsidiaries.[15]

---

compiled by the Kiel University "Institut für Weltwirtschaft" for the same year are 48.6% imports from Germany and 50.1% exports to Germany (NA Microcopy T-84, roll 135, 1437835, 1437885).

13. Jócsik points out that by 1943 the German share of both Romanian exports and Romanian imports amounted to 90% (*German Economic Influences*, p. 25).

14. Report prepared by Dr. Schomacker, NA Microcopy T-84, roll 136, 1438712.

15. Iván Berend and György Ránki, "Die deutsche wirtschaftliche Expansion und das ungarische Wirtschaftsleben zur Zeit des zweiten Weltkrieges," pp. 330, 334, and 336. Further details regarding aircraft manufacture can be found in Berend and Ránki, "Hadianyaggyártás Magyarországon," pp. 709 ff. Hungary shipped about 300,000 pieces of ammunition to Germany per month. I have found only vague data concerning the production of aircraft in Hungary. The farming out of German aircraft manufacture, especially the Messerschmidt 109, began in 1941. According to a report dated October 1942, Hungarian plants were producing 50 Messerschmidt 109s and 50 Messerschmidt 210s per month in addition to miscellaneous types; less than one-third of this production was retained for the Hungarian air force (NA Microcopy T-77, roll 712, 1930169). By 1944 about 550 airplane bodies and 650 engines were produced monthly in Hungarian factories (presumably only while this production was not interrupted by Allied bombing and the Red Army). According to Berend and Ránki the production of airplane bodies and engines did not exceed 893 and 679 respectively during the entire year 1944 ("Hadianyaggyártás Magyarországon," pp. 713–14). An American intelligence report, dated Sept. 29, 1943, notes that the monthly production of the

A significant commodity in the case of Germany's economic relations with many European countries, but not with Hungary, was
manpower. In the summer of 1943 there were about 6,000 Hungarian industrial workers employed in Germany. While Germany
requested 15,000 agricultural workers in 1943, Hungary had agreed
to send only 5,000, of whom 1,600 eventually reported to their place
of employment in Germany. A German agent in Hungary complained of the difficulties raised by the Hungarian authorities in the
matter of recruitment of agricultural workers.[16]

Until 1941 Hungary supplied Germany with a variety of agricultural produce, especially cereals like wheat and sweet corn. After
1941 Hungarian exports of cereals became almost insignificant, primarily because of the unusually poor harvests of 1941, 1942, and
1943. The level of Hungarian exports to Germany was maintained
only because of sizeable increases in deliveries of oil and bauxite. In
the fiscal year 1939–40 exports of wheat and flour from "Trianon"
Hungary to Germany totaled 277,300 tons. In 1940–41 these exports
amounted to 20,900 tons and in 1941–42 to nothing at all. "Only by
pressure," reported a German official to Ribbentrop in August 1942,
"did we succeed in obtaining a promise from the Hungarian
Minister-President regarding certain amounts of bread and fodder
regardless of the circumstances," presumably from the next harvest.[17]
In November 1942, the Hungarian government offered to make up
for the deficiency in cereal exports by increasing the value of fruits
and vegetables exported from 46 million to 66 million reichsmarks
and by increasing the number of cattle exported to 56,000.[18] A mem-

---

plant at Csepel was 70 to 80 Junkers, 250 to 300 Junkers at Szigetszentmiklós, and
about 20 Dornier near Debrecen, not to mention the production of lesser plants in
Hungary (OSS report no. 575533 on Hungary, NA Record Group 226).

16. Gerhard Misch to Dr. August Heinrichsbauer, June 12, 1943, NA Microcopy T-84,
roll 136, 1439518. See also report by Consul Barkóczi, June 9, 1942, which confirms these
numbers (Political Section, Ministry of Foreign Affairs, Hungarian National Archives,
K63, bundles 187–88, tétel 21). Lajos Jócsik, whose work is otherwise favorable to
Hungary and minimizes Hungarian contributions, writes that 37,990 Hungarians were
employed in Germany (without specifying the period or the religion of the workers)
(*Germany Economic Influences*, p. 31).

17. Report by Emil Wiehl to Rintelen, Berlin, Aug. 6, 1942, NA Microcopy T-120,
roll 2565, 313920–21; same report reproduced on roll 93, 105501. See also memorandum
by Hudeczek for Ribbentrop on prospects for German-Hungarian economic relations
in fiscal year 1942–43, Aug. 7, 1942, NA Microcopy T-120, roll 2564, 313066.

18. Telegram from Jagow to Berlin, Nov. 21, 1942, NA Microcopy T-120, roll 93,
105893. It should also be noted, however, that although rationing had been in effect
since September 1941 and the rations had been reduced several times, bread portions

orandum at the end of the fiscal year 1942–43 makes it clear that 31,869 of the promised 56,000 head of cattle had not been shipped, although some cattle, complained the Germans, had been shipped to Switzerland.[19]

The statistics on exportation of cereals quoted above did not take into account the territories recently regained by Hungary. When Hungary was granted the Bácska, after the joint operations against Yugoslavia in April 1941, it was in exchange for the entire excess of cereal harvest of that province. This excess was to be divided between Germany and Italy in the ratio of 60 to 40 percent. A "secret protocol" to this effect was signed in Budapest on May 21, 1941, and a German team of experts was allowed into the Bácska to make the necessary statistical estimates.[20] In the summer of 1942 Kállay agreed to allow another team of German experts to examine the results of the harvest in the Bácska.[21] In 1941–42 the excess harvest in the Bácska amounted to 340,000 tons, and 60 percent of this was shipped to Germany;[22] but here too the production declined to a point where there was nothing to spare for export. In February 1942, for instance, Jagow was instructed to try and obtain more from the Bácska; if cereals were not available, Germany would like 35,000 tons of sugar instead of the 10,000 promised: after all, argued Carl Clodius, the chief of the Trade Section of the Reich Foreign Office, the Finns were depriving themselves for the sake of the "common cause" to the point of hunger.[23]

The following table affords a rapid survey of Hungarian agricultural exports to Germany in the period 1938 through 1943.[24]

---

were increased twice during 1943 and flour portions once. István Pintér, "A Kállay kormány 'hintapolitikája' és az anti-fasiszta ellenállási mozgalom" [The "pendulum policy" of the Kállay ministry and the anti-Fascist resistance movement], p. 478.

19. NA Microcopy T-120 roll 2564, 313156–57.

20. Note by Erdmannsdorf to Reich Foreign Office, May 9, 1941, NA Microcopy T-120, roll 2563, 312179–89; also telegram from Clodius to Berlin, July 15, 1942, NA Microcopy T-120, roll 2564, 312846–47.

21. Telegram from Clodius to "Sonderzug," July 17, 1942, NA Microcopy T-120, roll 93, 105374.

22. Report by Wiehl to Rintelen, Berlin, Aug. 6, 1942, NA Microcopy T-120, roll 2565, 313920–21. The figures given by Clodius are somewhat at variance with these. He indicates that only 270,000 tons of corn were shipped to Germany and Italy, leaving a deficit in corn shipments that was never made up.

23. Clodius to Budapest, Feb. 19, 1942, NA Microcopy T-120, roll 2563, 312634–36.

24. From "Der Aussenhandel Ungarns, 1941–1943," prepared by the Statistisches Reichsamt, NA Microcopy T-84, roll 135, 1438084 ff., 1438229 ff.

	1938	*1939*	*1940*	*1941*	*1942*	*1943*
Wheat, in tons	237,349	231,281	56,544	90,614	18,743	104,680
Flour, in tons	21,425	49,058	36,121	30,729	39,450	35,691
Corn, in tons	79,171	46,225	1,403	32,731	46,629	36,425
(Head of) pigs	195,974	355,022	154,368	42,828	29,722	45,320
(Head of) cattle	43,759	35,810	50,274	30,866	40,769	—

Overall Hungarian production in this same period was steady,[25] but relatively speaking there was a steep decline; the size of Hungary almost doubled in this period, and while the newly acquired or regained territories had little agricultural significance, except for the Bácska, an additional population of about three million had to be fed. In May 1941, the total population of Hungary had risen to 14.7 million. The yield per acre of most agricultural produce declined in the early 1940s.[26]

Official economic talks between Germany and Hungary, encompassing shipments of all kinds of goods from Hungary and questions of credit, took place about once every six months during the war. The German negotiator on these occasions was usually Carl Clodius, the chief of the Trade Section of the Reich Foreign Office. Clodius was regarded by some of the Hungarian parties involved as a "gentleman," as far as National Socialist officials went; Kállay wrote, in his memoirs, that Clodius was "a very decent man, in whom I did not detect excessive enthusiasm for the cause he served." [27] Indeed, it appears from the dispatches Clodius sent to Berlin that in addition to wringing concessions from Germany's allies, which was basically his mission, he sometimes went out of his way to persuade Reich officials to meet certain requests of the allies. In a telegram dated August 2, 1942, Clodius complained that in "at least twenty or thirty instances" he had received a negative reply from the Reichswirtschaftsministerium. On the other hand, continued Clodius, "we are asking the Hungarians to make greater sacrifices." [28]

Clodius's attitude may explain his success; there can be no deny-

---

25. See NA Microcopy T-84, roll 135, 1438213 ff. An index based on harvests in the period 1929–38 gives only 83.1 for 1940, 84.1 for 1941, and 76.2 for 1942 (Berend and Ránki, "Die deutsche wirtschaftliche Expansion," p. 326).

26. NA Microcopy T-84, roll 135, 1438219 ff.

27. *Hungarian Premier*, p. 290.

28. Telegram from Clodius to Berlin, NA Microcopy T-120, roll 93, 105481. On July 28, 1942, Clodius had wired: "Ich halte es nicht für richtig ungarische Wünsche im Hinblick auf Nichtzusage vom Getreide abzulehnen, weil wir Ungarn ohnehin schon

ing that Germany's requests from Hungary were often substantially met. Perhaps a good indication of Hungarian compliance was that German exports to Hungary did not match Hungarian exports to Germany. There remained a deficit of payments which continually increased during the war. These loans—for that is what these deficits amounted to—were readily granted by the Hungarian government, often without interest. In July 1941, the government authorized a maximum deficit of 200 million reichsmarks without interest.[29] By January 1942, the Hungarian minister of finance was prepared to raise the amount of the credit from 200 to 300 million reichsmarks, requesting only that his decision not be made public, "as it might cause difficulties with the National Bank."[30] But Lipót Baranyai, the strongly anti-Nazi president of the bank, was obliged to resign in 1943. Even by June of 1942 the German deficit reached 430 millions of reichsmarks.[31] In the summer of 1942, an official of the Reich Ministry of Economy, Dr. Erik Landfried, turned to Count Weizsäcker, suggesting that the Hungarians be asked to grant credit up to 1,000 million reichsmarks. Commenting on the Hungarian proposal that in order to alleviate the deficit some German shareholders ought to surrender their shares in Hungarian industrial concerns, Dr. Landfried declared that the proposal was unworthy

nicht einmal so viel liefern wie für die notwendige Aufrechterhaltung der ungarischen Kriegswirtschaft im deutschen Interesse erforderlich ist" (NA Microcopy T-120, roll 2564, 312885).

29. Telegram from Clodius (in Rome) to Berlin, July 31, 1941, NA Microcopy T-120, roll 91, 103901–4; see also telegram from Clodius to Berlin, July 9, 1941, NA Microcopy T-120, roll 2563, 312303).

30. Telegram from Clodius to Berlin, Feb. 14, 1942, NA Microcopy T-120, roll 2563, 312611–12). About the minister of finance, Lajos Reményi-Schneller, Kállay wrote that he was strongly pro-German, "but it was not my experience that he failed to represent our case energetically and according to my instructions in those negotiations" (*Hungarian Premier*, p. 290). It appears from the interrogations conducted by Martin Himler, that Reményi-Schneller received pay for his services from National Socialist Germany (*Igy néztek ki a magyar nemzet sírásói*, p. 163). This evidence is corroborated by a German agent in Hungary who agreed that Reményi-Schneller was the only truly pro-German member of the Hungarian cabinet: "Im Verlauf des Gesprächs bezeichnete sich Remény-Schneller als das einzige Kabinettsmitglied, das stets auch dann, wenn es unpopulär sei, die deutsche Linie im Kabinett vertrete. Alle übrigen Kabinettsmitglieder wären von einem deutschen Sieg nicht überzeugt. Der grösste Gegner in der ungarischen Staatsführung sei jedoch zweifellos der jetzige Nationalbank-Präsident" (memorandum by Helmut Triska to Martin Luther, Sept. 30, 1942, on a conversation with Reményi-Schneller, NA Microcopy T-120, roll 2565, 313835).

31. Memorandum by Schnurre, June 2, 1942, NA Microcopy T-120, roll 93, 105636.

of an ally.[32] Hence, although only a few shares were returned to the Hungarians, the Hungarian leaders once again granted Germany a substantial increase in credit. By the end of 1943 the German debt to Hungary exceeded 1,035 million reichsmarks.[33] It appears probable (we cannot know, for accurate accounts were not kept in 1944) that the "voluntary" Hungarian contributions in 1944 would have more than doubled that sum. All these debts were tabled by the National Socialist officials of the German Ministry of Finance as a Hungarian "contribution" to the common cause. Their settlement was a matter that should be discussed "only after the victorious war." [34]

While the amount of the German debt tends to indicate that the Hungarian government was accommodating, to say the least, it may also be an indication of German pressure. Kállay, in his anxiety to be fair, points out that the German government and the Reich Foreign Office in particular never intervened in the economic negotiations.[35] The statement is patently erroneous, for the German negotiators did not represent private interests but were officials of the German government, the Foreign Office in particular; but the implication of the statement, that no political pressure was applied on Hungary during these negotiations, is also mistaken. In a dispatch on July 20, 1941, Clodius reported that he had made a small concession to the Hungarians which "had to be done if only for psychological reasons, in order not to give the Hungarians the undesirable impression that they had to bow completely to the German demands. As for the rest, all the major German requests have been put through." [36] A few days later, in summarizing the achievements during the negotiations in Hungary, Clodius described these negotiations as a "significant step in the assimilation of Hungary into the German plans for the economic reconstruction of Europe under German leadership." [37] Some phases of the negotiations were diffi-

32. Dr. Landfried to Weizsäcker, July 30, 1942, NA Microcopy T-120, roll 2564, 312908–9; there is also a paraphrase of this letter, by Wiehl to Clodius, dated July 31, 1942, and reproduced on 312913–14 of the same roll.

33. Berend and Ránki, "Die deutsche wirtschaftliche Expansion," p. 352. According to a German report on Hungarian economy, dated July 19, 1944, the German debt to Hungary had reached 1,100 million reichsmarks by the end of 1943 (NA Microcopy T-84, roll 136, 143713).

34. Quoted by Berend and Ránki, "Die deutsche wirtschaftliche Expansion," p. 351.

35. Kállay, *Hungarian Premier*, p. 285.

36. Telegram from Clodius to Berlin, July 20, 1941, NA Microcopy T-120, roll 2563, 312268.

37. Telegram from Clodius (in Rome) to Berlin, July 31, 1941, NA Microcopy T-120, roll 2563, 312304; also reproduced on roll 91, 103901–4.

cult, wrote Clodius, precisely because the influential Hungarian personalities became aware of the German plans for economic assimilation. Occasionally, Germany was not reluctant to use outright political pressure to attain economic ends: evidence of this is the memorandum on German-Hungarian economic relations prepared for Ribbentrop, in which reference is made to the use of outspoken political pressure (*entsprechenden politischen Druck*). The memorandum does not explain, however, just what this pressure consisted of and admits that it was to little avail.[38] A year later Clodius told Kállay: "Take care, Mr. Premier! The conviction is beginning to gain ground in Berlin that it is not good policy for us to tolerate Hungary's independence; for we are getting incomparably much more from the occupied countries, especially Czechoslovakia [*sic*], and also from Rumania which grows and works for us as we want." [39] Clearly, Clodius was threatening Kállay with a German occupation of Hungary. It was perhaps on this same occasion that Clodius reported to Berlin that he had found the Hungarian government more recalcitrant than usual.[40] At the end of this chapter I shall have occasion to quote a German document concerning "ruthless" exploitation of the Hungarian economy. It appears, then, that the German negotiators were not loath to apply political pressure; they refrained from doing so when the desired ends could be attained without its application.

It would appear, if one is to judge by the complaints of certain National Socialist officials, that the Hungarian government or at least certain elements in Hungary did practice a form of economic sabotage.[41] Perhaps the most convincing witness, in this instance, is the Fascist Italian minister to Budapest, Filippo Anfuso; he records

38. Memorandum prepared by Hudeczek, Aug. 7, 1942, NA Microcopy T-120, roll 2564, 313066.

39. Kállay, *Hungarian Premier*, p. 285.

40. Telegram from Clodius to Berlin, Dec. 7, 1943, NA Microcopy T-120, roll 2564, 313176.

41. I have no room, in this study, to discuss industrial sabotage. I am aware of two such attempts before the German occupation in March of 1944, both unsuccessful. An attempt by alleged Hungarian agents of the British Secret Service to blow up an ammunition factory in Györ was the most nearly successful; the agents were caught and sentenced to death before their plans could be carried out. See Jenő Lévai, *A Margitkörúti vészbírák* [The bloodthirsty judges on the Margit boulevard], pp. 40–49; see also Abwehr Report, July 1, 1942, NA Microcopy T-120, roll 691, 311933–34. Dezső Sulyok relates that the workman commissioned to place the explosives, being a good party man, checked with Károly Peyer, the leader of the Social Democrats, who denounced the project (*A magyar tragédia*, p. 403).

in his memoirs that Bárdossy gave the Germans only a fraction of what they asked for but that Kállay refused even that fraction, "while confusing them by promising them everything."[42] But the prime minister and the government officials were probably not the only elements in Hungary bent on limiting contributions of goods to Germany. While undoubtedly there had been a series of poor harvests, one may wonder about the cause of these. The poor harvests may have been the result of a deficient collection of the produce as well as the lower yield of the soil. Is it possible that the Hungarian peasant was consciously perpetrating sabotage of the German war effort? Was the Hungarian peasant actively anti-Nazi? The Reich officials who complained about the relatively bad harvests in Hungary were more inclined to blame the Jews: "Even though the harvests more than suffice for the country's own needs, still one has to blame the poor organization, and lastly, but not least, the Jewish panic-propaganda, which have permitted a situation to develop that can hardly be controlled any longer by ordinary means."[43] This analysis was provided by the German minister in Budapest in December 1941, when the Bárdossy cabinet was still in power and there was little official encouragement given to even a passive form of resistance. In 1943, Dr. Gerhard Misch, one of the numerous German "economic observers" stationed in Hungary, complained that it was very difficult to estimate the results of the coming harvest because the Hungarian authorities were concealing the concrete data.[44]

Although it is absurd to blame the poor harvests on the influence of the Jews, especially after 1942, when the few Jewish landholdings had been confiscated,[45] a sociological analysis of the problem may be possible. One could argue, for instance, that the system of landholdings between-the-wars provided little incentive for the individual peasant, who in most cases could not work his own land. In fact, 54.6 percent of the agricultural area in Hungary belonged to the wealthy landowning class constituting 1.7 percent of the landown-

42. *Du Palais de Venise,* pp. 221, 226.

43. Letter from Jagow to Berlin, Dec. 4, 1941, NA Microcopy T-120, roll 2563, 312551–52.

44. Confidential report by Gerhard Misch to Heinrichsbauer, June 11, 1943, NA Microcopy T-84, roll 136, 1439525. Misch adds that the capacity for export of crops depends not so much on production as on the collection of the produce.

45. Altogether 820,000 *holds* (1 *hold* is equal to 1,405 acres) of land owned by Jews were expropriated in consequence of the laws of 1939–IV and 1942–XVI (*Tanulmányok a Horthy-korszak,* p. 156).

ers.[46] It is partly the inequality of landholdings in Hungary which led many western as well as Marxist observers to refer to the country in that period as a feudal of semifeudal regime.[47] The wealthy landowners were mostly aristocrats whose interests were represented in the upper house of the Parliament. The role of the upper house in this period makes it clear that the Hungarian aristocracy was, in general, pro-British and anti-Nazi.[48] It is not impossible then that— besides the Hungarian peasant's lack of incentive for production— the powerful landowning class made its political sympathies felt through its controlling influence over the country's agricultural production.[49]

The "Jewish influence" argument can be upheld with some justifi-

46. These and other interesting data regarding land distribution in Hungary are given by John Kosa, "Hungarian Society in the Time of the Regency (1920– 1944)", pp. 253–65. Kosa also notes that the social system prevailing in Hungary until 1944 is often called semifeudal (p. 253). A Hungarian legal publication defines the Hungarian state in the Horthy era as monarchical and Fascist (*Tanulmányok a Horthy-korszak*, p. 22). With regard to land distribution, see pp. 134 ff. of this work.

47. Horthy himself told his interrogators, in broken English, on Oct. 15, 1945, exactly a year after he relinquished power: ". . . the whole world spoke of Hungary as a novelty, as a 'feudal Hungary'. I don't know why they say 'feudal Hungary', because we were absolutely a democratic state and until the last moment we had our parliament, the only state in Europe. Had it until the last moment with absolute democratic representation for parliament, and in that atmosphere a corrupt man couldn't live" (interrogations, NA Record Group 238, World War II Crimes Records).

48. Regarding the upper house, Kállay wrote: "In the Upper House I could be much franker about my policy and my intentions. I could be absolutely sure of secrecy. It was certain that in this company there was no informer carrying tales to the Germans. The entire membership of the Committee [on foreign affairs?] was anti-German or, as they called it at the time, Anglo-Saxon in its sympathies. The committee was sharply opposed to any trespassing into politics by the army, and its members showed no trace of anti-Semitism. It is a curious phenomenon that this body, composed partly of indirectly elected and partly of nominated members, should have been more representative of the country's mentality and incomparably more aware of its true interests than the deputies in parliament elected by ballot on the basis of a wide suffrage" (*Hungarian Premier*, p. 186).

49. The economist Iván Kádár writes that the curtailment in the production of war materials was not due to the attitude of the ruling classes but resulted from the lack of raw materials and the increasing resistance of the workers ("A munkásosztály helyzete a Horthy-rendszer idején" [The conditions of the working class during the Horthy regime], p. 258). It is clear, however, that the author was referring to industrial workers. The same author also states on p. 214 ff. that while real wages declined the "intensity" of work increased. This statement seems to contradict his thesis that the resistance put up by the workers must account for the decline in production. A Swiss writer who visited Hungary in the winter of 1942–43 claims that economic, social, and labor conditions were improving in Hungary (Pierre Thomas, "Coup d'oeil sur la Hongrie en guerre," pp. 52–61).

cation when it comes to Hungarian industry. A German "Survey of the Government and Economy of Hungary," compiled in April 1940, pointed out that five families of Jewish extraction exercised a controlling influence over Hungarian industry: the Manfréd Weiss, Fülöp Weiss, Jenö Vida, Pál Biró, and Ferenc Chorin families.[50] In another report on Hungary compiled in October 1941, the Association of Hungarian Manufacturers was described as an uncontrolled para-government exercising its influence over the Hungarian economy and politics by invisible means. While the present leaders of the association were all Aryans, the author conceded, the former leaders (and here he mentioned my father, "still visible in the background") continued to exercise a nefarious influence.[51] What the German agents in Hungary failed to note, and perhaps to notice, was that all these "Jewish" industrialists and bankers made no effort to hamper the German war effort or the Hungarian contributions to it. On the contrary: the German orders for goods were conscientiously filled. The captains of Hungarian industry hoped to avert the military occupation of Hungary by full-fledged economic collaboration.[52]

Paradoxically enough, although Hungary was primarily an agricultural land, her economic significance to Germany during the war did not reside in her agricultural resources. We have seen that Germany obtained only a limited amount of produce from Hungary after 1941. Furthermore, Germany could turn elsewhere for produce: to France, Poland, the Ukraine, and so on. The alternatives were far fewer when it came to certain mineral resources, especially oil and bauxite.

In 1937 Hungary produced 13.3 percent of the world's bauxite production.[53] In 1942 the exports of bauxite to Germany amounted to 865,000 tons or more, whereas the total production was just under one million tons.[54] In the beginning of 1942 Hungary had agreed to ship one million tons of bauxite to Germany each year for the

50. NA Microcopy T-84, roll 135, 1437953. It should be noted, perhaps, that most members of these families were Christians and that three of the persons named were titled members of the Hungarian aristocracy. Pál Biró was no longer in Hungary.

51. Report by Dr. Janovsky, NA Microcopy T-84, roll 136, 1439137–38.

52. Miksa Fenyö to author. Before 1938 Miksa Fenyö was executive director of the Association of Hungarian Manufacturers.

53. Basch, *Danube Basin,* p. 228.

54. Berend and Ránki, "Die deutsche wirtschaftliche Expansion," p. 327. The German statistics shown in the table below indicate that 926,123 tons were exported to Germany that year.

coming twenty-five years.[55] But the production in 1943, as in 1942, fell short of the one-million mark, and consequently so did the exports to Germany. The table below provides a quick survey of the variations of Hungarian bauxite exports to Germany, in tons.[56]

1938	1939	1940	1941	1942	1943
358,290	568,644	641,782	714,697	926,123	870,931

Only a portion of the 1.3 million tons Hungary promised to ship to Germany to make up for the deficiency in 1942 and 1943—the promise was made during the Vienna negotiations a day or two before the German occupation of Hungary[57]—could be delivered during 1944. The same applied to the 180,000 tons of manganese ore promised to Germany early in 1944.[58] Whereas Germany needed about 500,000 tons of manganese a year, the Hungarian production, most of which was shipped to Germany, amounted to little over 100,000 tons in 1943.[59]

For Germany the most important Hungarian export item was oil. It appears that neither the Allied nor even most Hungarian economists suspected the full significance Hungarian oil production assumed in the minds of Hermann Göring, Albert Speer, and Ribbentrop. It was an American oil company, Standard Oil of New Jersey, which initiated the exploratory borings in Hungary and which hoped to exploit the promising deposits just as the war broke out. Before 1938 Hungary produced no oil whatever; and in the first couple of years of the war, while Standard Oil was in charge, the production fell far short of meeting domestic Hungarian needs. But production increased rapidly, although Hungarian oil production never attained a level comparable to the Romanian. In 1942 Ro-

55. Note by Nickl to Clodius, Apr. 23, 1942, NA Microcopy T-120, roll 93, 105156–67; see also the memorandum prepared by Hudeczek for Ribbentrop, Aug. 7, 1942, NA Microcopy T-120, roll 2564, 3131066–67.

56. "Der Aussenhandel Ungarns, 1941–1943," Statistisches Reichsamt, Nov. 1944, NA Microcopy T-84, roll 35, 1438084. The statistics for Hungarian production of aluminum (one suspects, however, that these figures include production of untreated bauxite ore) are as follows: *1939*, 400,200; *1940*, 561,700; *1941*, 823,400; *1942*, 988,500. The 1942 level of production was almost maintained in 1943 and 1944 (NA Microcopy T-84, roll 135, 1438130–32).

57. Telegram from Clodius to Berlin, Mar. 20, 1944, NA Microcopy T-120, roll 2564, 313250, 313310 ff.

58. Note from Clodius to Ribbentrop, Feb. 23, 1944, NA Microcopy T-120, roll 2564, 313236.

59. Berend and Ránki, "Die deutsche wirtschaftliche Expansion," p. 329.

mania shipped about 2,500,000 tons of oil to Germany,[60] Hungary
about one-twentieth that amount. Nevertheless the Hungarian oil
wells soon became the second most important source of oil within
the German sphere of influence. The significance of this source of
oil is attested to by the amount of German paperwork I have found
on the subject among the records of the German Foreign Office,
the Wehrmacht, and other organs of the Reich government; perhaps
every second German document on the Hungarian economy pertains
to the exploitation of Hungarian oil resources.

Statistics vary on the production of oil in Hungary. The table below, however, is presumably accurate, because it was compiled by
German authorities in 1944, when most of the Hungarian records
and data were in their possession. Although these numbers pertain
only to oil produced by wells owned by MAORT (the former
Hungarian-American Oil Corporation), the production of all other
Hungarian wells was negligible.

MAORT Oil Production in Thousands of Tons

1937	*1938*	*1939*	*1940*	*1941*	*1942*	*1943* [61]
1,366	37,254	141,848	249,590	421,600	665,201	837,711

These numbers indicate that until 1941 Hungarian oil production
was meaningless to Germany, being insufficient to meet Hungary's
domestic needs. In March 1941 an official of the Standard Oil Company informed the first secretary of the American legation that the
Hungarian government refused to furnish Germany 60,000 tons of
crude oil from the year's output. The Hungarian requirements, according to this official, were 394,000 tons a year which could be curtailed, under the rationing system then in effect, to 330,000 tons.
While the Hungarian production promised to be sufficient in 1941
to fulfill the country's requirements in gasoline, it was not sufficient
to provide Hungary with the necessary additional supplies of kero-
sene, diesel oil, and lubricants.[62] Hungary's yearly requirement was
estimated at 400,000 tons by Hungarian sources in 1942 (for instance by Gen. Jenő de Bor of the Ministry of Defense), which is

60. See NA Microcopy T-120, roll 59, 47696.

61. NA Microcopy T-84, roll 135, 1437969. Total Hungarian production was estimated in thousand tons as follows: *1938*, 42.8; *1939*, 143.8; *1940*, 253.5; *1941*, 422.4;
1942, 668.4; *1943*, 840.8 (Na Microcopy T-84, roll 135, 1438130–32).

62. Dispatch from Travers to Department of State, Mar. 29, 1941, NA Record Group
59, General Records of Department of State, 864.00 P.R./203.

credible if one considers that, unlike in March of 1941, Hungary was at war in 1942.[63] According to German computations, Hungary's requirements in time of peace (1937) had been about 285,000 tons, of which 280,000 had to be imported. Neubacher, the German minister in Belgrade, estimated Hungarian requirements in 1942 at only 240,000; [64] another German source, Cap. Anton Krautzdorfer, who was the "Officer of Military Economy" stationed in Budapest, estimated these requirements at about 330 to 350,000 tons.[65] In either case the discrepancy between Hungarian and German estimates is sizeable. This discrepancy may account for the fact that Reich officials often suspected the Hungarian authorities of concealing oil resources or of withholding oil that was not really needed. In a conversation with German Foreign Office officials on November 26, 1941, Professor Bentz of the Reichstelle für Bodenforschung maintained that he was confidentially informed Hungary could produce 550,000 tons in 1942 but the government forbade it and would not allow a production in excess of 480,000 tons. In fact, the German estimates of Hungarian production tended to be somewhat above the actual figures until the pertinent records were seized in 1944. German estimates of Hungarian needs, on the other hand, were probably underestimates.[66]

Beginning in 1942 Hungarian exports of oil to Germany became significant. The following table shows the amounts, in tons, of oil exported to Germany.

1938	*1939*	*1940*	*1941*	*1942*	*1943* [67]
2	0	643	51,381	125,418	203,629

Total Hungarian exports, including those to certain neutral countries, exceeded the exports to Germany by about one-third.

63. NA Microcopy T-84, roll 135, 1437963–64. General de Bor indicated to Reich officials that Hungary was prepared to ship to Germany all production in excess of 400,000 tons.

64. See telegrams from Clodius and Neubacher to Berlin, Sept. 10 and 11, 1942, NA Microcopy T-120, roll 93, 105703–4.

65. Ibid. The detailed war diaries and situation records from 1941–44 of the "Wehrwirtschaftsoffizier" stationed in Budapest are reproduced on three rolls of microfilm: NA Microcopy T-77, rolls 711, 712, 713.

66. Statistics on Hungarian oil production, 1942 and 1943, NA Microcopy T-84, roll 135, 1437963.

67. "Der Aussenhandel Ungarns, 1941–1943," Statistisches Reichsamt, Nov. 1944, NA Microcopy T-84, roll 135, 1438122. The pertinent statistics in Komlós, *Az elárult ország*, pp. 55–56, do not always appear reliable. The same can be said about some of the

The table above also shows that the official of Standard Oil who stated in 1941 that Hungary would refuse to ship oil to Germany in 1941 was misled, or rather made a mistaken prediction. In July of 1941 Clodius was sent to Budapest for trade negotiations. On July 14 he telegraphed to Berlin that the Hungarian government had an almost pathological fear of the alienation of the corporation which owned Hungary's only oil supply. "I would like to bring up the request for the takeover of the property by Germany . . . only if I am authorized to support our request with political pressure without regard to the expected consequences inside the country." [68] Ribbentrop's top-secret instructions were that Clodius should refrain from applying political pressure without regard to the consequences but rather should do his best to attain the desired end.[69] It was Göring who insisted; oil supplies for the German air force had to be assured. Extensive correspondence between Clodius and the Reich Foreign Office on the subject of these negotiations, between July 24 and 31, shows that Bárdossy at first categorically refused to grant the Germans even a minority share of the holdings of the Hungarian-American Oil Corporation. But Ribbentrop's estimate of the situation proved correct; Bárdossy eventually changed his mind, and a solution satisfactory to the Reich was reached.[70] Hungary agreed to a takeover of a certain portion of the shares by a German consortium, *en attendant* "a later definitive settlement of the question of ownership between Germany and Hungary." [71] The debate was summarized in a memorandum prepared by Clodius on August 16, 1941:

> . . . the German request that Hungary should agree to the purchase of the shares now in American possession of the only large Hungarian oil company, MAORT, by a German group at first encountered considerable resistance. The significance of MAORT, which provides all of Hungary with oil, is for

statistics quoted by Berend and Ránki in "Die deutsche wirtschaftliche Expansion," p. 328. The above sources sometimes overestimate Hungarian shipments to Germany; Kállay, on the other hand, claims that Hungary had the largest number of private cars and trucks on the road of any country in Europe: "That was done on purpose to leave as little gasoline as possible to Germany" (*Hungarian Premier*, p. 303). I have not been able to find reliable statistics on the number of private vehicles.

68. NA Microcopy T-120, roll 1168, 469000o.

69. Telegram from Wiehl to Budapest, July 18, 1941, NA Microcopy T-120, roll 1168, 469002.

70. See NA Microcopy T-120, roll 1168, 469003 ff., and roll 91, 103885–940.

71. Telegram from Clodius to Berlin, July 31, 1941, NA Microcopy T-120, roll 91, 103901.

Hungary about the same as that of the Ruhr coal mining for Germany. The Hungarian government argued that the American participation represented purely a capital interest, whereas Germany as owner of the majority would certainly intervene very actively at once. . . . Inasmuch as the Hungarian oil deposits are the largest in Europe after those in Rumania and Russia compliance with the German request was of great importance for Germany's oil supply. The Reichsmarschall therefore repeatedly and urgently asked that this request be put through with the Hungarian government.[72]

In another message to Ribbentrop, Clodius mentioned the conversations he had had with the German economic experts Keppler and Neumann: "Both gentlemen declared that we must insist on compliance with our demand, if necessary, by supplying the strong political pressure required . . ." and, furthermore, "for business reasons, no German company could be expected to take over an enterprise during the war, and afterwards to cede the majority of the shares." [73]

The main theme of Bárdossy's conversations with Ribbentrop in November 1941 was increased shipments of Hungarian goods, especially oil.[74] These German requests were repeated during Ribbentrop's visit to Hungary in January of 1942.[75] Subsequent negotiations indicate, however, that while Germany was able to obtain most of the oil supplies requested, she did not have a controlling influence in the management of the MAORT company or in the production of Hungarian oil. Each time German and Hungarian economic experts met, that is biannually and sometimes quarterly, the quantities of oil and by-products to be shipped to Germany had to be agreed upon anew.

Economic relations between Germany and Hungary seem to have remained fairly steady throughout most of the war. At times Hungarian officials cooperated only grudgingly. For instance, Reich officials did not object to a Belgian-Hungarian trade agreement in June of 1943, for it was hoped this way "goods will come out of Hungary

72. *DGFP*, series D, 13 : 320–21.

73. Ibid.

74. Memorandum prepared by Clodius for Ribbentrop, Jan. 4, 1942, NA Microcopy T-120, roll 92, 104479. See also minutes of meeting (by Rintelen) between Ribbentrop and Bárdossy in Berlin on Nov. 26, 1941, NA Microcopy T-120, roll 614 (Loesch Collection), F90146–59. The Hungarian minutes are partly quoted in Karsai, *A budai vártól*, p. 61.

75. NA Microcopy T-120, roll 92, 104479.

which otherwise would never be brought out"; furthermore, "Germany had to supply Belgium anyway." [76] During the economic negotiations in December of 1943, even the conciliating Clodius reported that he had found the Hungarian government more difficult to handle than before.[77] On the other hand, the negotiations conducted between German and Hungarian economic experts in Vienna, March 16–19, 1944, were entirely successful from a German point of view; [78] yet this Hungarian compliance with German requests could not stall the imminent German occupation of Hungary.

The German occupation of Hungary signified, as could be expected, the total exploitation of Hungary's economic resources. We shall have occasion to make incidental references to certain business transactions after March 1944 in the last chapters of this study. A general and adequate characterization of economic relations in the last year of the war is provided by the minutes of an interoffice conference on April 19, exactly a month after the German troops had marched into Hungary. This conference took place in the office of Clodius on the Wilhelmstrasse:

> Following the special instructions of the Minister of Foreign Affairs Clodius pointed out that it was a question of a quick and relentless exploitation of the economic resources of the country. . . . We agree on the fact that no Hungarian contribution of any significance must be neglected simply because of a lack of means of payment. . . . The Hungarian agriculture must be set to work to supply German requirements to the utmost. . . . The representative of the Ministry of Supplies will examine in what areas the shipments of Hungarian raw materials can be increased even further. Here too the objective is to extract everything possible for the German war economy.
>
> The needs of the army of occupation will be provided, according to the agreement still in effect, both in money and in kind, by Hungary. Furthermore, the Hungarian government will provide 100 to 200 million pengö for the construction of airfields. . . . We will also do our best to comb through Hungary ruthlessly for any available labor force and make it work

76. Memorandum by Clodius, June 21, 1943, NA Microcopy T-120, roll 2564, 313284.
77. Telegram from Clodius to Berlin, Dec. 7, 1943, NA Microcopy T-120, roll 2564, 313176.
78. Telegram from Clodius (in Vienna) to Berlin, Mar. 20, 1944, NA Microcopy, T-120, roll 2564, 313250.

for the German war economy. We will start with the deportation of Jewish workers.[79]

I think it is hardly necessary to elaborate except, perhaps, to observe that apparently some officials of the German Foreign Office still had no clear understanding of the basic purpose of the deportations.

During the last year of the war and the German occupation of Hungary from March 1944 to about December 1944, the Hungarian economy assumed paramount importance for Germany. The German sphere of influence had shrunk to a point where Hungary, or parts of that country, was almost the only foreign territory of significance under German control. And observers have noted that Hitler seemed more anxious to hold out in western Hungary than anywhere else, perhaps in order to retain his last source of oil.[80]

79. Memorandum by Clodius, Apr. 15, 1944, NA Microcopy T-120, roll 2564, 313463–65. In 1938 a pengö was worth $0.19 or $0.294 at the official rate of exchange (L. D. Schweng, *Economic Planning in Hungary Since 1938*, p. 21). 100 pengö was the equivalent of 60.90 reichsmarks early in 1944 (NA Microcopy T-84, roll 136, 1438704).

80. For instance, Warlimont, *Inside Hitler's Headquarters*, p. 499.

6. The Defeat of the Hungarian Forces on the Don River

The German offensive in the summer of 1942 almost became the triumphal march Hitler had hoped for in 1941. Territories already once conquered were reconquered. The whole of the Ukraine, including the Donets basin, became occupied territory. Army Group A crossed the Kerch peninsula and reached the Caucasus. The German Sixth Army of Army Group B crossed the Don River and, in September, reached the Volga River near the outskirts of Stalingrad (Volgograd).

For the next four months the war, the eastern campaign at least, was waged around Stalingrad.[1] German and Soviet reinforcements were poured in and consumed at Stalingrad. German heavy artillery was removed from other sectors of the front and brought to bear on Stalingrad; the city, suffering the fate the German High Command had envisaged for Moscow and Leningrad, was reduced to rubble.

Stalingrad was strategically important. Its capture would have achieved the isolation of the Soviet armies in the Caucasus. By the same token, its capture would have meant the virtual encirclement of the Soviet armies in Russia proper; Allied help by way of Murmansk or Archangelsk could scarcely have compensated for the loss of access to oil reserves in the Caucasus and in the Caspian basin. More importantly, the capture of Stalingrad—the city bearing the name of the Soviet leader—may well have broken Soviet morale; and the longer the siege lasted, the greater the implications of a victory and the more urgent its capture to Hitler and the German General Staff.

There were commanders, in the German military hierarchy, who soon realized that a prolonged siege of Stalingrad would be a tactical error. The Germans were setting a trap for themselves. The siege was a departure from the mobile warfare at which the Germans excelled. The siege presented Marshal Chuikov with the opportunity to threaten the encirclement of the German forces, for the Soviet military leaders could not have counted on the Germans allowing them-

I wish to thank Dr. Jaroslaw Pelenski for his many helpful suggestions regarding this chapter. Most of this chapter is derived from my article "The Allied Axis Armies at Stalingrad," *Military Affairs* 29 (Summer 1965): 57–72.

1. The Soviet offensive at Stalingrad, the battle of El Alamein, and the Anglo-American landings in North Africa occurred almost simultaneously. Militarily, however, the battle of Stalingrad was the most significant.

selves to be encircled.[2] The Soviet Union was given time to mount carefully the counteroffensive.

An even greater mistake, on the part of the Germans, was their failure to assure the flanks of the Sixth Army. Between units of the Sixth Army south of Stalingrad and units of Army Group A at Mozdok, several hundred miles farther south, there was one German division and the Fourth Armored Army consisting, for the most part, of the Fourth Romanian Army (plus some German armored units). The northern flank of the Sixth Army was held by the Romanian Third Army. To the northwest along the Don River line was held by the Italian Eighth Army. Farther along the Don, to the northwest of the Italian army, was the Hungarian Second Army. It was common knowledge that these allied armies had only inferior gear. Germany was unable to supply the allies with the weapons and equipment they lacked, in particular with antitank weapons which could cope with the Soviet tanks.[3] After the Soviet attacks in November and December 1942, Hitler reproached the army leaders for not having supplied the Italians and Romanians with antitank weapons,[4] but his reproaches did not solve the problem for the Hungarians who were to feel the next blow of the Red Army. Nor could the Germans, having extended the front several thousand miles, afford to place significant reserves behind the allied armies: three or four German divisions were incorporated into the allied armies, and two or three more (including the Forty-eighth Armored Corps) were held in reserve.

The Soviet counteroffensive was an evident move against the two Romanian armies on the flanks of the Sixth Army.[5] The two-pronged attack began on November 19. On the twenty-first, both Romanian

2. The British military observer, J. F. C. Fuller, explains: "The distribution of the German forces automatically shaped the Russian plan of campaign. . . . Once the flanks of the salient were pierced, the objectives were to be the Stalingrad-Stalino and Stalingrad-Novorossisk railways—Paulus' lines of supply. . . . The idea that, in the face of these attacks . . . on his communications, Paulus would continue the siege of Stalingrad very naturally never entered Marshal Zhukov's head, who, with General Vassilevsky as his Chief of Staff, organized these vast operations" (*The Second World War, 1939–1945*, pp. 253–54).

3. Joachim Schwatlo Gesterding, "Probleme der Naht," p. 49.

4. *KTB, OKW*, 2 : 1954.

5. The Soviet military historian B. S. Telpuchowski does not conceal the fact that the Russian attacks at points held by the four allied armies, although dictated by circumstances, did not neglect the consideration that these were inferior forces backed by inadequate German reserves (*Die Sowjetische Geschichte des grossen Vaterländischen Krieges*, pp. 174–75).

armies having been overrun, the Soviet units met at Kalatsch on the Don, closing the ring around the Sixth Army. Early in December the German High Command created Army Group Don, under the command of Field Marshal Fritz Erich von Manstein, the task of which was to regain control over the territories held prior to the Soviet counteroffensive and to reestablish contact with the German army at Stalingrad. Manstein realized the former task was next to impossible but almost achieved the latter. On December 21 the Fourth Armored Army of this Army Group Don reached to within seventeen miles of the Sixth Army. By then, however, the Soviet attack which had overrun the Italian Eighth Army after December 16 had penetrated so deeply into German occupied territory as to threaten not only the lines of communication of Army Group Don but also the capture of Rostov and thereby the lines of communication of Army Group A, still clinging to the Caucasus. Hence the effort to relieve the Sixth Army besieged at Stalingrad had to be shelved, and the German forces had to evacuate the Caucasus and the sub-Caucasian steppes. About a month later, in January 1943, a Soviet offensive overran the Hungarian Second Army and the remainder of the Italians, advancing toward Kharkov.

The Hungarian military authorities, and the German ones even more so, should have been alerted by the events of the past two months and the very similar tactics used by the Red Army vis-à-vis Romanians and Italians; how could the Red Army have hoped to achieve surprise? [6] It is true that in an official report on the Soviet Union in the period from May to December 1942 the chief of the Hungarian military intelligence still concluded that in its "present situation" the Red Army was unable to deliver an attack which might influence the outcome of the war! [7] Nevertheless, Soviet attacks directed against the sectors held by the Italians and the Hungarians had been predicted since November 30.[8] Around the middle of December, Ribbentrop told Sztójay that there seemed to be a regret-

6. According to a Hungarian military historian, the Soviets nevertheless did achieve surprise: "The German as well as the Hungarian leadership was surprised by the great Russian offensive of January 12, 1943—which had never been the case on the eastern front in World War I. The Russian camouflage must have been first-rate. The highest German command informed General Jány that only his southern flank would be affected by an eventual attack" (D. A. von Balvanyi, "Der Untergang der 2. ungarischen Armee am Don, 1943," p. 1057).

7. Political Section, Ministry of Foreign Affairs, Hungarian National Archives, K 64, bundle 86.

8. *KTB, OKW,* 2 : 1954.

table defeatist attitude in Hungary, unwarranted by the situation, which the Germans had well in hand. Kállay replied to Sztójay's telegraphic report that a certain feeling of defeatism was understandable but that it was not serious: proof of this was the fact that there had been less attempts at sabotage in Hungary than in any other European country.[9] Hitler sent the regent a telegram shortly before Christmas requesting him to instruct the Hungarian troops on the Don to put up a rigid defense if attacked.[10] On Christmas Eve Horthy replied that he would order tough resistance but complained that according to the report of the Second Army the Hungarian troops were not adequately equipped, thus lacking the means for prolonged resistance: "please let us have some assistance in this regard." [11] Horthy also remarked that the Hungarians had been assigned too long a sector of the front and were backed up by too few reserves. These deficiencies were insistently noted by several Hungarian commanders, both before and after the Soviet attack. On December 27 General Szombathelyi, chief of the General Staff, issued an order implementing Hitler's request. Our positions, read the order, must be held at any cost: "No one may retreat; there is no backward, only forward." [12] On that same day Hitler himself ordered "all possible measures" to support the Hungarian army in order to prevent the Red Army from "extending its penetration toward the north . . ." [13] But the German military authorities were slow in carrying out Hitler's order. While some antitank cannons had been transferred from the Second German Army to the Italian Eighth and Hungarian Second armies since December 4,[14] in January 1943 the Hungarians were still short of large caliber antitank weapons able to cope with the heavily armored Soviet tanks.

The Hungarian troops were spread on a thin line along the Don, in the winter, when the thickly frozen river constituted no obstacle whatever; the soldiers were short of weapons and equipment, includ-

9. Report by Ghyczy read at the cabinet meeting of Dec. 22, 1942, Political Section, Ministry of Foreign Affairs, Hungarian National Archives, K 63, bundles 187–88, tetel 21.

10. Ránki, *Emlékiratok és valóság*, p. 225.

11. Copy of Horthy's letter to Hitler, received by the OKW, NA Microcopy T-77, roll 778, 5504023–24. This is one of the Horthy letters not printed in the *Confidential Papers of Nicholas Horthy.*

12. Ránki, *Emlékiratok és valóság*, p. 225.

13. *KTB, OKW*, 2 : 13171. In May 1942 Hitler had already ordered that the Hungarians be supplied with antitank artillery (Halder, *KTB*, 2 : 437).

14. *KTB, OKW*, 2 : 1067.

ing clothing items such as clean uniforms, underwear, and boots.[15] It is true that the Hungarian lines were no thinner than the Romanian or Italian lines had been,[16] but the almost total lack of mobility made it extremely difficult for the Hungarians to send rapid reinforcements to the trouble spots. In any case, there were few reserves. The Russians were numerically superior, not to mention their manifold superiority in tanks and artillery. German intelligence reported that the Soviet units began their attack on January 12 with six heavy divisions, three infantry brigades, and three tank brigades in reserve; this may well have been an underestimate, because the German leadership did not think it necessary, on the basis of this information, to throw in the reserves or bring up reinforcements. By January 19 the Soviets had engaged nine heavy divisions, six brigades, and five tank brigades against the Hungarian Second Army and the Italian Alpine Corps.[17] The Soviet historian Telpuchowski writes that the Soviet leadership had assembled an overwhelmingly superior force: three times as many soldiers and ten times as much artillary faced the Hungarian army in the Ostrogozhsk-Rossosch sector of the front.[18]

On the fourteenth of January, two or three days after the beginning of the Soviet attack,[19] the Hungarian Twelfth Light Division was reported in full flight.[20] On the fifteenth and sixteenth of January the two-pronged attack of the Soviet forces was making further

15. Sulyok, *A magyar tragédia*, pp. 386 ff.; see also Ránki, *Emlékiratok és valóság*, pp. 226–27.

16. According to Andreas Hillgruber in *KTB, OKW* (2 : 31), the nine Hungarian and one German divisions constituting the Hungarian Second Army held a line of 160 kilometers, or 16 kilometers per division. A German military observer, Horst Scheibert, noted ten Hungarian and two German divisions held a line of 190 kilometers, thus corroborating Hillgruber's statement (*Zwischen Don und Donez*, p. 10). General Nagy, the Hungarian minister of defense, claimed that some Hungarian divisions held a line of 26 to 29 kilometers, while bearing only five to six thousand rifles (*Végzetes esztendők*, p. 104). In fact, General Nagy blamed the defeat, in the account he gave of it to the defense committees of the House of Parliament, on 1) the extended front lines; 2) the failure to allow the timely intervention of reserves (ibid., p. 129). It must be noted that the sectors held per division would not have been excessive but for the weakness of the Hungarian units.

17. NA Miocrcopy T-78, roll 333, 6291097.

18. Telpuchowski, *Die Sowjetische Geschichte*, p. 209.

19. According to the account given by the German historian, Andreas Hillgruber, the Soviet attack began only on Jan. 14, which would make the Hungarian collapse seem all the more rapid ("Der Einbau der verbündeten Armeen," p. 673).

20. NA Microcopy T-78, roll 333, 6290724.

progress "due to the rapid collapse of the Hungarian units."[21] On the seventeenth and eighteenth of January, the Hungarian nineteenth and twenty-third divisions reportedly abandoned their positions along the Don without having been attacked.[22] Gen. Italo Gariboldi, in command of the neighboring Italian units, requested permission to withdraw his four Italian and two German divisions "in armonia" with the Hungarian Second Army.[23] Most of the Hungarian Third Army Corps and its commanding officer, fighting to the north, capitulated in the first days of February; the Russians claimed 17,000 of its 60,000 troops killed.[24] Other units of the Hungarian Second Army had ceased to offer resistance long before.

The collapse of the Hungarian army led its commander, Gen. Gusztav Jány, to issue on January 24, 1943, what is a most extraordinary order in the annals of Hungarian military history. "The Hungarian Army lost its honor," began the order,[25] because with the exception of a few individuals it had not accomplished what everyone could expect it to accomplish. The enemy was superior, it was true; to lose a battle would have been a misfortune, but not a disgrace. "The disgrace consisted in the panic-stricken, cowardly flight of the troops, on account of which the German allies and our fatherland bear us contempt. They have good reasons for feeling so. No one will be allowed," continued the order, "to return home, even if wounded or ill: everyone will recover here or perish. Order and iron discipline will be reestablished, by summary executions if need be." General Jány concluded his order with a sentence meant as an insult to the anti-Semitically inclined Hungarian junior officer: "Characteristic of the events of the last few days is that the Jewish labor service companies march in close order and in good discipline, whereas the so-called regulars give the impression of a horde sunk to the level of brutes."[26]

The reputation of Hungarian arms sank low indeed. Whereas before the war Hitler tended to conceive of the Hungarians as heirs to

21. Ibid.
22. NA Microcopy T-78, roll 333, 6290726.
23. Gariboldi to commander Army Group B, Jan. 17, 1943, NA Microcopy T-501, roll 333, 1097.
24. NA Microcopy T-78, roll 333, 6290815, 6290819–20.
25. A German translation of this order is reproduced on NA Microcopy T-78, roll 333, 6290713–16. In contrast to General Jány, Colonel Adonyi notes that "no disgrace affected the honor of the Hungarian soldier; by his heroic deeds he proved himself worthy of his ancestors" (*A magyar katona a második világháborúban,* p. 53).
26. NA Microcopy T-78, roll 333, 629016.

the martial virtues of the Huns and of the early Magyars, he now felt the Hungarians performed poorly on the battlefield. Henceforth he graded Germany's allies on the Russian front as follows: Romanians first, Italians second, and Hungarians last.[27] During Hitler's next encounter with Horthy, on April 16, 1943, Hitler did not mince his criticisms of the Hungarian army. He claimed that only ten to fifteen thousand German prisoners, at the most, fell into the hands of the Russians at Stalingrad.[28] The allies had let the Germans down,

> not because they were inadequately equipped—this was not the case—but because they were not spiritually up to the situation. . . . Concerning the Hungarian army the Führer mentioned the commander-in-chief of the Hungarian army as an exception because he had flown everywhere in his "Storch," at great personal risk, to help his attacked units. According to the reports he had seen, however, the Hungarian troops had fought very poorly.[29]

If recriminations among the Axis partners were not uncommon before the battle of Stalingrad, they became rather frequent as a result of it. The German accusations were often answered by the Hungarian commanders. General Jány himself, although like many Hungarian generals at least partly of German descent, noted that the task of the Hungarian forces seemed to have been the protection of German units, and if no weapons were available the "living mass" of Hungarian soldiers was expected to soften the Russian blow.[30]

Hitler's poor opinion of the Hungarian performance in the eastern campaign was not entirely deserved. The rout of the Hungarian Second Army was not exclusively the result of Hungarian weakness or incompetence. General Jány had asked for the intervention of the "Cramer Group," the mostly German reserve force behind the Hungarian lines, as early as January 12; Soviet units had broken already through the Hungarian lines on January 13, but it was only on January 16 that Hitler authorized the intervention of the reserves

27. Entry for May 8, 1943, *Goebbels Diaries*, p. 356.

28. According to Soviet sources the number of German prisoners taken at Stalingrad was about 91,000; see in particular Marshal Vasili I. Chuikov, *The Battle for Stalingrad* (New York: Holt, Rinehart, and Winston, 1964), p. 263.

29. Ambassador Paul Schmidt's minutes of the meeting between Hitler and Horthy, Ribbentrop also present, Apr. 16, 1943, NA Microcopy T-120, roll 618 (Loesch Collection), F13163–64.

30. Karsai, *A budai vártól*, p. 262.

with, as we know, negative results.[31] Defense Minister Vilmos Nagy happened to be in Berlin on January 16, and on his request Field Marshal Keitel promised reinforcements, including tanks, for the Hungarian Second Army; but these reinforcements, even if promised in earnest, could have arrived only too late. Nagy explained that the lack of reserves was one of the basic causes of the defeat.[32] Furthermore, several Hungarian units, although encircled, kept fighting until annihilated. Other Hungarian units were used by German commanders as their rear guard, on the principle that they were less valuable. According to a Hungarian citation, General Oszlányi was decorated (about a year after the event) because his unit, the Ninth Light Division, had been the last of all of the Axis forces to leave the Don River, "thus enabling the orderly withdrawal of sizeable German forces from the Voronezh bridgehead." [33] In the case of the Thirteenth Light Division (Hungarian), both Hungarian and German military leaders seem agreed that it left the front only after having received orders to that effect and that it covered the breakout of the German 168th Alpine Division from Ostogozhsk at the cost of grievous loses to itself.[34] Furthermore, the defeat can be explained, in part, by factors we have already mentioned: the poor equipment, temperatures as low as minus thirty-eight degrees centigrade,[35] the lack of heavy antitank artillery. But perhaps the most important single factor in the Hungarian defeat was the low morale. While neither the troops nor the officers could have been aware of the true intentions of the Kállay government, the secret contacts between his government and representatives of the Anglo-American powers in particular, nevertheless troops and officers could not help but sense they were not receiving adequate logistical support either from the German or the Hungarian logistical commands. They may also have realized that the relationship between Hungarian participation in the campaign against the Soviet Union and Hungarian national interest was not clear; as Chief of Staff Szombathelyi stated, the

31. Ibid., pp. 241–47.

32. Nagy, *Végzetes esztendők,* pp. 119–21, 129.

33. NA Microcopy T-78, roll 333, 6290754. When General Greiffenberg, the new German military attaché in Budapest, read this item in the *Pester Lloyd* he wrote to General Heusinger to find out if the Hungarian citation was correct and deserved. General Heusinger replied he did not know but, in any case, it was best to let sleeping dogs lie.

34. OKW report of Oct. 28, 1943. NA Microcopy T-28, roll 333, 6290779.

35. Karsai, *A budai vártól,* p. 243.

Hungarians have entered the war for "purely idealistic" (ideological?) reasons.[36] It was a question of morale; the Hungarian soldier, like his Romanian or Italian comrade, could not see the connection between fighting on the Don River and the defense of the country.[37] The Hungarian soldier was not particularly interested in the "crusade against bolshevism," especially after he saw the chances of victory recede into the distance of the Russian steppes.

While the political situation in Hungary may have had an impact on the performance of Hungarian troops at Voronezh and the Don River, it is certain that this performance had an impact on the policies of the Kállay government. Tactically speaking, the Germans lost the battle of Stalingrad on November 19, 1942; but it was only in late January and early February 1943 that the liquidation of the German Sixth Army became an undeniable fact, almost simultaneously with the rout of the Hungarian army. The extent of the Hungarian losses is somewhat difficult to estimate. Ferenc Adonyi computes these losses at 35,000 dead, 35,000 wounded, and 26,000 prisoners or missing.[38] A report by Nagy, dated February 23, 1943, gives a total of 70,000 for all types of casualties, including number of missing or prisoners;[39] but in his memoirs Nagy writes that only about 60,000 or 70,000 men remained out of a total of 200,000.[40] Even so, the figure of 200,000 does not include the Jewish labor service, which may have numbered as much as 50,000 in the Ukraine and most of which perished during the rout. The lower estimate cited by Horthy during the meeting with Hitler at Salzburg in April 1943, may have been, however, closer to reality (he had no reason to underestimate the number of Jewish victims on the occasion): he had to "confess blushingly" that most of the 36,000 Jews in labor battalions he sent to the front "had perished during the Russian advance."[41] Ribbentrop's comment was: they probably joined the Russians.

These events accelerated, if they did not initiate, attempts by the Kállay government to dissociate Hungary from the National Social-

---

36. Memorandum by Szombathelyi, Feb. 12, 1943, *Confidential Papers of Nicholas Horthy*, p. 212.

37. Gesterding, "Probleme der Naht," p. 51.

38. Adonyi, *A magyar katona a második világháborúban*, p. 53.

39. Quoted in Karsai, *A budai vártól*, p. 261.

40. Nagy, *Végzetes esztendők*, p. 128.

41. Minutes of the meeting by Paul Schmidt, Apr. 16, 1943, NA Microcopy T-120, roll 618 (Loesch Collection), F13182.

ist cause.[42] Mussolini, in response to the news of Stalingrad, had advised a settlement à la Brest-Litovsk.[43] As we know, Hitler disregarded this advice. Nevertheless, when Mussolini learned that the Italian units remaining in Russia were to be used as occupation divisions only, he felt piqued. Gen. Vittorio Ambrosio was instructed to inform the German assistant chief of staff, Gen. Walter Warlimont, that the Italian Army Corps being reorganized in Russia must be used not in duties in the rear but in the front lines.[44] In contrast, the Hungarian leaders insisted (to the relief of the Germans) that the remaining Hungarian units be employed in the rear only and not be allowed to come into contact with Soviet regulars.[45] More important perhaps is the fact, so difficult to document, that before 1943 less than a dozen persons in Hungary had predicted Germany would lose the war:[46] after the events at Stalingrad and on the Don there were quite a few, and some had the courage of openly censuring the government for its apparently unaltered course.

42. An official of the Office of Strategic Services, the American intelligence organization of World War II, concluded that Hungary had been collaborating completely with Germany since the dismemberment of Czechoslovakia, but that following February 1943 there came a new period "marked by the Government's effort to reduce its commitment to the German war effort." During this period the ruling group was pursuing a policy of "partial belligerent collaboration" with Germany by attempting to keep the Hungarian troops in Russia far behind the fast-receding fighting front and by making repeated demands for the return of all Hungarian military units to Hungary (Office of Strategic Services, *The Hungarian Coup d'Etat of 15 October 1944*, p. 8).

43. Ugo Cavallero, *Commando Supremo*, p. 417. Ciano noted in his diary: "Sopratutto Mussolini tiene a far sapere a Hitler (lo ha già detto a Göring) che giudica indispensabile arrivare ad un accordo con la Russia o quanto meno fissare une linea difensive che possa essere tenuta con poche forze" (Diario, 2 : 255–56).

44. F. W. Deakin, *The Brutal Friendship*, p. 205. All Italian troops on the eastern front were repatriated in the course of spring 1943.

45. Memorandum by Szombathelyi, Feb. 12, 1943, *Confidential Papers of Nicholas Horthy*, pp. 211 ff.; see also NA Microcopy T-78, roll 333, 6290771.

46. See, for instance, the opinion of Csécsy, *Ha Hitler győzött volna*, p. 5.

7. Attempts to Negotiate with the Enemy

Official and semiofficial attempts to maintain or establish secret contacts with the Anglo-American powers were made by the Hungarian government even before Hungary became actively involved in the war. Contact with the United States in particular was maintained throughout the war, albeit without signal results. After the events discussed in chapter 6—the battle of Stalingrad and the rout of the Second Army at Voronezh—Hungarian efforts to reach the Allies and to negotiate were redoubled.

Count Pál Teleki's plans regarding a Hungarian government in exile in the event of an international conflict engulfing Hungary, or in the event of German occupation, are related by a former Hungarian minister to the United States, János Pelényi. Teleki acted on a memorandum submitted by Pelényi in April 1939. Five million dollars were transferred from the Hungarian National Bank into the custody of Pelényi; the sum was earmarked to finance an eventual Hungarian government in exile to be headed by the regent, by Prime Minister Teleki, or by some other prominent political personality. A hundred thousand dollars were withdrawn from this sum and deposited elsewhere, perhaps in Switzerland. Eventually, however, Pelényi received instructions to deposit the money at the Federal Reserve Bank in New York, and the project for a Hungarian government in exile came to nought. After Teleki's suicide most members of the Hungarian government were confident of a German victory, while many were hopeful of one, and could see little use for another Hungarian government in the Allied camp. Pelényi himself resigned from his post when Hungary adhered to the Tripartite Pact in November of 1940.[1]

1. John Pelenyi [János Pelényi], "The Secret Plan for a Hungarian Government in the West at the Outbreak of World War II." Count Teleki's instructions to Pelényi, dated Mar. 17, 1940, mentioned the following persons as authorized to take over funds sent to Pelényi: Count Gyula Károlyi, Count Pál Teleki, Count Sándor Khuen-Héderváry, György Barcza, Lipót Baranyai, Count István Bethlen, or Ferenc Keresztes-Fischer. Except for Károlyi or Teleki, two persons would have to be present, besides Pelényi himself, to take charge of the funds. Teleki's letter mentioned Royall Tyler, an American who had been the League of Nations' representative in Hungary in the early twenties and who had taken a liking to Hungarians, as authorized to replace one of the persons listed.

There were other attempts to establish secret contacts with the Anglo-American powers before Hungary became a participant in the war, the best known of these being the venture of Tibor Eckhardt, the leader of the Smallholders party. Eckhardt left Hungary on March 7, 1941, and reached the United States in a roundabout way (via Egypt, for instance). Eckhardt relates that "more than a hundred" Gestapo agents crowded the railroad station at the time of his departure from Budapest, and it was only thanks to his friend József Sombor, the chief of the Budapest police force, that he managed to get away.[2]

Eckhardt's journey seems to have worried some Reich officials. It was generally suspected that Eckhardt was bearing instructions received from Count Teleki or from the regent himself. The American minister in Budapest, Herbert Pell, reported in October 1941 that Eckhardt's "proposed departure and the reason therefore were known, debated and largely approved in informed circles, including the Regency and the Government. . . . In consequence Dr. Eckhardt's action appears more as a natural outcome of responsible Hungarian desire than of an individual political peregrination."[3] At about the same time Adm. William D. Leahy, the American ambassador at Vichy, reported he had been told Horthy had entrusted Eckhardt with a "mission."[4] It is not surprising, therefore, that the German Foreign Office should have regarded Eckhardt's trip with suspicion and Eckhardt himself as a dangerous individual.[5] Dr. Eckhardt, however, in a private conversation with me, denied he had been entrusted with any mission by Admiral Horthy: he had left Hungary because he foresaw Hungary's fate. Admiral Horthy, on his part, declared during an interrogation he underwent in Wiesbaden, after the war, that although Eckhardt had been the leader of an opposition party he considered Eckhardt a "correct" man; furthermore, noted the interrogator, Horthy "denied . . . that the trip to the United States had an official purpose."[6]

2. *Recollections of Tibor Eckhardt,* pp. 244–45.

3. Dispatch from Herbert Pell to Department of State, Oct. 11, 1941, NA Record Group 59, 862.20211.

4. Telegram from Leahy to Department of State, Oct. 13, 1941, NA Record Group 59, 864.00/1028.

5. Telegrams from Thomsen (in Washington) to Berlin, Sept. 27, 1941, and Nov. 3, 1941, NA Microcopy T-120, roll 92, 104240, 104340–42.

6. Interrogation of Admiral Horthy, Sept. 1, 1945, NA Record Group 59, DeWitt C. Poole Interrogations. During these interrogations Horthy used the term "correct"

Whether Eckhardt's journey was officially sanctioned or not, soon after his arrival in the United States he established contact with the Department of State.[7] For almost a year Eckhardt maintained contact with the department as the leader of an "independent Hungary" movement. In October 1941 Eckhardt and other leaders of this movement, including Pelényi, Antal Balasy, Antal Zsilinszky, Viktor Bátor, and Count Kálmán Almássy were deprived of their Hungarian citizenship.[8] This gesture of the by-then largely germanophile Hungarian government did not disabuse those who felt that Eckhardt had been entrusted with a special mission; it was possible to assume, on the contrary, that this gesture was merely meant to reinforce Eckhardt's position among Hungarian exiles, many of whom were prone to criticize him for his pro-Horthy and "reactionary" stand. According to Elek Karsai, who is referring to a German document, Eckhardt was informed by the returning American minister, Herbert Pell, that the measure taken against him was only for the sake of form and that he would be rehabilitated when the time came.[9]

Eckhardt's organization may be regarded as a semiofficial arm of the Hungarian government, although its failure to cooperate with other groups, notably that of Count Mihály Károlyi, impaired its efficiency. Eckhardt uncompromisingly refused to "sit together with Communists,"[10] and the "independent Hungary" movement disbanded in July 1942.[11] Eckhardt, however, maintained contact with Hungarian diplomats in Lisbon throughout most of the war and bolstered the hopes Otto Hapsburg had conceived (likewise encour-

---

rather often. The context makes it clear he meant "honorable," the supreme virtue in the eyes of the regent.

7. See memorandum on conversation with Eckhardt, Oct. 27, 1941, NA Record Group 59, 864.00/1030: "Mr. Eckhardt outlined at some length his general aims, along the lines covered by previous memoranda in our files." I have been unable to locate these "previous memoranda." Kállay wrote that Eckhardt later received "authorization to represent the Hungarian cause in America" through the Hungarian minister in Lisbon, Andor Wodianer (*Hungarian Premier*, p. 369).

8. Dispatch from Herbert Pell to Department of State, Oct. 11, 1941, NA Record Group 59, 862.20211.

9. *A budai vártól*, p. 128.

10. Eckhardt to author. It should be noted the Count Károlyi was equally uncompromising. "After endless discussions," he writes, "I started the New Democratic Hungary Movement, to which the majority of our countrymen all over the world belonged. . . . I refused to collaborate with the dissident diplomats in London as long as they were in touch with Tibor Eckhardt, who started a movement of Free Hungarians in New York" (*Faith without Illusions*, p. 301).

11. Sulyok, *A magyar tragédia*, p. 472

aged by President Roosevelt) for a return to power, if not as emperor of a new Hapsburg empire, at least as the head of some form of Danubian or east European federation.[12]

Count Mihály Károlyi, a leftist and reform-minded politician who had been Hungarian prime minister and president for a brief period after the collapse of the Austro-Hungarian monarchy, was the leader of a rival organization with headquarters in London. Certain well-known Hungarian personalities, such as Rusztem Vambéry and Professor Oszkár Jászi, both of whom lived in the United States, sympathized with Count Károlyi's movement.[13] Hence, after the demise of the "independent Hungary" movement left-wing elements equally opposed to Nazi Germany and to the Horthy regime remained the only organized group of significance. Rusztem Vambéry wrote about the Horthy regime in the following terms: "Hungary is in actuality a dictatorship without a dictator. It is a dictatorship of a clique, backed by the military, the civil service and the judiciary, outstanding representatives of which the clique includes. It is a Fascist regime without a Fascist philosophy of its own, screened by a sham constitutionalism."[14] György Páloczi-Horváth, another member of Count Károlyi's group and an agent of the British Special Operations Executive in Turkey, described Hungary as a feudal, oppressive regime. A Hungarian peasant, he reports, told him that "we should like to fight the Nazi-Fascists but all of them, Hitler and Horthy, Goering and Kállay, Papen and Bethlen alike."[15] While the aims of this group were no doubt praiseworthy and unselfish, it accomplished no more than Dr. Eckhardt's, intent as it was on preventing a compromise which might result in Allied support or condonement of the "semifeudal" or outright feudal regime of Admiral Horthy. Károlyi's group offered no alternative that proved practicable given the diverging views of the three Allied powers, and it found itself excluded

12. Imre Kovács, "Kiugrási kisérletek a második világháborúban" [Attempts at bailing out during World War II], p. 105.

13. Eckhardt owed his relative lack of popularity among Hungarian emigrants in part to the fact that he had been a leader of the "Awakening Magyars," an anti-Semitic organization, in the twenties.

14. *The Hungarian Problem*, p. 30. Hungarian historians writing in the period from 1948 to about 1958 interpreted the "Horthy era" in very similar terms. "Fascist" was the epithet most commonly applied to Horthy and the Hungarian ruling class. The antagonism these elements may have manifested vis-à-vis Nazi Germany was seldom taken into account. Hungarian collaboration with Germany was described as the result of the betrayal of the ruling class, rather than the result of German pressures.

15. *In Darkest Hungary*, p. 157.

from the left-wing cabinets set up in Hungary after the war. Left-wing Hungarian individuals who had sought refuge in the Soviet Union, including such (by now) well-known names as Mátyás Rákosi, Ernő Gerö, and György Lukács were far more successful in this respect.[16]

It may be argued that since Eckhardt had emigrated to the United States on his own initiative he could not be considered a spokesman for the Hungarian government; but bona fide elements of the Hungarian government also attempted to establish contact with the Anglo-American powers as early as 1942. Antal Ullein-Reviczky, chief of the Press Section of the prime minister's office, hence responsible for the censorship of foreign news, was probably the most effective of these elements. I have pointed out in a previous chapter that the Reich officials strongly objected to Ullein-Reviczky, because of his British wife and because he was suspected of feeding information to the Turkish legation in Budapest. In his memoirs Ullein-Reviczky makes no mention of this alleged activity. He does claim, however, that about this time—he is not specific about the date—he began to form a diplomatic "second front" consisting of some consular attachés and reliable newspapermen. Their task was to establish contact with the Allies and "interpret Hungarian public opinion to them;"[17] in other words, largely a matter of propaganda. Unfortunately Ullein-Reviczky mentions the name of only one of his collaborators, Aladár Szegedy-Maszák, then the assistant chief of the Political Section of the Foreign Ministry. Szegedy-Maszák, however, has indicated that he has no recall of such activity in 1942 and that he had never been a close associate of Ullein.[18] Andor Gellért, who had been transferred from his Berlin post as press attaché to Stockholm some time during 1942, has been suggested as one of Ullein's "contact men." But Dr. Gellért was equally unspecific in response to a query addressed to him, stating merely that there was no official "diplomatic second front" but that certain members of the League

16. So were certain other leftists who had remained in Hungary between the two wars and who were arrested en masse in the summer of 1942, during the ministry of Miklós Kállay. See Pintér, "A Kállay kormány 'hintapolitikája,'" p. 471. Even more important is the work of Gyula Kállai, today speaker of the Hungarian House of Representatives, *A magyar függetlenségi mozgalom, 1936–1945* [The Hungarian movement for independence].

17. *Guerre allemande,* p. 127.

18. Aladár Szegedy-Maszák to author, Dec. 26, 1966.

of Revision may have assumed such a role.[19] The fact remains that Gellért did carry on conversations with British and American citizens in Sweden, as did Aladár Szegedy-Maszák, who followed Gellért to Stockholm for a brief visit.[20] A dispatch from the American minister in Stockholm, dated October 30, 1942, stated, that a reliable "informant" had given him a favorable description of Hungary's attitude toward the Allies, a description which, incidentally, was corroborated by a "local Soviet diplomat." [21]

I have also found a report indicating that Andor Gellért had established contact with Vilmos Böhm, who had been defense minister in the Károlyi government in 1919 and who, while living in Sweden, had a number of friends among eminent members of the Labor party in Great Britain. Böhm reassured Gellért on the score of the Soviet Union; his friends told Böhm that the Soviet Union would become, by the end of the war, one great cemetery, lacking the strength to penetrate into central Europe! [22]

American and German documents corroborate the claims of Ullein-Reviczky. The German Abwehr continued to keep a check on Mrs. Ullein's activities.[23] The American minister in Ankara cabled on December 2, 1942:

> A member of Hungarian Legation in Turkey, who recently returned from a visit to Budapest, has approached an officer of this Embassy with suggestion that there are now many influential Hungarians willing and anxious to collaborate with

19. Andor Gellért to author, July 7, 1967.

20. Kovács, "Kiugrási kísérletek a második világháborúban," p. 98; also Juhász, *Magyarország külpolitikája,* p. 264.

21. NA Record Group 226, Hungary, Records of the Office of Strategic Services, 27730.

22. Letter from Stockholm, July 29, 1942, Political Section, Ministry of Foreign Affairs, Hungarian National Archives, K 64, bundle 86 (1942). The first sentence of this letter, "the correspondent of the *Pesti Hirlap,* Andor Gellért, who was here recently . . . ," is crossed out and replaced by "one of my reliable informants . . ." See also Kovács, "Kiugrási kísérletek," p. 98.

23. The following report from Abwehr III to Abwehr I, classified "geheime Reichssache" and dated Dec. 10, 1942, may serve to illustrate Germany concern: "Gegen den U.-R. besteht starken Verdacht nachrichtendienstlicher Betätigung zu Gunsten des Gegners . . . Frau U.-R. ist geburtige Engländerin und Tochter des ehem. engl. General-konsuls in *Istanbul Cumberbeach.* Sie war vor einigen Wochen längere Zeit in Istanbul und unterhielt dort enge Beziehungen zu gegnerischen N.D. [Nachrichtendienst] Kreisen" (NA Microcopy T-120, roll 688, 311964). A report by J. Klahr Huddle in Bern, dated Oct. 19, 1942, quoting Alan Dulles, stated that Ullein-

our Government if opportunity can be arranged. Hungarian official, who has again returned to Budapest on business stated that if suggested collaboration were of interest to American Government he would very probably be able to arrange for visit to Turkey of a respectable Hungarian Government official who would be prepared to discuss details. It was indicated that Hungarians preferred to deal with a responsible member of Embassy rather than with members of some United States Government organization. In view of standing of Hungarian official in question I believe proposal to be a serious one and I would appreciate Department's instructions with regard to attitude to be taken towards it.[24]

Whether the "respectable Hungarian Government official" was a reference to Ullein-Reviczky, I cannot say. At any rate, this contact was to prove fruitful. Long before the report of the American minister, the Hungarian minister in Ankara reported he had been approached by a British citizen named Szilagyi, originally a Jew from Hungary, and that Szilagyi tried to persuade Heribert Thierry, first secretary of the Hungarian legation, that the Hungarian government should denounce the war before the Romanian does.[25] Before examining further developments in Turkey, let me discuss two other points of contact between the Hungarian government and the Allies.

In September and October 1939, and even later, tens of thousands of Poles fled their homeland. Slovakia being actively engaged on the side of Nazi Germany, there were only two exits left open: the narrow stretches of Poland's common border with Romania and Hungary. Most of the Poles who fled to Hungary remained but a short while;[26] they were allowed to proceed to France or Great Britain, via Yugoslavia, where many of them formed Polish volunteer units. According to one source, 140,000 Poles escaped to Hungary; 110,000 left the country right away, whereas about 15,000 remained through-

---

Reviczky, "who until lately was decidedly pro-Axis, is now doing all he can to make contacts in the few remaining neutral countries, with the United Nations' representatives, or with neutrals who are on good terms with the Anglo-Saxons" (NA Record Group 59, 864.00/1046).

24. Telegram from Kelley to Department of State, NA Record Group 59, FW 740.00119 E.W. 1939/1195.

25. Dispatch from Vörnle to Budapest, Sept. 21, 1942, Ministry of Foreign Affairs, Political Section, K 64, bundle 86 (1942), Hungarian National Archives.

26. Kállay gives the total number of Polish refugees as "more than 150,000," of whom about 100,000 crossed the Hungarian border with Yugoslavia within a few

out the war.[27] The Hungarian policy toward the Polish refugees was not consistent: most military refugees were disarmed and interned, some were not. On the whole, however, the Poles, especially the Polish officers, were treated in a friendly fashion, as indicated by the indignant German reports on the subject: "Hungary is helping the Polish brothers in truly amazing fashion," wrote one German agent, alluding to the fact that Poles and Hungarians cooperated throughout history, more often than not. "Projects to bring up Polish children in Hungarian families have been introduced, and other assistance projects. Most exacerbating is the help offered Polish officers . . ." [28] In November of 1939 the Germans reported the presence of about 45,000 Polish refugees in Hungary.[29] Another report dated June 12, 1942, described the committee for Polish refugees in Hungary as operating with practically unlimited funds and as being shielded by the Ministry of Interior, whereas the Poles without funds were interned but well provided for. On the other hand, read the report, at times terror was used toward the refugees, presumably in the case of persons suspected of being Communist agents.[30] Nevertheless, the Polish refugees who remained in Hungary often became the go-betweens for the Poles who had fled to the West and the underground in Poland.[31] The Poles seemed grateful for the treatment accorded them by the Hungarian authorities. The Polish government in exile in London intervened several times in 1943 to support the Hungarian efforts to reach an armistice with Great Britain.

Another outside contact maintained by the Hungarian government, for a while at least, was with certain Latin American countries

---

months (*Hungarian Premier*, p. 331). According to Imre Kovács there were 210,000 Polish refugees in Hungary, including 70,000 Jews (*D'une occupation à l'autre*, p. 16). Commensurate figures are given by Andor Kun who quotes the Sept. 13, 1943, issue of the *Dzennik Zolnierza*, a Polish émigré paper appearing in London (*Enyhítő körülmények Magyarország bünperében*, p. 41).

27. András Rácz, *Les réfugiés polonais en Hongrie pendant la guerre*, pp. 5–6, 27.

28. Unsigned report to Ausland W. Pr., Sept. 29, 1939, NA Microcopy T-77, roll 1026, 248918.

29. Report to Ausland W. Pr., Nov. 8, 1938, NA Microcopy T-77, roll 1026, 2498927–28.

30. Report by German military attaché in Budapest, NA Microcopy T-77, roll 1026, 2499022.

31. The Countess Listowel writes that mail from the Polish underground reached Lisbon thanks to the Hungarian diplomatic pouch and courier Tamás András (*Crusader in the Secret War*, p. 172); also Rácz, *Les réfugiés polonais*, p. 60.

that had signed the Pact of Rio de Janeiro with the United States. Hungary was about the last Axis country to break relations with Brazil and did so reluctantly. Among the reasons for Hungarian reluctance were the appeals of the Hungarian minister in Rio de Janeiro,[32] who happened to be Miklós Horthy, Jr., the younger son of the regent. Germany and Italy had asked the Hungarian government to break diplomatic relations with Brazil in February 1942, but Bárdossy asked that the request be reconsidered.[33] The Hungarian cabinet seems to have theoretically agreed to break relations on March 3, as Karsai states,[34] but it was not until May 2 that she actually broke with Brazil, Uruguay, and Paraguay.[35] Then the young Horthy asked to be accredited to the Chilean government, but he was unsuccessful.[36] In June he was able to find transportation across the Atlantic to Lisbon, and he arrived in Budapest on October 17, 1942.[37]

Around Christmas of 1942 the young Horthy read a speech over Radio Budapest in Portuguese; the speech was addressed to his friends in Brazil and the peoples of Brazil and Portugal. It contained a sentence to the effect that small nations are not always masters of their own destiny. I don't know whether anybody in Brazil, or on the Allied side, was duly struck by this pronouncement, but every Hungarian broadcast seems to have been monitored by the Germans, and the Reich officials took note. The German minister in Budapest was instructed to mention the matter to the Hungarian Foreign Ministry, which he did several times.[38] Hungarian officials finally responded to the minister's protests with the excuse that the young Horthy had, while an adolescent, suffered a brain concussion as a result of a fall from a polo horse and this concussion had permanently affected his mental faculties. This rumor, originally spread by Arrow-Cross elements, seems to have found wide acceptance among people

32. Ambassador Horthy to author; he was accredited to Uruguay and Paraguay, as well as to Brazil.

33. See telegram from Mackensen (in Rome) to Berlin, Mar. 3, 1942, NA Microcopy T-120, roll 92, 104652.

34. Karsai, *A budai vártól*, p. 236; see also telegram from Jagow to Berlin, Mar. 4, 1942, NA Microcopy T-120, roll 92, 104653.

35. Note by Woermann, May 5, 1942, NA Microcopy T-120, roll 92, 104943.

36. Miklós Horthy, Jr., to author.

37. Karsai, *A budai vártól*, p. 185.

38. See report by Jagow, May 29, 1943, NA Microcopy T-120, roll 94, 106290-91.

who had never met the young Horthy.[39] Ribbentrop finally gave instructions that the matter be dropped.[40]

The young Horthy's radio speech is significant because, he has assured me, he had shown the text of the speech to his father and the regent had endorsed it contents. The young Horthy added that there never was a serious disagreement between the regent and himself. He did not tell me, but it is easy to surmise, that it was he who influenced his father to stiffen resistance to German demands, particularly in 1944.

Although Hungary broke relations with Brazil soon enough to satisfy German expectations, relations with Chile (and, of course, with Argentina) were maintained for a long while. On March 27, 1943 Jenő Ghyczy, the undersecretary of the Ministry of Foreign Affairs, told Werkmeister that Hungary did not feel obliged to break relations with Chile, since Bulgaria and Japan, although Germany's partners, were not at war with the Soviet Union.[41] When the German minister repeated his request in April, Kállay promised to comply. But on May 17 Ghyczy again told Werkmeister Hungary did not feel obliged to break relations with Chile.[42]

In the meantime the negotiations in neutral countries, especially in Turkey, seemed nearing a solution. András Frey, a Hungarian journalist, correspondent of the moderate *Magyar Nemzet,* was sent to Istanbul. Frey's voyage was delayed by visa difficulties, but he finally arrived in Istanbul on or about February 1, 1943.[43] According to Kállay, Frey had been sent to present the following concrete proposals to representatives of the Anglo-American powers: (1) Hungary

39. According to another Arrow-Cross rumor, the young Horthy had an affair with "Frici" Goldberger, the daughter of a Jewish industrialist. Ambassador Horthy, who told me he was willing to discuss his affairs, denied that this one had ever taken place. An SD report on the subject, transmitted by Schellenberg and dated Sept. 3, 1942, reads: "Liebe zu der Tochter des jüdischen Industriellen Goldberger zwischen ihm [Horthy] und seine Mutter gewisse Differenzen bestanden. Ob diese Freundschaft noch besteht, ist gegenwärtig nicht festzustellen" (NA Microcopy T-120, roll 1096, 452395).

40. Note by Rintelen to Steengracht, May 29, 1943, NA Microcopy T-120, roll 94, 106298. In a conversation on June 10, 1943, Sztójay apologized for the young Horthy's speech: "Im übrigen sei der Gesandte von Horthy gesundheitlich nicht auf der Höhe" (NA Microcopy T-120, roll 94, 106356–59).

41. Telegram from Jagow to Berlin, NA Microcopy T-120, roll 94, 106115–16.

42. Telegram from Werkmeister to Berlin, NA Microcopy T-120, roll 94, 106257.

43. Macartney, *October Fifteenth,* 2 : 141; see also Kállay, *Hungarian Premier,* pp. 369–70, and Kertesz, *Diplomacy in a Whirlpool,* p. 67.

undertook not to fight the Anglo-Americans or the Poles should their units reach the border of Hungary; (2) "Hungary was in principle prepared to take action against the Germans." Kállay seems to have relied on Ullein-Reviczky's memoirs for a summary of these instructions.[44] Frey now writes that the story of an unconditional surrender offered by Kállay was invented in his presence by an official of the Hungarian Foreign Office and a British agent, because Kállay did not dare or was unable to make a move in that direction.[45] The American dispatches from Turkey seldom mention András Frey, which leads me to assume that Frey (perhaps following the contacts indicated to him by Ullein-Reviczky) entered into negotiations only with British representatives. In only one instance does the American consul in Istanbul refer to the matter: on March 7, 1943, the consul praised Frey for having maintained contact and been of "great assistance" to the British and "other Allied" governments.[46] The British reply was noncommittal: the British government requested that two senior officials be sent to Istanbul. Kállay, in turn, was reluctant to comply with the British request, ostensibly because the contact man on the British side was György Páloczy-Horváth, a left-wing Hungarian ex-journalist in the British secret service, stationed in Istanbul, whom Kállay distrusted.[47] I am inclined to question, therefore,

44. Kállay, *Hungarian Premier*, pp. 369–70. Ullein-Reviczky wrote: "1) L Hongrie ne compte pas opposer de résistance aux troupes anglo-américaines et polonaises au cas où celles-ci se présenteraient sur les frontières hongroises pour pénétrer dans le pays. Comme contrepartie la Hongrie ne demande *rien*. Il est toutefois entendu qu'une telle attitude ne saurait être observée du côté hongrois qu'envers les formations regulières des armées alliées, et non pas envers des bandes de partisans. 2) La Hongrie est, en principe, prêt à faire aussi des choses punitives contre les Allemands, à condition qu'une coopération pratique puisse préalablement être établie entre nos armées. 3) Le but de la présente offre n'est pas de sauver le régime hongrois actuel, mais uniquement le peuple hongrois" (*Guerre allemande*, p. 177).

45. András Frey to author, Oct. 2, 1967. Frey adds that the story can now be told; he did not wish to embarrass Kállay—who died in New York in October 1966.

46. NA Record Group 226, Hungary, Records of the Office of Strategic Services, 64222. The same praise is accorded to György Páloczi-Horváth, attached to the "British embassy" in Istanbul, and to Dr. Ferenc Albert Vali.

47. "What made things particularly disagreeable for us was that the British had designated to conduct the negotiations with us an individual of Hungarian origin named George Páloczy-Horváth, at that time employed by the organization which the British had established in Istanbul for counterespionage and sabotage in the Balkans. . . . Everyone in Hungary knew that he was a spy of Gömbös in former days and that later he became a left-wing Socialist with strong sympathies for Moscow. In Serbian affairs he was Tito's *homme de confiance*. The British only discovered in December, 1944, what we knew at that time, that Páloczy-Horváth was regularly passing on information to the Russians" (*Hungarian Premier*, p. 371).

the conclusions of some historians writing in the West and in Hungary who regard Miklós Kállay as a hero of anti-German resistance; [48] such an evaluation, while not altogether incorrect, is nevertheless unwarranted in its exaggeration.

Nevertheless, the steps taken by the Hungarian government elicited a change in the British attitude toward Hungary. Until the spring of 1943 the British government followed a tough line toward Horthy and other members of the Hungarian government; the Hungarian-language broadcasts of the British Broadcasting Corporation apostrophized Horthy in terms rather similar to those used in regard to Hitler or Mussolini. On April 6, 1943, the British ambassador in Washington presented an aide-mémoire which was a reappraisal of Germany's lesser allies, the "minor satellites." The appraisal of Hungary is remarkable: "Hungary has succeeded in preserving a greater degree of independence than any other satellite in South Eastern Europe." The document also discusses political opposition within Hungary, "democratic" and conservative:

> Leaders of these organizations have been surprisingly outspoken and speeches have been made inside and outside the Hungarian Parliament condemning the present orientation of Hungarian policy. The Primate, Cardinal Serédi, has also denounced Nazi conceptions publicly. Baranyai, the Governor of the National Bank, has recently resigned in protest against Hungarian concessions to Germany. There have been not unsuccessful efforts in Hungary to moderate the persecution of the Jews. . . .
>
> Although His Majesty's Government do not consider that any early and decisive change in Hungarian policy is likely, the general background seems favorable for some slight modification of the rigid attitude which His Majesty's Government have hitherto adopted towards Hungary.[49]

The modifications suggested were simply a more friendly attitude toward Hungarian peace feelers and reassurance regarding the territorial integrity of Hungary; that is, Hungary would not be "torn to pieces" any further than she had been torn to pieces by the Treaty of Trianon. Another remarkable facet of this British document is simply the fact that evaluation of events and conditions inside Hungary was by and large correct, a credit to the British intelligence service.

48. See, for instance, Nagy-Talavera, *The Green Shirts and the Others*, pp. 181 ff.
49. *FRUS 1943*, 1 : 486–89.

The German intelligence or counterintelligence service was per-
forming equally well with regard to Hungarian affairs. Hungarian
authorities during the war, as well as writers on this period of Hungarian history, thought very highly of its performance. Such an
estimate of the Abwehr, or of the Sicherheitsdienst, needs to be qualified. The German intelligence service was effective in Hungary
mostly because of the large number of German agents active there
under various guises and because of the large number of National
Socialist sympathizers in Hungary. Yet the Reich government was
not immediately aware of everything the Hungarian government did,
or contemplated doing, even concerning foreign policy. Thus the
Germans had only a vague knowledge of András Frey's mission to
Turkey. In mid-March the German minister in Budapest received instructions to check up on a broadcast by Eduard Beneš concerning
Hungarian feelers in neutral countries and on similar news received
from "very secret sources. . . . According to these sources at the beginning of February a prominent Hungarian and Refrey [sic] the
foreign affairs editorialist of the *Magyar Nemzet,* have stayed in Istanbul on a secret mission in contact with American and British officials." [50] Werkmeister, filling in for Jagow, replied as follows:

> The name of the editorialist of the *Magyar Nemzet* in question
> is not "Refrey," but Andreas Frey. He went to Istanbul about
> two months ago and has so informed the Press Attaché of the
> German Legation. Hence his mission was not "secret." Accord-
> ing to our Press Attaché his reportage was objective and com-
> pletely in the Axis spirit. Frey is a very intelligent half-Jew.[51]

Werkmeister was irritated, no doubt, by what he deemed excessive
distrust on the part of certain German agencies. Actually, the distrust of these German agencies was not unwarranted, but their information was garbled. Their main suspect, in fact, was not Frey or
Refrey, but Professor Albert Szent-Györgyi, recipient of the Nobel
Prize in biology. The documents Hitler showed to Horthy during
their meeting in April at Salzburg related mainly to the alleged
betrayal perpetrated by Kállay, the instruments of which had been
Professor Szent-Györgyi and his colleague, Professor Gyula Mészáros.
Szent-Györgyi had been invited by the Turkish government to

50. Telegram from Woermann to Budapest, Mar. 15, 1943, NA Microcopy T-120,
roll 94, 106077–78.
51. Telegram of Mar. 17, 1943, NA Microcopy T-120, roll 94, 106079.

hold conferences; he took advantage of this opportunity to carry out a political mission, apparently prescribed by himself and on his own initiative. Although he paid a visit to Kállay prior to his departure (this being the first occasion the two met), the witnesses and historians concur that Szent-Györgyi's mission was not expressly endorsed by Kállay. During his interrogation in September 1945, Horthy declared, convincingly enough, that "it would have been silly for Kállay to have used a man like Szent-Györgyi, whom he had not met before, and who had no acquaintance with diplomatic affairs." [52] On the other hand, it is difficult to believe that Szent-Györgyi would have invented *ex nihilo* everything he told the Americans.[53] In Istanbul he met a representative of the Socony-Vacuum Oil Company, and here is what he communicated to the representative in a memorandum:

> Before leaving my country, I visited the Prime-Minister, told him to come out this way to try to talk to Mr. Steinhardt [the American ambassador in Ankara] and asked him whether I could do any favor to him. He asked me to tell Mr. Steinhardt that
>
> 1) he is not giving one soldier or one gun any more to Germany,
> 2) he has to shout now and then against the Jews but he is doing practically nothing and is hiding 70,000 Jewish refugees in the country,
> 3) he could not follow till now a different policy because in that case Hungary would have been occupied by the Germans and mobilized totally against the Allies and the Jews exterminated.[54]

In the course of the memorandum Szent-Györgyi also mentioned that Ullein-Reviczky had indicated to him specific terms regarding a possible armistice and that he himself had sufficient influence to sway "the policy of the government at the right time any way desired." [55] The dispatch of the American ambassador enclosing this memorandum, dated February 13, reached Washington on March 16 after a

52. Interrogations of Horthy, NA Record Group 59, DeWitt C. Poole Interrogations.

53. Since Szent-Györgyi has not given me information on this subject, it is difficult for me to arrive at an accurate estimate of the situation.

54. Dispatch from Steinhardt to Washington, Feb. 13, 1943, NA Record Group 59, 864.00/1057.

55. Ibid.

voyage of over a month; the memorandum does not appear to have
been taken seriously by the Department of State. The British seem to
have taken the activities of Szent-Györgyi rather more seriously. According to the British aide-mémoire already referred to, he "appears
to enjoy a certain independence and in many respects he seems to
be a person with whom discreet contact might usefully be maintained
through suitable underground channels." He was to be informed,
therefore, that his views had been transmitted to London and that
the British government was pleased to note certain favorable developments in Hungary.[56]

Szent-Györgyi's activities were also taken seriously by the Reich
leaders who came to know about it. Many writers believe that, in his
"naïveté," Szent-Györgyi had transmitted his peace proposal to a
Gestapo agent.[57] There is reason to believe, however, that the Reich
leaders were informed of the mission by Szent-Györgyi's colleague,
Professor Mészáros. It appears Mészáros was active on behalf of the
Vienna office of the German Abwehr and received 300 Turkish
pounds every month for his services.[58] In defense of Mészáros be it
said that the information he gave the Abwehr was less than correct.
Furthermore, he continued to be held "guilty" by the German Foreign Office, along with Szent-Györgyi, for having "established contact with the enemy" and was refused a German transit visa on the
next occasion.[59]

These negotiations and German suspicions were part of the background of the Hitler-Horthy conversations at Klessheim Castle near
Salzburg in April 1943. Horthy's visit to Hitler may have been suggested to Ribbentrop by Jagow. Jagow hinted to the Italian minister
in Budapest, Filippo Anfuso, on April 7 that he had not only proposed that Horthy be invited to Germany but had also suggested that
Kállay be replaced by Imrédy, whom the Italian minister regarded,
with some justice, as strictly at the order of the Germans.[60] Nothing

56. Aide-mémoire, British Embassy to the Department of State, *FRUS 1943*, 1 : 488–89.

57. For instance, Macartney, *October Fifteenth*, 2 : 142.

58. "Geheime Reichssache" report from Grote to the OKW, July 16, 1943, NA Micro-copy T-120, roll 688, 311975. It was about this time that "Operation Cicero," a German spy operation affecting the British embassy in Ankara, became effective. See Elyesa Bazna, *I Was Cicero;* see also L. Moyzisch, *Operation Cicero*.

59. See pencil note by Feine, of the Reich Foreign Office, on a memorandum requesting that Mészáros be cleared, dated Jan. 31, 1944, NA Microcopy T-120, roll 688 311980.

60. Anfuso to Ciano, Apr. 7, 1943, Lisbon Papers, NA Microcopy T-816, roll 2197.

came of the proposal regarding Imrédy, but Horthy was invited to Germany, since his visit was in order anyway. On April 12 and 13 Hitler had received Marshal Antonescu, and quite recently he had received visits from leaders of the satellite countries; and these yearly or twice-a-year visits had become almost a ritual. But Antonescu's visit is particularly pertinent to our topic, because Hitler had talked to Antonescu in terms similar to those he was to use vis-à-vis Horthy, only more respectful. The Romanian and Hungarian governments were once more vying for the favors of the great powers. Marshal Antonescu's foreign minister, Mihai Antonescu, had also been sending out peace feelers toward the allies in January and February 1943 and had convinced the Italian minister in Bucharest, Renato Bova Scoppa, to make joint attempts at peace negotiations; Bova Scoppa's efforts, however, did not go beyond Mussolini and Ettore Bastianini, the new Italian foreign minister, who were, as we have already seen, determined to remain faithful to National Socialist Germany, at least for the time being. In fact, it seems the Romanians had been the first to contact Allied officials in the neutral countries of Europe, and Kállay authorized the Hungarian contacts partly to keep up with the "rival." [61] It is clear, however, that the Romanian attempts at "bailing out" were more successful in the long run.

Horthy received Hitler's invitation on about April 10; the invitation specified that the discussions were to center on the military situation and the fate of the Hungarian troops still near the eastern front.[62] Horthy came armed with a memorandum prepared by Andor Szentmiklóssy of the Hungarian Foreign Ministry. This memorandum stated that Hungary remained true to the Axis cause; that Hungary felt threatened by the hatred of her neighbors; that Hungary could serve the Axis cause best by securing her own frontiers; that Hungary was the factor which preserved order in the Carpathian basin; that Hungary could not afford to send troops for the occupation of former Yugoslav territories; that because of the large number of Jews in Hungary, the problem was especially serious in that country and could not be resolved by deportations.[63]

61. Csatári, *Forgószélben*, pp. 225 ff.; see also Hillgruber, *Hitler, König Carol, und Marschall Antonescu*, pp. 168–69, 171.

62. Macartney, *October Fifteenth*, 2 : 149.

63. This memorandum is printed in the *Confidential Papers of Nicholas Horthy*, pp. 231–44, and in *Horthy Miklós titkos iratai*, pp. 373–86. A portion of this memorandum is also printed, in somewhat different words (apparently a retranslation from the German) in *Magyarország és a második világháború*, pp. 417–18; the editors of this

Horthy did not have an opportunity to make much use of this memorandum. Hardly had he shaken hands with the chancellor when he was confronted with a series of loudly enunciated accusations; it is true, however, that these accusations were directed not so much against him, the regent, as against his government and especially his prime minister. The principal of these accusations: Szent-Györgyi had handed a note to the American ambassador in Ankara, presumably under instructions from Kállay. This note mentioned, among other things, that Hungary was on her way to total disorganization; that the expected defeat would result in unrest and probably in a general bloodbath; that Hungarians disliked national socialism.[64] Hitler also referred to similar Hungarian activities in Switzerland, involving a "whole series of Hungarian personalities," specifically naming Béla Varga, a member of the Parliament who had taken a trip there.[65] Ribbentrop, who was present during most of the conversations, read out the documentary evidence twice, on April 16 and on April 17. He also showed the regent some of the intercepted and decoded telegrams, adding that although he retained confidence in the regent he had lost all confidence in Kállay.[66] Horthy replied that

> he will investigate the matter. He admitted that Professor Szent-Györgyi had visited Kállay, but he added, that he would vouch his head on it that Kállay gave no political instructions of the kind mentioned by the Reich Minister of Foreign Affairs. Horthy intimated that Werkmeister [first secretary of the German legation in Budapest] may have been at the source of this report, since Werkmeister sees people who are not received by Horthy.[67]

During his interrogation by American authorities in Bavaria after the war, Horthy said "he told Hitler to ask a boy of ten years if it is possible when a Prime Minister wishes to make such a thing that he chooses a professor that he never saw in his life to go to Turkey

---

documentary compilation note that the memorandum bore neither a date nor a signature and refrain from ascribing it to anyone.

64. Partly charred minutes of the Hitler-Horthy conversation recorded by Ambassador Schmidt, Apr. 16, 1943, NA Microcopy T-120, roll 618, F-13171 (hereafter cited as Minutes).

65. Minutes, Apr. 16, NA Microcopy T-120, roll 618, F-13177.

66. Minutes, Apr. 17, 1943, NA Microcopy T-120, roll 618, F-40109–10.

67. Minutes, Apr. 17, 1943, NA Microcopy T-120, roll 609, F-40098–99. Horthy distrusted Werkmeister more than he distrusted other German officials; see memorandum by Weizsäcker to Ribbentrop, Apr. 15, 1942, NA Microcopy T-120, roll 92, 104848–51.

to speak to the American and English Ambassador for us. It was really ridiculous." [68]

Another accusation raised by Hitler was Kállay's toying with the concept of a "Balkan bloc." On February 10 the Hungarian minister in Ankara, János Vörnle, reported on the conference which had taken place at Adana between Churchill and the Turkish foreign minister, Numan Menemencioglu. The latter, according to the Hungarian minister's report, had declared that Turkey would be a factor for "peace and order" in Europe after the possible downfall of Germany and that he would like to form a "bloc" of states comprising Turkey, Greece, Bulgaria, Yugoslavia, Romania, and Hungary. Although Menemencioglu mentioned Hungary several times, Churchill raised no objections.[69] Kállay was pleased with this report. Such a "Balkan bloc" would have served to keep Soviet influence out of the Balkans and away from the Straits, and this in itself would have sufficed to endear the project to Kállay. But he also saw in this project—as he later hinted to Mussolini—an opportunity to draw closer to England, whom he regarded as Turkey's ally.[70] During their conversations in Rome in early April of that year, Kállay told Mussolini: "my opinion is that we must not recoil from all such discussions, because in any case discussions with the Turks would be interesting; such conversations would be all the more interesting as the Turks seem to orient themselves towards the Anglo-Saxon powers.[71] But Kállay also informed the German minister in Budapest about the Turkish proposal, adding that he wanted to tell the Turks he was very interested in it and explaining that this might be a way of bringing Turkey closer to the Axis! Although I have not been able to find the pertinent instructions issued by the Reich Foreign Office, it is clear that Ribbentrop disapproved of the project and that Kállay was so informed. According to the German minister in Budapest, Kállay was astonished at the unfavorable German reaction, but he was nevertheless prepared to comply with the German request and drop the

68. Horthy interrogation, Aug. 27, 1945, NA Record Group 238, World War II War Crimes Records.

69. Vörnle to Budapest, Feb. 10, 1943 (*Magyarország és a második világháború*, pp. 410–12).

70. *Hungarian Premier*, pp. 277–78.

71. Minutes of conversation between Kállay and Mussolini, Apr. 1, 1943. NA Microcopy T-973, Hungarian Collection, roll 1. The "Balkan bloc" project came to nought: Foreign Minister Sükrü Saracoglu ordered the negotiations broken off because of Anthony Eden's coolness toward it.

matter. The matter was dropped by everyone concerned, including the Hungarian and the Turkish governments, but not by the Reich leaders. For one thing, Jagow did not believe Kállay had been earnest about dropping the idea of a Balkan bloc.[72] Hitler mentioned the matter to Horthy on April 16, and Ribbentrop repeated the reproach on April 17. Ribbentrop accused Kállay of having been all too willing to join a Balkan pact, although he must have known the initiative came from England, Germany's "archenemy," and from her allies (actually, the initiative seems to have come from Turkey). He had even sent Szent-Györgyi back to Turkey to carry on further negotiations.[73] Ribbentrop commented: the present conflict could not be won by diplomatic shenanigans.[74] In the telegram Ribbentrop dispatched to the German ambassador in Rome for the information of Bastianini, Ribbentrop made only a delicate reference to certain "defeatist tendencies" condoned by the Kállay cabinet. The main point of the conversations, according to this telegram, was the "senseless project" of a confederation of Balkan states; if Germany should fail to achieve it, how could those states hope to thwart bolshevism? [75]

The German leaders also complained of Kállay's attitude with regard to Hungarian troops being trained in France. As the American Office of Strategic Services well knew, some Hungarian personnel, especially pilots, were stationed in France.[76] On April 3 Colonel Fütterer, the German air attaché in Budapest, reported he had been told by Gen. János Vörös "that the Hungarian flyers being trained in France must on no account be used in raids." This official communication, noted Fütterer, "shows again clearly that Hungary is prepared to take part only in the fight against Russia." [77] This incident was still fresh in the mind of the Reich leaders when Horthy came to Klessheim, and Ribbentrop cited it as another example of Kállay's untrustworthiness. Horthy answered that the French representative in Budapest, Count Robert de Dampierre, whom he described as a pleas-

72. Telegrams from Jagow to Berlin, Mar. 11, 1943, NA Microcopy T-120, roll 94, 106069; Mar. 29, 1943, NA Microcopy T-120, roll 94, 106119; Apr. 3, 1943, NA Microcopy T-120, roll 4, 106125.

73. Minutes, Apr. 17, 143, NA Microcopy T-120, roll 609, F-40110; see also Minutes, Apr. 16, 1943, roll 618, F-13171.

74. Minutes, Apr. 17, 1943, roll 609, F-40113.

75. Telegram from Ribbentrop to Rome (classified "geheime Reichssache"), Apr. 20, 1943, NA Microcopy T-120, roll 94, 106172–77.

76. NA Record Group 226, Hungary, Records of the Office of Strategic Services, 82874.

77. Telegram from Fütterer to Berlin, NA Microcopy T-120, roll 94, 106124.

ant cripple (*sympatischen Krüppel*), had objected, declaring that Hungary had not been at war with France and therefore should take no part in her occupation.[78] Horthy repeated this argument on May 9 in his letter to Hitler.[79]

Hitler and Ribbentrop did not fail to bring up the matter of the Hungarian Jews. During the April 16 conversations, Ribbentrop remarked that once again two "full Jews" had been elected to the upper house. Horthy replied that on constitutional grounds there was nothing he could do about that and, furthermore, there were a number of baptized Jews in Hungary, many of whom were valuable elements of society. "He had done everything that could be done against the Jews, but one couldn't murder them or let them die, after all. The Führer replied that wasn't necessary. Hungary could place Jews in concentration camps, just as Slovakia had done." [80] It is entirely possible Horthy did not know that the majority of the Jews of Slovakia had already been exterminated.[81]

The Jews were again a topic on April 17. They were responsible for black-market activities, said Hitler. "As Horthy replied, what should he do with the Jews after he had withdrawn from them all means of livelihood—he cannot kill them, after all—the Reich minister of foreign affairs explained that the Jews had to be either destroyed or brought into concentration camps. There was no other alternative." [82]

78. Minutes, Apr. 16, 1943. NA Microcopy T-120, roll 609, F 40101. Count Robert de Dampierre himself became the object of a German-Hungarian controversy when he was relieved from his post at the time of the German occupation of Vichy territory. In May 1942 an SS report signed by Schellenberg had described Dampierre as "absolutely" pro-British and pro-de Gaulle (NA Microcopy T-120, roll 350, 262362–65). At the time of the occupation, the Reich Foreign Office requested that the Hungarian authorities prevent the count from reaching a neutral or enemy country. Kállay replied that it would be unheard of to detain a foreign diplomatic representative against his will (see telegram from Jagow to Berlin, Dec. 15, 1942, NA Microcopy T-120, roll 93, 105932–35). It seems the count was not particularly impressed by the treatment the Hungarians accorded him. In an article on his diplomatic career, he dismissed his station in Budapest in a single paragraph and refers to Hungary in 1942 as "Nazi Hungary" ("De l'Autriche impériale à la Hongrie nazie").

79. NA Microcopy T-120, roll 94, 106272–76.

80. Minutes, NA Microcopy T-120, roll 618, F 13181.

81. In Slovakia large-scale deportations began on Mar. 26, 1942. By Mar. 31, 1943, 57,545 Jews had been deported, mostly to camps at Sered and Auschwitz; the majority were exterminated (Raul Hilberg, *The Destruction of the European Jews*, pp. 465 ff.).

82. Hitler continued, on the subject of the Jews: "Sie wären wie Tuberkelbazillen zu behandeln, an denen sich ein gesunder Körper anstecken konne. Das wäre nicht grausam wenn man bedenke, dass sogar uschuldige Naturgeschöpfe wie Hasen und

Horthy's visit, in Goebbels's words, "was conducted in a very heated atmosphere . . . The Führer was very outspoken." [83] But there was one pleasant episode during the talks on April 16. Horthy told Hitler that during sleepless nights he had thought up a system for making submarines more effective. According to Horthy the weak point of the submarine was that it had a very limited scope of vision. To overcome this handicap the submarine would need a cranelike device which, with the help of the countervailing wind, could lift a sailor a hundred meters into the sky; if all the submarines would shoot up their cranes at a certain time, they would be able to scan a large part of the ocean.[84] Hitler thanked Horthy for the suggestion and explained the principle of radar.

The outcome of the talks was that Horthy promised to undertake a thorough investigation of the charges mentioned by Hitler and "report" on the results of this investigation. The official communiqué, of course, did not mention Horthy's promise, nor was any reference made therein to the nature of the unpleasant arguments. But this communiqué gave rise to an additional disagreement. The phrase stating that Hungary and Germany would continue their struggle against the Anglo-American Allies until final victory was apparently added in Germany in disregard of the original wording of the communiqué which mentioned only the Soviet Union.[85] The German leaders, on the other hand, objected to the omissions in the Hungarian communiqué purporting to be a translation of the German one.[86]

Rehe getöt werden müssten, damit kein Schaden enstehe. Weshalb sollte man die Bestien, die uns den Bolschewismus bringen wollten, mehr schonen" (Minutes, NA Microcopy T-120, roll 609, F-4106–7). This document, as many others quoted in this study, is also reproduced in facsimile in *The Destruction of the Hungarian Jewry: A Documentary Account*, ed. Randolph L. Braham, 1 : 1965–96.

83. *Goebbels Diaries*, p. 335.

84. Minutes, Apr. 16, NA Microcopy T-120, roll 609, F-40096–98.

85. Kállay, *Hungarian Premier*, p. 184. See also telegram from Harrison (in Berne) to Washington, NA Record Group 238, 864.00/1066.

86. See note by Rintelen to Weizsäcker (at Fuschl), Apr. 22, 1943, NA Microcopy T-120, roll 94, 106183; also Juhász, *Magyarország külpolitikája*, p. 284.

8.   Continuation of Peace Efforts

While Horthy had to withstand Hitler's browbeating at Klessheim Castle, the secret negotiations continued in the capitals of neutral countries. Any well-organized account of these negotiations would prove misleading, for the negotiations themselves were not well organized but fumbling, bumbling, intermittent, and at times absurd efforts on the part of elements of the Hungarian government to find some miraculous way out of its well-nigh hopeless predicament. It would be purposeless to attempt to keep track of the numerous more-or-less official Hungarian representatives engaged in this activity. The flurry may indicate that the Hungarian Ministry of Foreign Affairs was worried lest its efforts to escape from the war pass unnoticed by the Allies, or perhaps the number of peace representatives was intended to compensate, in some way, for the lack of any radical alteration of Hungarian war policies. The major effort to reach the Allies, as we have seen, had taken place in Istanbul. In Lisbon contacts were established, or perhaps kept, between the Allied representatives, on the one hand, and the Hungarian minister Andor Wodianer, who was related to the regent; the representative of the Hungarian League of Revision, Ernő Tamás,[1] and another Hungarian diplomat and friend of the regent, Sándor de Hollán,[2] on the other hand. In Madrid the Hungarian minister Ferenc Ambró was regarded by the German agents there as a pro-British "decadent" aristocrat who probably also established contact with Allied representatives.[3] In Stockholm Andor Gellért continued his efforts on behalf of Ullein-Reviczky and the Minister of Foreign Affairs; Ullein-Reviczky himself became

1. The League of Revision was a propaganda organ composed of liberal and conservative elements alike to publicize the Hungarian position with regard to the Treaty of Trianon. Macartney attaches importance to the negotiations in Lisbon where Francis Deak, an American officer of Hungarian origin, asserted he was "the only authorized channel" in 1943; Macartney does note, however, that Deak's mission failed, like all the others (*October Fifteenth*, 2 : 204).

2. Military attaché in Portugal to chief of the intelligence branch, G-2, Sept. 14, 1943, and Adolf A. Berle to assistant chief of staff, G-2, Oct. 19, 1943, *FRUS 1943*, 1 : 500–1.

3. Telegram from Hans Heinrich Dieckhoff (in Madrid) to Berlin, Sept. 25, 1943, NA Microcopy T-120, roll 94, 106640–41; see also telegrams from Dieckhoff to Berlin, Oct. 8 and Oct. 18, 1943, NA Microcopy T-120, roll 97, 106709 and 106742.

the Hungarian minister to Sweden in September 1943 and made repeated attempts to explain the Hungarian predicament to Allied officials in Sweden. Switzerland became an anthill of subversive activity, perhaps because Allied government agencies, especially the British secret service and the American Office of Strategic Services, were so well represented there. Among the Hungarians who may have established contact with Allied agents there (Allen Dulles, Royall Tyler, and others), either on their own initiative or on the biddance of Kállay or Count Bethlen, was the new Hungarian minister to Bern, Baron György Bakach-Bessenyey, transferred in late August from Vichy to replace a pro-Axis minister.[4] In an aide-mémoire, the British embassy informed the Department of State on April 20 that the Hungarian minister in Vichy had attempted to get in touch with the British and United States ministers in Bern through the Brazilian minister. The British minister, Clifford J. Norton, and his "United States colleague declined to have anything to do with the matter . . . Mr. Norton's attitude has been approved and he has been instructed, in the event of further approaches being made, to continue for the present to take the same line."[5] The Hungarians were not discouraged. The same aide-mémoire mentions an approach attempted by György Barcza, former Hungarian minister to Great Britain. The British minister was again instructed to have no dealing with the man, but "other arrangements" were being made to find out "discreetly what if anything he may have to say."[6] According to Kállay, Barcza was sent on a special mission to Switzerland with his approval "at the very end of 1942" with instructions to negotiate but to oppose any suggestions regarding the return of Count Mihály Károlyi or regarding a leftist regime.[7] Barcza's trip is also mentioned in the German documents.[8] Other Hungarian negotiators in Switzerland included Dezső Laky, who had been food minister in the Teleki cabinet;[9] Baron Gábor Apor, the Hungarian minister to the Vatican;[10] Béla Varga, a Catholic clergyman and member of Parliament

4. I have also found a German report to the effect that Bakach-Bessenyey was in touch with Sokolin, Stalin's "informer" in Switzerland (telegram from Manfred Killinger (in Bucharest) to Berlin, Nov. 2, 1943, NA Microcopy T-120, roll 94, 106791).

5. *FRUS 1943*, 1 : 490–91.

6. Ibid.

7. Kállay, *Hungarian Premier*, p. 384.

8. See Telegram from Jagow to Berlin, Apr. 10, 1943, NA Microcopy T-120, roll 94, 1061390–94.

9. Komlós, *Elárult ország*, p. 24.

10. See telegram from Harrison (American minister in Bern) to Department of State, July 22, 1943, NA Record Group 59, 864.00/1086.

whose name had been mentioned by Hitler during the conversations at Klessheim; a certain Abbott Gerinczy who may have come to Switzerland at the instance of the regent; Lipót Baranyai, who was soon to be replaced as president of the Hungarian National Bank in the course of a swing to the right of Kállay's pendulum maneuvers; [11] Baron Albert Radvánszky, also an official of the Hungarian National Bank and described as the confidential representative of the Kállay-Bethlen group; [12] François Honti, ex-minister to France who, in Switzerland, established contact with the representative of General de Gaulle; [13] and perhaps others. Illustrative of these negotiations was a telegram from the American minister in Bern I found among the records of the Department of State:

> X. recently received a visit from Y. whom X. has known for a number of years and considers trustworthy and definitely anti-German. Y. claimed to speak solely for himself and not for his Government. However X. feels satisfied Y. had consulted and spoke with knowledge of his government. . . . Y. has now asked X. to arrange for him to see my British colleagues and myself. We have both told X. that we are not prepared to see Y. I shall maintain this attitude, in all such cases unless instructed otherwise.[14]

It was, indeed, the policy of the Department of State, at this time, to pay little attention to "enemy aliens" and their propaganda efforts. In any case, the negotiations in Switzerland, official or unofficial, led to no concrete results.

Kállay himself had made an attempt to strike out on an independent course during his long-postponed (since November of 1942) visit

11. See report by Kocher to Berlin, Nov. 30, 1943, NA Microcopy T-120, roll 1096, 452474.

12. Karsai, *A budai vártól*, p. 266. François Honti notes that more than one million Swiss francs were given to Radvánszky and Bakach-Bessenyey to finance the diplomatic ventures (*Le drame hongrois*, pp. 29–30). A German "charge sheet," elaborated in February 1944, mentions some of the Hungarian agents by name: Baranyai, Radvánszky and Tamás Kállay active in Switzerland, as well as Ferenc Ambró in Madrid and Andor Wodianer in Lisbon ("Geheime Reichssache" memorandum, NA Microcopy T-120, roll 99, 109780).

13. Pintér, "A Kállay kormány 'hintapolitikája,'" p. 487.

14. Telegram from Harrison (in Bern) to Department of State, Apr. 13, 1943, NA Record Group 59, 864.00/1060. In another telegram, dated June 30, 1943, Harrison provided the key to the code: "'A' referred to in my telegram 3879 June 30"—obviously he was referring to a different but equally secretive dispatch—"is Hungary; 'W' is de Barza [*sic*]; 'X' is Kállay; 'Z' is Bethlen. I received the memorandum from Elmer to whom it was handed by 'W'" (NA Record Group 59, 874.00/1080).

to Rome in the first days of April.[15] Kállay's concept was similar to
the one Mihai Antonescu had imparted to the Italian minister in
Bucharest, Renato Bova Scoppa. If I have understood Kállay's discreet hints correctly (this time the information is derived not from
Kállay's memoirs but from the original and contemporary minutes
of his conversations with Mussolini), he had advised Mussolini to
persuade Hitler to attempt a diplomatic settlement of the war and,
should Hitler remain unconvinced, to take the initiative in this
regard:

> I pointed out in this conversation that the foreign countries feel
> the lack of a more active Axis diplomacy, because, in my opin-
> ion, we have to take up defensive positions in the war and we
> must profit of the available time to find the way to peace or
> even to establish the necessary conditions for a victory itself by
> greater diplomatic activity. And I miss, first of all, the Latin
> initiative, because if there is room only for German and Ameri-
> can diplomacy, it cannot convey the spirit of latinity which
> Hungary also follows, and which must be preserved in this world
> crisis.[16]

If this language is not altogether lucid, well, it was not meant to be.
But there can be little doubt that Kállay expected the German leadership to turn down any suggestions regarding peace negotiations;
Kállay certainly would not have ventured to make any suggestions
regarding peace, however veiled, directly to the Germans. Furthermore, Kállay wished to see Italy break away from Germany: this is
what was meant by "Latin initiative." The reference to the "spirit of
latinity which Hungary also follows" could only be interpreted in the
sense that if Italy breaks away then Hungary will too; for Hungary
can hardly be described as a Latin country. Kállay's general concept,
expressed in deliberately obscure terms, was to return to the diplomacy of before the war, when Fascist Italy had been Hungary's
strongest ally. It is quite probable that, as Filippo Anfuso writes,
Kállay was disappointed in Mussolini, who was too faithful to Hitler.[17]

Mussolini understood Kállay's hints and returned to the topic at
the end of their conversations, declaring that the rumors regarding

15. Hitler was, of course, aware of Kállay's visit to Rome, but he did not know
what to make of it. See Minutes, Apr. 16, 1943, NA Microcopy T-120, roll 89.

16. Minutes of the meeting between Kállay and Mussolini, Apr. 1, 1943, NA Microcopy T-973, Hungarian Collection, roll 1.

17. *Du Palais de Venise*, p. 228.

Italian attempts at a separate peace were false. Separate peace for Italy was not possible because (1) Italy must remain faithful to Germany as a matter of honor; (2) Italy would derive no political advantage from it; (3) the conditions were not favorable,[18] presumably a reference to the military situations in Tunisia, where the Axis surrendered on April 5. Mussolini had already suggested to Hitler the advisability of reaching a "Brest-Litovsk" with the Soviet Union, a solution Hitler declined to consider.[19] Mussolini saw no possibility for a diplomatic solution on the western, or rather southern, front; he was removed [20] from power on June 25, 1943 (by which time the Allies had occupied most of Sicily), less than three months after he had told Kállay the conditions were not favorable for peace and Italy would derive no political advantage from a separate armistice.

When Marshal Pietro Badoglio's emissaries concluded an armistice with the Allies on September 8, Hungary was out of step. Marshal Badoglio had told Anfuso, the Italian minister to Budapest, during his visit to Rome on July 25, that should Italy "unhook" herself from the war Anfuso would be warned in order to enable the Hungarians to "avoid surprises." They even devised a password to be used on the occasion.[21] But both Anfuso and the Hungarian government were caught by surprise when the Italian surrender was announced over the radio.

During his audience with the pope, Pius XII, on April 2, Kállay tried another approach. In the message Baron Apor had been instructed to deliver to the pope on March 7, a few weeks before his visit, Kállay had discussed only the "dangers" of bolshevism.[22] In their conversations the pope acknowledged the existence of such dangers but declared the Germans seem to have fallen further away from God than the Russian people! This declaration is one of the few instances indicating the pope had come to a clear conclusion regarding the moral implications of the war; it also indicates the pope knew what was happening in Germany and in occupied terri-

18. Minutes of the meeting between Kállay and Mussolini, Apr. 1, 1943, NA Microcopy T-973, Hungarian Collection, roll 1.

19. The suggestion was first made to Göring in December 1942 (F. W. Deakin, *The Brutal Friendship* [Garden City, N. Y.: Doubleday, 1966], 1 : 89, 97, 104, 249).

20. Mussolini had meant that such an armistice would lead to the downfall of both fascism and himself. Had Mussolini known that Franco would remain in power for at least twenty-seven years after the war, he might have acted differently.

21. Anfuso, *Du Palais de Venise*, p. 261.

22. These instructions are reproduced, in facsimile, in Karsai, *A budai vártól*, following p. 268.

tories. When Kállay brought up the topic of peace, the pope noted that the chances for his successful intervention were slight, because Hitler was probably not an acceptable partner for the Allies; His Holiness nevertheless authorized Kállay to tell Mussolini he was ready to intercede for peace. Mussolini's reply, during a second meeting of the two leaders, was discouraging.

Though Hungarian representatives had put forth peace feelers in Italy and practically all the remaining neutral countries of Europe, the most significant developments took place in Turkey, where negotiations had first been attempted. In April an attaché of the British embassy in Ankara had a conversation with a Hungarian representative identified as Charles Schrecker.[23] The Hungarian reiterated that if the Anglo-Americans invaded the Balkans Hungary would not resist. But Schrecker specified certain conditions: (1) there should be no Serb, Croatian, Czech, or Romanian unit involved in the occupation of Hungary; (2) the Russian army should not attack; (3) Budapest should not be bombed. "If England should be prepared to accept these conditions as against Hungary's commitment not to fight against an Anglo-American army, the days of proceedings should be fixed, a meeting of experts prearranged, which would take place as soon as the situation would be ripe for it." [24] The Hungarian emissary was told that before the British government would consider entering into discussions with Hungary the Hungarian government should give proof of a "totally changed attitude." The Hungarian reply, on May 12, was: "What change of attitude would be considered in England as sufficient proof to justify entering into discussion?" [25] I have not found a copy of the British reply, either to the Hungarian question or to the specific proposals relayed by Schrecker. It is clear that the British were still reluctant to negotiate separately with the Hungarians.

Nevertheless Kállay undertook to institute certain measures he felt would meet the approval of the Anglo-American powers. The most important of these concerned Hungarian military participation.

23. Charles Schrecker first approached the Netherlands minister in Ankara, claiming he had come with the knowledge of Kállay, to deliver a message (aide-mémoire, British embassy to Department of State, Apr. 20, 1943, *FRUS 1943*, 1 : 490–91). I have found no trace of a Charles Schrecker in recent Hungarian history, nor do I know who might have used this name as an alias.

24. Dispatch from Steinhardt (American minister in Ankara) to Department of State, June 3, 1943, NA Record Group 59, 864.00/1075.

25. Ibid.

The disaster at Voronezh had already eliminated half of the Hungarian Second Army from the conflict—no merit of government policy. A considerable portion of the remaining troops was brought back to Hungary; while nine light divisions remained, or were sent out, as occupation forces, eventually the Hungarian minister of war explicitly stated no further forces could be made available for the purpose.[26] It was also understood that these forces were not to enter into contact with Soviet regulars.[27] Hitler and the German General Staff went along with the Hungarian specification but suggested that Hungary send, in addition, or perhaps in exchange for her troops in Russia, three divisions to occupy Serbian territory and thereby relieve German forces stationed there for front-line duty. The Hungarian chief of the General Staff Szombathelyi agreed to the German request and promised to send Hungarian troops to German (and Italian) occupied Yugoslavia beginning June 1, 1943. Vilmos Nagy, who was still minister of war, objected, and so did Kállay, who may have been acting on the advice of some of the Hungarian representatives in neutral countries.[28] At the cabinet meeting on March 10, 1943, the minister of interior, Ferenc Keresztes-Fischer, even threatened to resign if the German request were allowed. He feared Hungary might further antagonize the Serbs (who were not apt to forget the massacres at Novi Sad),[29] with whom Hungary had often tried to establish better relations, as well as the Anglo-Americans who would look askance at any Hungarian contribution to the German war effort.

The matter was brought up once again after Minister Nagy had been compelled to resign. The new minister of defense, Gen. Lajos Csatay, favored the idea of sending Hungarian troops to the Balkans.[30] The minister of interior and the new minister of foreign affairs, Jenő Ghyczy—appointed by Miklós Kállay in order to evade the onus the

26. Quoted by Karsai, *A budai vártól*, p. 279.

27. See above, chap. 6.

28. Nagy, *Végzetes esztendők*, pp. 132–33. See also Karsai, *A budai vártól*, pp. 278–79. A note by Grote of the German Foreign Office, dated Mar. 5, indicates the Hungarian government had declined to send troops to the Balkans even before the cabinet meeting of Mar. 10, NA Microcopy T-120, roll 94, 106042–43. Kállay may also have remembered the warning of Szilagyi (see above, p. 119, chap. 7). Royall Tyler strongly objected to this alternative in conversations with György Bakach-Bessenyey in Switzerland (Kovács, "Kiugrási kísérletek," p. 108).

29. Interestingly enough, a recent Yugoslav "official" history of the war, in English, makes no mention of the massacre at Novi Sad (Ahmet Donlagić, Žarko Atanacković, and Dušan Plenča, *Yugoslavia in the Second World War* [Belgrade: 1967]).

30. See telegram from Pappenheim to Berlin, Sept. 6, 1943, NA Microcopy T-120, roll 94, 106565–67.

Germans attached to the secret Hungarian peace feelers—continued to object strongly. The military leaders, Csatay and Szombathelyi, were not able to convince the cabinet, or the regent, and reportedly complained to Colonel Pappenheim, the German military attaché in Hungary, about the "cowardice of the government." Szombathelyi even added that he was ashamed to travel to Hitler's headquarters— where his visit was expected—under the circumstances.[31] Szombathelyi was particularly disappointed by his government's adamant attitude; he had submitted a long memorandum advocating that Hungary send troops to the Balkans, as the German government had requested, even though he recognized that the Axis could not win the war; by this means the recall of all Hungarian troops in Russia could be secured, he had hoped.[32] An additional consideration, which Szombathelyi may have considered but did not express in his memorandum, was that since an Allied landing was expected in the Balkans the Hungarian troops would have a chance to establish friendly contact with an Anglo-American military force sooner. Ultimately the Hungarian government remained unfavorable to the idea of sending Hungarian occupation troops to Serbia or Yugoslavia. The German minister's recommendation to his government was that, should Hungary persist in this attitude, Germany ought to reestablish Trianon Hungary—in other words, take away the territories granted Hungary by the two Vienna awards, as well as Ruthenia and the Bácska.[33]

Hungary had also undertaken diplomatic steps to secure the withdrawal of the Hungarian troops remaining in the Soviet Union, ostensibly to help defend the country against a possible attack from the Balkans. The German front in the East was rapidly receding, and it was not always possible to avoid encounters between the Hungarian occupation forces and regulars of the Red Army; even the Hungarian commander, Gen. Géza Lakatos, who seems to have agreed with the general policy of his government, was reluctant to order retreat in the face of the enemy, as such an order would have resulted in demoralization. Thus an encounter occurred, for instance, in early August 1943, but the German military bulletin praising the stand of the Hungarian units involved was censored by the Hungarian censorship, presumably to minimize Hungarian military participation.

31. Telegram from Pappenheim to Berlin, Sept. 15, 1943, NA Microcopy T-120, roll 94, 106605; same document reproduced on NA Microcopy T-77, roll 883, 5632212.

32. Nagy, *Végzetes esztendők*, pp. 167 ff.

33. Telegram from Jagow to Berlin, Sept. 17, 1943, NA Microcopy T-120, roll 94, 106606.

Ernst von Jagow bitterly complained to his superiors: until that time the Hungarians had tried to forget the fact that their country was at war with Great Britain and the United States, but now it seemed the Hungarian government also wanted to detach itself from the war against Russia.[34]

Indeed, Hitler's reproaches at the Klessheim meeting did not seem to have achieved the desired results. Horthy had "promised" Hitler to send a report on the findings of his investigation. Accordingly, Horthy wrote a letter on May 9, almost a month after his visit (perhaps with the help of Kállay). It was one of the regent's more courageous letters. He reiterated his trust in Kállay. The measures already taken against the Jews were adequate, he explained, although the regent did add that as soon as the "possibility for their deportation" was created Hungary would deport them. The regent reminded Hitler of Hungary's economic and military contributions to the Axis cause. He then complained of the activities of the Arrow-Cross party, whose leaders he designated as "high traitors" and who were, he implied, abetted by the National Socialist German Workers party. But, concluded the regent, nothing could happen in Hungary against his will, and he was "determined to preserve law and order under all circumstances." [35] The letter indicated clearly that Horthy was not willing to grant Hitler's principal request, the dismissal of Kállay. In a conversation on June 21, Horthy told the German minister that his prime minister might not be the most competent person for the post but that he enjoyed his, Horthy's, fullest trust. He preferred to stick by a man in whom he had full confidence and who was his friend.[36] And Hitler continued to regard Horthy as a valuable ally: witness the yacht Hitler announced as a present to Admiral Horthy on his seventy-fifth birthday (although the yacht was not delivered until considerably later).[37]

34. Telegram from Jagow to Berlin, Aug. 7, 1943, NA Microcopy T-120, roll 94, 105605–6.

35. Summary of Horthy's letter to Hitler, Ribbentrop to Jagow, May 25, 1943, NA Microcopy T-120, roll 94, 106272–76. Horthy's letter to Hitler is also printed in *The Confidential Papers of Nicholas Horthy*, pp. 249–55.

36. Telegram from Jagow to Berlin, June 21, 1943, NA Microcopy T-120, roll 94, 106394–97.

37. When Jagow transmitted Hitler's congratulations on the occasion of Horthy's seventy-fifth birthday, he also told Horthy that Hitler still intended to reply to Horthy's letter of May 9; Horthy told Jagow that he certainly did not expect a reply to his explanations (telegram from Jagow to Berlin, June 20, 1943, NA Microcopy T-120, roll 94, 106391).

Kállay, however, remained out of favor with Hitler and the German leaders. As early as April 24 Ribbentrop ordered Jagow and other members of the German legation in Budapest to adopt an attitude of complete reserve vis-à-vis Kállay and Ullein-Reviczky who had also been "compromised" by Kállay's suspicious activities.[38] On May 3 Ribbentrop's instructions went a step further: "I ask you not to accept any invitations from Mr. Kállay and to have no social intercourse with him whatever, otherwise our standpoint that we have no more trust in him would be watered down. . . ." [39]

In a further telegram, on May 5, Ribbentrop instructed Jagow to adopt the same attitude vis-à-vis Ullein-Reviczky.[40] Ullein-Reviczky, however, was appointed Hungarian minister to Stockholm the following month, and his place in the press office was taken by Mihály Arnóthy-Jungerth. Once again events in Hungary and in Romania took a parallel course; the Romanian foreign minister was accorded the same treatment by the German representatives there.[41]

In the case of Kállay the snub was reciprocated; he refused to see the German minister. The principal reason why he relinquished the office of foreign minister in July 1943, writes Kállay, "was to insert an intermediate person between myself and the German minister so that I would not have to receive démarches from him personally," and to "gain time to prepare my answers to German communications." [42] The evidence concerning this new attitude does not come from Kállay alone; an SS officer named Ernst Kienast corroborates the evidence by indicating reasons for Kállay's resentment. Kienast was told by a Hungarian counterintelligence agent that the Hungarians were able to decipher Italian diplomatic codes and that a dispatch by Filippo Anfuso, the Italian minister in Budapest, reported that Jagow was hoping the Kállay government would fall within a couple of months.[43] But since this intercepted dispatch was dated May 17 it is clear that the feud between Kállay and the German minister in Budapest was initiated by the latter, on Ribbentrop's instructions (dated May 3). It is not true, then, that it was after the appointment

---

38. Telegram from Ribbentrop to Jagow, NA Microcopy T-120, roll 94, 106185–86.
39. Telegram from Ribbentrop to Jagow, NA Microcopy T-120, roll 94, 106200–1.
40. NA Microcopy T-120, roll 94, 106210.
41. See Ribbentrop's telegram to Rome, May 3, 1943, NA Microcopy, T-120, roll 94, 106202–3.
42. Kállay, *Hungarian Premier*, p. 355.
43. Report by Kienast to Berlin, June 8, 1943, NA Microcopy T-175, roll 119, 2645174–76.

of Jenő Ghyczy as minister of foreign affairs that the Wilhelmstrasse forbade the German minister to see Kállay personally.[44] This is but one of the many inaccuracies that mar the documentary value of Kállay's memoirs.

The role of the Fascist Italian government in the German-Hungarian quarrel is not entirely clear, but it appears that Mussolini attempted to mediate by explaining the Hungarian position to Hitler in favorable terms. On May 14 Kállay instructed Zoltán Máriássy, the Hungarian minister in Rome, to remit a note of thanks to Mussolini for his "attitude full of understanding" and for his valuable advice regarding the Hungarian-German misunderstanding. The note gives no clue as to how the Duce came to find out about that misunderstanding, that is, about the Hungarian peace feelers. But the note explains that the Hungarian diplomatic efforts in neutral countries had been designed only as a propaganda measure to counter attacks by Romania and, to a lesser extent, by Slovakia! Nor was the note merely intended to alleviate German and possible Italian suspicions. He could not hide his impression, continued Kállay,

> that behind the annoying German-Hungarian misunderstanding lay motives of a different kind, although not on the Hungarian side. These might be summarized in the following manner: 1) the Germans cannot conceive that Hungary, in spite of her most ancient and fullest trust as an ally, should remain a sovereign and independent state, claim to be such, and be able to follow her own lines of policy because of this.[45]

This statement could be read, perhaps, as an appeal to Mussolini to help preserve Hungary's independence in the face of German pressure. Whether Mussolini read it as such and whether he would have been prepared to give Hungary effective help in this sense, I cannot say. At any rate it does not seem that Hitler seriously contemplated the occupation of Hungary at this point.[46]

44. Kállay, *Hungarian Premier*, p. 355.
45. Memorandum of the Hungarian government, NA Microcopy T-816, Lisbon Papers, roll 2197.
46. There are indications, however, that Hitler did consider the incorporations of parts of Hungary into the Reich. For instance, during one of his "table conversations" in 1942, he declared, "We shan't succeed in preserving the German minorities in Hungary except by taking over control of the State—or else we shall have to withdraw our minorities from Hungary" (Trevor-Roper, *Hitler's Secret Conversations*, p. 275). See also Goebbel's observations, below.

It is clear, however, that Hitler and other German leaders continued to be exacerbated with some of the policies of the Hungarian government. On May 7 Goebbels noted that Horthy had so far fulfilled none of the "promises" he made on the Obersalzberg: "possibly the Führer was too brusque . . ." Goebbels also noted that the Jewish problem was being solved least satisfactorily in Hungary. During the talks at Klessheim, Horthy had brought up a "number of humanitarian counterarguments which of course don't apply at all to this situation. You just cannot talk humanitarianism when dealing with Jews . . ." Hitler was only partly successful in winning Horthy over to his point of view; "from all this the Führer deduced that all the rubbish of small nations (*Kleinstaatengerümpel*) still existing in Europe must be liquidated as fast as possible." [47] But it was only after the Italian surrender that Hitler took concrete steps to avert a Hungarian defection.

During the summer of 1943 serious negotiations between Hungarian and Allied representatives were resumed. The British government, as we have seen, had usually followed a more rigid policy toward Hungary than the American. But an official of the Department of State noted, in July 1943 that

> the British have recently informed us that they are inclined to be less harsh in considering these Hungarian overtures . . . In view of the sensitiveness of the Czechoslovak Government and, to a lesser degree, the Yugoslav Government on questions regarding the treatment of Hungary, and in consideration of the special position of Soviet Russia as regards the Hungarian question, it would appear to be advantageous to let the initiative, if anything is to be done in this matter, come from the British.[48]

If anything, the Department of State seems to have stiffened its attitude. In the aide-mémoire of April 6, the British had suggested a modification of the rigid line adopted vis-à-vis Hungary.[49] In its reply on April 28 the Department of State implied that efforts to this end might be premature and might result in the liquidation of the useful elements in Hungary. Nevertheless, the modification proposed by the British would be a good thing in terms of "psychological warfare." [50]

There was no consistent American policy with regard to Hungary.

47. *Goebbels Diaries*, pp. 352, 357.
48. Memorandum by C. W. Cannon, July 6, 1943, NA Record Group 59, 864.00/1090.
49. British embassy to Department of State, *FRUS 1943*, 1 : 487–88.
50. Aide-mémoire, Department of State to British embassy, *FRUS 1943* 1 : 492.

Certain State Department officials regarded the British reevaluation of Hungary's position as "very significant" news and as further evidence that the British were adopting a softer line on Hungary.[51] Often the American line was even "softer": a memorandum by a high-ranking Department of State official, C. W. Cannon, about Hungary's postwar territorial problems in the Bácska, Transylvania, Slovakia, and Ruthenia, seems to favor granting several of these disputed areas to Hungary, including Ruthenia because, stated the memorandum, the Hungarians may be in a better position and more willing to defend this territory against Soviet encroachments than the Czechs![52] These considerations, though pragmatic enough, disregarded military realities; we must, however, refrain from excessively criticizing the Hungarian statesmen who held on to similar illusions.

About this time an official of the Hungarian Foreign Ministry was sent to pick up a radio transmitter in Ankara.[53] On August 17, László Veres, the official of the ministry, and Dezső Ujváry, the Hungarian consul in Istanbul, notified Sterndale Bennett, the British

51. "The Hungarian Government has stood out as far as possible against German demands such as the sending of more troops to Russia, the shipment of wheat to Germany, and the enforcement of anti-Jewish legislation in Hungary. The Hungarians are under constant pressure, but they have persisted in their resistance as much as is compatible with Hungarian security (telegram from Winant to Department of State, Aug. 13, 1943, quoting a British Foreign Service official, NA Record Group 59, 864.00/1094).

52. Memorandum by C. W. Cannon, Aug. 16, 1943, NA Record Group 59, 864.00/1094.

53. It appears that two or more radio transmitters were picked up by Hungarian agents in Ankara on different occasions. László Veres brought a shortwave transmitter and receiver from Istanbul in September 1943, and this set was placed in the basement of the Budapest police headquarters (Kertesz, *Diplomacy in a Whirlpool*, p. 69). Alexander St.-Iványi, who took care of many escaped Allied prisoners-of-war, refers to a set brought over to him or his group by the representatives of the Polish General Bor and "left behind by the U.S. Legation" ("Our Man of Destiny in 1944," p. 33). One set was picked up by a former Hungarian military attaché in Ankara, Col. Otto Hátz (consular dispatch from Istanbul, June 16, 1944, NA Record Group 226, 79428). The dealings and double-dealings of Colonel Hátz kept the German Abwehr and Sicherheitshauptamt preoccupied. As Hátz's activities in Sofia and Ankara became suspicious to certain German authorities, Jagow reported: "Streng vertraulich kann mitgeteilt werden, dass Oberst Hátz seit langem eng und zuverlässig mit deutschen Militärstellen zusammen arbeitet, insbesondere aber einer der besten Mitarbeiter unserer Abwehr ist. Seine Deutschfreundlichkeit steht ausser Zweifel" (telegram of Dec. 4, 1943, NA Microcopy T-120, roll 94, 106854). The German minister in Sofia agreed: "Hatz ist an sich sehr deutschfreundlich und von diesem Gesichtspunkt aus zuverlässig. Er hat uns schon sehr viele wertvolle Dienste geleistet. An seiner Glaubwürdigkeit dürften keine Zweifel bestehen. Dagegen ist er ein Mann, um den sehr viele Frauengeschichten spielen und der sehr viel Geld verbraucht" (telegram to Berlin, Dec. 14, 1943, NA Microcopy T-120, roll 94, 106867-69). Further telegrams regarding

minister in Istanbul, of Hungary's willingness to capitulate.[54] It seems they were not expressly empowered to do so, but the Hungarian government did not renege on the offer. Under cover of darkness on September 9, a day after the Italian surrender, the Hungarian representative and the British ambassador, Sir Hugh Knatchbull-Hugessen (witnessed by György Páloczi-Horváth) signed the conditional armistice on board a vessel in the Sea of Marmara; [55] the condition was that Hungary would lay down her arms if and when Anglo-American troops reached her border. Further stipulations, as cited by Kállay, were (1) the Hungarian government should confirm the capitulation; (2) Hungary's surrender would be kept secret until it became effective; (3) Hungary must reduce her military cooperation with Germany, withdraw from the Soviet Union, and assist Allied aircraft flying in Hungarian air space; (4) Hungary must progressively diminish economic cooperation with Germany; (5) Hungary must resist any German attempt to occupy the country; (6) Hungary must eventually place resources at the disposal of the Allies; (7) an Allied air mission would be dropped in Hungary at the suitable moment to make the necessary advance preparations in connection with Hungary's surrender; (8) radio contact would be established between the Allies and the Hungarian government.[56]

Hátz's questionable activities are reproduced on roll 94, 106931–33. The German minister in Sofia, Beckerle, telegraphed to Berlin on Mar. 22, 1944: "Hatz hat die Sachlage so dargestellt, dass die Engländer bezw. Amerikaner mit einem Angebot zur Mitarbeit an ihn herantreten seien und dass nach den verschiedenen Zwischenverhandlungen dieses Angebot auf Weisung seiner vorgesetzten Stelle abgelehnt worden sei, um den Gegner über die Bündnistreue Ungarns nicht in Zweifel zu lassen . . ." (NA Microcopy T-120, roll 1025, 405263). The German Foreign Office now completely mistrusted Hátz (see note by Altenburg to Wagern, Apr. 24, 1944, NA Microcopy T-120, roll 1025, 405265; and Wagern to Schellenberg, June 29, 1944, NA Microcopy T-120, roll 1025, 405272–73), but the SS continued to support him because he had not resigned, as many Hungarian military attachés had done, when the Sztójay government took over (see letter by Schellenberg to Geiger, June, 1944, NA Microcopy T-120, roll 1025, 405268–69). The German Foreign Office noted with some satisfaction, in mid-November 1944, that Hátz had defected to the Russians by airplane. "Es besteht sich nunmehr, dass der sattsam bekannte Oberst Hatz, zuletzt Generalstabschef des 6. Ung. Korps, zu den Russen übergelaufen ist. Ich habe ständig von ihm gewarnt . . .", cabled Veesenmayer to Berlin on Nov. 17, 1944 (NA Microcopy T-120, roll 1025, 405274). The correspondence regarding Hátz was one set of documents Ribbentrop attempted to use to discredit Himmler and his operations.

54. Kállay, *Hungarian Premier*, p. 373; see also Ullein-Reviczky, *Guerre allemande*, p. 177.
55. Karsai, *A budai vártól*, pp. 332 ff.; Pintér, "A Kállay kormány 'hintapolitikája,'" p. 483; Maxime Mourin, "Les tentatives de décrochage de la Hongrie dans la deuxième guerre mondiale"; also Kovács, "Kiugrási kísérletek," pp. 99–100.
56. Kállay, *Hungarian Premier*, pp. 373–74.

It is difficult to say whether or not Hungary actually surrendered to the Anglo-Americans on September 9, 1943, as several authors have claimed.[57] While it is true that Hungary abided by some of the points listed in the conditional surrender, the condition initially set by the Hungarians themselves, that the Anglo-American forces reach the borders of Hungary, was never realized. As Professor Stephen Kertesz noted, the military situation precluded a Hungarian surrender to the Anglo-Americans.[58] Prime Minister Kállay himself writes of the "breakdown in the negotiations." The reason for this breakdown, explains Kállay in a passage using italics, was that "the English would not recognize the fact that *resistance in Hungary was an official operation undertaken with the knowledge* of the Regent and under the direction of the Premier." [59] It is doubtful that the Anglo-Americans themselves regarded the transaction of September 9 as anything more than "psychological warfare"; the Soviet government was bound to disapprove of a unilateral action. The Soviet Union was kept faithfully informed about the Hungarian peace feelers. On August 26 the British minister in Moscow told Molotov about the approach made by Veress who claimed to represent Kállay, Minister of Interior Keresztes-Fischer, and members of the Hungarian General Staff. Veress offered unconditional surrender. "Molotov appeared to be somewhat suspicious," reported Clark Kerr, the British minister, "and asked many questions as to who Veress represented and how the British government viewed the matter." [60] During the October 25 session of the Moscow meetings, the subject discussed was "Peace Feelers from Enemy States." According to the minutes of the meeting,

> Mr. Molotov said that in regard to Hungary there had been some disagreement with the British Government which he hoped to liquidate. He said that the Soviet Government was opposed to

57. Whether the surrender was conditional or unconditional is yet another moot point. Cordell Hull wrote that the "principle of surrender should be flexible. In some cases the most severe terms should be imposed. I had Germany and Japan in mind in this connection. In other cases we would have preliminary informal conversations that would result in substantial adjustments away from the terms of unconditional surrender. Here I had in mind Italy and the Axis satellite states, Rumania, Hungary, Bulgaria and Finland" (*Memoirs of Cordell Hull,* p. 1570).

58. "The truth is that in this period of the war, the military situation did not make possible the conclusion of an armistice treaty with Hungary" (*Diplomacy in a Whirlpool,* p. 211, n. 59).

59. Kállay, *Hungarian Premier,* p. 380.

60. American ambassador in the USSR to Department of State, Aug. 27, 1943. *FRUS 1943,* 1 : 497–98.

any negotiations except on the basis of unconditional surrender of the Hungarian Government, and that while they were most interested in interfering with the German war machine on any territory, whether Hungary or Rumania, he did not believe that half measures or negotiations were of any value.[61]

Anthony Eden thereupon agreed that the Soviet Union had a primary interest in the matter, since both these countries were fighting against the Soviet Union. The American secretary of state raised no objection.[62]

It appears likely, however, that, despite the shortsightedness of the Hungarian government, feelers had also been extended toward the Soviet Union. An unsigned German memorandum, elaborated just before the German invasion of Hungary in March 1944, refers to "information received" regarding contacts between Hungarian officials and Sokolin, a Soviet representative in Switzerland.[63] I have also found some references to negotiations between Hungarian officials and representatives of Tito in late 1943 or early 1944,[64] but the information contained in the German reports is so garbled that these cannot be accepted as evidence. The editors of the volume, *The Confidential Papers of Nicholas Horthy*, seem to feel that negotiations between Hungary and the Soviet Union did take place, through mediators (perhaps in Stockholm), in February 1944. "Official propaganda of the Hungarian government," the editors wrote, "tried to advance these negotiations with the Soviet Union when they represented the situation as if the Hungarian units were not fighting against the Soviet Army." [65] Finally, in Stockholm Ullein-Reviczky was instructed to establish contact with Madame Kollontai, the Soviet minister there. Ullein-Reviczky succeeded in doing so and reported—two weeks before the German invasion of Hungary—that Madame Kollontai's attitude had been encouraging: if the Hungarians should turn against the Germans, the Soviet Union would not interfere with Hungary's social system and would insure the

61. Minutes of Moscow meeting, Papers of Cordell Hull, Library of Congress, container 79.

62. Ibid.

63. "Geheime Reichssache" memorandum, about Feb. 1944, NA Microcopy T-120, roll 99, 109780; see also telegram from Manfred Killinger (in Bucharest) to Berlin, Nov. 2, 1943, NA Microcopy T-120, roll 94, 106791.

64. OSS reports dated Feb. 19 and Apr. 7, 1944, NA Record Group 226, OB 11365.

65. *The Confidential Papers of Nicholas Horthy*, p. 267; see also Macartney, *October Fifteenth*, 2 : 213 ff. Romanian officials were also in contact with Soviet officials, in Stockholm in particular.

country's territorial integrity.[66] This information comes from the records of the Hungarian intelligence bureau; but if the Hungarian intelligence was aware of this contact, so was the German intelligence, since their sources of information were identical.[67]

Some of the conditions set in the "armistice" agreement with Great Britain were fulfilled by the Hungarian government. In the first place (and after a delay of about one month, which indicates hesitations), the agreement was confirmed through Andor Wodianer and Sir Ronald Campbell, the Hungarian and British representatives in Lisbon.[68] However unsuccessfully, the Hungarian government continued its efforts to recall the Hungarian units in the East.[69] Hungarian antiaircraft artillery did not fire at Allied aircraft flying over Hungarian territory.[70] On the other hand, neither Budapest nor any part of Hungary was bombed by the American or Royal Air Forces until after the Germans occupied the country. An American pilot, who had to bail out over Hungarian territory, showed his captors the orders he had received forbidding him to drop bombs on Hungarian territory.[71] During the Moscow talks on October 19 and 20, 1943, Major General H. L. Ismay stated the Allies hoped to reach airfields near Rome, which would allow them to bomb Austria, Bavaria, Czechoslovakia, and Romania; significantly, he made no mention of Hungary.[72]

The measures undertaken and carried out by the Hungarian government were not energetic or effective enough to satisfy the Allied powers. On the other hand, they were definitely subversive in the eyes of the National Socialist leaders. The occupation of Hungary was now imminent.

66. Csatári, *Forgószélben*, p. 345.

67. Dr. Elek Karsai to author.

68. Kertesz, *Diplomacy in a Whirlpool*, pp. 68–69; Kovács, "Kiugrási kisérletek," p. 103; Juhász, *Magyarország külpolitikája*, p. 300.

69. "Following a very subtle maneuver by furloughs and evacuations due to health conditions, the Hungarian army succeeded in recuperating about 10,000 men since the summer of 1943" (OSS reports dated Feb. 29 and Apr. 10, 1944, NA Record Group 226, OB 11553).

70. German requests for garrisoning western Hungary with flying units were refused, but these were made as early as February 1943. József Kun, "Magyarország német katonai megszállásának előkészítése és lefolyása, 1943 szeptember–1944 március" [The preparation and execution of Hungary's military occupation by Germany, September–March 1944], p. 44.

71. Kállay, *Hungarian Premier*, p. 390.

72. Papers of Cordell Hull, Library of Congress, container 79: "Most Secret Protocol."

9. The German Occupation

On September 3, 1943, the Badoglio government in Italy signed an armistice with the Allies (which became effective on September 8), and henceforth the National Socialist leaders used the name Badoglio as a byword for treason. The Italian action was warning enough, and various measures were adopted to prevent similar "treachery" on the part of Germany's remaining allies. That same month Hitler ordered the elaboration of a plan for the occupation of Hungary and Romania.[1] While the plans regarding Romania never reached a final stage, mainly because of Hitler's absolute confidence in Antonescu, those regarding Hungary were brought up to date several times and finally carried out.

The Italian surrender disconcerted the Kállay government. We had seen that Kállay had been the very person, back in April 1943, to hint to Mussolini that diplomatic steps ought to be taken to end the war and that Hungary would follow Italy's lead along such a path. Mussolini had brushed Kállay's suggestion aside. While Mussolini was no longer Italy's Duce in the summer of 1943, the Hungarian government could nevertheless hope to remain advised of any diplomatic steps contemplated or taken by the Italian government. In fact, Filippo Anfuso, the Italian minister in Budapest, and the Italian Foreign Ministry reached an agreement on July 25, 1943, that Anfuso and the Hungarian government would be notified in case of an Italian surrender.[2] On July 31 the American Consul General in Istanbul reported that he had it on "good authority" that on his visit to Turkey the new Italian Foreign Minister had spoken to János Vörnle, the Hungarian Minister in Ankara. The Italian Minister asked Vörnle "if his government wanted him to include Hungary in

1. On Sept. 23, 1943, Goebbels noted in his diary: "as regards the possibilities of treachery by other satellite states, Horthy would like to desert us, but the Führer has already taken the necessary precautions against this . . ." (*Goebbels Diaries*, p. 480). The German intentions could be guessed. In an article which appeared in the Sept. 18 issue of the *Daily Telegraph*, an expert on central European affairs figured that the occupation of Hungary by German troops was "almost inevitable" (quoted in dispatch from London to Department of State, Sept. 22, 1943, NA Record Group 59, 864.00/1106). While it is not known on what day Hitler gave out the instructions, the plan for "Operation Margarethe"—the occupation of Hungary—was drafted by the army General Staff (Wehrmachtführungsstab) on Sept. 30. (*KTB, OKW*, 4 : 198).

2. Anfuso, *Du Palais de Venise*, p. 228.

the [expected] peace negotiations."[3] Whether or not Vörnle relayed the question to Budapest, it seems the Italian surrender caught the Hungarian government by surprise. Quick thinking and quick action would have been necessary, but the Hungarian government seemed quite unable to reach a decision that would have reversed the policy of compliance with German demands it had been pursuing for almost two and a half years.[4] Two days after the proclamation of the Italian surrender it was perhaps too late already; the German forces had repressed most manifestations of resistance in central and northern Italy and were ready to cope with other eventualities. Jagow reported on September 9 that some prominent elder politicians, such as Count Móricz Eszterházy, would have liked to provoke a German occupation of Hungary under some pretext or other and thereby earn the good will of the Allies.[5] According to a later (December 17, 1943) report of the Office of Strategic Services, Hungarian "propagandists" in Switzerland were asking "if the Allies really wish them to capitulate and be occupied; if so, when they should capitulate. They further ask what assurance there is that they would be rewarded for suffering the nightmare of German occupation and revenge."[6] In fact, however, the Hungarian government did nothing beyond continuing the efforts already begun to arrive at a conditional armistice with the Anglo-American powers. It was merely a coincidence that an armistice of this sort was signed by British and Hungarian representatives in Turkey on September 9, the day after the Italian armistice was announced.

3. *FRUS: The Conferences at Washington and Quebec, 1943* (Washington: G.P.O., 1970), p. 524.

4. Kállay's comment: "Immediately after Italy's surrender I convened a ministerial council and announced that all agreements which bound us to the Italo-German Axis had, by Italy's act [of surrender] become automatically non-operative. Hungary had recovered her moral freedom, and her policy would now be determined exclusively by her own needs and decisions." But the ministers did not think the time was ripe for a breakaway from the German alliance (*Hungarian Premier*, p. 206). These statements seem to be contradicted by Stephen Kertesz: "The political division of the Hungarian Foreign Ministry, having received news of the Italian armistice in the absence of the prime minister and the foreign minister, immediately set about drafting a government announcement. This stated that the Tripartite Pact ceased to be valid after the collapse of Italy and Hungary had regained her liberty of action. But Kállay and Ghyczy did not see their way clear to accept this course, for they feared German reprisals" (*Diplomacy in a Whirlpool*, p. 66).

5. Telegram from Jagow to Berlin, Sept. 9, 1943, NA Microcopy T-120, roll 94, 106576.

6. Records of the OSS, NA Record Group 226, Hungary, 53552.

The Hungarian attitude toward the two Italies became under-
standably ambiguous. The Hungarian minister in Rome, Zoltán
Máriássy, was instructed to remain there, presumably to await the
arrival of the Allies.[7] While Filippo Anfuso was appointed Italian
ambassador to Berlin, the first counselor of the legation, Baron Carlo
de Ferraris, was recognized by the Hungarian government as Italy's
true representative in Budapest. On September 27 the German
ambassador to the Fascist Republic, Rudolf Rahn, was instructed to
inform the recently liberated Duce that Hungary was the only country not to recognize the new Italian (Fascist Republican) government,
but the Reich government had already decided to take up the matter
with the Hungarian government.[8] Kállay, apparently anxious to
demonstrate his objectivity regarding the Germans and not particularly concerned with facts and precision, notes in his memoirs that
this was the first occasion during his regime that Germany tried to
intervene in Hungarian foreign policy.[9] The Hungarian government
responded to the German intervention by informing Ribbentrop:
"We have taken note from your telegram of the fact communicated
by you that Mussolini has founded the North Italian Fascist Republic. We take this occasion to inform you that we always possessed
in Mussolini a true friend of the Hungarian cause"; the new representative of the Fascist Republic, Raffaele Casertano, was received
and accredited by the Hungarian government, along with the royalist
representative, Baron de Ferraris.[10] But no Hungarian diplomat was
sent to represent Hungary at Salo, the seat of the new Fascist Republican government. Thus two Italian legations functioned in Budapest
side by side. The Italian Cultural Institute was left in the hands of
its royalist administrators despite Fascist attempts to have them ex-
pelled.[11] Only when the German troops occupied Hungary on March
19, 1944, did the royalist Italian representatives cease to exercise
diplomatic functions.[12] In fact, these representatives were arrested by
the Gestapo on the very first day, and the papers of their legation
were scattered; I have found some among the extant records of the

7. Dispatch from Johnson (in Stockholm) to Department of State, Oct. 1943, NA
Record Group 59, 864.00.
8. Telegram from Hilger to Rahn, NA Microcopy T-120, roll 94, 106650.
9. Kállay, *Hungarian Premier*, p. 215.
10. Ibid., pp. 216–17, 220.
11. NA Microcopy T-821, *passim*.
12. Kertesz, *Diplomacy in a Whirlpool*, p. 67; also Anfuso, *Du Palais de Venise*,
p. 276.

German SS (NA Microcopy T-175) and others among the Italian records eventually captured by the Allies at "Aktensammelstelle Süd," near Munich.[13]

There is, among the German documents which fell into Allied hands after the war, a flood of reports on Hungary in the fall of 1943, all unfavorable from a National Socialist point of view. The Hungarian attitude toward the Italian Fascist Republic was but one grievance of German or pro-Nazi Hungarian observers. Generally speaking, these observers agreed with SS officer Herrmann that "it can be said with some certainty that Hungary will go the same way as Italy in the very near future." [14] This same SS officer recommended Archduke Albrecht as Hungary's next premier, especially since the archduke had declared that he refused to deal with any German agency but the SS.[15] Another SS officer, Kienast, who reported regularly on Hungary, described the recent attempts of the Kállay government to dissociate Hungary from the war. Kállay's efforts, wrote Kienast, to make speeches emphasizing his loyalty to the Axis "have a ludicrous effect and obviously find no believers in the Reich." [16] Kienast also mentioned the reopening of the proceedings against the officers responsible for the mass shootings at Ujvidék (Novi Sad) and noted that this was the first response to the decision the Allies had taken at Moscow, that war criminals would be tried and condemned at the place of their crimes.[17] Furthermore, reported Kienast, Horthy was becoming senile; he accepted everything he was told uncritically, so that he was even less reliable than formerly. Witness the case of Béla Jurcsek: Horthy had accused Jurcsek, well known for his National Socialist sympathies, of being an agrarian reformer! [18] One of

13. In its attitude toward the Italian royalist representatives, the Hungarian government managed to stay one step ahead of the Romanian. The Italian minister to Bucharest, Bova Scoppa, was allowed to remain in Romania as the representative of royalist Italy, but Mussolini's Republican-Fascist regime was recognized as early as September 25 (Hillgruber, *Hitler, König Carol und Marschall Antonescu*, p. 173).

14. Report dated Sept. 24, 1943, NA Microcopy T-175, roll 65, 2581453.

15. Other government (German) agencies, such as the Foreign Office, were reluctant to deal with the archduke lest they antagonize the Hungarian government.

16. Kienast to Gottlob Berger, Dec. 11, 1943 (geheime Kommandosache), NA Microcopy T-120, roll 350, 262332 ff. A further report by Kienast to Himmler, date Jan. 3, 1944, complains of the "privileges" granted Jews, especially Zionists, in Hungary (NA Microcopy T-175, roll 59, 2574568).

17. Kienast to Gottlob Berger, Dec. 11, 1943, NA Microcopy T-120, roll 350, 262332 ff.

18. Ibid. Incidentally, Horthy became 75 on June 15, 1943. Hitler sent Horthy a yacht as a birthday gift. Hitler's letter of congratulations to Horthy is reproduced on

the informers of the German government, the SS in particular, was Gen. Jenő Ruszkay, a retired Hungarian officer of German descent. According to Ruszkay, Hungary was a belligerent state in name only; in fact she was neutral and anglophile. Horthy was a plaything of the existing circumstances: he had solved neither the Jewish nor the agrarian problem.[19] Goebbels, too, received reports about developments in Hungary, and he found these anything but comforting. "Influential circles in Hungary are at work for a direct break with us. The Regent is trying to create the impression that he is neutral about these efforts. That is, however, in no wise the case. I even regard him as the mainspring of this development. . . ."[20]

I found most of these charges summarized in a long memorandum, classified as *geheime Reichssache,* unsigned and undated, but written "ten months after the April visit of Horthy"—that is, in February 1944. This memorandum noted that Kállay did not believe in the possibility of a German victory, that he felt the Anglo-Americans had only the Soviet Union to fear, and that he was still intent on negotiating with the enemy. Half a dozen of the Hungarian "secret" negotiators were listed by name, and there was even a reference to negotiations with Soviet agents in Switzerland.[21] Another report, prepared by Gerhard Feine [22] of the German Foreign Office in September 1943, was an exception in the sense that it admitted there was no positive proof of Hungarian dealings with the Allies. On the other hand, noted Feine, there were Hungarian officials who believed in a German victory and in the alliance with Germany; and he even named two, Gen. Lajos Csatay and Gen. Ferenc Szombathelyi: "Ambassador Jagow and his military attaché evaluate Csatay as a thoroughly reliable person and an earnest advocate of our common cause who also possesses the courage to fight for his convictions. In the Chief of the General Staff Szombathelyi he has an assistant who is prepared to follow the same way." [23] It is ironic, perhaps, that soon after the German troops marched into Hungary Szombathelyi was forced

NA Microcopy T-120, roll 94, 106383–86. Horthy's two letters of thanks, dated June 18 and Oct. 15, 1943, are reprinted in *The Confidential Papers of Nicholas Horthy,* pp. 258–60. The letter of Oct. 15 was also an occasion for Horthy to reassure Hitler on the score of Hungarian loyalty.

19. Summary by Venn of a report by Ruszkay, fall of 1943, NA Microcopy T-175, roll 119, 2644772.

20. *Goebbels Diaries,* p. 507.

21. NA Microcopy T-120, roll 99, 109769–82.

22. Formerly an official of the German legation in Belgrade.

23. Memorandum by Feine, Sept. 17, 1943, NA Microcopy T-120, roll 94, 106623. An SS officer's estimate of Csatay, at the time of his appointment, reads as follows:

to leave his post and go into hiding, while Csatay was only reluctantly tolerated by the German authorities who were still not completely in command of the situation.

The new German military attaché in Budapest, Gen. Hans von Greiffenberg, reported on an audience granted him by Horthy on October 15, 1943. The regent read from notes. He mentioned the fear of air raids in Budapest, Hungary's only large city. He declared it was Churchill's fault there could be no peace between England and Germany. He remarked that the reports of a number of German personalities had given a false picture of conditions in Hungary. He concluded his observations, according to Greiffenberg, by banging on the table: "I will never sway from the correct path by even a single step," he declared. "The honor of Hungary has never suffered a blemish in her thousand years of history, and I know how to preserve her honor. I can guarantee you that the country is solidly in my hands, and will remain solidly in my hands." [24] The regent did not mean to fool Greiffenberg or the Germans: he truly believed, it seems, that honor would not allow him or Hungary to sway from the alliance with Germany, no matter how politic or desirable such a course might be. He also truly believed that his leadership rested on the general support of the Hungarian people. The events of October 15, 1944, exactly a year later, were to give incontrovertible evidence regarding the weakness of the support on which Horthy's rule rested; and perhaps only Horthy was surprised at this discovery. As for Hitler, he too seemed to be convinced of Horthy's popularity but not of his determination to maintain what he assumed to be Hungary's honor.

The most significant of the many reports on Hungary, if only because of their author, were the ones compiled by Edmund Veesenmayer, the future "plenipotentiary" of the Reich in Hungary. Veesenmayer had visited Hungary once before, in the spring of 1943, and had submitted a lengthy report of his observations at that time.[25] In the fall he was sent once again on a mission to Hungary. He was

---

"Politisch hat er sich nicht hervorgetan, ist ausgesprochener Truppenführer, steht aber den rechtseingestellten Militärs Nahe, gilt als absolut deutschfreundlich und als ausgesprochen antisemitisch" (report by Kienast, June 10, 1943, NA Microcopy T-175, roll 119, 2645177-79).

24. Telegram from Greiffenberg to Berlin, Oct. 15, 1943, NA Microcopy T-120, roll 94, 106730-31.

25. This report, dated Apr. 30, 1943, is reproduced on NA Microcopy T-175, roll 65, 2581460-73; see also Elek Karsai, "Edmund Veesenmayer's Reports to Hitler on Hungary in 1943."

instructed by Ribbentrop to "examine on location the practical possibilities of exercising German influence on the internal political
developments in Hungary."[26] Veesenmayer came to Budapest in
November 1943. His was clearly a biased report full of contempt for
the Hungarians. The very national anthem of the Hungarians, stated
Veesenmayer, was composed by a German (Ferenc Erkel). The
bridges that were the pride of Budapest had been built by German
engineers.[27] The greatest Hungarian painter was of Bavarian stock
(probably Mihály Munkácsy was meant). The Hungarians, continued
Veesenmayer, have no national force: their country had seldom seen
independence since 1526, the year of the battle of Mohács. Then
Veesenmayer's report turned to more practical considerations. Horthy, he stated must be turned into a soldier of the Führer. History
may repeat itself: Hungary may become another Italy, Horthy another Mussolini, Count Bethlen a Badoglio. Hence a reliable ministry should replace the one in power. Horthy, whom Veesenmayer
still regarded favorably from a National Socialist point of view,
would want to remain at the head of the state, if only to preserve his
dynasty, and would therefore accept any prime minister imposed on
him, even Gen. Jenő Ruszkay or Béla Imrédy.[28] The Hungarian
army, thought Veesenmayer, was reliable; no Hungarian soldier
would turn his weapon against a German. Hence, there still were
elements in Hungary on whom Germany could count. Veesenmayer's
recommendations, set forth in eight points, were based on these and
similar half-true observations, and by and large would be adopted by
the National Socialist leadership at the crucial moment in March
1944.[29] The changes necessary in Hungary—and this was the gist of
Veesenmayer's report—could be carried out only by outside intervention, that is, with the assistance of the German military.

   The Hungarian demarches concerning the recall of Hungarian
troops in Russia were anything but reassuring. Chief of the General
Staff Szombathelyi made three visits within a few months to Hitler's

26. Note by Hencke to Sonnleithner, Sept. 17, 1943, NA Microcopy T-120, roll 94,
106620.

27. Budapest's most beautiful and oldest bridge, the Lánchíd (Chainbridge), was
built by the Scottish engineer Adam Clark.

28. Recently there appeared a monograph on this key personality: Péter Sipos,
Imrédy Béla és a Magyar Megujulás Pártja [Béla Imrédy and the Hungarian Renaissance party].

29. Report from Veesenmayer to Steengracht (geheime Reichssache), NA Microcopy
T-120, roll 94, 106873–910. Substantial excerpts from this report are printed in Karsai,
A bduai vártól, pp. 346–62.

headquarters at the Wolfsschanze, in September and November 1943 and again in January 1944.[30] Each time Szombathelyi was instructed to request the return of the Hungarian units remaining on the eastern front, about nine light divisions engaged in antipartisan operations, under the pretext that these units were not equipped to fight regulars of the Red Army while unable to avoid such encounters at times, and also because some of the Hungarian units were placed far to the north and had not been allowed to retreat toward Hungarian territory. Gen. Kurt Zeitzler, the chief of the General Staff (1942–44), had not wanted to receive Szombathelyi the third time, but Hitler agreed to see him in order to "tell him off" (*anzupfeifen*).[31] During this last visit Szombathelyi also met with Wilhelm Keitel and told him Hungary intended to defend the line of the Carpathians with Hungarian units alone. Marshal Keitel found this idea rather ludicrous, as it was inconceivable that the German lines should have to withdraw so far west![32] Nevertheless Horthy repeated the same argument in a letter to Hitler on February 12, 1944. In the preamble Horthy stated that it was only natural for a country, whether Germany or Hungary, to prefer to fight wars outside its own borders, one implication of this statement being that Germany might prefer to fight the war on Hungarian territory. Hungary, of course, wanted to avoid such a course:

> The ridge of the Carpathians means an obstacle to the Russian army hard to overcome, and the Hungarian army will have it easier to hold this line than hold up a thrust by greatly superior arms and war material in the plain country. It is my firm conviction that we shall be able to hold this front alone, without taking recourse to German aid, in which case our centralized war industry and the supply lines important for both of us would perhaps not become as exposed to air-raids.[33]

30. For the September visit, see Kaltenbrunner to Hewel, Sept. 17, 1943, NA Microcopy T-120, roll 94, 106619; and telegram from Colonel Pappenheim to Berlin, Sept. 21, 1943, also roll 94, 106633. With regard to the visit in January, see Keitel's telegram to Szombathelyi, Jan. 17, 1944: "Kräfte zur Verfügung. Zu meinem Bedauern kann daher ihrem Wünsch nach Verlegung des Ung. Röm. 8 Korps nach Süden noch nicht entsprochen werden" (NA Microcopy T-77, roll 883, 5632136, 5632160). At the same time, however, the German High Command found sufficient forces to undertake Operation Margarethe.

31. Memorandum by Grote for Ribbentrop, Jan. 22, 1944, NA Microcopy T-120, roll 99, 109723.

32. Nagy, *Végzetes esztendők*, p. 186.

33. *Confidential Papers of Nicholas Horthy*, p. 268.

Horthy concluded his letter with a request for the return of the Hungarian troops in Russia. This argument was repeated a third time in a memorandum Szombathelyi elaborated for Keitel's benefit on February 14.[34] Gen. Géza Lakatos, the actual commander of the Hungarian forces on Soviet territory, also received instructions to visit Hitler's headquarters in order to endeavor to secure permission for the withdrawal of Hungarian troops. Lakatos met Hitler on March 12, 1944, at which time the National Socialist leaders had already set the date for the occupation of Hungary. When Lakatos mentioned the Hungarian intention to defend the Carpathians, he reports, Hitler began to shout in a fit of fury: "And you want to defend the Carpathians with your own troops; but the Russians are always able to detect the weakest sections of the front and they never fail to attack precisely there with their main forces!" [35]

The Hungarian government had also resorted to a somewhat desperate effort to recall directly some of its troops from the eastern front despite a chain-of-command agreement with Germany. The Hungarian order for retreat "presupposed" German agreement. On November 12, 1943, Szombathelyi had telegraphed to Keitel: "In the hope that my repeated requests in this regard will find understanding there, I have already transmitted the order [for the withdrawal of the Eighteenth and Nineteenth light divisions] to the commander of the Hungarian occupation troops." [36] Szombathelyi, however, allowed himself to be persuaded to retract his order: the same day, on November 12, the German military attaché could report that Szombathelyi, having "modified" his order, agreed that the "Hungarian movements would take place only by agreement of both German groups." [37] According to Kállay, the Germans had responded by threatening the Hungarian commanders with use of "any means" to prevent a Hungarian withdrawal.[38] Although a Hungarian withdrawal was pre-

34. Nagy, *Végzetes estendők*, p. 187.

35. Quoted from memory by Lakatos, June 2, 1961, Hungarian National Archives, notes of General Lakatos.

36. NA Microcopy T-77, roll 883, 5632204. According to the Hungarian military historian József Kun, the order for the withdrawal of the eighteenth and nineteenth light divisions came from the local commander, that is, General Lakatos, whereas the request from the Hungarian General Staff for German agreement to the withdrawal arrived only later. Kun does not claim, however, that Lakatos had not requested or received Szombathelyi's permission for issuing the withdrawal order in the first place ("Magyarország német katonai megszállásának előkészítése és lefolyása," p. 44).

37. Telegram from Greiffenberg to Abwehr I, Nov. 12, 1943, NA Microcopy T-77, roll 883, 5632206–7.

38. On Mar. 1, 1944, Kállay wrote to Ullein-Reviczky, then Hungarian minister in Stockholm: ". . . le gouvernement hongrois persiste dans sa volonté de ramener nos

vented, the German commanders were not entirely satisfied, because it seemed to them the Hungarian logistical commands were not supplying their own troops adequately, while the troops themselves often mentioned their inadequate supplies as an excuse for not getting involved in serious fighting.[39] Whatever the case may have been, the Hungarian divisions had to remain near the front, and Horthy's letter to Hitler remained unanswered, at least until March 15.

Another source of disagreement between German and Hungarian military authorities was the new Hungarian policy toward partisans. An order issued by General Lakatos on October 23, 1943, was wholly at variance with the policy of the Wehrmacht and the Waffen SS which qualified partisans as "bandits" not entitled to treatment as prisoners of war if captured. Lakatos's order mentioned "chivalry" and "humanity," terms which SS officers found offensive, either because they saw therein a criticism of National Socialist methods or because they felt this was simply a Hungarian effort to create an alibi in the eyes of the Allies. The order issued by Lakatos read, in part:

> The Hungarian spirit of chivalry and the type of just warfare inherited from our forefathers does not tolerate the commission of cruelties or inhumanities toward our vanquished enemies; and therefore we must pay particular attention that in fighting and defeating the enemy we do not commit unnecessary murders, and we must especially avoid the destruction of entire villages as a means of reprisal.[40]

Furthermore, stated the order, the Hungarian soldier must differentiate between partisans and innocent civilians, as otherwise he might only encourage the civilians to join the partisans. Reprisals were to be carried out only by special German units (that is, the SD!).[41]

soldats dans le pays. Une fois des ordres furent déjà depêchés en ce sens, mais les Allemands ripostèrent par un contre-ordre et se déclarèrent prêts à empêcher le retour des nôtres par n'importe quel moyen" (Ullein-Reviczky, *Guerre allemande*, p. 149).

39. On Dec. 15, 1943, Greiffenberg, the German military attaché in Budapest, submitted a report on the Hungarian army which reads in part as follows: "Die Sicherungsdivisionen klagen in erster Linie über ihre geringen Gefechtsstärken. Abhilfe ist trotz unserer Bemühungen und des Drangens des ungarischen A.O.K. bisher in ausreichenden Masse nicht erfolgt. Die von ungarischer Seite angegebenen Transportgründe sind nicht stichhaltig. . . . Insgesamt lässt sich sagen dass sowohl die Besatzungstruppe als auch die Heimat nur mit halbem Herzen beim Einsatz im Ostraum ist" (NA Microcopy T-77, roll 883, 5632169–70).

40. Translation (German) enclosed with a report from Schellenberg to Wagner (German Foreign Office), Jan. 17, 1944, NA Microcopy T-120, roll 1096, 452942–48.

41. Ibid.

About the turn of the year, the pendulum policy of the Kállay government seemed to take a swing to the right. Kállay himself appears to have been overwhelmed by a certain feeling of hopelessness due to the slowness of the Anglo-American advance up the boot of Italy and the rapidity of the Soviet advance. Kállay made several strongly pro-German speeches, and a reconciliation between him and Béla Imrédy, the leader of one of Hungary's National Socialist factions, was effected. On the German side, Jagow received instructions to renew social relations with Kállay.[42] Yet despite this apparent resignation of the Hungarian government to its alliance with Germany, preparations for Operation Margarethe continued on the German side.

In fact, it did not appear to the German authorities that Kállay's attitude had basically changed. A somewhat mystifying SS report, on the margins of which the initials of Himmler appear, described the attitude of Kállay in March 1944 as one of outright sabotage. According to this report, on March 7 General Szombathelyi called on Colonel Czlenner, chief of the Transportation Division of the Hungarian General Staff, and told him Kállay wished that German military transports across Hungary be sabotaged. Colonel Czlenner indignantly refused, referring to the military significance of the forty daily German transports in the southern sector of the eastern front and pointing out that the supplying of the German troops in the southern sector was also in the interest of Hungary. Thereupon Szombathelyi declared that he too rejected Kállay's proposal. Nevertheless, Colonel Czlenner had the impression that the chief of the General Staff would have been quite willing, on his part, to sabotage the German transports. The colonel reported the incident to Gen. Jenő Ruszkay that very day, although he must have known Ruszkay sent reports regularly, as on this occasion, to the German Army High Command or to Heinrich Himmler. I have found no corroboration of this interesting document elsewhere, not even in Kállay's memoirs. It might be noted, incidentally, that Kállay does not appear to have known, as early as March 7, of the German preparations for Operation Margarethe; hence, this sabotage plan—if indeed there was such a plan—could not have been designed to protect Hungary from such a German invasion.

The plans for Operation Margarethe had undergone several re-

---

42. Veesenmayer felt that his advice had been disregarded and complained bitterly; see letter from Kienast to Himmler, Feb. 5, 1944, NA Microcopy T-175, roll 59, 1574542-43.

visions. The units initially earmarked for the operation had to be sent to the front to cope with emergencies. Hitler had proposed to use Slovak, Croatian, and Romanian troops along with the German units. During Antonescu's visit to Hitler on February 26, 1944, Hitler hinted at Romanian cooperation in case of Hungarian "betrayal." [43] Antonescu asked for compensation in terms of Transylvanian territory, but Hitler would not agree, because he was intent on securing the cooperation, not the antagonism, of the Hungarian people. On March 7 the Red Army was only about a hundred miles from the borders of Hungary: Hitler felt he could delay no longer. During a conference at his headquarters on that day, it was decided that Operation Margarethe would begin on March 19,[44] a Sunday, and that assistance from Germany's satellites would be dispensed with. According to the Nuremberg trial proceedings, it was Ernst Kaltenbrunner, the chief of the Gestapo, who persuaded Hitler to be more "moderate" and not to allow the intervention of Romanian and Slovak units.[45] While Hitler continued to use the threat of an occupation by Hungary's neighbors during Horthy's visit on March 18, it is clear that this part of the project did not get beyond the planning stage, and later reports of a Romanian division on Hungarian soil were unfounded.

One of the main tasks of the operation was to insure that Hungarian economic activities continued unhampered—an aim clearly incompatible with an attack by the satellite countries. Keitel's special order of March 11 reads: "Jeglicher Eingriff der Truppe in das Wirtschaftsleben ist strengstens verboten"—it is strictly forbidden for troops to interfere with the economic life: "The chief administrative task of the German commands in Hungary is the securing of the continuation of work in the entire agriculture, the oil industry and the most important armaments factories and pertinent plants working in the German interest." [46]

Another important task, added Keitel, was the immediate arrest and deportation of former Anglo-American, French, Polish, and Yugoslav prisoners of war who had found refuge in Hungary.[47] The

43. Karsai, *A budai vártól,* p. 406.

44. Ibid., p. 406.

45. *Trial of the Major War Criminals,* 11 : 230, and 18 : 60–61.

46. Besondere Anordnungen Nr. 1 zum Stichwort "Margarethe," Mar. 11, 1944, NA Microcopy T-77, roll 790, 5519580–82. This order was repeated by Keitel on Mar. 19 (NA Microcopy T-120, roll 99, 109834–35).

47. Same order. Kállay estimates the number of Anglo-American and French POWs who had escaped to Hungary at 2,000 (*Hungarian Premier,* p. 336). About 800 French

first enclosure to this order indicates that the German Army High Command counted on continued Hungarian support against the Soviet Union. Nevertheless, stated the enclosure, all Hungarian soldiers must be disarmed and restricted to their barracks: "Any Hungarian resistance against the command operations of the German Army must be ruthlessly broken up by the immediate use of all weapons. The leaders of the resisting units must be shot during the combat, while the other soldiers are to be taken prisoners." [48]

The second enclosure to the order provided a summary of Hungarian history, especially after 1918; it bears no classification mark; hence, we may assume it was meant for the German enlisted man to read or hear. It explained that Hungary had regained considerable territories recently, thanks to Germany; the Hungarians had not shown gratitude, however, but asked for more. This spirit of ingratitude had already manifested itself earlier in Hungarian history when the Hungarians forgot to thank Prince Eugen of Savoy who was alone responsible for having liberated them from the Turks.[49] This historical survey did not fail to mention the threat posed by the largely unhampered activities of the Jews in Hungary.[50]

A Führer directive was issued under the top-secret markings "Chefsache" and "geheime Kommandosache" the following day. This directive explained the reasons for the contemplated operation: Kállay's negotiations with the Allies, the dominating influence of the Jews and of the "reactionary" or *jüdisch-versippte* and corrupt elements within the Hungarian aristocracy, and even the participation in the general betrayal of some high-ranking Hungarian officers. The betrayal was supposed to have been carried out the previous year simultaneously with the Italian betrayal, but the quick and energetic countermeasures of the German armed forces in Italy had

---

prisoners-of-war escaped to Hungary and some of them collaborated in writing a grateful testimonial, *Refuge en Hongrie, 1941–1945*. A German report, dated Nov. 12, 1943, states that over 200 Englishmen were allowed to move about freely in Hungary (NA Microcopy T-77, roll 883, 5632495–96). St.-Iványi writes that it was he and well-known members of the Hungarian aristocracy, such as Count Mihály Andrássy, Count József Károlyi, and Count Antal Sigray, who took care of the Allied citizens and escaped prisoners-of-war ("Our Man of Destiny in 1944," pp. 32–33). One of these escaped prisoners, Jerome Caminada, published an interesting book which indicates, among other things, that the fate of people like himself was not invariably good in Hungary (*My Purpose Holds*).

48. Enclosure no. 1 to order of Mar. 11, 1944, NA Microcopy T-77, roll 790, 5519583. This enclosure is *not* printed literally in *KTB, OKW*, vol. 4, pt. 1, which contains detailed information regarding Operation Margarethe.

49. Enclosure no. 2 to order of Mar. 11, 1944, NA Microcopy T-77, roll 790, 5519585.

50. Ibid.

frightened the traitors in Hungary.[51] The directive then proceeded to state that the German troops would march into Hungary and set up a truly national Hungarian government which would undertake to persuade every element within the country to contribute to the common cause (*gemeinsame Sache*). Finally, the directive specified the tactics of the operation: the occupation of Hungary up to the Tisza River was to be carried out by four groups of forces marching concentrically toward Budapest.[52] A special operation bearing the code name Trojan Horse was also discussed: troops would be sent to the Budapest area by way of the Danube and by train, ostensibly as German units on their way to the eastern front. Together with some airborne battalions of the Brandenburg Division, which would be landed at one of the Budapest airports, these troops would occupy strategic positions in Budapest and insure the cooperation of the Hungarian government.[53] A final paragraph in the directive noted that the concentration of troops to the south and southwest of Hungary was to be explained as preparations for an antipartisan operation in Croatia, whereas the concentration in the north and northwest must be explained as maneuvers in preparation for a spring offensive on the eastern front.[54]

A further directive issued by Keitel, on March 13, makes it clear that the German High Command expected some resistance. This directive stated that Hungarian enlisted men who resisted were to be interned and deported to Germany for labor service, whereas Hungarian volunteers would be accepted into the German army as *hilfswillige* (*Hiwis*)—assistants. With regard to Hungarian officers who resisted, "if, despite the basic order, these should fall alive into our hands, they must be disarmed, placed under strict surveillance and sent as soon as possible . . . to the Reich where they will be placed in special camps [concentration camps]." [55]

51. Führer directive, Mar. 12, 1944, NA Microcopy T-77, roll 791, 5519591. Unless we have overlooked significant evidence, it would seem that the above accusations are mostly fantasy.

52. On March 25, Gen. Walter Warlimont issued an order placing the area east of the Tisza under German control—and under the command of General Both (NA Microcopy T-77, roll 791, 5519623). General Löhr was to be in charge of the entire occupation operation (Führer directive, Mar. 12, 1944, NA Microcopy T-77, roll 791, 5519592–93).

53. This group to be commanded by General Pfuhlstein.

54. NA Microcopy T-77, roll 791, 5519595.

55. Draft of OKW directive (marked "Chefsache" and "geheime Kommandosache"), Mar. 13, 1944, NA Microcopy T-77, roll 790, 5119572–74. This directive is not printed literally or summarized in detail in *KTB, OKW*.

The Hungarian secret service does not seem to have been particularly well informed about the German plans. Some Hungarian agents in Austria reported a concentration of German troops in the area of Wiener-Neustadt and Eisenstadt, forty to fifty troop transports detraining there each day since early in March. Some German officers had been overheard to say the troops were destined for an occupation of Hungary. On March 13 the Hungarian assistant chief of staff asked the German air attaché, Gen. Kuno Heribert Fütterer (in the absence of the army attaché), about the meaning of the concentration of troops. Fütterer was astonished (perhaps genuinely), cabled to Berlin, and was informed the German troops were preparing for maneuvers. The Hungarian officer seemed prepared to apologize, indicating the cabinet was somewhat nervous because neither Horthy nor Szombathelyi had received replies to their letters. Jenő Ghyczy, the minister of foreign affairs, repeated to Jagow that the incident was harmless and that the Hungarian authorities were not really worried; in fact, "the Hungarian government knows there is not the slightest possibility that the rumor might be true." [56] Kállay and other members of the Hungarian government nevertheless felt the Germans were massing in order to intimidate Hungary. When the German military authorities requested permission for 100,000 troops to cross Hungary, the Hungarian government refused; [57] but obviously this refusal had no effect on the success of the Trojan Horse operation. On March 17 the railroad tracks twenty-five kilometers north of Ujvidék (Novi Sad) were blown up; [58] hence, it is clear that someone, perhaps Hungarian or Serb partisans, knew about the German plans. But this incident was to hamper German operations very slightly.

A further conference regarding Operation Margarethe, with the participation of Hitler, Himmler, and Ribbentrop, was held at Klessheim Castle on March 15. At this conference Himmler pre-

56. Telegram from Jagow to Berlin, Mar. 15, 1944, NA Microcopy T-120, roll 99, 109813–15; also József Kun, in "Magyarország német katonai," p. 65. Kállay notes that when he asked Jagow about the meaning of the German troop concentration around Vienna, Jagow responded that he did not see why the Hungarians should be concerned, unless they had a bad conscience (*Hungarian Premier*, p. 408).

57. Kállay, *Hungarian Premier*, pp. 408–11. According to Kállay (pp. 410–11), there were only 1,719 German soldiers stationed in Hungary until March of 1944. The Office of Strategic Services, however, received information, dated Feb. 4, 1944, to the effect that 15,000 German officers and men had recently infiltrated into Hungary in addition to large numbers of air force personnel (NA Record Group 226, Hungary, Records of the Office of Strategic Services, 11365).

58. J. Kun, "Magyarország német katonai," p. 69; see also *KTB, OKW*, 4 : 199.

sented a lengthy memorandum prepared by the SS embodying many of Veesenmayer's recommendations for a political, or perhaps a diplomatic, approach to exerting German influence in Hungary.[59] Hitler decided on a compromise. While maintaining the provisions regarding a military occupation of Hungary, he decided to reach Horthy, invite him to Germany, and persuade him to cooperate. Should Horthy refuse to cooperate, at least the visit would serve the purpose of leaving Hungary without effective leadership at the time of the invasion. The invitation would specify that Hitler wanted to talk over the topics mentioned in Horthy's letter of February, especially the military topics; thus the top military leaders in Hungary could be included in the invitation.

Horthy received Hitler's invitation that very evening, after a gala performance at the Budapest opera house (March 15 being a Hungarian national holiday). Hitler asked to see Horthy at Klessheim to discuss the military and the political situation, in particular the points Horthy had raised in his last letter. The visit would have to take place Friday or Saturday, that is, within three days, as the critical situation of the eastern front demanded the presence of the Führer. A reply was requested by Thursday noon.[60] Horthy hesitated. Kállay and Csatay seem to have advised him against accepting the invitation, whereas Ghyczy and Szombathelyi were in favor of it. Horthy decided to accept. "Details may have slipped my mind," he writes in his *Memoirs*, "but I still remember twice putting my revolver in my pocket and twice taking it out again before leaving the train. I knew that I would not be searched as Hitler's generals were; but justice was to be meted to him by a higher tribunal. I left my revolver in my carriage." [61] The assassination of one state leader by another would indeed have been a novel turn in contemporary history, so unprecedented, in fact, that it is difficult to accept Horthy's reminiscences literally.

Horthy arrived at Klessheim on March 18, accompanied by Ghyczy, Csatay, and Szombathelyi. Thus Hungary was indeed momentarily deprived of military leadership. Hitler's plan for the occupation of Hungary had run smoothly so far. It would continue to run smoothly: Operation Margarethe was to be a bloodless blitz, the most cleverly

---

59. *KTB, OKW,* 4 : pt. 1, 199.

60. Telegram from Ribbentrop to Jagow, Mar. 15, 1944, NA Microcopy T-120, roll 99, 109819–20. Horthy, *Memoirs,* pp. 210–11.

61. *Memoirs,* p. 212.

devised and most successfully executed of all German plans during the war.

The important conversations between Hitler and Horthy took place in private. Ambassador Paul Schmidt, an interpreter who sat in on many top-level meetings, was simply—to use Schmidt's own words—"dismissed" by the "fractious" Horthy from the conference room.[62] Horthy, who had been Emperor Francis Joseph's naval aide for many years, spoke German at least as well as Hungarian and felt no need of an interpreter. Nevertheless, the account of the meeting by Paul Schmidt, an account based largely on circumstantial evidence, comes from the "nearest" and most disinterested source. Paul Schmidt was standing in the hall "when suddenly the door of the conference room flew open, and to our surprise the aged Horthy came rushing out, very red in the face, and began to climb the stairs to the first floor." [63] To detain Horthy, "a most convincing fake air-raid was staged, which even included a smoke screen over the castle, as an excuse for preventing Horthy's special train from leaving"; although the air raid fooled no one, Horthy was obliged to stay. Conversations were resumed. Ribbentrop told Schmidt, the interpreter, that if Horthy did not give way Schmidt would not have to accompany him to the frontier, as Horthy would be detained as a prisoner. But eventually Horthy did promise to replace the Kállay government, and Schmidt noted the contrast between Horthy's and Antonescu's attitudes; the latter had categorically refused to dismiss his foreign minister at Hitler's request.[64]

Horthy's own account, as published in his memoirs, is based essentially on that of Schmidt, but Horthy had given several accounts of this important episode. The earliest of these is one given the assembled members of the Crown Council upon Horthy's return to Budapest on March 19. The minutes of this assembly record that, at Horthy's protest

62. Schmidt, *Hitler's Interpreter*, p. 270. Horthy gives the following account of the incident: "We went straight to his [Hitler's] study, followed by Paul Schmidt, Hitler's interpreter. I had nothing against Herr Schmidt, whom I considered an intelligent and kindly man, and to whom we now owe the account of the exceedingly dramatic events of my stay at Klessheim which he has recorded in his book, but as none of my people were present and as no interpreter was needed between myself and Hitler, I queried his presence and he withdrew. Later I regretted this, for, had I not protested, there would have been a witness to our talk" (*Memoirs*, p. 213).

63. Moreover, Horthy told Hitler, "if everything has been decided already, there is no point in my staying any longer. I shall leave at once!" (Schmidt, *Hitler's Interpreter*, p. 271.).

64. Ibid.

and in reply to his indication in what way Hungary would be able to bear up against such a military occupation as planned by the Reich, Hitler replied that he had plenty of reserves to act with the proper effect against this, and there would be also the Rumanians, the Slovaks, and the Croatians, against the Hungarians. The Regent retorted that Hitler had better use these reserve divisions in the fight against the Russians, and for his part he believed for the time being the invasion was a mere bluff. The Regent then rose and went to his rooms.[65]

Horthy gave several additional accounts of the meeting during interrogations in connection with the Nuremberg trials. The affidavit Horthy signed in connection with the trial of Veesenmayer and other officers of the German Foreign Ministry was not printed in the various series of documentary publications pertaining to the trials; hence, it may be worth discussing here. Hitler informed him at Klessheim, declared Horthy on May 27, 1947, that Hungary was to be occupied by German troops. He protested and wanted to leave, but his train had been disconnected, and Horthy asked whether he should consider himself a prisoner:

> Since obviously they did not want to allow things to come to an open breaking point they continued the comedy-playing: Hitler sent Keitel out to try and rescind the order for the occupation, Keitel came back and said that unfortunately that was no longer possible. Thereupon Ribbentrop came up with a communiqué which he wanted to give out to the newspapers, to the effect that Hitler, in accord with myself, has ordered the occupation of Hungary.[66]

The real historiographical controversy centers around the problem of just what Horthy did agree to at Klessheim. Among the records of the German Foreign Office I have found the draft of a "superseded" protocol dated Klessheim, March 18. Although superseded, the document gives at least an indication of the initial German demands. The demands included the formation of a Hungarian cabinet that would be prepared to contribute the entire economic potential of the country for the war effort. The cabinet would be presided over by Béla Imrédy, and the minister of defense would be Jenő Rátz; all other leading officials would likewise be designated in

65. *Confidential Papers of Nicholas Horthy,* p. 282.

66. Affidavit, May 27, 1947, NA Record Group 238, World War II War Crimes Records.

agreement with the Reich government. In order to assist the new
cabinet in its internal task, German troops would occupy the country.
A German plenipotentiary would be appointed to insure that the
Hungarian government operates in accord with the Reich government. Most important perhaps, the regent would issue a proclamation to the Hungarian people, immediately after the German troops
marched in, instructing the population and the authorities to receive
the German troops in a friendly manner and to support the measures
adopted by them; the regent would issue similar orders to the Hungarian army as well.[67] To what extent did the regent agree to these
demands? Horthy himself provides certain clues to the reply:

> When I announced that I did not want to have anything to do
> with the whole matter and would like to resign, Hitler answered
> with the promise that he will withdraw the German troops from
> Hungary as soon as an acceptable prime minister has been
> designated in Hungary. Since at that time I still believed in this
> promise, I decided to try once again.[68]

This version of the events seems to indicate that an agreement, even
though unsigned and unwritten, was reached. The minutes of the
Crown Council, on March 19, also imply that whereas the encounter
between Hitler and Horthy had been stormy at first the storm subsided: Hitler, it is reported, saw Horthy out to his private train "and
took leave of him with a friendly smile." [69] The historian György

67. NA Microcopy T-120, roll 99, 109832–33; also György Ránki, "The German Occupation of Hungary," pp. 269–70; and *KTB, OKW*, 4 : pt. 1, 230–31.

68. Affidavit, May 27, 1947, NA Record Group 238, World War II War Crimes
Records. Another account given by Horthy, more succinct, was recorded by the DeWitt
C. Poole Mission even earlier, on Sept. 1, 1945: "Hitler charged that Hungary was
about to betray Germany just as Italy had done. Horthy denied the charge, since
Hungary had never committed an act of betrayal in its entire history, he asserted.
When convinced that the war was lost, Horthy said, he would inform Hitler first of
all that it was time to sue for an armistice. He further appraised Hitler that he (Hitler)
was despised by the entire world and that if he invaded Hungary, the Hungarian people would be added to the list of those who hated both Hitler and the German people.
Hitler delayed Horthy's return to Budapest, and when he (Horthy) did return he was
virtually in custody . . ." (Interrogation of Nicholas Horthy, NA Record Group 59,
General Records of the Department of State). The interrogators noted, however, that
Horthy "was plainly worried lest he be considered a war criminal."

69. Hitler had even told Horthy that he had always "liked Hungary very much, he
said even the idea was ridiculous that he wanted to turn Hungary into a province.
The case of Bohemia was different. Bohemia was a part of the Holy Roman Empire of
the German Nation and later on of the Austrian Empire" (*Confidential Papers of
Nicholas Horthy*, pp. 284–85).

Ránki argues that while Horthy never signed the "protocol" he nevertheless agreed to at least some of its provisions.[70] Elek Karsai, another Hungarian scholar, points out that Horthy, Ghyczy, and Szombathelyi all sent telegrams from Klessheim asking the Hungarian authorities to receive the German forces in a friendly manner.[71] A German historian writes that Horthy agreed to all of Hitler's important demands after Hitler consented to the withdrawal of the German troops once a "national" (that is, right-wing) cabinet had been sworn in.[72] These authors seem to base their argument in part on the war diary of the German Army High Command. According to this dairy, Horthy had twice refused to reach an agreement with Hitler; yet, at the end,

> against expectations, the regent once again went to see the Führer, on his own initiative, toward 8 o'clock in the evening. After this renewed conversation he declared that he understood the views of the Führer fully and therefore will comply with his requests. Thereupon, toward nine o'clock Horthy and his company left on their return voyage.[73]

It is permissible to doubt the accuracy of the account provided by the war diary, since it was compiled during the war. The war diary does not state that Hitler threatened Horthy with the use of Romanian, Slovak, and Croatian units. The tense relations between Hungary, Romania, and the satellite states of Croatia and Slovakia explain why such a prospect must have appeared as particularly dreadful to the Hungarians. The Romanian occupation of 1919–20 had left an unpleasant impression on Hungarians of all classes. Horthy himself explained to one of his ministers in the new right-wing Sztójay cabinet that this was the circumstance which, while continuing to refuse outright collaboration, nevertheless forced him to take cognizance of the German decision to occupy Hungary.[74] The meeting at Klessheim remains a rather obscure episode in German-Hungarian relations, nor does it seem likely that further documents

70. Ránki, "German Occupation of Hungary," p. 271.

71. Karsai, *A budai vártól*, p. 441.

72. Andreas Hillgruber, "Das deutsch-ungarische Verhältnis im letzten Kriegsjahr," p. 82.

73. *KTB, OKW,* 4 : pt. 1, 200–201, 230.

74. This argument is accepted by Karsai, *A budai vártól*, p. 433. Other accounts favorable to Horthy were published by Hungarian authors soon after the German defeat. General Nagy, who appears to have had access to firsthand information, believes Horthy did not give in to Hitler's demands (*Végzetes esztendők,* pp. 190 ff.).

or revelations will come forth to shed more light on the matter. On the whole, it is possible to agree with Gerald Reitlinger's judgment that at Klessheim "all went well. The seventy-six year old Regent, Admiral Horthy, showed even less spirit than might have been expected of a man in his uncomfortable position." [75]

It cannot be denied that as a result of the Klessheim conversations Hitler felt reassured, and the regent was not written off; the forces singled out for Operation Margarethe were somewhat reduced at the last minute (which may also indicate that if Marshal Keitel had really intended to do so the entire operation could still have been called off). The "propaganda flight" of units of the German air force over Budapest was canceled; the leaflets scheduled to be dropped on Hungarian troops were not dropped. It was also decided that the Castle (*Vár*) and the Fort (*Citadella*) in Budapest would not be occupied, and the group led by General Pfuhlstein would remain, for the most part, outside the city limits. Furthermore, two divisions, the 100th Jagd Division and the 21st Armored Division, and two smaller units, the 301st and 507th armored battalions, would not take part in the operation. Hitler also felt there was no need to disarm the Hungarian forces, that the occupation of Hungary up to the Tisza River, but including the airport at Debrecen, could be carried out smoothly.[76]

There remained for Operation Margarethe a sizable German force. From the south: the 8th Cavalry Division, the 42d Alpine Division, three motorized regiments (Grenadier Regiment 92, the Brandenburg Regiment, and the SS Police Regiment 5), one brigade (SS Brigade 201), and an armored battalion (the 202d). From the southwest: the 1st Alpine Division, the 367th Infantry Division, and the 18th SS Armored Grenadier Division. From the northwest: the

75. *The SS: Alibi of a Nation*, p. 349. François Honti wrote: "Horthy était un personnage plutôt qu'un caractère. Il tenait de son état militaire des allures martiales donnant l'impression d'énergie, mais il était vacillant dans les moments décisifs. On le vit bien en mars 1944 lorsque Hitler le somma de donner son assentiment à l'occupation allemande de la Hongrie: en invoquant son serment à la Constitution, il refusa d'abord de légaliser ce coup de force, puis finit par ratifier le fait accompli" (*Le drame hongrois*, p. 29).

76. "1. Reichsverweser v. Horthy hat sich bereiterklärt, deutschen Forderungen zu entsprechen. Anordnungen an ungarische Wehrmacht sind bisher nicht erteilt und werden voraussichtlich nicht vor 19. 3., mittags, ergehen. 2. Es bleibt bei deutscher militärischer Besetzung. Ungarische Wehrmacht vorläufig in Kasernen zusammenhalten, nicht entwaffnen. Gemeinsame Wachen stellen, Eingriffe vermeiden . . ." (directive, Mar. 18 ["geheime Kommandosache" and "Chefsache"], NA Microcopy T-77, roll 791, 5519627–28). This document is summarized in *KTB, OKW*, 4 : pt. 1, 231–32.

Armored Training Division, the 16th Armored Grenadier Division, a battalion of the Wiking Armored Division, a heavy artillery battalion (the 997th), and a militia battalion. From the north: three reinforced regiments (from the Grossdeutschland, Feldherrnhalle, and Brandenburg divisions), as well as engineering and sappers units. The 21st Armored Division and at least two battalions of paratroopers were also to take part in the operation.[77] The spearhead of Operation Margarethe would be the Trojan Horse transport group, which included SS troops and which was to entrain in the evening of March 18. German sappers would engineer a "sabotage" by blowing up the tracks in the vicinity of Budapest, so as to force the troops to detrain there around two o'clock in the morning. Their march into Budapest would begin at four o'clock, simultaneously with the concentric advance of all the other units.[78]

The Allied intelligence services must have sensed events in Hungary were nearing the denouement. One of the stipulations of the agreement signed by British and Hungarian representatives in Turkey on September 9 had been that an Allied mission would be dropped on Hungary at an opportune moment to prepare the way for Hungary's surrender. The moment seemed opportune. Accordingly, on March 17, a three-man American team took off from Brindisi in Italy and was dropped by parachute in southwestern Hungary. Howard K. Travers, erstwhile first secretary of the American legation in Budapest, had been approached regarding the mission but declined; [79] thus the mission was composed entirely of military personnel, a colonel being in charge.[80] The team was met by a Hungarian unit and driven to Budapest on March 17.[81] The three Americans, Col. Florimund Duke, Maj. Alfred Suarez, and Capt. Guy Nunn, were taken to Gen. István Ujszászy, the chief of the Hungarian counterintelligence service. The American colonel's instructions seem to have been to return to Bern, leaving the other members of the team and a radio set in Hungary. But before the mission could accomplish anything German troops marched in, and the American soldiers were

77. *KTB, OKW,* 4 : pt. 1, 222.

78. Ibid., passim.

79. Secretary Travers expressed surprise when I told him the mission was, in fact, carried out.

80. Kertesz, *Diplomacy in a Whirlpool,* p. 72. Kertesz states the team had four members.

81. J. Kun, "Magyarország német katonai," p. 55; see also St,-Iványi, "Our Man of Destiny in 1944," p. 34.

handed over to the Sicherheitsdienst and taken away to Berlin.[82] The British may have planned a similar mission, which did not even have time to get off the ground.[83]

It was only during Horthy's visit at Klessheim that the Hungarian government received definite information regarding German intentions. According to a prearranged signal, Minister of Foreign Affairs Ghyczy sent a telegram to Assistant Foreign Minister Andor Szentmiklóssy on March 18: "Tell my wife I am well"—meaning, the Germans were coming.[84] During the night, Kállay summoned some of the military leaders who had remained in Hungary to his office, and it seems he seriously considered defending the country. The military leaders, with the exception of Gen. István Náday, either refused to consider such a course or deemed resistance useless.[85] Even Gen. József Bajnóczy, the deputy chief of the General Staff, who was not pro-Nazi, argued that an order to fight against the Germans could only be given by the regent or, in his absence, by the chief of the General Staff. They were out of the country at Klessheim. Even if they did give such an order, the army commanders would not obey. Furthermore, argued Bajnóczy, he had just received a telegram from the chief of the General Staff to the effect that the German troops were to be treated as friends. After the meeting, Bajnóczy found the German military attaché waiting in the antechamber. "What is the

82. "Two days later," quotes St.-Iványi, "the Germans crossed the border from Austria and we were prisoners for thirteen months in Belgrade and other German prison-camps" ("Our Man of Destiny in 1944," p. 34). "Zweck sollte Vereinbarung sein, Ungarn aus dem Krieg an Seite Deutschlands herauszubringen. Amerikanischer Oberst sollte nach Bern zurück, Verbindungsleute mit Sonderapparat in Ungarn blieben. Inhalt der geheime Verhandlungen im einzelnen bekannt. Unterlagen vorzeitig verbrannt. Deutscher Einmarsch verhinderte Fortführung der Aktion. Amerikaner wurden SD übergeben, befinden sich derzeit in Berlin. Nachricht über Vorgänge erhielt SD durch anständiger ungarische Offiziere, nach dem ich vorher bereits Winkelmann mit einem Vertrauensmann von mir zusammengebracht hatte, der den ganzen Vorgang bis ins Detaille schilderte. . . . Bemühe mich derzeit, Vernehmung Szentmiklosys [sic] durch SD zu ermöglichen. Reichsführer -SS dürfte laufend und eingehend unterrichtet sein" (telegram from Veesenmayer to Berlin, Apr. 20, 1944, NA Microcopy T-120, roll 1096, 45294–50). The story of the American mission, its purpose, its achievement, and its final fate, is still by and large a mystery. We must hope that one or another participant will eventually publish revelations.

83. Kertesz, *Diplomacy in a Whirlpool*, p. 72.

84. Karsai, *A budai vártól*, p. 439.

85. Ibid., p. 440. The following officers were present: József Bajnóczy, Béla Miklós, Szilárd Bakay, István Náday, János Vörös, Sándor Magyarossy, Vilmos Hellebronth. Only the last three can be described as definitely pro-German.

decision," asked Greiffenberg, "will there be military resistance or not?" Bajnóczy replied that there would not be resistance. "Gott sei's Dank!" exclaimed Greiffenberg.[86] It is possible that Kállay's concern over the safety of the regent also prevented him from taking effective measures. The regent's train, as we have seen, left Klessheim around 9:30 P.M. on March 18. At 1:00 A.M. it arrived in Vienna, where it was held up until at least four in the morning, the moment when the German troops began their advance into Hungary. By the time the regent's train crossed the Hungarian border, German troops were near the Hungarian capital,[87] in fact, the regent was greeted by a German honor guard upon his arrival in the Hungarian capital. During the night, however, the regent's exact whereabouts were not known to Kállay.

The Hungarian generals refused to take action against the Germans for a number of reasons. Kállay himself notes that twenty-one of the twenty-nine top-ranking officers of the Hungarian army were of German ("Souabian") descent; it would have been better said that a majority of these officers sympathized with National Socialist Germany. Furthermore, some of the Hungarian officers had already received Szombathelyi's instructions to the effect that the Germans were to be greeted in a friendly manner; [88] these instructions were duly transmitted to the Hungarian field commands. Prime Minister Kállay soon gave up all thought of resistance. In the early hours of March 19, a German general appeared in his office and read a message from Field Marshal Keitel to the effect that should Hungarian forces oppose German troops Hungary's neighbors would be asked to intervene.[89]

As a result, German troops marched into Hungary unopposed. Since the end of the war, Miklós Kállay has often been criticized for not having organized Hungarian resistance. It may be argued that resistance could only have been organized by the military hierarchy, and the military seemed altogether unwilling to undertake such a task. But the Kállay government had been in power for two years: it nevertheless failed to obtain the necessary ascendancy over the military and to insure, by judicious selection of military personnel, that if

86. Dr. Elek Karsai to author.
87. *KTB, OKW,* 4 : pt. 1, 230.
88. Karsai, *A budai vártól,* pp. 440–42.
89. Kállay, *Hungarian Premier,* p. 421.

it came to a showdown between Hungary and Germany the Hungarian army could still be relied on to obey orders. Had Kállay made the necessary changes in military personnel, the resistance could, and perhaps should, have been organized.

To advocate resistance, however, does not imply faith in the eventual success of such resistance. Some authors believe that resistance might even have been successful. In his article on the German occupation of Hungary, György Ránki declares that "had the Hungarian government resolved to resist, it had means to do so," partly because the German army was by then hard pressed and unable to muster significant reserves.[90] The evidence, however, tends to show that the Hungarian army could have offered only token resistance. While it is true that the German reserves were exhausted, it is obvious that Germany had sufficient strength left to occupy Hungary. Had it been necessary to withdraw forces from the front, it is not impossible that the German leaders would still have ordered the occupation: the war against the Jews, in this case the Jews of Hungary, was of primary importance.[91] But in any case the Hungarian army posed no real threat to the Germans. According to a German report compiled early in March, the Hungarian army had an overall strength of 450,000 men of whom 90,000 were in Russia: "the efficiency of the units is limited, the training incomplete, the equipment deficient. Only part of the weapons can be described as modern (the divisions have no heavy antitank artillery.)"[92] These forces, moreover, were scattered throughout the country, a limited concentration of troops being stationed alongside the Romanian border. Furthermore, preparations for resistance should have started weeks ahead. Had the Kállay government ordered resistance at the last moment, it is doubtful whether the majority of the local commanders would have made even a pretense of obeying that order: the utter unreliability of the Hungarian army in the face of a German threat became obvious a few months later, on October 15, when the overwhelming majority of the Hun-

90. "The German Occupation of Hungary," p. 267. The military historians, Jenő Czebe and Tibor Pethö, argue that Hungary should have ordered total mobilization, concentrated her troops along the Carpathians in the East, and held that area or joined the Russians on the other side of the mountains (*Hungary in World War II,* p. 30).

91. Gerald Reitlinger writes: ". . . Hitler's chief motive in securing Hungary was the extermination of European Jewry, the obsession that always transcended his military strategy" (*The SS: Alibi of a Nation,* p. 350).

92. NA Microcopy T-77, roll 791, 5519600–601. This document is summarized in *KTB, OKW,* 4: pt. 1, 214

garian army sided with the new Arrow-Cross government, in disregard of its oath of loyalty to Regent Horthy.[93]

On March 19 the Hungarian army offered not even token resistance; there is considerable disagreement as to whether any shots were fired at all. Some Hungarian authors claim shots were fired at the German troops at the airport near Budapest and perhaps also at Sopron, Győr, and Székesfehérvár.[94] Others, however, know of no incidents whatever: "Not only did the German occupation encounter no resistance," writes Ránki, "but owing to the unpreparedness of the antifascist front, the occupational forces did not have to fight any spontaneous resistance of the people either." [95] The German sources seem to support Ránki's account. "Widerstand würde nirgends geleistet"—nowhere was there resistance. Only the Hungarian garrison at Ujvidék (Novi Sad) was disarmed,[96] apparently because the German units involved did not realize that their orders had been changed. In fact, it seems the German units marching into Hungary were sometimes greeted with cheers, and the German leaders had every reason to be satisfied. "When their country was occupied," writes Gen Walter Warlimont, "the vast majority of Hungarians continued to treat the Germans as allies . . ." [97] We may well agree with the statement in the war diary of the German Army High Command, that the choice of date for Operation Margarethe was once again a manifestation of Hitler's sure political instinct; [98] the gain of a country, this time, seems to have cost National Socialist Germany not even the bones of a single grenadier.

Yet there was at least one incidence of resistance. In the early hours of March 19 the Gestapo was already busy rounding up Hungarian political figures of the left, Jewish industrialists, and certain members of Horthy's and Kállay's entourage. When a squad of SS men drew up

93. Maj. Ferenc Adonyi states that from a military standpoint it would not have been possible to defend Hungary against the Germans on Mar. 19, 1944 (*A magyar katona a második világháborúban*, pp. 59 ff.).

94. The most noteworthy of these authors is József Kun because he seems to contradict, in this respect, other historians writing in Hungary at the same period. Kun's statements seem to be made with ill-concealed national pride ("Magyarország német katonai," p. 75). But see also Imre Kovács, *D'une occupation à l'autre,* p. 15; and Dezső Geleji, *Magyarország 1944-ben* [Hungary in 1944], p. 36.

95. "German Occupation of Hungary," p. 274; see also Kállai, *A magyar függetlenségi mozgalom,* p. 211.

96. *KTB, OKW,* 4 : pt. 1, 234.

97. *Inside Hitler's Headquarters,* p. 413.

98. *KTB, OKW,* 4 : pt. 1, 246.

in front of the apartment house of Member of Parliament Endre Bajcsy-Zsilinszky it was met with revolver shots. The gun battle ceased only after Bajcsy-Zsilinszky fell wounded and unconscious. When Bajcsy-Zsilinszky was finally released by the German and Hungarian authorities in October 1944, it was again he who organized the first serious group of resistance fighters.[99] In a letter to Kállay, dated February 12, 1944, Bajcsy-Zsilinszky had argued that a forceful occupation of Hungary by the Germans would be better for Hungary than one borne "with meekness and patience; because the forceful occupation will win the honor and the future of the country maybe by suffering, possibly by very grave torments, blood and destruction to our unfortunate fatherland, but it will separate us from the fate of the German Reich." [100] But the occupation, except for Bajcsy-Zsilinszky's lone heroic act, was borne with meekness, and the fate of the defeated Hungary was quite as painful as that of the German Reich.

99. He was arrested, however, by the Arrow-Cross police before his group was able to cause any damage. He was executed in the early hours of Dec. 24, 1944, in the prison yard at Sopronkőhida near Sopron. His political career is discussed in some detail by Jenő Lévai in *Hősök hőse* [The hero of heroes] (Budapest: 1969). Eyewitness accounts and documents about Bajcsy-Zsilinszky are collected in Károly Vigh, ed., *Kortársak Bajcsy-Zsilinszky Endréről* [Contemporaries write about Endre Bajcsy-Zsilinszky]. See also Sulyok, *A magyar tragédia*, pp. 506–7.

100. Dr. Elek Karsai to author.

10. Submission to the German Occupation and the Extermination of Jewish Citizens

While the history of Hungary during most of World War II may be a challenge to the researcher because of the scarcity of pertinent documents, the contrary seems to be true of Hungary in the period of the German occupation. The student of Hungarian history in 1944 faces a superabundance of documentation. There may be two reasons for this: first, there was the prolixity of the new German representative in Hungary, the "plenipotentiary" Edmund Veesenmayer, who sent lengthy reports to Berlin several times a day; second, a greater volume of both Hungarian and German records survived from the last stages of the war, as there remained less time for their destruction.

The German occupation, we have seen, was carried out swiftly and smoothly. On the very first day of the occupation, on March 19, the Gestapo rounded up most of the prominent but politically undesirable elements. These undesirables included Allied prisoners of war escaped from Germany; [1] the members of the royal Italian legation; liberal or left-wing politicians, including some members of Parliament; [2] politicians who did not belong to any left-wing or liberal organization but were known for their anti-Nazi views; leading Jewish industrialists; eventually, government officials implicated in "treasonable" (i.e., pro-Allied) activities, including two prominent officials of the Ministry of Foreign Affairs, Aladár Szegedy-Maszák and Andor Szentmiklóssy; and three officers of the Hungarian counterintelligence service, Gen. István Ujszászy, Col. Gyula Kádár, and Maj. Kálmán Kéri.[3] If I may be allowed to insert an autobio-

1. By April 7, 812 escaped French POWs had been arrested, as well as 5,450 Polish, 39 English, 11 American, 16 Belgian, 12 Dutch, and 180 Soviet prisoners of war (telegram from Veesenmayer to Ribbentrop, NA Microcopy T-120, roll 100, 110089–90).

2. The deputies arrested were Endre Bajcsy-Zsilinszky, Károly Rassay, Kálmán Rátz, Károly Peyer, Count Apponyi, Gusztáv Grátz, Géza Malasits, Dezső Laky, and Lajos Szentiváni. The following members of the upper house were arrested: Lipót Baranyai, Antal Sigray, Iván Csekonics, Ferenc Chorin, Móricz Kornfeld. Later the deputies Ferenc Nagy, Ernő Bródy, and Aladár Huszár were also arrested. Iván Boldizsár, *The Other Hungary*, p. 57.

3. The reports of the chief of the SS in Hungary, Otto Winkelmann, (filed among the documents of the German Foreign Office) also regularly mentioned the arrests of "Communists," "Trotskyites," and "Allied spies"—mostly Hungarian Jews.

graphical note here—because I feel it is necessary to reveal the derivation of the author's personal involvement in his work—my father had been warned early Sunday morning, March 19, that the Germans were coming; he had sufficient presence of mind to leave our residence on the Svábhegy (now Szabadsághegy) in search of a hiding place. My family and myself hid for the entire duration of the German occupation, about eleven months, in as many different locations in Budapest; at times we were together, at other times not.[4]

The Kállay cabinet resigned on March 19, and Miklós Kállay found refuge within the Turkish legation;[5] Horthy's task was to find a prime minister acceptable to the Germans. He hesitated. In February 1941, before Hungary had taken the fatal step which engulfed her in the world war, Horthy had told the American minister in Budapest that:

> he personally would submit to any fate rather then accede to the surrender of Hungarian sovereignty. Should Germany demand a change in the personnel of the Government which would make Hungary but a puppet State, he would refuse to comply and would appoint a Government beyond the frontiers of the country, leaving Hungary no legally constituted Government within her territory.[6]

But times changed. Hitler did demand a change in the personnel of the Hungarian government; in fact, Hungary was reduced to a puppet state, but Horthy did not appoint a government in exile. Nor did he resign. It is true that Horthy did not even consider appointing Ferenc Szálasi, the leader of the extreme right-wing Arrow-Cross party, as Hungary's new prime minister. It may be that Szálasi was likewise not the Germans' favorite candidate, for the Germans obviously needed a government which had some popular support and which could maintain order; yet Szálasi was one of the few people who knew in advance of the German invasion. In his

4. Miksa Fenyö, *Az elsodort ország* [A country adrift], p. 50 and *passim*.

5. Kállay left the Turkish Legation late on Nov. 19, 1944, and was immediately arrested by the Arrow-Cross government then in power. He was detained in prisons and camps, including the Mauthausen and Dachau concentration camps. Kállay died in New York City in 1966.

6. Memorandum of a conversation between Minister Montgomery and Regent Horthy, Feb. 14, 1941, NA Record Group 59, General Records of the Department of State, 711.64/19.

diary Szálasi wrote: "The [Hungarian] General Staff is asking the party leader of the National Socialist party [i.e., Szálasi himself] that he should inform them of his permanent residence in order that he be informed of immediate serious changes." [7] It seems. then, that Szálasi was the favorite candidate of the Hungarian General Staff. Still, he had to wait until October 16 to accede to power. Furthermore, Horthy refused to appoint Béla Imrédy as prime minister despite Veesenmayer's explicit request.[8] He hesitated until March 23, and Veesenmayer was on the verge of losing patience, advocating an all-out German occupation and the elimination of the regent himself. Horthy, according to the cables sent by Veesenmayer, told lies and was physically not up to his task.[9] Finally, on the twenty-third, Horthy appointed Gen. Döme Sztójay as prime minister. While Veesenmayer may have preferred Imrédy, who was politically able as well as reliable from the German point of view, there could be no objection to Sztójay. Sztójay had been Hungarian minister in Berlin for many years, and all this time he seems to have served German interests at least as well as the Hungarian ones. As Macartney writes, Sztójay was a "completely wholehearted believer in Germany's invincibility, and thus constituted something of a Trojan horse in Hungary's diplomatic fortress." He was popular in Berlin, adds Macartney, "and if a Minister's duty is to cultivate good relations with the country to which he is accredited, Sztójay performed it well." [10]

Horthy, having complied with Hitler's principal request, the replacement of Kállay, went into a kind of retreat. Kállay, in his memoirs, never criticizes the regent, whose faithful servant he remained to the last, except in this one instance. When Horthy re-

7. The Szálasi diary (Dr. Elek Karsai to author).

8. Telegram from Veesenmayer to Berlin, Mar. 20, 1944, NA Microcopy T-120, roll 99, 109866–67.

9. Ibid.; also *Trials of War Criminals before the Nuernberg Military Tribunals,* 13 : 338–41.

10. "Hungary's Declaration of War," p. 156. During an interrogation in Bavaria on Aug. 27, 1945, Horthy remarked about Sztójay: "He was before an officer, a General. So I thought what I command he do it. He was not quite right with his heart and he asked me not to nominate him, but didn't know another one to trust, and he was absolutely a correct man, and I told him he must, and he came and he tried everything to get these imprisoned people [here Horthy must have been referring to Ujszászy, Kádár, and Kéri]. But he couldn't do anything. It became always worse and worse" (Interrogations, NA Record Group 238, World War II War Crimes Records). It might be noted that the regent made these declarations before a Hungarian tribunal sentenced Sztójay to death.

turned from Salzburg, Kállay "begged" him to abdicate, but Horthy refused.[11] It has been averred in recent studies that Horthy wanted to abdicate but was dissuaded from so doing by Kállay. This is probably false; in view of Kállay's general faithfulness toward the regent, there is no reason to doubt his testimony, as stated in his memoirs, in this specific instance. Horthy's resignation would have precluded the possibility of his interventions on behalf of the Jews of Budapest in the coming summer, to be sure. On the other hand, the gesture of resignation might have served to impress upon the Hungarian bureaucratic apparatus and the Hungarian public the illegitimate nature of the German intervention; and the bureaucracy and the public might have hesitated to follow the lead of a quisling government. I do not say so with assurance: for the coup d'état of October 15 indicated that Horthy had few dedicated followers left. Is it not possible, however, that Horthy lost support precisely because he had not taken a stand a bit earier, on March 19? Perhaps the next best course of action for Horthy would have been simply to take no part in public affairs; then the public could have assumed that Horthy was no longer master of his own person (which, in a sense, was true). During a cabinet meeting on March 29, when the soon-to-be-proclaimed "Jewish Laws" were discussed, the new prime minister declared it was not necessary to ask for the regent's approval, as the regent had already given him a free hand in this matter.[12] If the regent had indeed done so, one might assess such a declaration as a total abnegation of responsibility. But Horthy's retreat was not complete. While the German authorities were intent on keeping Horthy away from public affairs —Veesenmayer even received instructions to "isolate him completely in the Burg"[13]—he made several public appearances in the weeks immediately following the German occupation of his country. He visited the Ludovika military academy in Budapest when a new class of officers received their commission, and on May 9 he witnessed military maneuvers near Budapest and seemed

11. Kállay, *Hungarian Premier*, p. 433. Publicly, especially during the cabinet meeting of Mar. 19, Kállay entreated Horthy not to resign.

12. *Vádirat a nácizmus ellen* [Charge-sheet against naziism], ed. Ilona Beneschofsky and Elek Karsai, 1 : 50–51.

13. Telegram from Altenburg (in Fuschl) to Veesenmayer, Apr. 2, 1944, NA Microcopy T-120, roll 99, 110047, also, *Trials of War Criminals before the Nuernberg Military Tribunals*, 13 : 341–42.

to "have a good time." [14] On April 15 Horthy and Csatay signed an appeal to the troops in which the customary slogans were repeated: "fighting shoulder to shoulder with the German comrades, the true and honorable allies . . ." [15] Thus Horthy gave the lie to those who had the kindness to assume he was under some sort of house arrest.

The German occupation of Hungary led to measures that illustrated a technique developed to a fine point in the occupation of other European countries. The *Gleichschaltung* process seems to have been carried out in Hungary more rapidly than elsewhere. By March 29 the opposition parties, that is, the Social Democrats, the Smallholders party, and the Peasants' Union were dissolved by order of the minister of interior.[16] New ministers were installed, and higher-ranking government officials throughout the country were replaced by individuals well known for their pro-German sentiments. Although Sztójay's cabinet did not include members of the Arrow-Cross party, the fanatic group of Hungarian National Socialists, the German authorities had reason to be satisfied with the cooperation afforded by the new Hungarian cabinet. A few days after the German invasion, the Hungarian army was still regarded as unreliable by the Germans; Ribbentrop and Veesenmayer could not agree on whether or not the Hungarian army ought to be disarmed.[17] For once, however, the regent threatened to resign if Hungarian troops were not allowed to leave their barracks.[18] So the Hungarian army was rehabilitated, while the pretense of keeping politics out of the army was dropped. General Szombathelyi felt obliged to go into hiding after the German forces entered the country and was replaced, on April 19, by Gen. János Vörös. At first Horthy had told Vörös that such was the wish of the Germans, but when Vörös refused to accept the appointment on those terms Horthy was compelled to tell him it was also his own wish. Vörös then accepted the appointment but only on condition that he be allowed to carry out the "necessary changes" in personnel among the generals and in

14. Entry for May 9, Diary of János Vörös, Hungarian Collection, NA Microcopy T-973; hereafter cited as Diary of Vörös.

15. Telegram from Veesenmayer to Ribbentrop, Apr. 15, 1944, NA Microcopy T-120, roll 100, 110164.

16. Telegram from Feine (in Budapest) to Berlin, Mar. 29, 1944, NA Microcopy T-120, roll 99, 109987.

17. Telegram from Ribbentrop to Veesenmayer, Mar. 25, 1944, NA Microcopy T-120, roll 99, 109965–69.

18. Telegram from Veesenmayer to Ribbentrop, Mar. 26, 144, NA Microcopy T-120, roll 99, 109958–59.

the headquarters of the General Staff.[19] In May retired Gen. Károly
Beregfy, described as having "good comradely relations with German
officers," General László, "who had been dismissed because of his
too strongly pro-German attitude," and General Ruszkay, described
as pro-German and "an enemy of the Jews" (*Judengegner*) were recalled for active duty.[20] By May 30 Veesenmayer had grown quite
impatient with Csatay and had changed his mind regarding Ruszkay
as well, describing both of them as "continually disturbing factors"
in all important decisions to be taken.[21] Veesenmayer was then instructed by Ribbentrop to try to effect the replacement of General
Csatay as minister of defense without, however, provoking the resignation of the regent;[22] Veesenmayer did not succeed, and Csatay remained in the cabinet until October 16. Csatay was not, however,
outspokenly anti-National Socialist. The few outspokenly anti-National Socialist elements in the Hungarian military had already been
sent into retirement.

Similar steps were taken in the economic sphere. The instructions
Hitler had given to Veesenmayer specified that all Hungarian poten-
tials must be exploited for the common war effort.[23] Several plants
producing goods of strategic importance were simply taken over by
German authorities;[24] in most cases, however, such measures were

19. Apr. 18–19, Diary of Vörös. Veesenmayer's comment on the appointment: "Vörös
ist ausgesprochener antisemit" (telegram to OKW/WF/st/AG Ausland, Apr. 20, 1944,
NA Microcopy T-77, roll 883, 5632104).

20. Telegram from Veesenmayer to Ribbentrop, May 13, 1944, NA Microcopy T-120,
roll 100, 110337–39; also telegram from Veesenmayer to Berlin, May 15, 1944, NA
Microcopy T-77, roll 883, 5632090–91. This telegram also mentions the promotion
of Colonel Bartalis, who stood "for the complete participation of Hungary in the
War."

21. NA Microcopy T-77, roll 883, 5631689–91; also telegram from Veesenmayer to
Ribbentrop, May 30, 1944, NA Microcopy T-120, roll 100, 110440–41.

22. Telegram from Altenburg to Veesenmayer, May 4, 1944, NA Microcopy T-120,
roll 1096, 452959. General Ruszkay quarreled with the leadership of the Arrow-Cross
party and was no longer favored by the Germans. He continued, however, to send
long reports and suggestions to Himmler. On June 4, 1944, he proposed that Prime
Minister Sztójay be supported by a strictly "National Socialist" cabinet (NA Microcopy T-175, roll 59, 2574508–14).

23. Hitler to Veesenmayer, Mar. 19, 1944, NA Microcopy T-120, roll 99, 109870–71.
The same instructions specify that all German representatives, including that of the
SS, report to Veesenmayer and that the occupation forces remain under military command, ultimately under the chief of the OKW. See also *Trials of War Criminals before
the Nuernberg Military Tribunals*, 13 : 336–37.

24. The economic exploitation of Hungary was discussed in a report by Winkelmann, the chief of the SS in Hungary, who deplored Veesenmayer's "anti-Hungarian"
policies: "Ich stehe nach wie vor auf dem Standpunkt, dass mein Verhalten eher die

unnecessary, as the Hungarian economic leadership put no obstacles in the path of German exploitation.

Freedom of the press was further curtailed; about 120 newspapers and periodicals were banned outright, whereas other newspapers that had hitherto maintained a moderate stand now felt obliged to support National Socialist views.[25] The works of a good many writers of Jewish faith or Jewish origin were banned by decrees published in May and June 1944.[26] Generally speaking, German supervisors, advisors, coordinators swarmed into Hungary and established a shadow government that insured the proper execution of the Gleichschaltung process.

The German occupation meant, of course, that Hungary ceased to be any kind of a refuge for Jews. Professor Andreas Hillgruber,

---

Billigung des Führers findet, als die einseitige Festlegung Veesenmayers auf Imredy und seine ständige Sorge, die Ungarn irgendwie oder irgendwo zu kranken." Nevertheless, it appears from the remainder of this same report that it was Winkelmann rather than Veesenmayer who felt no compunctions about confiscating Hungarian machinery and even plants. Veesenmayer had told Winkelmann he could not confiscate Hungarian property. Winkelmann replied that he could, "sehe er ja. Ich möchte den mal sehen, der mich wieder mit Gewalt herausbringe. Nachdem ich aber praktisch der Besitzer sei, wäre ich bereit, mir den Verlag nochmal formell so übergeben zu lassen, dass die Ungarn ihr Gesicht währten. Ich wäre auch bereit, den Ungarn gegenüber zu erklären, dass mein Zupacken nicht formell richtig gewesen wäre. Ich würde aber immer so handeln, wenn meine berechtigten und höflich vorgebrachten Wünsche nicht erfüllt würden" (report of May 8, 1944, NA Microcopy T-175, roll 59, 2574520–21). The occupation of Hungary was also the occasion of a protracted and rather well-documented quarrel between Speer and Ribbentrop. Speer wanted to send an "economic plenipotentiary" to exploit Hungarian resources. Ribbentrop insisted his man, Veesenmayer (with whom, incidentally, he did not always agree either), was quite competent in the matter, being a "specialist in economic and industrial affairs," especially as applied to Hungary (Veesenmayer's expertise was of very recent date). Ribbentrop won the round: while various German economic experts were sent to or remained in Hungary, Hitler agreed with Ribbentrop that Veesenmayer should retain ultimate authority in all matters (*Neue Reichskanzlei* file entitled "Neuordnung in Ungarn," NA Microcopy T-120, roll 2488, E-263886-953).

25. For quotes from and an analysis of the radical right press of Hungary during the war, see Nicholas M. Nagy-Talavera, "The Second World War As Mirrored in the Hungarian Fascist Press."

26. Included in the list were the works of Béla Balázs, Lajos Biró, Sándor Bródy, Ernő Szép, Dezső Szomory, Milán Füst, Oszkár Jászi, György Lukács, Frigyes Karinthy, Menyhért Lengyel, Miksa Fenyö, Mihály Földi, Oszkár Gellért, etc. The poet Miklós Radnóti (who achieved fame posthumously) was carried off to the work camps at Bor in Serbia; he was killed later while being transferred from one camp to another. Several writers of Jewish origin suffered a similar fate (Komlós, *Elárult ország*, pp. 80, 90, 124). For a complete roster of blacklisted writers, see *Vádirat a nácizmus ellen*, 1 : 279–81.

in a learned article on German-Hungarian relations during the last
year of the war, dismisses the matter of the deportation and extermination of nearly half a million Jews in one sentence.[27] It is true
that the survivors have already given a fairly complete account of
the fate of the Hungarian Jewry. Yet the subject cannot be dismissed;
it was the most important "problem" the German occupation force
felt incumbent upon itself to "solve," and it was also the issue
around which Hungarian official resistance, such as it was, eventually centered.

The first anti-Jewish measures were published in March. At a
luncheon given by Sztójay and the entire Hungarian cabinet on
March 25, Veesenmayer was told the cabinet would soon introduce
measures to increase war production, release the undelivered corn
to Germany, and tackle the Jewish problem.[28] On March 29, the
national pawnshops were ordered closed to make it more difficult for
Jews to pawn their belongings.[29] On March 31 an order appeared
compelling Jews—that is, all people of Jewish descent—to conspicu-
ously display a star cut out from "canary-yellow" cloth on their outer
garment whenever on the street.[30] The failure to comply with this
regulation would result in internment (but some persons of Jewish
faith who had the will to resist and never wore the yellow star did
manage to elude detection and survived.) Veesenmayer was pleased;
he reported to Ribbentrop that considering the local conditions the
Hungarian developments must be described as unusually quick.[31]
On April 7 the under secretary of the interior László Endre instructed the police to prevent Jews from purchasing lard or sugar
(later on extended to many other goods there seemed to be a shortage
of), to disconnect their telephones, to confiscate their radios and so
on.[32] All stores, offices, and warehouses owned by Jews (perhaps more
than a third of all such establishments in Hungary) were ordered

27. Andreas Hillgruber, "Das deutsch-ungarische Verhältnis im letzten Kriegsjahr."
Hillgruber's article is aptly criticized by György Ránki in "A német-magyar viszony az
utolsó háborús évben és az europai biztonság" [German-Hungarian relations in the
last year of the war and European security].

28. Telegram from Veesenmayer to Ribbentrop, Mar. 25, 1944, NA Microcopy T-120,
roll 99, 109928–29.

29. Telegram from Feine (in Budapest) to Berlin, Mar. 29, 1944, NA Microcopy
T-120, roll 99, 109986.

30. *Vádirat a nácizmus ellen,* 1 : 53.

31. Telegram of Mar. 31, 1944, NA Microcopy T-120, roll 99, 110018–20.

32. Ibid.

closed. Eventually the Jews of Budapest were allowed to shop or be on the streets only a few hours each day. The order for the deportation of the Hungarian Jews was issued to higher-echelon police officers by the Hungarian Ministry of Interior on April 7:

> The Royal Hungarian Government will cleanse the country of Jews within a short space of time. I order the cleansing activity to take place by provinces; as a result of this the Jewish population will be collected in the designated camps without regard to sex or age. In the cities and larger towns a part of the Jewish population will be collected in houses to be designated as "Jewish houses" by the authorities, that is in the ghettoes. . . .
>
> The Jews will be collected by the police having jurisdiction in the area and by the Royal Hungarian gendarmerie. The gendarmerie will assist the regular police inside the cities if necessary. The German security police will be on location in an advisory capacity; one must insist particularly on collaboration with the German police.[33]

The order then proceeded to enumerate the provinces in which the "collection process" was to take place. First came the district of Kassa (Košice) in northeastern Hungary, and nearest the eastern front; then from east to west (more or less), the districts of Marosvásárhely (Tirgu-Mures), Kolozsvár (Cluj), Miskolc, Debrecen, Szeged, Pécs, Szombathely, Székesfehérvár, and lastly Budapest.[34]

The appearance of sovereignty was preserved; the order for deportations did not emanate from the German occupation authorities. A circular issued by Undersecretary Endre Baky to the agencies and branches of the Ministry of Interior on April 19 explained that the German Sicherheitsdienst would participate in the execution of the anti-Jewish regulations;

> but the activities of this organization would be confined to insuring the security of the German troops in the rear area and aims to help the Hungarian authorities only because of the special experience gained in the struggle against the Jews and against bolshevism; it does not, however, wish to interfere with

33. Order number 6163 of 1944 (quoted in Karsai, *A budai vártól*, pp. 471–72; also in *Vádirat a nácizmus ellen*, 1 : 124–25; and in Lévai, *Black Book*, p. 112).
34. Ibid.

the Hungarian authorities or to infringe upon Hungarian sovereignty and independence.[35]

At the Nuremberg trials Veesenmayer testified in his own defense that:

> had the Hungarians consistently refused to meet German demands concerning the solution of the Jewish question, the solution would not have taken place. Pressure would certainly have been applied, but as 1944 was already a year of "crisis," no force would have been available to collect and deport one million persons. This is obviously a task of such dimensions that it could only be carried out in three months, and then only with the wholehearted and enthusiastic support of the entire administrative organization and the armed forces of Hungary.[36]

Veesenmayer's statement is about half true. Just a month before the beginning of the deportations, and event though 1944 was a year of "crisis," Hitler had found sufficient armed strength to invade Hungary and was prepared to dispose of Hungarian resistance has such resistance taken place. On the other hand, a month or two later, when the regent finally intervened energetically to halt the deportations of Jews, Hitler preferred not to insist for the time being. Undoubtedly, as Lévai notes in his English-language book on the fate of the Hungarian Jewry (and also in his Hungarian-language monographs on the same subject), the "sellout" of the Jews was facilitated by twenty-five years of anti-Semitic propaganda in Hungary, the rousing of the "rabble's rapacious instincts" when this rabble stood to profit materially from the expulsion of the Jews, as well as the lack of physical resistance on the part of the Jews.[37]

The question remains, whence did the initiative for the deportations come, who was ultimately responsible for the murder of nearly half a million Hungarian Jews? It is true that much of the deportation program was carried out, enthusiastically, by the two undersecretaries within the Ministry of Interior, Endre Baky and László Endre.[38] The order for the ghettoization, as we have seen, was signed by one of them. Similarly, it was the pertinent Hungarian ministries

---

35. *Vádirat a nácizmus ellen,* 1 : 185–86.

36. Quoted in Lévai, *Black Book,* p. 114.

37. Ibid., p. 139.

38. Horthy is reported to have observed, when learning of their nomination, that they both had been his men at Szeged in 1920.

that issued the censorship measures, the orders regarding the renewed Hungarian military contributions, or even the orders regarding the exploitation of Hungary's economic resources. The Hungarian Fascist press went so far, in its support of the anti-Semitic measures in particular, as to state it was the "patriotic duty or every Hungarian to denounce any Jew who did not comply with or tried to evade the new regulations.[39]

This does not mean, however, that the Hungarian authorities were solely accountable for the extermination of Hungarian Jews. It is doubtful that individuals like Endre Baky and László Endre could have risen to power without a German occupation (even though both had held responsible positions in the between-the-wars period). The German shadow government was everywhere; most assuredly it supervised the execution of the measures against the Jews. Ribbentrop instructed Veesenmayer on April 11 that a trustworthy German, perhaps a Sicherheitsdienst agent, be picked to "lead or control" the Hungarian expert for Jewish affairs in the Ministry of Interior.[40] Veesenmayer replied that the application of the Hungarian laws against the Jews was assured by the fact that an SD specialist worked in close cooperation with László Endre, the undersecretary of the interior in charge of Jewish affairs.[41] The deportations themselves could not have been carried out without German participation; and they were carried out at German instigation. In early April, during conferences between Hitler, Speer, and Milch, it was decided to ask the Hungarian government for a Jewish labor contingent of 100,000 men.[42] When Veesenmayer relayed to Sztójay the German request for Jews, the Hungarian government did not refuse. It is useless to speculate what would have happened had the request been turned down by the Hungarian government. Sztójay promised to make 50,000 able-bodied Jews available to Germany by the end of April and another 50,000 in May.[43] At any rate, the Hun-

39. The Apr. 16, 1944, issue of the *Magyarság*, quoted in *Vádirat a nácizmus ellen,* 1 : 197.

40. Telegram from Altenburg (for Ribbentrop) to Veesenmayer, NA Microcopy T-120, roll 100, 110105.

41. Telegram from Veesenmayer to Ribbentrop, Apr. 22, 1944, NA Microcopy T-120, roll 100, 110234. The "SD Specialist" may have been Eichmann himself (Lévai, *Black Book,* p. 107; also Hilberg, *Destruction of the European Jews,* pp. 530–31).

42. Minutes of a conversation between Hitler and Speer, Apr. 9, 1944 (printed in *Vádirat a nácizmus ellen,* 1 : 133–34).

43. Telegram from Veesenmayer to Ribbentrop, Apr. 14, 1944, NA Microcopy T-120, roll 100, 110133.

garian military authorities informed Veesenmayer on April 15 that 5,000 Jews could be made available immediately and 5,000 more could be provided every three or four days until the quota had been fulfilled.[44] Veesenmayer's request was soon superseded. On April 23 Veesenmayer cabled to Berlin and to Eichmann, who was still in Germany, that beginning mid-May it would be possible to transport 3,000 Jews daily from northeastern Hungary and, if the transport system allowed, simultaneously from other ghettos as well. Destination: Auschwitz.[45] Himmler felt Auschwitz was the logical place: "the open labor assignment [of Jews] in the plants of the Reich is out of question, because it would make illusory the completed evacuation of Jews from Reich territory and the effected exclusion of Jews from the plants in the Reich." [46] And, according to the testimony of Dieter Wisliczeny (the German SS police chief on Hungarian territory) at Nuremberg:

> In Ruthenia over 200,000 Jews were affected by these measures [ghettoizing]. Consequently, impossible food and housing conditions developed in the small towns and rural communities where the Jews assembled. On the strength of this situation Eichmann suggested to the Hungarians that these Jews be transported to Auschwitz and other camps. He insisted, however, that a request to this effect be submitted to him either by the Hungarian government or by a member thereof. The request was submitted by State Secretary von Baky. The evacuation was carried out by the Hungarian police.[47]

The gas chambers and crematories at Auschwitz had not been in use since the fall of 1943; they were now reactivated.[48] But the Hungarian authorities could claim, when accused of misdeeds, that they had been asked to furnish Jews for labor, not for extermination. When the papal nuncio asked the Hungarian prime minister why, if the Jews were being deported to furnish the Germans with manpower, were women and children included in the deportations, the answer was something to the effect that the morale of the Jewish

44. Telegram from Veesenmayer to Berlin, Apr. 15, 1944, NA Microcopy T-120, roll 1306, 487111.

45. NA Microcopy T-120, roll 1306, 487115–16.

46. *Trials of War Criminals before the Nuernberg Military Tribunal,* 13 : 1071–72.

47. *Trial of the Major War Criminals,* 4 : 367.

48. Rezsö Kasztner, *Der Bericht des jüdischen Rettungskomitees aus Budapest, 1942–1945,* p. 30.

laborer was higher if he had his family near him.[49] In fact, not all National Socialist elements in Germany were pleased with the proceedings; Speer, for one, seems to have been disgruntled. It was revealed on May 26, at one of his ministerial conferences, that only two trainloads of employable Jews had been forwarded from Auschwitz out of some 140,000 who had been shipped there during the twelve preceding days.[50]

While the attitude of the Hungarian Jews in this period is not, strictly speaking, a chapter of German-Hungarian relations, the matter has received so much attention that the subject might seem conspicuous by its omission. The thesis of Professor Hannah Arendt,[51] that the failure of the Jews to resist persecutions accounts, in part, for the fate they suffered, has been subjected to repeated criticisms. The general argument that the Jews failed to resist can hardly be disputed with regard to the Jews of Hungary. Gerald Reitlinger, for one, writes that the rounding up of the Jews for deportation was carried out, not by the German SS or even by the Hungarian gendarmerie, but mostly by the Jewish councils.[52] I found a report among the records of the Office of Strategic Services, dated October 1944, the incongruity of which struck me as almost comic. This report stated there were 100,000 Jews in the Budapest "underground." [53] The informant must have simply meant there were many Jews living under assumed names, with false certificates of birth, or in Christian homes, and so on; this kind of "underground" existence had little to do with resistance.

The true fate of the European Jewry was not universally known in March 1944. According to Jöel Brand, who organized rescue operations involving Hungarian Jews, the Jewish leaders were informed of the deportations in Poland by hundreds of memoranda as early as 1942 and 1943; and the warnings were passed on to the Allies.[54] For various reasons the Department of State and the British

49. See note of the Hungarian government to the nuncio, dated June 30, quoted by Jenő Lévai in *L'église ne s'est pas tue; le dossier hongrois, 1940–1945*, p. 30.

50. Reitlinger, *The SS: Alibi of a Nation*, p. 355. Initially about one-third of the estimated one million Jews had been expected to be capable of work (report by Thadden on a visit to Budapest, May 25, 1944, NA Microcopy T-120, roll 4203, K209059).

51. See in particular Hannah Arendt, *Eichmann in Jerusalem* (New York: Viking Press, 1963).

52. *The Final Solution*, p. 460.

53. OSS report in NA Record Group 226, Hungary, 107060.

54. Alex Weissberg, *Advocate for the Dead; the Story of Joël Brand*, p. 31.

Foreign Office saw fit to suppress this information.[55] The people within the occupied territories were often even less well informed. But while the ultimate fate of the Jews may have not been generally known, practically everyone in Hungary must have known that the Jews had been or were being deported from the countries occupied by Germany.[56] Yet the leaders of Hungarian Jewry seemed prepared to cooperate with the Germans. Perhaps they felt that the Hungarian authorities, who had spared most of them until this time, would continue to protect them from the Germans; [57] perhaps they also felt the German authorities themselves were not as bad as their reputation. For instance, the two Gestapo officials who had come to speak to a gathering of Jewish leaders the day after the beginning of the occupation appeared to be well-behaved, gentlemanly fellows.[58] They came to reassure the Jewish leaders and to order the formation of a *Judenrat*—a Jewish council.[59] A Jewish council was formed, modeled on those the German occupation forces had sponsored in other countries. The purpose of the council, as these forces saw it, was to relay and execute their orders; often these orders came directly from the German authorities and not through the intermediary of the Hungarian government.

Definite news about concentration camps and gas chambers arrived only later. In April 1944 two Slovakian Jews managed to escape from Auschwitz and reached Switzerland. The Swiss authorities hesitated to allow the publication of the information brought by the two escapees, but eventually this information was published, early

55. Arthur D. Morse, *While Six Million Died* (New York: Random House, 1968), passim. Interestingly enough, the Hungarian secret service intercepted Allied telegrams from the British and American embassies in Bern giving details regarding the deportations in Hungary, including the news that one and a half million Jews had been exterminated already! (Telegram from Veesenmayer to Ribbentrop, July 6, 1944, NA Microcopy T-120, roll 100, 110651–55.)

56. Ernő Munkácsi, *Hogyan történt* [How it happened], p. 11.

57. Ibid., pp. 14–15.

58. Jenő Lévai writes: "[Eichmann] virtually hypnotized the Jewish Council and, through that body, the whole Hungarian Jewry. As long as no desperate reports were received from the provinces, the Jews of Budapest placed unbounded confidence in the specious German promises" (*Black Book*, p. 88).

59. Munkácsi, *Hogyan történt*, p. 17. The council was composed of Dr. Károly Wilhelm, Dr. Niszon Kahán, Dr. Samu Csobádi, Samu Kahán-Frankl, Fülöp Freudiger, and Samu Stern. On May 8 Undersecretary Endre appointed a new Jewish council composed of the following members: Samu Stern, Dr. Ernő Pethö, Dr. Károly Wilhelm, Dr. Béla Berend, Samu Kahán-Frankl, Fülöp Freudiger, Sándor Török—a writer who was supposed to represent the Christianized Jews—Dr. József Nagy, and Dr. János Gábor (*Vádirat a nácizmus ellen*, 1 : 197).

in July, in the *Journal de Genève* and the *Gazette de Lausanne*. Earlier, in May, Fülöp Freudiger, one of the leaders of the Hungarian Jews and a member of the council, was told of the two Slovakians' experience in a Hebrew letter from surviving coreligionists in Bratislava.[60] The so-called "Notebooks from Auschwitz" were also copied and sent to Hungarian clergymen such as Jusztinián Cardinal Serédi, the chief Roman Catholic prelate in Hungary, Bishop László Ravasz, the chief dignitary of the Reformed Church, and to the regent himself.[61]

While the Jewish council exhorted the Jews of Hungary, orally and by way of newsletters, to obey,[62] some of its members and some of the followers, preferred to adopt a less passive attitude. The most significant of the rescue attempts were the deals negotiated with the Gestapo officials stationed in Hungary. Toward the summer of 1944, SS officials, including Himmler, no longer seemed to regard the extermination of the European Jewry as an unalterable dogma of national socialism and were prepared to make deals. The price attached to the liberation of Hungarian Jews, per capita, varied but was not meant to elicit an automatic refusal. The resources of the Hungarian Jews themselves, however, would have been insufficient by far to pay for their own redemption, especially since the SS officials felt these resources could be acquired without negotiations. Help had to come from Jewish organizations outside the German sphere [63] or from the Allied governments themselves. At one point the SS asked for trucks, and these could only be supplied by the Allies. All things considered, the requests were made with some tact; Himmler never asked for weapons and even promised the trucks would not be used against the Anglo-Americans who, in the

60. Munkácsi, *Hogyan történt*, pp. 78–87; and Lévai, *Black Book*, pp. 175, 229.
61. Munkácsi, *Hogyan történt*, p. 111.
62. Exhortations to obedience were published, for instance, in the Apr. 6, 1944, issue of the *Magyar Zsidók Lapja* [The bulletin of the Hungarian Jews] (*Vádirat a nácizmus ellen*, 1 : 115).
63. Lévai writes: "It has not been possible to get to the bottom of all the facts concerning the vast Zionist rescue-attempt and the reasons for its failure. It must however be said that the aid given to Hungarian Jewry by foreign quarters was too scanty by far. To this day the competent leaders of the Hungarian Jews have been unable to ascertain the exact amounts—both with regard to their sum total and the use they were put to—that were received from abroad for this purpose. World Jewry has still to determine, who or what is responsible for the fact that the opportunity of rescuing one million Jews by paying 2 million dollars was missed" (*Black Book*, p. 284). It should be noted that Lévai was probably mistaken, with regard to both his estimate of the number of Hungarian Jews and the price set on them by the Germans.

meantime, made good their landing on the coast of Normandy. Obviously the Soviet leaders would not have been prepared to accept such proposals; but there is no indication that Anthony Eden, who received these proposals, ever consulted with the Soviet leaders, and therefore the onus of refusal must rest with Eden and the Anglo-American Allies.[64]

Among the reports of the Office of Strategic Services, I found one which described, albeit in somewhat confused terms, the Jews-for-trucks negotiations, in particular the mission of Joël Brand and "Bandi" Grosz, sent to the Near East by Rezső Kasztner to contact the British authorities there.[65] Having reached Turkey safely, the two agents continued to Aleppo in Syria, where they were arrested and detained by the British authorities. There is no doubt the two agents were actually arrested, but a report among the records of the Reich Foreign Office states that Brand had not really been arrested, the news of his arrest having been broadcast only to allay Soviet suspicions while the western powers were ready to conclude a deal with the German government;[66] the German leaders sometimes projected their hope of lack of cooperation between the western powers and the Soviet Union as an accomplished fact. The Gestapo, according to the OSS report, "wanted thousands of trucks and supplies or $2,000 per Jew."[67] While a number of authors, from Lévai to Gerald Reitlinger, write of the price being $200 dollars a head, the OSS report is the earliest I could find on the subject, and furthermore, the price of $2,000 seems more commensurate with the original proposal of 10,000 trucks. According to Ira Hirschmann, the American "special agent" sent by President to negotiate, the deal involved 10,000 trucks to be loaded with 2,000,000 cakes of soap, 200 tons of cocoa, 800 tons of coffee, and 200 tons of tea.[68] Later on,

64. On Mar. 30, 1944, when Eden was asked in Parliament if he knew of an instance in which 1,400 Jewish refugees had been refused admittance to Palestine by British authorities, he declared that he did not (*Vádirat a nácizmus ellen*, 1 : 82).

65. OSS report in NA Record Group 226, Hungary, 85291. According to Ira Hirschmann, the name of Brand's companion was André György, and he was a "double agent" (*Caution to the Winds*, p. 173). Regarding Joël Brand, see also Weissberg, *Advocate for the Dead*.

66. Telegram from Veesenmayer to Ribbentrop, July 22, 1944, NA Microcopy T-120, roll 4203, K209219. It is possible that this interpretation originated with Hungarian Jews who, while knowing the British were not deluding the Soviets, nevertheless attempted to prolong the brief amnesty granted the Hungarian Jews.

67. OSS report in NA Record Group 226, Hungary, 85291.

68. *Caution to the Winds*, p. 174. According to Kasztner, the Germans had asked for 200 tons of tea, 800 tons of coffee, a million boxes of soap, 10,000 trucks, and

however, the German SS, realizing the difficulties involved in obtaining trucks, seemed prepared to accept goods from neutral countries, goods that were blocked by the Allies: chrome, nickel, ball bearings, and so on.[69] The message regarding the deal, whatever the terms, eventually reached Moshe Shertok, the head of the Political Office of the Jewish Agency, who was then in Cairo. Shertok delivered the message to Anthony Eden. Eden, as we have seen, procrastinated and eventually rejected the offers. He regarded the German move—or so he expressed himself in public—as a propaganda move,[70] and the deal was denounced in the London *Times* and over the broadcasts of the BBC. It was a shameless attempt, claimed the British Broadcasting Corporation, to weaken the Allies, whose sympathies for the Jews are well known. The British and American governments would not consider such proposals even if it could help the Hungarian Jews.[71] Hence, the deportations in Hungary proceeded on schedule. By July about 400,000 Jews had been deported from the Hungarian provinces.[72] The last deportation train left on July 8. No one at that time, however, realized that

---

some wolfram in exchange for 1 million Jews (*Der Bericht des jüdischen Rettungskomitees*, p. 36). On July 4 my father noted in his diary, "Can a £1,000 bill [per Jew] abolish the differences between the Aryan and Semite races?" (*Az elsodort ország*, p. 41).

69. Note from Becher to Himmler, NA Microcopy T-175, roll 59, 2574473. It is entirely possible, however, that Himmler did not adopt Becher's solution.

70. "1. Die andere Seite hatte an den Ernst unseres Verhandlungswillens nicht geglaubt. Sie meinte, wir wollten ihr Einverständnis nur zu propagandistischen Zwecken benutzen. 2. Durch die eingehenden Besprechungen und dadurch, dass im gleichen Moment bedingungslos 300 Stück über die Grenze rollten, ist diese Auffassung korrigiert" (note from Becher to Himmler, Aug. 25, 1944, NA Microcopy T-175, roll 59, 2574472). The 300 "pieces" of merchandise were Hungarian Jews released from Bergen-Belsen and shipped to Switzerland.

71. Telegram from the "Sonderzug" to Veesenmayer, July 20, 1944, NA Microcopy T-120, roll 4203, K209218.

72. Estimates regarding the number of victims vary considerably. Lévai gives an exact figure, 434,351, for the number of Jews deported from Hungary by July 8 (*Black Book*, pp. 250–51). According to Hilberg, 437,402 Jews had been deported by July 8 (*Destruction of the European Jews*, p. 547). Furthermore, according to Lévai, 618,007 Hungarian Jews were deported and killed during the German occupation. An additional 63,000 had been killed during the war. There were about 260,000 Hungarian Jews left on December 1, 1945 (*L'église ne s'est pas tue*, p. 15, note; also Lévai, *Black Book*, pp. 470–72). According to Dieter Wisliczeny, the number of Jews deported by July 8 exceeded 476,000 (Kasztner, *Der Bericht des jüdischen Rettungskomitees*, p. 65). Gerald Reitlinger, however, believes that the figure of 381,600 Jews deported by June 30 is more reliable (*Final Solution*, p. 460). The statistics regarding the actual exterminations are even more hazardous. It is clear that a not insignificant proportion of the deported Jews survived but never returned to Hungary.

this trainload had been the last; close to 300,000 Jews still remained in Hungary, that is, in Budapest. There the Jews survived at least until October. In October 1944, after Ferenc Szálasi, the leader of the Arrow-Cross party, came to power, the persecutions were renewed. Before Budapest became surrounded by the Red Army, many of the surviving Jews were marched to concentration camps, where they perished, if they had not already perished en route; many others were shot during pogroms organized by the Arrow-Cross militia in Budapest itself.

Reszö Kasztner, who was mainly responsible for the deals with SS agents, particularly with Wisliczeny, Krumey, Hunsche, and Becher, published a report of his activities in 1946. In this report he gives an account of the failure of the Brand mission and of his own. The report also mentions, however, that as a result of the negotiations he undertook, 318 Hungarian Jews, including many prominent Zionists, were able to leave the Bergen-Belsen concentration camp in North Germany and reach Switzerland in August 1944. In December 1944 another group of Jews numbering 1,355 was allowed to reach Switzerland (causing some dismay to the Swiss authorities), in token of German good faith in the negotiations.[73] These numbers may seem insignificant in relation to the number of Jews who perished; the deal was, nevertheless, the largest successful rescue operation involving Hungarian Jews. Dr. Kasztner, having survived the war in Budapest, emigrated to Israel. There he was tried on various charges stemming from his rescue operation and was acquitted of those charges;[74] he died, however, at the hands of a fanatic assassin.

Another rather well-known rescue operation involved the members of the Weiss and Chorin families, owners of the largest industrial concern in Hungary. The records of the SS and of the Reich Foreign Office contain extensive documentation on the subject.

73. Kasztner, *Der Bericht der jüdischen Rettungskomitees*, pp. 90–92. Ernő Munkácsi describes this report as one-sided in *Hogyan történt* (p. 59). He also notes that while many eminent Zionists were included among the group taken to Bergen-Belsen for ulterior release, there were many others who had been selected because they had handed over their valuables (p. 58). My sister Panni could have left with the group for 20,000 pengő. She was unable to muster that amount (Miksa Fenyő, *Az elsodort ország*, p. 45, entry for July 5). Gerald Reitlinger gives the number of Jews taken from Bergen-Belsen and released in Switzerland as 1,684, and he notes that another 1,100 Jews reached Switzerland in February 1945. Himmler received 5 million Swiss francs in exchange (*The SS: Alibi of a Nation*, p. 357).

74. Jenő Lévai notes that Kasztner's honesty and talent should not have been questioned. Lévai does accuse Kasztner of dictatorial manners and of the yearn to be regarded as the lone savior of the Hungarian Jewry (*Black Book*, pp. 267 ff.).

Basically, however, the deal was simple. Ferenc Chorin, acting as the head of the Weiss, Kornfeld, and Chorin families and negotiating with Kurt Becher, the SS representative, leased his property to the "H. Göring Werke" on May 17 for a period of twenty-five years in exchange for a plane ride to Lisbon for forty-six relatives and friends.[75] The deal, it is clear, was conducted with the knowledge and approval of the Führer.[76] Ferenc Chorin felt obliged to write a letter to the regent explaining his decision.[77] But the decision did not require an explanation; there was little to prevent the German agents from taking over the Csepel Island works (also called the Manfred Weiss works) without consulting the owners except, perhaps, an intermittent concern for legality. The reproach of some western critics that the Chorin and Weiss families managed to save themselves while others perished is misplaced.[78] Had the possibility arisen, Ferenc Chorin would doubtless have attempted to save others; but the significant portion of the deal was not that the largest concern in Hungary passed temporarily into German hands (and Chorin knew well that the "twenty-five year" clause was sheer nonsense) but rather that the forty-six individuals whose life had been redeemed were indeed brought back from the concentration camp at Mauthausen or elsewhere and allowed to fly to Lisbon on June 25 by special airplane, as per agreement.

75. See correspondence between the Reich Foreign Office and the Sicherheitsdienst, July 1944, reproduced on NA Microcopy T-120, roll 3124, 505340 ff.; furthermore, see NA Microcopy T-120, roll 4203, K209144–211. See also OSS reports on Hungary, Record Group 226, 104280, 107062, 109833, Report 104280, in particular consists of about fifty pages. Letters addressed to "Dear Neutral Trade Department" on the subject of the Weiss estate are included in OSS report 106289 (Dec. 5, 1944). Allied and particularly OSS interest in the "Chorin deal" may have been due to the fear that Chorin might feel inclined to transfer additional assets to the Germans for the redemption of three hostages left in Vienna. See also Elek Karsai and Miklós Szinai, "A Weiss-Manfréd vagyon német kézbe kerülésének története" [The history of the German acquisition of the Manfréd Weiss fortune].

76. "Mit Zustimmung des Führers sei einer Gruppe ungarischer Juden die Ausreise nach Portugal gestattet werden" (report by Thadden to Wagner, no date, NA Microcopy T-120, roll 4203, K209210–11).

77. The Chorin letter to Horthy, dated May 17, 1944, is printed in *The Confidential Papers of Nicholas Horthy*, pp. 291–93.

78. The German authorities intercepted an English-language telegram from Lisbon (author not indicated): "More Hungarians refer 01800 expected arrive tomorrow. Members Party already arrived known leading bankers financiers Budapest their money power must facilitated evacuation while hundreds thousands other Jews being delt [sic] different manner including force labour" (NA Microcopy T-120, roll 4203, K209200). It is interesting that the author of this telegram did not seem to be aware of the fact that Jews were being exterminated.

The Jews who remained in Budapest in July 1944 were saved, in part, because of a change in the attitude of the regent. This change itself was the result of several factors. In April and early May the regent had steadfastly refused to believe reports regarding concentration camps and the ultimate fate of the Hungarian Jews. The apostolic nuncio in Hungary, Monsignore Angelo Rotta, visited Prime Minister Sztójay and sent memoranda on behalf of the Jews on at least four different occasions, without appreciable results.[79] The nuncio seemed reluctant to approach the regent, either because Horthy appeared to be out of the picture or because he was a member of the Reformed Church. Bishop Ravasz did call on the regent on two occasions and informed him about the roundup of the Jews in the provinces. The regent told the bishop that when he had heard of certain excesses committed against the Jews in the town of Nyíregyháza he dispatched the two undersecretaries (presumably László and Baky) to investigate and restore order; this, to his knowledge, was done. It is possible, continued the regent, that a few hundred thousand Jews will have been deported from the country, "but not a single hair of theirs will be twisted." [80]

The change in the regent's attitude must have occurred sometime in May. One of the factors influencing this change may have been his increased awareness of the fate of the deported Jews, thanks to confidential reports and to items appearing in foreign newspapers.[81]

79. "Toute démarche," wrote the nuncio on May 15, 1944, "est jusqu'à présent restée sans effet. La Nunciature a même toutes les raisons de croire que l'on envisage d'en venir à la déportation (camouflée ou non) de centaines de milliers de personnes. Nul n'ignore ce que la déportation signifie dans la pratique. . . . Le simple fait de persécuter des hommes pour le seul motif de leur origine raciale constitue une violation du droit naturel. Si Dieu leur a donné la vie, personne au monde n'a le droit de la leur retirer ou de leur refuser les moyens nécessaires à la conserver: à moins qu'ils n'aient commis des crimes" (quoted by Lévai in *L'église ne s'est pas tue,* pp. 21–23). On Apr. 14, 1944, Veesenmayer cabled to Berlin: "1./ Habe weisungsgemäss Sztójay betreffend Intervention des Nuntius Mitteilung gemacht. Sztójay hatte dafür Verständnis und hat auch seither den Nuntius nicht mehr empfangen und zugesagt, Angelegenheit dilatorisch zu handeln. Ich selbst werde nach Übergabe Beglaubigungschreibens wohl Gelegenheit haben, Nuntius kennen zu lernen und alsdann nicht versäumen ihm in geeigneter Form das Nötige zu sagen" (NA Microcopy T-120, roll 1096, 452951).

80. Notes by Bishop Ravasz, quoted by Albert Bereczky, *A magyar protestantizmus a zsidóüldözés ellen* [Hungarian Protestantism against the persecution of the Jews], pp. 15–16; also quoted in Munkácsi's *Hogyan történt,* p. 142.

81. In an affidavit signed on May 27, 1947, Horthy stated that he found out about the extermination of the Jews "gegen Ende June 1944, als ich ausführliche Berichte von Vernichtungslager Auschwitz bekam. F[rage]. Was haben Sie dann getan?

Psychological factors must have played a part; Horthy eventually realized that he was not, strictly speaking, a prisoner of the Germans and he gained self-confidence. Practical factors also played a part. The regent felt—and this argument is brought out in his *Memoirs*—that there was little he could do for the Jews dispersed in the provinces. It should be mentioned, however, that many Jewish men between the ages of eighteen and forty-eight had been drafted into the forced labor battalions of the Hungarian army; and while the treatment of these laborers worsened during the German occupation, especially as a result of an ordinance issued on June 7, 1944, according to which they were to be treated essentially as prisoners of war, nevertheless (or perhaps precisely because of this ill treatment), they were to avoid deportation at least until the Arrow-Cross assumed power in October.[82] Furthermore, large numbers of Hungarian Jews concentrated in the capital could perhaps be saved by energetic diplomatic or even military intervention.[83]

An important factor in the regent's change of attitude was the advice or intervention of certain personalities and leaders of foreign states, including the pope. Among the pleas from foreign leaders came one from the king of England [84] and another from the king of Sweden.[85] In June, for the first time, the representatives of several

---

A[ntwort]. Solange die Deportationen auf dem Land stattfanden, war ich, da meine verschiedenen Proteste an Veesenmayer erfolglos waren, gegenüber der deutschen Übermacht machtlos. Als nun auch die Deportationen aus der Hauptstadt drohten, war die Sache etwas anders. Die ungarischen Streitkräfte die durch das Land verstreut waren, waren so minimal, dass an einen Widerstand gegen die deutschen Massnahmen nicht zu denken gewesen wäre. Die Streitkräfte in Budapest waren auch minimal aber sie unterstanden einem verlässlichen, vorzüglichen Offizier, General Bakay, auf den ich mich verlassen konnte, und konnten deshalb, solange die Deutschen es noch nicht zu einem offenen Bruch kommen lassen wollten, um die Farce des souveränen, Ungarischen Staates noch nicht zu zerstören, mit einigem Erfolg eingesetzt Werden" (interrogation of Admiral Horthy, NA Record Group 238, World War II War Crimes Records).

82. Karsai, *"Fegyvertelen álltak az aknemezőkön,"* 1 : xciii; also Martin Broszat, "Die jüdischen Arbeitskompanien in Ungarn."

83. Interrogation of Admiral Horthy, NA Record Group 238, World War II War Crimes Records; also Horthy, *Memoirs*, p. 219.

84. Ribbentrop's protests against "foreign intervention" seem rather weak: "Ich bitte Sie," he cabled to Veesenmayer, "der ungarischen Regierung mitzuteilen, dass es nicht opportun ist, auf die verschiedenen ausländischen Angebote zugunsten der dortigen Juden einzugehen" ("Geheime Reichssache" telegram, July 3, 1944, NA Microcopy T-120, roll 2721, E-420979).

85. One message from the king of Sweden was delivered, in the first days of July, by Raoul Wallenberg, the Swedish diplomat who volunteered his services and who was to play such an important role in saving the lives of many Budapest Jews during

neutral countries also intervened in a more concrete way. The
Swedish minister asked that three to four hundred Jews who were
Swedish citizens be allowed to leave the country. The Swiss government offered to take ten thousand Jewish children, with 10 percent
adult accompaniment, in addition to nine families totaling thirty
to forty individuals once a week.[86] The efforts of the neutral governments represented in Budapest redoubled as the persecutions
were renewed in October. The Portuguese, Spanish, and Turkish
legations were involved in the rescue attempts, as were the San
Salvadorian and Costa Rican governments whose closest representatives were in Switzerland, but it was the Swedish and Swiss legations
that handed out the greatest numbers of "protective letters" and
that, along with the apostolic nuncio, saved the lives of the greatest
number of Jews.[87] Since Monsignore Rotta's repeated queries to the
Hungarian government not only proved fruitless but eventually
went unanswered (the Hungarians resorted to one of Ribbentrop's
favorite techniques, "dilatorisch zu behandeln"), on June 25, 1944,
the pope himself addressed a message directly to the regent (the
Allied forces had entered Rome on June 4):

---

the days of the Arrow-Cross regime after Oct. 15 (Munkácsi, *Hogyan történt,* pp.
180 ff.). There are several monographs on Raoul Wallenberg and his mission, the best
being perhaps Josef Wulf's *Raoul Wallenberg;* see also Jenő Lévai's *Raoul Wallenberg, hjälten in Budapest* (Stockholm: 1948); and the article by Jacques Sabille, "La
tragique épopée de Raoul Wallenberg, héros suédois de la dernière guerre."

86. The Hungarian government, noted Veesenmayer, adopted a "positive" attitude
toward these offers. By positive, Veesenmayer meant the Hungarians were inclined to
comply with the requests (telegram from Veesenmayer to Berlin, June 29, 1944, NA
Microcopy T-120, roll 4357, K215093; also reproduced on NA Microcopy T-120, roll
100, 110593–94). The reply to Veesenmayer's telegram was as follows: "Im Hinblick auf
die vom Reich bisher konsequent verfolgte Linie in der Judenpolitik,—die darauf
hinausgeht, eine Auswanderung von Juden möglichst zu unterbinden und, soweit sie
zugelassen wird, von einer wertvollen Gegenleistung abhängig zu machen,—sowie im
Hinblick auf unsere Araber-Politik schlagt Gruppe Inland II vor, die Ungarische
Regierung durch Gesandten Veesenmayer zu bitten, den Schweizern und Amerikanern
zu antworten, einer Auswanderung nach Palästina könne unter keinen Umständen
zugestimmt werden . . . Eine Rück-Antwort auf diese Stellungnahme dürfte erst in
etwa 14 Tagen bis 3 Wochen zu erwarten sein und bis Ende dieses Monats ist die
Judenaktion in Ungarn im gros abgeschlossen, sodass die Intervention dann im
Wesentlichen gegenstandlos geworden ist" (unsigned memorandum of the Reich
Foreign Office, July 6, 1944, NA Microcopy T-120, roll 1306, 487147–50). See also
telegram from Veesenmayer to Berlin, Sept. 15, 1944, NA Microcopy T-120, roll 3131,
E509820.

87. More than 30,000 protective letters were issued by the various neutral governments, including the apostolic nuncio; as often as not, however, these letters did not
serve their purpose (Lévai, *L'église ne s'est pas tue,* p. 63).

We are asked from several sides to interpose Our authority to prevent the continuation and worsening of the suffering of a great many unfortunate people owing to their nationality or their race, and who live among a noble and chivalrous nation. Because of Our affection toward all human beings, Our paternal heart cannot remain unimpressed by these appeals. Because of this We turn to Your Highness, appealing to His noble feelings, hoping that Your Highness will do everything in His power to spare renewed mournings and renewed sufferings to these unfortunate people. Pius XII.[88]

The prince primate of Hungary, Jusztinián Cardinal Serédi, as well as the leaders of the Protestant churches, threatened a public denunciation of the deportations unless these were halted by the Hungarian government.[89] The cardinal even drafted a pastoral letter which was to be read from the pulpit the Sunday after its receipt. The government got wind of this sabotage effort and put strong pressure on the cardinal to change his attitude. The Catholic leaders eventually reached an agreement with the Hungarian government whereby the latter would not permit further deportations and the pastoral circular was retracted by the cardinal. Similar agreements were arranged between the Hungarian government and the Protestant leaders. Accordingly, on Sunday, July 16, both Catholic and Protestant clergymen simply told their congregation that their respective churches had taken steps on behalf of the Jews, especially the Christianized Jews, and would continue to take such steps.[90] As the Hungarian government seemed to live up to the agreement and did not allow further deportations of Jews, the various churches refrained, with the exception of certain individual clergymen, from denouncing the persecutions in specific and unmistakable terms.

A memorandum by Count Bethlen, Hungarian prime minister in the period 1921–31 and still Horthy's respected counselor, was

---

88. Quoted in Lévai, *L'église ne s'est pas tue*, pp. 83 ff. A different view of the attitude of the churches is expressed in Róbert Major, "The Churches and the Jews in Hungary."

89. While the cardinal had already intervened repeatedly on behalf of the Christianized Jews, he was prodded by the apostolic nuncio and by the archbishop of Győr, Vilmos Apor, to take an energetic stand on behalf of all persecuted Jews (Lévai, *L'église ne s'est pas tue*, pp. 83 ff.).

90. Munkácsi, *Hogyan történt*, pp. 146 ff. With regard to the Catholic Church, see Lévai, *L'église ne s'est pas tue*, pp. 103–12. With regard to the Protestants, see Bereczky, *A magyar protestantizmus a zsidóüldözés ellen*, pp. 23–24.

forwarded to the regent sometime in June 1944. This memorandum
suggested that the Sztójay cabinet be dismissed and the deportation
of the Jews prohibited. Count Bethlen even outlined the tactics
necessary to carry out these measures, tactics which were adopted,
by and large, by the regent.[91]

It is clear that the intervention of Count Bethlen, of the pope and
the various churches of Hungary, and of certain foreign leaders left
a deep impression on Horthy; but it cannot be argued that these
interventions were solely responsible for the regent's change of
heart. The regent had been disturbed by the news of persecutions
even prior to these interventions. According to a German intelligence report described as "reliable," Horthy had told the new Swiss
minister in Budapest, around mid-May, that he was not responsible
for the measures against the Jews and that he would have those who
were responsible arrested "at a given moment." [92] Early in June
Horthy wrote a letter to his prime minister regarding the treatment
of the Jews:

> Above all it is clear that I was not in a position to prevent
> anything that was a German measure in this line or a govern-
> ment measure enacted on German demand, so that in this re-
> spect I was forced to a positive [*sic*] attitude. Although in this
> way not only could I obtain no advance knowledge of the
> measures taken, but even subsequently I was not informed of
> everything; nevertheless of late I have received information to
> the effect that in many respects more had been done here than
> even by the Germans themselves, partly in such a brutal, and
> sometimes inhuman manner as has not even been done in
> Germany.

In fact the German authorities produced a documentary film about
the roundup and entraining of Jews in Hungary which was shown
in Switzerland and perhaps in other neutral countries; the point of
the documentary was that it showed not a single German soldier or

91. This memorandum is printed in *The Confidential Papers of Nicholas Horthy,*
pp. 308–14. At one point Bethlen suggested: "Hungarian soldiers on the front having
taken the oath to Miklós Horthy would fight only under his command, but would
lose their combat value if any attempt were made to remove the Regent from his post.
For this reason loyalty to the person of the Regent should be inculcated on the troops
and the officer corps at the front, repeatedly through all the days."

92. Telegram from Ribbentrop to Veesenmayer, May 18, 1944, NA Microcopy T-120,
roll 100, 110372–73.

SS man but a good many uniformed agents of the Hungarian government.[93]

> It is therefore my resolute demand [continued Horthy] that on the part of the Government urgent measures be taken to end that in branches of professions, thus e.g. in particular engineering and medical work, further in trade in general, or in occupations where special learning or experience is required . . . the Jews concerned should not be removed from their domiciles, nor should measures be taken against them hampering them in their work, or putting obstacles in the way of their occupation. . . . I request you to inform the cabinet of the contents of my manuscript, and take action for their realization without delay.[94]

Horthy also ordered, in this message, that the two undersecretaries of the interior, Baky and Endre, be relieved of their duties.[95]

Horthy first raised the question of Hungarian sovereignty in a conversation with General Greiffenberg on May 5.[96] On June 6 Horthy wrote a letter to Hitler on the same topic. It was to be delivered by Sztójay, who had been invited to visit the Führer. Sztójay did not take the letter but undertook to tell the Führer about its contents. He complained that two and half months had elapsed since the meetings at Klessheim, and the German troops had not

93. Lévai, *Black Book*, p. 305; also Komlós, *Elárult ország*, p. 99. It is true that the effectives of Eichmann's "Sonderkommando" and of the Gestapo in general were so limited in Hungary that it scarcely could have accomplished what it did accomplish without the help of the Hungarian authorities, especially the gendarmerie (Munkácsi, *Hogyan történt*, p. 112). On the other hand, the Hungarian authorities were not invariably cooperative. A set of instructions sent by Hitler and Ribbentrop to Veesenmayer regarding rewards to Hungarian collaborators indicates these authorities may have needed encouragement: "Der Herr RAM lässt Sie verständigen, dass der Führer sich zu vorbezeichnetem Drahtbericht dahin geäussert hat, dass, wenn in Ungarn Einheimische uns bei den Massnahmen gegen die Juden behilflich seien, wir vielleicht aus jüdischen Kapital diesen Einheimischen Dotationen geben könnten. Dadurch wurde die Mitarbeit der Ortseinwohner aktiviert werden" (telegram from Altenburg to Veesenmayer, May 17, 1944, NA Microcopy T-120, roll 1306, 487123).

94. *The Confidential Papers of Nicholas Horthy*, pp. 301–3. While Horthy's style of writing, in Hungarian, may not have had literary merits, the strange syntax and word usage in the excerpt above is probably the fault of the translator. See also telegram from Veesenmayer to Ribbentrop, June 21, 1944, NA Microcopy T-120, roll 100, 110557–58.

95. *The Confidential Papers of Nicholas Horthy*, pp. 301–3.

96. Telegram from Veesenmayer to Berlin, May 6, 1944, NA Microcopy T-120, roll 100, 110312.

been withdrawn from Hungary as Hitler promised. Instead, thousands of innocent people were under arrest, including several high-ranking officers. Indeed, the three officers arrested by the Germans, Ujszászy, Kádár, and Kéri, had become the subject of persistent complaints on the part of Horthy, Sztójay, and other officials of the Hungarian government. On the part of Horthy, the complaints illustrated his concern for and strong faith in the honor of the Hungarian officer class; but perhaps his insistence on their release was also a legitimate way of venting his fury at the Germans and at his own real or imagined impotence. After all, the arrest of the three officers seems, in relative terms, only a minor blow at Hungarian sovereignty. As regards Prime Minister Sztójay, this was the first time he and the German authorities disagreed.[97]

In his letter to Hitler, Horthy had also enumerated the recent Hungarian economic, financial, and military contributions.

> Since March 19th of the current year we have sent out 2,700 officers and 119,654 men. . . . One has to fear our troops on the front will learn of the circumstances that at home many thousands of German troops carry on a comfortable, carefree life, while they have to run into death. . . . There are now

97. Veesenmayer demanded the "disappearance" or arrest of Kádár and Ujszászy on or before April 14 (telegram from Veesenmayer to Berlin, Apr. 14, NA Microcopy T-120, roll 1096, 452951-52); apparently Sztójay hesitated. Kádár and Ujszászy were arrested by the German authorities on Apr. 18. Sztójay protested the arrest on Apr. 19 and about every other day thereafter. On May 8 General Greiffenberg, the German military attaché, reported that he had been summoned by Horthy who told him he would ask that Hitler return sovereignty to Hungary: "Es spielte dabei auf die Verhaftung und mögliche Aburteilung ungarischer Offiziere ohne Mitwirkung ungarischer Dienststellen an, was nach seiner Auffassung 'das Mitgehen auch uns wohlgesinnter Kreise in Hass verwandeln könnte'" (telegram to OKW, May 8, 1944, NA Microcopy T-77, roll 883, 5631721). On May 5 Ribbentrop had agreed, "in principle," to the transfer of the three Hungarian officers into Hungarian custody (memorandum of May 26, NA Microcopy T-77, roll 883, 5631701-2, 563176). But the officers remained in German custody, and Sztójay continued to protest (see, for instance, Veesenmayer to Berlin, June 8, 1944, NA Microcopy T-120, Roll 1096, 452990-91). The German authorities decided not to release the three officers, as they were the only witnesses to the Hungarian "betrayal," by which presumably the negotiations with the American Airborne mission were meant. "Diese Offiziere sind die einzigen Kronzeugen, die wie für die ungarischen Hochverratspläne haben" (note by Wagner, June 5, 1944, NA Microcopy T-120, roll 3155 E518646). Nevertheless, Ujszászy, Kádár, and Kéri were freed early in July, but Kéri was rearrested by the Germans on July 14. Ujszászy and Kádár were taken by the Hungarian military authorities into protective custody (July 7 and 14, Diary of Vörös).

250,000 German troops in Hungary who certainly would render good services at the front.[98]

Horthy made no mention of the Jews in his letter, nor did Sztójay bring up the matter in the course of his visit; but Hitler told Sztójay that until the Jewish problem had been completely solved the German troops would have to remain in Hungary.[99]

Sztójay was displeased with the result of his meetings with the German leaders. Veesenmayer's estimate of Sztójay had been of the highest order: Sztójay had always agreed to the principal German demands.[100] Now even Sztójay was complaining. Hungary was being discriminated against in a number of ways. A German plenipotentiary was active in Hungary (whereas there was no Hungarian plenipotentiary in Germany). Hungarian officers and public figures had been arrested and prosecuted without the participation or consultation of Hungarian authorities. Representatives of the Badoglio government had been arrested despite their right of asylum. The Gestapo was active on Hungarian soil. Travel to and from Hungary was controlled by German authorities. Homes, factories, and land

98. *The Confidential Papers of Nicholas Horthy,* pp. 305–6. Horthy was mistaken regarding the effectives of the German force stationed in Hungary. These were considerably less. Some time in July the Hungarian authorities specifically requested that the two SS divisions stationed in Hungary, the Eighth and the Twenty-second SS cavalry divisions, be released for the defense of the Carpathians. The German military command refused, because, for one thing, both divisions were still being outfitted: "Im übrigen sind sie die einzigen deutschen Verbände, die in Ungarn stehen und somit ein gewissen Druck auf Volk, Regierung und Wehrmacht aufüben können. . . . Als Begründung für die Ablehnung ist nur mangelnde Beweglichkeit und beschränkte Verwendungsmöglichkeit anzugeben" (telegram from military attaché to OKW Wehrmachtführungsstab, July 26, 1944, NA Microcopy T-77, roll 883, 5632043). On July 17 Horthy also wrote Hitler a letter containing the following passages: "Almost four months have elapsed since [the occupation of Hungary] and I should like to ask Your Excellency most urgently in accordance with your valuable promise to withdraw the occupying forces in the country, the special staff of SS, and above all the Gestapo which day after day, in a quite senseless manner, creates martyrs and transports Hungarian property by the wagonloads from the country." Horthy also mentioned his intention of setting up a new government "with a Three-Star-General at its head." "Finally," wrote Horthy, "I would remark that the further solution of the Jewish problem will be realized without the often unnecessary brutal and inhuman methods [sic]." This letter was not sent either, but its contents were read over the telephone by Veesenmayer to Ribbentrop, and Hitler, in response, threatened the gravest reprisals (*The Confidential Papers of Nicholas Horthy,* pp. 316–18).

99. Ibid., p. 306.

100. Telegram from Veesenmayer to Ribbentrop, May 10, 1944, NA Microcopy T-120, roll 100, 110316.

were taken over by German authorities without Hungarian consent. Germany's relations with Hungary, concluded Sztójay in a letter to Ribbentrop, were different from Germany's relations with Slovakia, Bulgaria, Romania, or Finland.[101] He would return to Hungary, he told Wilhelm Keitel, without so much as a minor concession on the part of the Germans. On the contrary, argued Sztójay, it seemed as if Hungary were losing more and more of its independence.[102] While Keitel informed Hitler of Sztójay's complaints, Hitler expressed no opinion on any of the particular issues. And a further memorandum on June 30 listing the Hungarian complaints and suggesting remedies was handled "dilatorily" on Ribbentrop's instructions.[103]

It was perhaps as a result of Horthy's message of early June that Sztójay called a cabinet meeting on June 23 to discuss the deportation of Jews. The two undersecretaries of the interior (not yet fired) were asked to report on the subject. Their report insisted the deportations were being carried out in a "humane" manner. Arnóthy-Jungerth, a well-meaning undersecretary of foreign affairs, remarked sarcastically "that one must really regret not having been born a Jew and not being able to take part in those picnics." [104]

At a meeting of the Crown Council a few days later, on June 26, it was decided to halt the deportations; [105] the question was, would the decision of the Hungarian authorities prevail over the determination of Eichmann, Veesenmayer, and the entire German leadership? In June the German authorities were already making preparations for the deportation of the Jews of Budapest, variously estimated at between 200,000 and 300,000. As early as May 27 Dr. Schmidt of the Reich Foreign Office wrote a note to Rintelen regarding the "unfavorable" reaction in neutral countries toward the deportation of Jews and the necessity of finding some excuse for proceeding against the Jews of Budapest. One could, suggested Dr. Schmidt, discover explosives in the headquarters of Jewish organizations or in the synagogues, find Jewish sabotage units and plans for a revolu-

101. Sztójay to Ribbentrop, June 7, 1944, NA Microcopy T-120, roll 100, 110516–21.
102. Report by Ritter on conversation between Keitel and Sztójay, June 7, 1944, NA Microcopy T-120, roll 100, 110495.
103. Memorandum by Hungarian minister in Berlin, summarized by Gustav Adolf Steengracht, NA Microcopy T-120, roll 100, 110617–20.
104. Quoted in Munkácsi, *Hogyan történt*, p. 164.
105. Ibid., p. 173; see also June 26, Diary of Vörös.

tion or for an attack on the police, discover black-market activities with foreign currency on a scale large enough to undermine the country's economy; the excuse for the undertaking must be something especially serious.[106] Dr. Schmidt's suggestions were forwarded to Veesenmayer. On June 6 an official of the Reich Foreign Office noted that the Normandy landings were a fortunate coincidence (!), and the date for the deportation of the Budapest Jews ought to be reset as "world propaganda" would now hardly notice the event.[107] Veesenmayer, however, was in any case not concerned about repercussions in other countries; he felt the roundup of the Budapest Jews would provoke the same amount of adverse reaction as the roundup of the Jews in the provinces had: very little.[108]

The deportations from Budapest had been scheduled for July 6. It was felt the entire action could take place in a day or two, since the Jews had already been gathered in houses designated as Jewish and the entire city public transportation system had been reserved for the operation. As the Budapest police seemed insufficient or not entirely reliable for the purpose, about five thousand gendarmes were brought to the capital city to help in the execution of the operation. But the regent intervened. He ordered a Hungarian division under the command of General Bakay to report to the capital. He called the director of the gendarmerie, General Faraghó, telling him to order the gendarmes out of the capital (even though a certain Colonel Ferenczy had been responsible for the activities of the gendarmerie in connection with the roundup of the Jews). In fact, Horthy had felt a plot was afoot. He had been informed that one of the rightist parties ("probably Baky and company"—Horthy told General Vörös) had concerted with the leaders of the Gestapo on how to get rid of the government, perhaps with the help of the SS.[109] One manifestation of the plot seems to have been the attempt to assassinate István Bárczy, a friend of the regent and secretary of

106. See also *Trials of War Criminals before the Nuernberg Military Tribunals,* 13 : 352–53.

107. Memorandum by Thadden to the chief of the Inland II Section, June 6, 1944, NA Microcopy T-120, roll 1306, 487139.

108. Telegram from Veesenmayer to Thadden, June 8, 1944, NA Microcopy T-120, roll 106, 487140.

109. June 29, Diary of Vörös. General Vörös told the regent he did not think a plot likely; certainly Szálasi's party stood on a much higher "moral plane." But General Vörös may have been not entirely sincere, as he had been warned earlier, on June 17, by Ministers Imrédy and Kunder (who were also right wing, of course), that Baky was

the cabinet (on June 28, 1944).[110] But the suspected plot was not Horthy's only motive for taking action. On July 5 he informed General Vörös he intended to *"prevent the further deportation of Jews from Hungary"* (the italics are those of Vörös), even though the general warned him to proceed with caution in order to avoid the "political complications" that might result from the delays in the solution of the Jewish question.[111] Since General Vörös did not, or pretended not to, believe in the possibility of a plot against the regent, he did not order military forces to Budapest as the regent had requested. But General Károly Lázár, the commander of Horthy's bodyguard, did; and General Baky's army corps, or sections of it, took up stations in the northern sectors of the city and around the railroad stations by 2300 on July 6.[112] The next day Horthy again summoned Vörös and asked him whether, in case of necessity, it would be possible to resist with arms the Gestapo and SS units stationed in Hungary. "I repeated," wrote General Vörös in his diary, "that our strength *is insufficient* to confront the Germans. Despite the difficult situation on the front the Germans still have enough strength to beat our resistance, especially with heavy armored vehicles." [113]

It must have been clear to Horthy that in the event of a crisis he could not rely on his chief of the General Staff, but the matter did not yet come to a test. Horthy gave orders to halt the deportations.[114] Still, Veesenmayer felt confident the deportations would eventually be completed: he held "all the political wires firmly in his hand," he boasted.[115] While General Vörös told the regent the

organizing and perhaps arming vigilante units for the Arrow-Cross party; see diary entry for June 17. See also telegram from Veesenmayer to Ribbentrop, July 6 and 8, 1944, NA Microcopy T-120, roll 100, 110660–65, 110673–74.

It seems that Ferenc Szálasi, the leader of the Hungarist Movement, or Arrow-Cross Party, was responsible for revealing the plot by the rival group around Baky and Imrédy on July 2 (Karsai, *Vádirat a nácizmus ellen*, p. xv).

110. Editorial comments in *The Confidential Papers of Nicholas Horthy*, pp. 318–19.

111. July 5, Diary of Vörös.

112. July, ibid. Vörös added, "all this was reported to me by General Lázár on the morning of the 7th, saying that he had not wanted to disturb my night's rest." See also Munkácsi, *Hogyan történt*, pp. 177 ff. My father, although in hiding, had a fairly accurate picture of these events (entry for July 7, *Az elsodort ország*, p. 65).

113. July 7, Diary of Vörös.

114. Telegram from Veesenmayer to Ribbentrop, July 6, 1944, NA Microcopy T-120, roll 100, 110651–55.

115. Telegram from Veesenmayer to Ribbentrop, July 9, 1944, NA Microcopy T-120, roll 4203, K209142–43.

Germans might send additional SS units to Hungary, Veesenmayer cabled the Führer that these would not be necessary.[116] Yet, despite the efforts of Veesenmayer and of certain other National Socialist officials, the regent stood firm and deportations were not resumed until after his demise; and the National Socialist leaders could not or did not wish to force the issue. Eichmann and his *Sondereinsatzkommando* finally departed from Hungary on August 30.[117] Horthy had told Veesenmayer that concentration camps would be set up for Jews in Hungary proper. But one of the Jewish leaders persuaded Horthy that this would be unwise, and the Red Cross, charged with the task of finding emplacements for such camps, was conveniently unable to find a single suitable location in six weeks of searching.[118]

In two instances the regent's order to halt the deportations was circumvented. The Jews on the outskirts of the capital were deported by order of the minister of the interior, Andor Jaross, and these deportations took place after the decision of the Crown Council on June 26.[119] In the other instance, the inmates of the Hungarian concentration camp at Kistarcsa were involved. On July 14 Eichmann managed to load over a thousand of the inmates on a train which took off toward Auschwitz. A member of the Jewish council called Horthy to inform him of the incident; Horthy gave orders, the train was halted, and the inmates returned to Kistarcsa. A second attempt by Eichmann was, however, successful; on July 19 the inmates were loaded on trucks, and the Hungarian authorities found out about the operation too late.[120]

Despite these incidents a change had set in in Hungarian-German relations. The German occupation continued, it is true. The Hungarian government continued to send troops to the eastern front; in fact, as far as the Hungarians were concerned, it was no longer the eastern front but the Carpathian Mountains, Hungary's own frontier, that had to be defended. The German authorities continued to exploit the resources of the Hungarian economy, without encount-

116. Ibid. The following German units were stationed in Hungary at the time: the 389th Infantry Division, the Eighteenth SS Cavalry Division, the Twenty-second SS Cavalry Division, and the Eighteenth SS Armored Grenadier Division ("Horst Wessel") (Hillgruber, "Das deutsch-ungarische Verhältnis," p. 85).

117. Lévai, *L'église ne s'est pas tue*, p. 51. Also, Karsai, *Vádirat a nácizmus ellen*, pp. xxv ff.

118. Lévai, *Black Book*, p. 325.

119. Telegram from Veesenmayer to Ribbentrop, July 9, 1944, NA Microcopy T-120, roll 4203, K209142.

120. Lévai, *L'église ne s'est pas tue*, pp. 41–42.

ering official or unofficial resistance. Politically, however, the regent and his advisers began to make attempts to regain Hungarian sovereignty and were at least considering the renewal of negotiations for an armistice. Perhaps these attempts were belated; but the causes for the failure of the Hungarian government and of the regent must be sought not in the events of the spring and summer of 1944, when Hungary was already overwhelmed with German might, but in the conditions and events preceding Hungarian entry into the war or even preceding the outbreak of the war itself.

11. The Abortive Coup of October 15, 1944

During the four months between July and October 1944 the regent and his advisers attempted to extricate Hungary from her predicament. It was not the first time, to be sure; we have seen that numerous such attempts had already been made in 1943, mostly without the knowledge of the regent. Now the predicament seemed even more hopeless, and it was a predicament which resulted, it cannot be denied, at least in part from the regent's oversights, his class prejudices, and his lack of competence. Admittedly his position was extremely difficult: he had taken command of the country in the wake of the Hungarian Commune, and he preserved an intense distaste for "bolshevism" even after the danger of a Communist takeover had receded far into the distance. Now it was becoming increasingly clear, even had the Anglo-American Allies not warned the Hungarian government to that effect,[1] that armistice or peace negotiations had to be conducted with the Soviet Union first of all and that Hungary would be occupied not by Anglo-American but by Soviet troops. Yet for two or three months longer, and as late as September, the regent and some members of his entourage continued to hope for some miracle (such as the dropping of Anglo-American paratroopers on Hungarian territory) that would have resulted in an Anglo-American or at least a joint Allied occupation. A substantial segment of Hungarian public opinion and some of the Hungarian leaders, reached by the propaganda of German and Hungarian newspapers and radio broadcasts, continued to believe in the possibility of a German victory;[2] their faith found confirmation in the fact that Germany eventually did produce some of the "secret weapons" of which she had boasted for so long and perhaps also in the fact that Hitler escaped yet another assassination attempt, the plot of July 20, as if by divine intervention. Many Hungarians, pro-German or pro-western, seemed to cultivate a belief in political or military miracles,

1. Archduke Otto of Hapsburg, for one, attempted to warn Hungary (along with Tibor Eckhardt) on Sept. 8, 1944, that this was the "last chance" for Hungary to break away from the Axis (Lukacs, *The Great Powers and Eastern Europe,* p. 623). Similar warnings came from Bakách-Bessenyey in Switzerland and from other Hungarian sources abroad.

2. Márton Himler, *Igy néztek ki a magyar nemzet sirásói,* passim.

a belief propagated by the press and other media.[3] And even if some of the Hungarian leaders knew the war was lost, they also knew they had compromised themselves too far, especially vis-à-vis the Soviet Union: by fighting or persuading others to continue fighting, they could enjoy a few more days of power, a few more days of respite.

Yet Horthy was determined to replace the Sztójay cabinet; it had failed to stand up to any of the German demands and would have proven definitely unreliable if secret negotiations with the enemy were to resume. Horthy was toying with the idea of setting up an "apolitical" (that is, military) government as early as July 5.[4] A few days later, in a conversation with Veesenmayer, Horthy complained of the inhumane treatment of the Jews, and he also hinted at the possibility of setting up some kind of a military dictatorship.[5] On July 11 Horthy told General Vörös he was determined to make the change; it is significant, perhaps, that of the five names Horthy mentioned in this connection, those of Generals Géza Lakatos, Lajos Csatay, Szilárd Bakay, Ferenc Farkas, and Jenő de Bor, only the first two were eventually retained to form the new cabinet.[6] In mid-July Horthy announced his intention of effecting changes in the cabinet even though the risk involved was great, for Hitler not only might refuse to condone a change in government but might forcefully intervene to prevent such a change. Indeed, Hitler reacted very unfavorably to the idea. He regarded the replacement of Sztójay as nothing less than treason. "In this case," cabled Ribbentrop to Veesenmayer, Hitler "would immediately recall Ambassador Veesenmayer and order such measures that would make the repetition of such events in Hungary impossible once and for all." The next paragraph in the cable (microfilm of the original manuscript), having undergone some revisions, bears the initials of Hitler himself in approval:

> The Führer expects that henceforth the measures against the Jews of Budapest will be carried out by the Hungarian government without any further delay, with the exceptions granted by the Reich government on the recommendation of Ambassador

3. Nagy-Talavera, "The Second World War As Mirrored in the Hungarian Fascist Press," pp. 179–208, passim.

4. July 5, Diary of Vörös.

5. Telegram from Veesenmayer to Ribbentrop, July 8, 1944, NA Microcopy T-120, roll 100, 110673–74.

6. July 11, Diary of Vörös.

Veesenmayer and in agreement with the proposals of the Hungarian government. These exceptions must not, however, result in any delay in the execution of the general anti-Jewish measures, or else the Führer will feel obligated to retract his agreement to these exceptions.[7]

Hitler's message concluded with a further warning that any departure from the "ways decided at Klessheim and instituted since then" might jeopardize the very existence of the Hungarian nation; it might be annihilated by bolshevism.[8] Thus the message implies that Horthy had actually assented, back on March 18, to some of the measures Hitler had ordered in connection with the occupation of Hungary.

The Führer's telegram was read to Horthy by Veesenmayer. Horthy interrupted at one point to remark that these were indeed strong words. After the lecture, Horthy told Veesenmayer he regretted having asked Veesenmayer to send a message in the first place, for surely the message must have been worded wrong and was misinterpreted by Hitler. Then, Horthy continued (according to Veesenmayer) with "long explanations" regarding the injustices committed by the Reich both against himself and against Hungary, and he threatened to resign, while warning Veesenmayer that 90 percent of the Hungarian people stood behind him. Veesenmayer in turn made a threat to the effect that Germany still had enough power to restore order in Hungary should the necessity arise, since Hitler's policy had always been to set aside sufficient reserves, and besides the Germans had many friends in Hungary. "After the conclusion of this conversation," wrote Veesenmayer, "Horthy was completely finished, his whole body trembled, and he was an old broken man."[9]

The language used by Hitler and Veesenmayer did not break or even intimidate the regent as much as it aroused him. On July 17 Horthy convoked Generals Csatay and Vörös and once again asked

7. July 16, 1944, NA Microcopy T-120, roll 4203, K209127–36; see also NA Microcopy T-120, roll 100, 10730–32. The exceptions mentioned in this telegram refer to Jewish artists, writers, scientists, for whom the Hungarian government had requested exemptions.

8. Ibid., roll 4203, K209130–31.

9. Telegram from Veesenmayer to Ribbentrop, "supercitissime," July 17, 1944, NA Microcopy T-120, roll 4293, 209133–34; see also NA Microcopy T-120, roll 100, 110136–37. Furthermore, see telegram of German military attaché in Budapest to the OKW Wehrmachtführungsstab, July 20, 1944, NA Microcopy T-77, roll 883, 5632060.

them "what would happen if we were to undertake armed resistance against the Germans here." Vörös told Horthy, as he had done on a previous occasion, that this would mean the end of Hungary's national existence (using terms very similar to those Veesenmayer had used) and that the best service Hungary could render the "cultured" western nations would be to hold up the onslaught of bolshevism. Horthy did not mention the conversation he had had with Veesenmayer shortly before but told the two generals the Germans were delaying the receipt of the letter he had written to Hitler! [10]

On his return to headquarters General Vörös briefed his staff, notably General László, about his conversation with the regent! In his diary he comments that he felt the regent was given poor advice by that "old clique" composed of Count Bethlen and Baron Rakovszky. The officers of the General Staff—and this is significant in retrospect, in view of the events of October 15—unanimously agreed that one must by all means avoid fighting against the Germans and restore smooth relations with them at the earliest opportunity.[11] Yet a few days later the German military attaché in Budapest complained that the general situation in Hungary was becoming increasingly unfavorable to German interests; even the Hungarian chief of the General Staff (that is, Vörös), who used to be the most loyal and influential partner of the Germans, now was talking about his "concern for Hungary" and his "responsibility in face of history." [12]

On July 22, that is, very shortly after the plot of July 20, Horthy dispatched Gen. Béla Miklós, his aide-de-camp, to Hitler's headquarters. Miklós was to deliver a message. Hitler seems to have been in an elated mood that day; he had escaped the assassination attempt, he felt, "as if by miracle." Besides, he was elated because everyone in Berlin appeared greatly relieved at his escape, and full harmony reigned between the party and the army! [13] Having explained these circumstances to General Miklós, Hitler finally came to inquire about the general's mission, and when informed of Horthy's design to form a government of generals, he disapproved. But Hitler's dis-

10. July 17, Diary of Vörös.

11. Ibid.

12. Telegram to OKW Wehrmachtführungsstab, July 23, 1944, NA Microcopy T-77, roll 883, 6532682.

13. Telegram from Schmidt to Veesenmayer on conversation between Hitler and General Miklós, July 24, 1944, NA Microcopy T-120, roll 4203, K209124. In another telegram of the same date Veesenmayer described Miklós as an anglophile (NA Microcopy T-120, roll 100, 110740).

approval was expressed in terms milder than those he had used previously. The German troops were not in Hungary, explained Hitler, to irritate the Hungarians but because Hungary was not strong enough to stand on her own feet. He had the feeling that "worlds separate him from Horthy." This war, continued Hitler, was not an ordinary war, "as for instance in the time of Maria Theresa"; this war would determine the fate of central Europe. If some catastrophe should befall Hungary, this would mean a catastrophe for the Balkans as well, since Germany would be cut off from her oil supply in Romania and her supply of raw materials such as manganese and copper in other Balkan countries. Should anyone ask what business does he have interfering in the internal affairs of Hungary, he would simply answer that he is entitled to interfere as the representative of the greatest power in Europe, the power that has fought the longest against bolshevism! [14] Seldom had Hitler been more outspoken. Then Hitler proceeded to discuss the military situation, which he regarded as more promising than in the preceding year. "Germany will use new weapons in great quantities. The enemy will lose their senses (*Den Feinden würden Hören und Sehen vergehen*)," he asserted. "Germany will build new U-boats, new fighter-planes, new bombers!" [15] According to the chief of the Press Section, Schmidt, Miklós was visibly and increasingly impressed, but he merely remarked, upon leaving, that Horthy would never break his word.[16] On July 28, after his return, Horthy appointed General Miklós to the command of the First Hungarian Army, operating in the Carpathians [17] (although Gen. Heinz Guderian would have preferred to see the pro-German General

14. Telegram from headquarters at the Brenner Pass to Veesenmayer, based on notes taken by Schmidt during the Hitler-Miklós conversation, July 24, 1944, NA Microcopy T-120, roll 100, 110774–77.

15. Hitler also deplored the Allied bombing raids over German cities and remarked, in justification of the German bombing of Rotterdam in May 1940: "Rotterdam sei bombardiert worden, weil aus der Stadt heftig geschossen wurde"—it is clear that Hitler did not remember the event correctly (telegram from Schmidt to Veesenmayer, July 24, 1944, NA Microcopy T-120, roll 4203, K209124).

16. "Miklos, der von der Darlegungen des Führers sichtlich in steigendem Masse beeindruckt wurde, wusste weiter nichts zu erwidern, als dass ein Treubruch Horthy's nie erfolgen wurde, und dass Horthy der 'Fixpunkt' sei, der das gesamte ungarische Staatswesen und Volk in seiner Person zusammenhalte" (same telegram, ibid., K209125–26).

17. July 28, Diary of Vörös. See also telegram to OKW Wehrmachtführungsstab, Aug. 2, 1944, NA Microcopy T-77, roll 883, 5632031.

Farkas in that position), and thus acquired a faithful man in an important post.

While Horthy hesitated to carry out the cabinet changes he desired, the Allies undertook repeated air raids against the city of Budapest, on an ever more formidable scale. Until the German occupation, Budapest had been bombed only twice, both times by the Soviet air force.[18] These Soviet raids, on September 4 and 17, 1942, had caused considerable alarm but only moderate damage. Until March 1944 the Hungarian government benefited from an unwritten agreement with the Anglo-American powers to the effect that there would be no bombing of Hungarian territory; and such bombing would have been difficult in any case, because until the end of 1943 Budapest was not within striking distance of any airfield occupied by the Allies. After the Allied invasion of southern Italy, and especially after the German occupation of Hungary, the Allies considered bombing both feasible and advisable. The Royal Air Force raided Budapest, and occasionally other Hungarian cities, at night. The American air corps raided in the daytime. The first serious raid was probably the one of April 3.[19] On April 13, 40 to 60 planes flew over Budapest at night, and about 540 flew over Hungary in the daytime, dropping bombs; there were about three hundred dead.[20] On this same occasion thirty-one Americans parachuted to safety, but four others were shot by the Hungarian troops and the population.[21] The Allies directed major raids against Hungary on April 17, May 5, May 11, June 2, June 13, June 14, June 26, July 2, and so on.[22] The raid on July 2 was on a scale comparable to the major raids directed against German cities in the same period:

18. *KTB, OKW*, 2 : 681, 775.

19. Karsai, *A budai vártól*, p. 465; see also, NA Microcopy T-120, roll 99, 110058–59.

20. Daily German military report, Apr. 13, NA Microcopy T-78, roll 332, 6289267.

21. Daily German military report, Apr. 14, ibid., 6289269. I have also found a German report on an incident (perhaps the same incident) in which a Hungarian regiment commander took the side of the Allied pilots threatened by the local population, arguing it was disgraceful and unchivalrous to attack unarmed soldiers. Furthermore, the pilots taken prisoner received "roast chicken and cake." But the chief of the Hungarian General Staff, warned by the German authorities, relieved this commander of his duties and instituted court-martial proceedings against him (telegram to OKW Wehrmachtführungsstab, July 20, 1944, NA Microcopy T-77, roll 883, 56325769; or NA Microcopy T-120, roll 100, 10715–17).

22. NA Microcopy T-78, roll 332, 6289275 ff. For a report on the bombings of June 13–14 and the destruction of oil refineries in Hungary, see OSS weekly "appreciation" report, NA Record Group 226, Hungary, 80331.

700 aircraft swept over Hungary.[23] The people of Hungary were told the raids were brought on them by the Jews, and Veesenmayer proposed to Ribbentrop and to the Hungarian authorities that ten "passing" Jews be shot for every Hungarian killed in an air raid.[24] While this threat of reprisals was not carried out, several thousand Jews of Budapest were relocated into houses near the industrial plants that were the primary targets of Allied bombardments. There were others in Hungary who believed the raids were brought about by the persecution of the Jews. Yet the raids did not stop when the deportations were halted. On July 14 there was another monster raid, directed mainly against Fantó, Shell, and other oil refineries, as well as against the Manfréd Weiss industrial complex on Csepel Island, just south of the capital.[25] Yet another massive raid took place on July 30; but, as the SS officer Kurt Becher reported to Himmler, the only casualties were twenty-eight Jewish labor service

23. Daily German military report, July 2, 1944, NA Microcopy T-78, roll 332, 6289411; see also Munkácsi, *Hogyan történt,* p. 174. On that Sunday (July 2) my father recorded in his diary: "There was an air raid at night, and there is an air raid in progress now, in the morning. Panni [my sister] and I are upstairs. The usual symptoms: my heart beats more quickly, my hands shake more than usual. But if I examine myself closely, I do not mind the attack. Perhaps justice is being done. Our powerful leaders should learn that there are some who are even more powerful. But nonsense. Because the powerful are no doubt safe in their air raid shelters, but the workers in the suburbs, and the many thousands of Jews in the concentration camps, where have they to go? The priests continue to recite the Mass in the shelters. The ancient Christians also proclaimed the gospel in the catacombs.

"The bombing has been going on for twenty-five minutes now without a break; I have the sensation they are aiming at this house, and will hit it any moment. Another wave of bombers; as if it never were to stop. How many aircraft? 500 heavy bombers, or perhaps more? Panni and I hit the ground and await the end. The end of the bombing, or our end? I would not like to perish. I would have to leave so many things behind. But I approve of the bombing, provided it does not hurt . . . whom? If I could pick them out personally. If I could become the justice-maker. But then in what way would I be better than those scoundrels against whom I protest? And how slight is the difference between justice and injustice!

"And I hate those people for the additional reason that they evoke such evil sentiments in me. . . . Three-quarters of an hour have passed since the beginning of the bombing . . . and now, as if the sound of the explosions was growing more distant. It is over; Hitler's Hungarian henchmen may continue their work" (*Az elsodort ország,* pp. 36–37).

24. Telegram from Veesenmayer to Ribbentrop, Apr. 3, 1944, NA Microcopy T-120, roll 100, 110065.

25. Daily German military report, July 14, 1944, NA Microcopy T-78, roll 332, 6289428–29, 6289437.

men.[26] The raids, which continued unabated in August and during much of September, undoubtedly served a purpose. The oil refineries were almost all incapacitated: of the seven big refineries producing a yearly 1,025,000 tons of oil, five were almost completely out of commission by November 1944 because of the bombings.[27] But civilian suffering was also considerable. The rumors regarding the dropping of fountain pens or dolls filled with explosives were plain nonsense,[28] but I also recall reading leaflets dropped from Allied aircraft deploring the fact that the railroad stations serving Budapest all happened to be "downtown"! There was not much the civilian population could do about that. Nor did it seem that the Allied aircraft took care to avoid bombing residential areas.

While the regent had decided to replace the Sztójay government early in July, his decision took no effect until late in August. Perhaps the decisive event was the Romanian surrender on August 23.[29] It should have been clear to the regent and his advisers that Romania would gain ascendancy in the eyes of the Allies unless something were done quickly. In fact, according to one observer, the British government had already hinted in December 1943 that whichever country got out of the war first would receive Transylvania.[30] Whether any member of the British government ever actually made such a declaration and, if so, whether the declaration really reached the ears of the Hungarian leaders (something which might have happened even if the declaration was never made), hardly seems important; the possession of Transylvania was clearly at stake. From the very beginning of the military campaign against the Soviet Union, rivalry with Romania—that is, the Transylvania problem—was foremost in the minds of certain Hungarian leaders. Romania,

---

26. Telegram from Becher to Himmler, Aug. 4, 1944, NA Microcopy T-175, roll 59, 2574474.

27. "Der Aussenhandel Ungarns 1941–1943" by the Statistisches Reichsamt, Nov. 1944, NA Microcopy T-84, roll 135, 1438207.

28. These rumors were taken seriously even by some of the German authorities: see, for instance, telegram containing German police report from Hungary, June 6, 1944, NA Microcopy T-120, roll 100, 110497.

29. Karsai, *A budai vártól*, p. 503.

30. The Countess Listowel [Márffy-Mantuano], *Crusader in the Secret War*, p. 190. Something to this effect was also intimated by an American consular dispatch from Istanbul, Mar. 14, 1944, OSS, NA Record Group 226, Hungary, 65575. The countess reports a fantastic plan she ascribes to Stalin in 1945, namely, the plan to make Count István Bethlen, deported to the Soviet Union after the Soviet occupation of Hungary, the president of a Transylvanian republic: a proposal which the veteran statesman is reported to have declined (p. 175, note).

like Hungary, had become Germany's subservient ally; and when the tide of war turned, after the battle of Stalingrad and the Allied victory in North Africa, Hungarian diplomats in conversations with Allied agents had hinted that Romania had served German interests better, both economically and politically.[31] Now, after the Romanians not only had surrendered but were participating in the operations against the retreating German forces, it looked as though the Romanians had definitely gained the upper hand in the competition for the good will of the Allies. Count Miklós Bánffy, a Transylvanian aristocrat, visited the regent on September 16 and told him it was peremptory to break with the Germans and to sue for an armistice as the Romanians had done.[32] It appears that Count Bethlen, scion of an ancient Transylvanian family, had already submitted a memorandum to Horthy on August 25, advocating the reestablishment of autonomy for Transylvania (in other words, partially surrendering Hungarian sovereignty).[33] Of course, it would have been too late in any case. In fact, at the second Quebec Conference, in September 1944, the western allies formally agreed to the commitment made by the Soviet government to the Romanian government a month or so earlier, namely, that Transylvania should be returned to Romania "subject to confirmation at the peace settlement." [34]

Other factors may also have played a part in the regent's decision: for instance, the renewed German attempts to deport the Jews of Budapest. The deportations were to take place on August 25 but were once again prevented by order of the regent.[35] Heinrich Himmler, the man directly responsible for carrying out the final solution, the most intransigent enemy of the Jews and other "inferior" peoples, had himself come to adopt a policy of compromises. On July 26 he had given instructions for deportations from Hungary to cease until further notice.[36] Hence Eichmann himself left

31. Ágnes Rozsnyói, *A Szálasi puccs* [Szálasi's coup d'état], p. 7. The thesis of Hungarian-Romanian rivalry is expounded in detail by Csatári in *Forgószélben*, passim.

32. Gyula Borbándi, "A zólyomi tárgyalások" [The negotiations at Zvolen], p. 137.

33. Report by Schellenberg, Aug. 27, 1944, NA Microcopy T-120, roll 4203, K209122–23.

34. Herbert Feis, *Churchill, Roosevelt, Stalin* (Princeton, N.J.: Princeton University Press, 1957), p. 417.

35. Telegram from German Military attaché to OKW Wehrmachtführungsstab, Aug. 24, 1944, NA Microcopy T-77, roll 883, 5631668–69.

36. Heinz Höhne, *The Order of the Death's Head* (New York: Coward-McCann, 1970), p. 566.

Hungary toward the end of the month, and eventually, on September 28, his entire *Sondereinsatzkommando* was disbanded.[37] This did not signify that the German and Hungarian National Socialists had once and for all abandoned their hopes of solving the Jewish problem in Hungary, or what remained of it. They were simply waiting for a more favorable opportunity, which came soon enough, at the time of Ferenc Szálasi's take-over of power on October 16.

On August 24, the day of the Romanian about-face, the new Hungarian cabinet was sworn in. It was a military cabinet, though perhaps not as military or as anti-Nazi as Horthy would have wished. Four soldiers whose names had been included on the original list for the new cabinet were dropped.[38] The new premier was Géza Lakatos. The minister of foreign affairs was another general, Gusztáv Hennyey. The cabinet might indeed have been apolitical had it not been for the fact that the pro-Nazi minister of agriculture, Béla Jurcsek, was retained, along with the perennial and equally pro-Nazi minister of finance, Lajos Reményi-Schneller. Hence the decisions taken at cabinet meetings could not be kept secret from the German occupation authorities. On August 28 Horthy informed Veesenmayer that he could not wait another six or eight weeks for Sztójay to recover (Sztójay was indeed unwell) and added that, in any case, Sztójay had been too weak in character and too inclined to compromise.[39] Veesenmayer was then introduced to the new prime minister, Lakatos, with whom he spent over an hour. Veesenmayer was favorably impressed, although he warned Horthy against taking an irrevocable decision;[40] but the irrevocable decision had already been taken.

Horthy's objectives in appointing the Lakatos cabinet seem to have been threefold: first, the restoration of Hungarian sovereignty in spite of the German occupation; second, the cessation of the persecution of the Jews; third, preparations for withdrawal from the war.[41]

37. Telegram from Veesenmayer to Berlin, Sept. 29, 1944, NA Microcopy T-120, roll 2721, E420965.

38. Telegram from Veesenmayer to Ribbentrop, July 15, 1944, NA Microcopy T-120, roll 100, 110718–21.

39. Telegram from Veesenmayer to Ribbentrop, "citissime mit Vorrang," Aug. 28, 1944, NA Microcopy T-77, roll 1096, 453002.

40. Ibid., 453003 ff. Veesenmayer continued to be favorably impressed with Lakatos in September "Keinesfalls ist jedoch die Regierung Lakatos als eine Badoglio-Regierung anzusehen" (report by Veesenmayer to Ribbentrop, NA Microcopy T-77, roll 883, 5631627–31).

41. Ágnes Rozsnyói, "October Fifteenth, 1944," p. 59.

But during the cabinet meeting on August 29, presided over by the regent, it was decided to continue to fight alongside the Germans and to hold the line of the Carpathians at any cost.[42] According to the then minister of foreign affairs, Gusztáv Hennyey, Horthy was even at that time concerned first of all, not so much with national survival but with Hungary's loyalty as an ally and his own code of honor.[43]

After considerable hesitation, and repeated German requests, the Hungarian government agreed to order its troops to invade the southern parts of Transylvania. According to the Vienna Award of August 1, 1940, Transylvania had been divided between Romania and Hungary, Romania being allowed to retain roughly the southern half. The Hungarian government was clearly reluctant to send its troops into this area, even after the Romanian surrender, because her claim to northern Transylvania was based on ethnic considerations, and invasion of the southern area might jeopardize Hungary's right to the northern one, in fact, would smack of imperialism. The Hungarian government knew that such an aggression could only alienate the Allies further (for the Hungarian government still seemed to entertain the hope that it might be allowed to retain part of Transylvania after the war). By the time the order to advance was issued, it made little difference. In fact, Gen. Lajos Dálnoki-Veress, in command of the Second Hungarian Army, received the order to advance at the same time as he received secret instructions to handle the matter dilatorily.[44] It is interesting, however, that Dálnoki-Veress himself has recently denied that the Hungarian advance was purposefully slow; on the contrary, he claims, the Hungarian troops advanced some seventy kilometers in three days and

42. Gusztáv Hennyey, "Ungarns Weg aus dem Zweiten Weltkrieg," p. 693; see also Ignác Ölvédi, "Adalékok Horthy és a Lakatos-kormány katonapolitikájához" [Data regarding the military policy of Horthy and the Lakatos cabinet].

43. Hennyey, "Ungarns Weg," p. 692.

44. Telegram from Schellenberg to SS Field Headquarters, Sept. 4, 1944, NA Microcopy T-120, roll 1096, 453013. The German authorities seemed to be aware of these secret instructions: "Am 1.9. begibt sich Generalstabschef Voeroes in Begleitung des Chefs Operationsabteilung Nadas zum Oberbefehlshaber der ungarischen Armee in Nordsiebenbürgen [Transylvania]. Voeroes soll versuchen, Veres dazu bewegen, von sich aus die zugesagte Offensive zu sabotieren, indem er mit militärischen Grunden, wie nicht genugend vorbereitet zu sein, ein Hinausschieben der Operationen motiviert. Oberst Nadas will versuchen, diesen Plan des Generalstabschefs zu durchkreuzen" (Kaltenbrunner to SS Field Headquarters, Sept. 2, 1944, NA Microcopy T-120, roll 1096, 453012).

defeated the Romanian resistance.[45] At about the same time, on September 6, the Red Army had already crossed the Carpathian Mountains and advanced into the southern parts of Transylvania.[46]

On September 7 the Crown Council met and decided to send Germany an ultimatum. The ultimatum simply stipulated that Germany send five divisions for the protection of Hungary within twenty-four hours and that four of these divisions should be armored. The request was reasonable, for nothing short of such assistance could stop the advance of the Red Army. Certain members of the Hungarian government felt the German authorities could not or would not comply with this request and would thus provide Hungary with a legitimate grievance (as if she did not already have a few legitimate grievances!) that would justify or even warrant armistice negotiations.[47] Even the terms of the eventual armistice were outlined at the meeting (but it is doubtful if the Allies would have found these acceptable).[48] Veesenmayer was officially informed of the Hungarian request and of the consequences should Germany not grant the request: clearly, the document was meant as an ultimatum.[49] But the German government did its best to comply with the Hungarian request. While it sent four divisions instead of the five requested, only one of which was armored, and while it took the German government considerably longer than twenty-four hours to send these, it nevertheless intended to comply with the Hungarian request and to hold the area against the attacks of the Red Army. Horthy summoned his secret council,[50] which included Lakatos, Hennyey, and Csatay from among the ministers, on September 10, and the council decided in favor of an armistice, regardless of the extent of the German help, which was in any case slow in coming. But when the proposal was presented to the cabinet as a

45. Lajos Dálnoki-Veress, "Lehetőségek és mulasztások 1944-ben" [Possibilities and omissions in 1944], p. 164.

46. Rozsnyói, "October Fifteenth, 1944," p. 65.

47. Ibid., pp. 67–67; Reitlinger, *The SS: Alibi of a Nation*, p. 362.

48. The terms of the armistice are quoted, not entirely without bias, by Hennyey in "Ungarns Weg," pp. 697–98.

49. Sept. 6 and 7, Diary of Vörös. The notations of Vörös indicate that Horthy and his advisors had already reached their decision on Sept. 6.

50. Besides the ministers, the secret council included Antal Vattay, Gyula Károlyi, István Bethlen, Móricz Eszterházy, Kálmán Kánya, Zsigmond Perényi, Vilmos Röder, Hugó Sónyi, Béla Teleki, Dániel Bánffy, and Gen. István Náday (Hennyey, "Ungarns Weg," p. 699, and Karsai, *A budai vártól*, p. 511). There is some disagreement between the two authors regarding the composition of this council.

whole it was turned down; furthermore, the cabinet threatened to resign should the regent decide to sue for an armistice in disregard of its recommendation.[51]

The regent was undaunted, but he had no clear concept of what kind of an armistice would be feasible and acceptable. He still seemed to be toying with the idea of a separate peace with the western Allies. Two spectacular missions were fitted out to reach territory occupied by the Anglo-Americans. The first of these missions flew in June and consisted of Prince Miklós Odescalchi piloting an aircraft which got lost and landed near Ancona, Italy, on territory still held by the Germans; the prince was captured and executed as a traitor.[52] The second venture was the flight of Gen. István Náday, accompanied by Col. Charles T. Howie and a pilot. Colonel Howie was a South African officer taken prisoner at Tobruk in North Africa who, having escaped from a German prisoner-of-war camp near Breslau, made his way to Hungary in 1943.[53] While offered the opportunity to proceed toward Turkey, he preferred to remain in Hungary where he thought he could perform more useful service; he may well have become, if he was not already, an agent of the British intelligence service. Colonel Howie went into hiding when the German troops occupied Hungary and rounded up Allied prisoners who had escaped to Hungary (some of whom were in camps and some not), but he was asked to visit Horthy several times in July and August 1944. On the night of September 22–23, Howie and Náday were flown to Foggia, near the spur of the Italian boot, in a "rickety old Heinkel . . . spirited away from the Germans," [54] piloted by a major of the Hungarian air force. After crash-landing near the Foggia airfield, the delegation was received by Field Marshal Henry Maitland Wilson, the Allied commander-in-chief in the Italian theater, who seemed to be in agreement with Churchill in advocating an Allied thrust through the "Ljubljana gap" and per-

51. Rozsnyói, "October Fifteenth, 1944," p. 68; see also Sept. 10 and 11, Diary of Vörös.

52. Kovács, *D'une occupation à l'autre*, pp. 35–37; Komlós, *Elárult ország*, p. 151. See also German police report, June 18, 1944, NA Microcopy T-120, roll 100, 110546–47.

53. Caminada, *My Purpose Holds*, p. 145.

54. St.-Iványi, "Our Man of Destiny in 1944," pp. 34–36. The author is incorrect regarding the date of the flight, given as Sept. 10. General Náday, according to a German report, was "der einzige Waschechte Jude" (except for General Koós) who retained his commission in the Hungarian army despite the discriminatory measures passed against Jewish officers in 1939 (report dated Aug. 26, 1942, NA Microcopy T-120, roll 691, 311944).

haps onto the Hungarian plains. Since that same night the Red Army had crossed the Hungarian frontier and was already on the Hungarian plains, there could be no question of peace or armistice with the western Allies only. In fact, General Náday declared that the Hungarian authorities realized the Soviet attack could not be stopped and that Soviet occupation of Hungary was inevitable. Therefore, Hungary was suing for peace and at the same time asking the western powers to mediate and moderate the expected hardships of a Soviet occupation.[55] The mission was not entirely without repercussions. Churchill made friendly allusions to Hungary in a speech delivered shortly after this incident on September 28.[56] During his visit to Naples on October 6, Churchill may have discussed the Hungarian flight mission with Field Marshal Wilson. A few days later in Moscow (on October 9), Churchill made a deal with Stalin, the famous percentage deal, according to which the two leaders apportioned the countries of southeastern Europe to the Anglo-American or the Soviet spheres of influence; and Churchill asked for, and was promised, "50 percent influence" in Hungarian affairs.[57]

A result of these secret missions and secret attempts at negotiations with the western powers was the Soviet suspicions and allegations regarding western influence in Hungary. The German intelligence service received several reports concerning alleged Anglo-American plans for a landing on the Dalmatian coast and even a parachute drop in the area of Lake Balaton.[58] Horthy received similar reports and was inclined to believe them.[59] Recently a Hungarian historian wrote that "western diplomacy was still flirting with the idea of a separate peace with Hungary and the occupation of the country by western troops, the latter being the principal object of both western govern-

55. Feis, *Churchill, Roosevelt, Stalin*, pp. 419 ff.

56. Lukacs, *The Great Powers and Eastern Europe*, p. 263.

57. See, among others, *The Reckoning: The Memoirs of Anthony Eden*, p. 559; and Winston S. Churchill, *Triumph and Tragedy* (Boston: Houghton Mifflin, 1953), pp. 226–27.

58. Note by Kaltenbrunner, Sept. 2, 1944, NA Microcopy T-120, roll 1096, 453010–11. See also telegram from Lorenz to Himmler, Sept. 2, 1944, NA Microcopy T-175, roll 130, 2659658–59.

59. Telegram from Schellenberg to SS field headquarters, Sept. 5, 1944, NA Microcopy T-120, roll 1096, 453018–19. This telegram also mentions that Horthy forbade any resistance in case of an Anglo-American landing and instructed General Béldy to fly to Switzerland to negotiate. On Sept. 21, however, Bakach-Bessenyey, the former Hungarian minister to Switzerland, cabled once again to the effect that Hungary had only one alternative: unconditional surrender (Hennyey, "Ungarns Weg," p. 701).

ment circles and Hungarian ruling class." [60] The only evidence to this effect, however, is the German intelligence reports and possibly Soviet intelligence reports. But if serious historical scholars relying on examination of documentary sources can make such assertions and believe that this was indeed the attitude of responsible western officials, it is difficult to blame the regent for practicing "wishful thinking" along the same lines. The fact remains, however, that Churchill's interest in Hungary proved to be a passing fancy and that the responsible officials in the West generally did not give a second thought to the fate of its ruling class.

Eventually, the Hungarians also made attempts to reach Soviet officials. Early in August a Jewish landowner named Rosenberg was picked to go across the front—presumably because of his knowledge of Russian and his acquaintance with Marshal K. Voroshilov—by Miklós Horthy, Jr., as an emissary; but Rosenberg changed his mind when he reached the Hungarian border, averring that the trip might prove risky. [61] About the middle of September a Hungarian mission, composed of Baron Ede Aczél, Imre Faust, and József Dudás, crossed the front line and ventured as far as Moscow; the aim of the mission, it seems, was simply to determine the feasibility of the trip and the attitude of the Sovet authorities. [62] But the successes of the Red Army in repelling the Hungarian counterattack at Arad and Temesvár (Timisoara) may have finally convinced the regent of the necessity for negotiating with the Soviet Union. An uprising having taken place in Slovakia, the anti-Nazi partisan forces controlled a considerable portion of that country in September 1944. The Hungarian Count Ladomér Zichy, who had an estate in an area under the control of the Slovak partisans, was instrumental in bringing about contact by mail between a Soviet officer and the partisans, and the regent. [63] On September 18 the partisans could vouch for direct contact with Moscow by aircraft. After some further hesitation on the part of the regent, a three-man delegation, composed of Géza Teleki, the son of the former prime minister, Gen. Gábor Faraghó, former Hungarian military attaché in Moscow, and Domokos Szentiványi, an official of the Hungarian Ministry of Foreign Affairs,

60. Rozsnyói, "October Fifteenth, 1944," p. 62.

61. Péter Gosztonyi, "A magyar-szovjet fegyverszüneti tárgyalások, 1944 október" [Hungarian-Soviet armistice negotiations], *Uj látóhatár* [New horizon] 12 (1969) : 401.

62. István de Szent-Miklósy to author. See also Rozsnyói, *A Szálasi puccs*, p. 47, and "1944 október 15. A Szálasi-puccs története" [History of the Szálasi coup d'état], p. 392.

63. For details see Borbándi, "A zólyomi tárgyalások."

was sent to Moscow.[64] Horthy also wrote a letter to Stalin, in English, in which he referred to the misleading information which led him to declare war on the Soviet Union in June 1941. It was not a matter of imperialism: "For the sake of justice, I would like to inform you, that we have never ever wanted to take but a single inch from anybody [*sic*], that was not ours by right." And Horthy begged Stalin "to spare this unfortunate country which has its own historic merits and the people of which has so many affinities with the Russian people."[65] The mission left on September 28 and arrived in Moscow on October 1. The negotiations for an armistice lasted until October 11. The mission and the negotiations were secret to a point where not even the "reliable" members of the Hungarian cabinet were informed of them until October 10.[66] The negotiations are discussed in some detail by Macartney in *October Fifteenth* and in an article he published in the *Vierteljahreshefte für Zeitgeschichte* entitled "Hungary's Way out of World War II";[67] these discussions are based on notes taken by General Faraghó as well as on the copies of communications sent and received by the mission and preserved by Géza Teleki. Molotov informed the other Allied governments of the terms proposed by the Soviet government, and these terms were approved by both the United States and the British governments; hence, the conditions presented to the Hungarian delegation by the Soviet government reflected the position of the Allies, or at least that of Great Britain and of the Soviet Union.[68] Churchill telegraphed to his "colleagues" on October 12 that "as it is the Soviet armies which are obtaining control of Hungary, it would be natural that a major share of influence should rest with them."[69] Cordell Hull writes in his memoirs that the Department of State protested against the "bilateral" nature of the decisions taken with regard to the armistice.[70] The Soviet government presented the Hungarian delegation with the terms of the armistice on October 8 in the name of the three main Allies; in fact, it was only on that date that Horthy

64. Rozsnyói, "October Fifteenth, 1944," pp. 73, 75.

65. Gosztonyi, "A magyar-szovjet fegyverszüneti tárgyalások," p. 416.

66. Hennyey, "Ungarns Weg," p. 703.

67. Macartney's article, "Ungarns Weg aus dem Zweiten Weltkrieg," was published in response to Hennyey's article of the same title. See also the article by Gosztonyi; "A magyar-szovjet fegyverszüneti tárgyalások."

68. Feis, *Churchill, Roosevelt, Stalin*, pp. 419 ff. See also Rozsnyói, *A Szálasi puccs*, p. 72.

69. Churchill, *Triumph and Tragedy*, p. 234.

70. *Memoirs of Cordell Hull*, p. 1461.

requested to know the terms.[71] The armistice signed by the Hungarian mission on October 11, and confirmed a few days later by another Hungarian agent, was qualified as provisional or preliminary. The principal terms of the preliminary armistice were the cessation of hostilities against the Soviet Union, the withdrawal of Hungarian troops and officials from territories acquired by Hungary after 1937, and participation in the fight against Germany.[72] The precise terms indicated that Hungary should undertake to fight against the Germans, whereas the Soviet Union would come to the Hungarians' assistance. While this provisory armistice undoubtedly led to the regent's proclamation of October 15, that proclamation made no mention of the fact that the Hungarian units were to turn their arms against the Germans. But before we discuss the events of October 15, certain factors have to be noted.

One objective of the Lakatos government since its appointment had been to halt the persecution of the Jews, and in this the government was fairly successful. The Sztójay government had promised the German authorities, shortly before its demise, that while it could no longer accept the removal of Hungarian Jews beyond the borders of the country the Jews of Budapest would be concentrated in camps set up especially for the purpose somewhere in the Hungarian countryside. The deportations were scheduled for early in September but, as we have seen, the Hungarian and Red Cross officials in charge of selecting suitable sites in Hungary procrastinated, no site was considered adequate, and the Jews of Budapest were allowed to remain in Budapest, at least for another month.[73]

Another main objective of the new Hungarian government was the reestablishment of Hungarian sovereignty, primarily in military matters; indeed, Hungarian military independence was a prerequisite for successfully carrying out an armistice, the terms of which were

71. Macartney, "Ungarns Weg aus dem Zweiten Weltkrieg," pp. 82, 89.

72. A German author noted in a recent account of these happenings: "Die Hände dieser drei Ungarn, Faraghos, Telekis und von Szent-Ivanyi, zitterten nicht, als sie die Verpflichtung unterschrieben, dass Ungarn nunmehr Deutschland den Krieg zu erklären und die deutschen Truppen zu entwaffnen und sie als Kriegsgefangene der Roten Armee auszuliefern habe" (Erich Kern [Kernmayr], *Die letzte Schlacht: Ungarn 1944–1945*, p. 46).

73. Negotiations regarding the deportations between the gendarmerie officer Lt. Col. Ferenczy and Veesenmayer are reproduced on NA Microcopy T-120, roll 2721, E-420950–51. Eventually Veesenmayer proposed that the deportations be undertaken either by applying more pressure on the Hungarian government or by "eigener Regie" (note by Wagner to Ribbentrop, Oct. 12, 1944, ibid., E-420950–51).

easily foreseeable. I cannot give here a detailed account of Hungarian military participation in the last twelve months of the war, but a brief examination of the position of the Hungarian army seems warranted.

On March 19 the German authorities were undecided regarding the future role of the Hungarian army; but a few days later, as the Red Army broke through at Tarnopol in the foothills of the Carpathians, Hitler decided to mobilize the Hungarian forces in the name of *Waffenbruderschaft*—comradeship in arms.[74] In the course of the next three or four months, several Hungarian divisions were sent to the East to fight in the front lines. Even during the first month of fighting, between April 17 and May 20, the casualty figures of the Hungarian First Army ran high: 12,135 killed and wounded and 3,441 missing.[75] By July 15, the casualties were estimated at 3,000 dead, 18,000 wounded, and 4,000 missing.[76] As a result of a heavy Soviet attack around July 23, the Hungarian units, and especially the Seventh Infantry Division, were split in two; the smaller section in the north was placed under German command and retreated toward Warsaw.[77] In the summer of 1944 altogether fourteen Hungarian divisions, in addition to three more occupation divisions, were sent out of the country.[78]

The dispatch of Hungarian divisions to the eastern front did not always proceed smoothly, and Horthy's decision, or rather indecision, regarding the First Cavalry Division is generally indicative of the dilemma of responsible Hungarian leadership throughout this period. The chief of the General Staff noted somewhere in his diary that he had indirectly advised the regent that "anything the Germans demanded that could be granted, and if it was also in the Hungarian national interest, should be granted right away, without hesitation. Whereas any request that does not fit these requirements should be decisively turned down, and the refusal should be allowed to stand." A week after Vörös noted this principle in his diary, the regent agreed to the dispatch of the First Cavalry Division to the eastern front, while expressing his resentment at the

74. Ránki, "German Occupation of Hungary," pp. 275 ff.

75. Telegram from military attaché in Budapest to OKW Wehrmachtführungsstab, May 20, 1944, NA Microcopy T-77, roll 883, 5632092.

76. Report dated July 15, 1944, Diary of Vörös, appendix.

77. Report on military situation, Aug. 9, 1944, Diary of Vörös, appendix. See also Czebe and Pethö, *Hungary in World War II*, pp. 38–41.

78. György Ránki, "L'occupation de la Hongrie par les allemands," p. 42.

tone of the directives received from German headquarters. On June 3, about another week later, the regent became insistent that the division remain within Hungarian territory. During the visit Vörös paid to the Führer headquarters, around June 5, Hitler insisted the division must fight in the Pripet marshes and not along the Carpathians; and Horthy agreed. The next day Horthy again insisted the division must be used along the Carpathians, that is, on Hungarian territory. That same afternoon, however, Horthy was persuaded to agree once and for all to the German request.[79] Vörös had understood the country's problem well: a weak regent, whose hesitations necessarily disconcerted those who counted on him to lead the struggle to regain Hungarian sovereignty. As he had done so many times in the past, the regent ultimately gave in to the German demand, but he had vacillated long enough to provide further ground for German distrust of him and his regime.

The subsequent history of the First Cavalry Division illustrates the disagreements between German and Hungarian commands on the local and even the higher echelons. On July 8 Vörös received a personal communication from General Vattay, commanding officer of the division, to the effect that after eleven days of continuous fighting the division had lost its striking capacity and that he himself was tired of arguing with arrogant young German generals.[80] Vörös requested the OKW's permission to withdraw the unit, and this permission was seemingly granted on July 24,[81] only to be rescinded by Keitel on July 27. "The Führer and the German armed forces expect the Hungarian troops to continue fighting until victory alongside the Germans and in the tradition of German-Hungarian commradeship in arms," wrote Keitel to Vörös; "it is completely impossible to withdraw these units for the moment." [82] During Gen. Heinz Guderian's visit to Horthy on August 1, the return of the First Cavalry Division was requested once again, Guderian agreed to the request,[83] and the repatriation of the division seems to have actually begun on August 23 (certainly not earlier).[84] By

79. Entries of May 21, June 3, 5, 8, and 9, Diary of Vörös.

80. Vattay to Vörös, July 8, 1944, Diary of Vörös, appendix.

81. Telephone report by General Homlok (in Berlin) to Vörös, July 24, Diary of Vörös, appendix.

82. Keitel to Vörös, July 27, Diary of Vörös, appendix.

83. Heinz Guderian, *Panzer Leader,* p. 368.

84. Minutes of a conversation with General Guderian at the Führer headquarters, Aug. 23, Diary of Vörös, appendix.

then the Red Army had occupied most of the foothills of the Carpathians in the south and in the east, and around September 22 the Soviet forces broke into the Hungarian plains. For a few days Hungarian units crossed the borders of Trianon Hungary in the direction of Arad and Temesvár (Timisoara). The clear danger of a Soviet occupation of Hungary seemed to result in an increased number of defections among the Hungarian troops. According to Maj. Gen. Hans Friessner, who was the highest ranking German commander in the southeast at that moment, more and more frequently Hungarian battalions would simply abandon their posts and leave their German comrades in the lurch.[85] Hence, noted Friessner, it became necessary to bolster the Hungarian units by integrating German units into them even on the lower echelons.[86]

The Soviet units continued to advance for a few more days and reached the Tisza River in northeastern Hungary on October 8, but a lull set in during the armistice negotiations in Moscow.[87] On October 15 the Soviet units were still much too far from the capital to offer the regent any effective assistance.

Almost for the first time in the war, manifestations of Hungarian partisan activity took place in August and September 1944. During the Kállay regime the Hungarian left had been partly persecuted, partly integrated into the government-approved Social Democratic party. There had been a few attempts at sabotage. There had also been a few antigovernment and antiwar demonstrations late in 1941 and early in 1942.[88] But these demonstrations were effectively silenced by mass arrests. The Communist party, illegal since 1919, numbered barely a dozen active members after these arrests.[89] Under the name of the Peace party, it managed, nevertheless, to print and distribute some handbills, especially in the second half of 1944. There had been some resistance activity in the early months of the German occupation, as the periodic reports of the chief of the SS

85. Hans Friessner, *Verratene Schlachten*, p. 110. General Friessner is one of a sizable group of retired German generals who seem to feel that to fight along with Hitler to the last was the only honorable attitude for Germans and Hungarians alike.

86. Ibid., p. 117.

87. The Allies also stopped bombing Hungary between Sept. 23 and Oct. 15 (Hillgruber, "Das deutsch-ungarische Verhältnis," p. 94).

88. Concerning the demonstration of Mar. 15, 1942, see telegram from Werkmeister to Berlin, Mar. 31, 1942, NA Microcopy T-120, roll 92, 104792.

89. Sándor Mucs, "A magyar fegyveres ellenállási mozgalom megszervezése és szerepe Magyarország felszabadításában" [The organization of the Hungarian armed resistance and its role in the liberation of Hungary], p. 36.

police in Hungary (General Winkelmann) indicate. A noteworthy incident, not mentioned in any Hungarian historical account, was the revolt in the military prison at Sátoraljaújhely, which broke out at the news of the German invasion; fifty prisoners were shot during the revolt, and thirty or forty more were condemned to death later on.[90] However, most persons arrested on suspicion of spying, sabotage, or left-wing political activity were probably innocent Jews. An opportunity for more action came during the uprising in Slovakia in the late summer of 1944; the Slovak insurgents were joined by a number of Hungarians, as were the partisans active in the mountains of Ruthenia and in the Bácska. For instance, Dr. Iván Boldizsár writes that he and a friend smuggled supplies to Titoist units twice a week.[91] And there were units of Hungarian partisans in Hungary itself.[92] The first serious partisan action in Budapest was a hand-grenade attack against an SS barrack on September 22,[93] and the most spectacular achievement of the Hungarian resistance was the dynamiting of the statue of Gömbös, the pro-German and pro-Nazi prime minister of the early 1930s, in Budapest on October 6, 1944.[94] There is a fairly extensive literature on the activities of Hungarian partisan groups and on the contributions of Hungarian partisans to other resistance movements. On the whole, however, the activities of resistance groups in Hungary had no significant effect on the outcome of the struggle between the regent and the National Socialists and contributed but little to the victory of the Red Army.

The events of October 15 have given rise to considerable polemical literature. While the polemicists naturally attempt to conceal the polemical nature of their investigations, the gist of their argument revolves around a clearly discernible issue: to what extent was Horthy responsible for the fiasco of his coup d'état on October 15— in fact, was the fiasco itself his true objective? Hungarian historians have often argued that Horthy was not only unable but also unwill-

90. Two telegrams from Veesenmayer to Ritter, Mar. 31, 1944, NA Microcopy T-120, roll 99, 110032 ff.

91. Boldizsár, *The Other Hungary*, p. 21.

92. According to Karsai one such unit exploded 7 trains, destroyed 7 locomotives and 72 railway cars, 1 bridge, 2 trucks, 385 soldiers, wounding 412 more and capturing 267. (*A budai vártól*, pp. 522–23). According to a report dated Aug. 16, 1944, 117 persons were arrested in the Baranya for partisan activities, although many were released shortly thereafter (mentioned in Elemér Sallai, "Die Befreiungskämpfe um Budapest," p. 153).

93. Miklós Dezsényi, *Hősök és árulók* [Heroes and traitors], p. 152.

94. Karsai, *A budai vártól*, p. 535.

ing to carry out a successful coup d'état, either because of a lack of physical or moral courage or because of his abhorrence of bolshevism and his sense of loyalty toward Germany. Other historians have argued that Horthy's proclamation of October 15 was forced upon him by the preparations of the Arrow-Cross party for a coup d'état of its own. Their argument has been that it was never Horthy's intention to "betray" Germany but that, on the contrary, he intended to remain true to his word to the last; and their argument has found support, perhaps to their own surprise, in the more recent testimonies of some Hungarians in exile and of the regent himself. Gusztáv Hennyey, who was the minister of foreign affairs in the Lakatos cabinet, declared in an article published in 1962 that Horthy never intended to undertake military action against Germany despite the stipulations of the "provisory" armistice signed in Moscow.[95] In an appendix to Hennyey's article, there appeared a reprint of a letter which Horthy had addressed to Chancellor Konrad Adenauer on November 3, 1954. In this letter Horthy stated (one really wonders whether Adenauer could have cared, although the letter was acknowledged) that it was absolutely not true that Hungary had been ready to stab Germany in the back in connection with the armistice of 1944 and that not once in her 1,000 years of history did Hungary ever betray an ally.[96] Yet there are other historians, including Macartney and some eminent historians writing in Hungary, who believe that the fiasco of October 15 was a bona fide fiasco: that Horthy hoped the armistice could be successfully carried out but that his hopes were thwarted by a variety of factors over which he had no control at the moment.

A number of significant incidents preceded the proclamation of October 15. On October 8, Gen. Szilárd Bakay, commander of the Hungarian forces stationed in Budapest, was kidnapped by the Gestapo.[97] On October 10, shortly after midnight, Horthy sent a telegram to Moscow, the text of which is rather confusing; but the gist of the telegram, nevertheless, was the authorization given the Hungarian delegation to sign the armistice. On October 11 Horthy also dispatched Maj. József Nemes across the front with an authorization to the Hungarian delegation in Moscow to "countersign"

95. "Ungarns Weg," p. 696.
96. Ibid., pp. 718–19.
97. Rozsnyói, "October Fifteenth, 1944," p. 82.

the "provisory" armistice.[98] Furthermore, on October 11, Horthy conferred with the commanders of the First and Second Hungarian armies, and it was agreed that at a given signal they should establish contact with the Soviet forces, whereas certain units would be ordered to withdraw toward Budapest and help defend the capital against the expected German countermeasures.[99] On that same day, Szeged, then Hungary's second largest city, fell into Soviet hands. The "provisory" armistice signed in Moscow was still not confirmed; telegrams sent by the Hungarian peace delegation from Moscow requesting the dispatch of an "older" or more experienced envoy could not be deciphered by the regent in Budapest, although the members of the delegation later insisted their telegrams had been ciphered without an error.[100] (Was the regent playing for time?) On October 12 Faraghó in Moscow sent Horthy a telegram requesting that an elder officer of the general staff be sent across the front line as a parliamentarian and informing Horthy that south of Szolnok the Red Army would not attack and that the Hungarian troops in this area could be safely withdrawn to Budapest.[101] On October 13 the regent dispatched three Hungarian parliamentarians, Gen. Antal Vattay, Col. Lóránt Utassy, and Maj. István de Szent-Miklósy, and they reached the Soviet headquarters (Marshal V. Malinovski) near Szeged on the same day; but the Soviet commander was not satisfied, because the three Hungarians were militarily uninformed about the strength and locations of units. Furthermore, the Hungarian units had not begun to withdraw as the Soviets had requested.[102] The same day the Sixth Army Corps, commanded by Gen. Ferenc Farkas, received orders to move to Budapest immediately. By October 14 the headquarters of the corps were in Budapest but not the troops, and the commander, whom Horthy informed of his intentions in a conversation at 11:00 A.M., was distressed to hear

98. Karsai, *A budai vártól*, pp. 538, 540. It appears, however, that Major Nemes left Budapest only on the following day, Oct. 12 (telegram from Horthy to Moscow, Oct. 11, reproduced by Macartney in "Ungarns Weg aus dem Zweiten Weltkrieg," p. 92).

99. Rozsnyói, "October Fifteenth, 1944," p. 86.

100. Telegrams from Horthy to Moscow, Oct. 12 and 13; and from the delegation in Moscow to Horthy, Oct. 13 (Macartney, "Ungarns Weg aus dem Zweiten Weltkrieg," p. 93).

101. Juhász, *Magyarország külpolitikája*, pp. 342–43.

102. Telegram from delegation in Moscow to Horthy, Oct. 14 (Macartney, "Ungarns Weg aus dem Zweiten Weltkrieg," pp. 94–95). See also Karsai, *A budai vártól*, p. 542.

the news of the armistice.[103] By October 14 Major Nemes had reached a Soviet headquarters. On October 13 Rudolf Rahn, the German ambassador to the Fascist Republic at Salo, had received instructions to proceed to Budapest for a special assignment; and Rahn arrived in Budapest the following evening. On October 15, at nine in the morning, the Crown Council met. During the meeting, General Vörös received coded instructions he did not understand at the time, but he later found that the instructions, to be sent to the commanders at the front, were to negotiate with the local Soviet commanders the orderly withdrawal of the Hungarian units.[104] This order indicates that Horthy's proclamation later that day had not been premeditated for long and was premature.

The next episode was perhaps the decisive one. It seems that Miklós Horthy, Jr., who had been active during the preceding months organizing a "bureau for bailing out" [105] (*Kiugrási iroda*) and establishing contact with left-wing elements, was approached by agents who claimed to be partisans of Tito. SS Maj. Otto Skorzeny, whose spectacular deliverance of Mussolini had earned him a reputation as a specialist in abductions, had been picked by Hitler for a similar mission in Hungary. Skorzeny had arrived in Hungary a couple of weeks before October 15; and so did, incidentally, Gen. Erich von der Bach-Zelewski, who prided himself on having just recently crushed the resistance of the Polish Home Army in Warsaw.[106] While the target of Skorzeny's mission had been designated as the regent, the German High Command soon realized that the regent's son would offer an excellent opportunity for extorting the regent's continued allegiance to the "common cause." [107] In the small hours of the morning of October 15 the young Horthy entered a building for his appointment with the actual or presumed agents of Tito.[108] The building was already surrounded by Skorzeny's detachment, and when two of Skorzeny's men entered the building,

103. Ferenc (Kisbarnaki) Farkas, *Tatárhágó visszanéz* [The Tatar pass looks back], pp. 152–53.

104. Oct. 15, Diary of Vörös.

105. István de Szent-Miklósy to author.

106. Otto Skorzeny, *Skorzeny's Secret Missions*, p. 200.

107. "This police action [*sic*] was probably inspired by the hope that the Regent, anxious to avoid seeing his son committed for trial, would abandon all thought of separate peace" (ibid., p. 201).

108. Horthy, Jr., explained in a letter to General Hennyey that he intended to secure his passage to southern Italy via Yugoslavia and territories held by Tito (Hennyey, "Ungarns Weg," p. 705, note).

Horthy's escort opened fire. After five minutes of shooting, Horthy and a friend were captured, rolled inside a carpet, driven off to the airport, and abducted by airplane.[109] The regent was notified, apparently by survivors of the Hungarian detachment which had escorted the young Horthy, in the midst of the meeting of the Crown Council. The prime objective of Skorzeny's mission was accomplished; while at first the coup de main served only to exasperate the regent, the implied threat against his surviving son's life eventually served to convince Horthy to desist from his intention of resisting the German forces. According to the report of General Winkelmann, the chief of the SS in Hungary, Veesenmayer, during the interview which took place at noon on October 15, told "the Old Man, in a very forthrightly manner, but without using the most callous terms we had agreed Veesenmayer should use, that at the slightest sign of treachery, his son would be stood up against the wall." [110]

At the same time the plot to set up an Arrow-Cross party government, to be headed by Ferenc Szálasi, entered its final phase. Operation Panzerfaust, the attack on the Vár by German armor, had not been scheduled but was planned for about October 24.[111] The political consensus between Szálasi, Veesenmayer, and Winkelmann was absolute.[112] The Arrow-Cross party undertook a campaign of handbills in September and October 1944. A proclamation in case of a take-over by Szálasi was preprinted in Vienna in three million copies, and these were shipped to Budapest.[113] The instructions received by Ambassador Rahn on October 13 were to proceed to

109. Skorzeny, *Skorzeny's Secret Missions*, pp. 202 ff.; also report by Winkelmann to Himmler, Oct. 25, 1944, NA Microcopy T-175, roll 59, 2574489–90.

110. Report by Winkelmann to Himmler, Oct. 25, 1944, NA Microcopy T-175, roll 59, 2574491 (hereafter cited as Winkelmann report).

111. Péter Gosztonyi, "Német katonai okmányok 1944 október 15 előtörténetéhez" [German military documents regarding the history of the events leading to October 15, 1944], p. 516.

112. "Nach Einsetzung der Regierung Lakatos, die für uns ein Alarmsignal des Verrats war [Winkelmann's estimate of the situation must have differed considerably from that of Veesenmayer], trat Szalasi mit mir in Verbindung. Wir haben unsere Ansichten, unsere Aufgaben und unsere Absichten in der ersten Stünde verglichen und in Übereinstimmung gebracht" (Winkelmann report, 2574486). See also Ránki, "L'occupation de la Hongrie," p. 51.

113. Winkelmann report, 2574487. Some of the leaflets fell from the lorry carrying them from Vienna, and the Arrow-Cross plot could have been prematurely revealed; but the leaflets were obligingly returned by a Hungarian policeman.

Budapest and help Szálasi and Veesenmayer carry out their coup.[114]
But on the morning of October 15 Szálasi had still not received
the signal from his German sponsors. On October 6 Winkelmann
ordered the arrest of the young Horthy and of three generals,
Szilárd Bakay, Károly Lázár, the commander of Horthy's bodyguard, and Kálmán Hárdy, the commander of the river forces and
a relative of the regent; the first two arrests, as we have seen, were
carried out on or before October 15. In the meantime, German
troops, especially armored units, were concentrated around Budapest.

At the meeting of the Crown Council on October 15, the "provisory" armistice signed in Moscow and twice confirmed was still
not discussed; instead, the discussion centered around the *desirability* of concluding an armistice. Prime minister Lakatos, who favored
the idea as did most of those present, insisted the German minister
be warned in advance; and Horthy answered he would tell Veesenmayer in person.[115] Thus Veesenmayer was summoned at noon and
was received by the regent in the presence of Lakatos and Hennyey.
Horthy complained in bitter terms of the behavior of the Gestapo
and of other German troops stationed in Hungary. Horthy accused
the Gestapo of having engineered the abduction of his son that
morning. He then informed Veesenmayer that the Hungarian government was compelled to sue for an armistice. For once Veesenmayer made no threats or counterthreats but insisted, before de-
parting, that Horthy receive Ambassador Rahn, who had flown in
from Salo "especially for the purpose." Horthy agreed, and Rahn
was introduced. As there were no witnesses to this meeting, the
historians must rely on the accounts given by Horthy and Rahn,
and especially that of the latter, whose account is far more detailed.
Ambassador Rahn told Horthy that Hungary would be occupied
by Russians and that Hungary could then no longer remain a feudal
and aristocratic state! Therefore, Horthy and Hungary were, in
fact, committing suicide. Horthy then replied, according to Rahn,
that Rahn was absolutely right and he wished Rahn had come ear-

114. Ribbentrop was serious; he cabled to Rahn and Veesenmayer a line from
Beethoven's *Fidelio,* telling them that they must vouch with their heads for the success of the enterprise: "Sie haften mit Ihrem Kopf dafür . . ." (Rudolf Rahn,
Ruheloses Leben, p. 263).
115. Hennyey, "Ungarns Weg," p. 706.

lier.[116] But by that time the regent's armistice proclamation had been read over the radio.

The armistice proclamation was clearly an appeal for the cessation of hostilities. It did not state that an armistice had been concluded in Moscow, but it did state that armistice negotiations were taking place at the moment, which may have been technically correct. One paragraph, instructing the Hungarian troops to turn their weapons against the Germans, had been deleted at the request of Prime Minister Lakatos after the cabinet meeting on the afternoon of October 14.[117]

At three in the afternoon the regent's appeal was repeated over the radio, and a general order, albeit distorted, was forwarded to the troops. Most authors feel that the orders to be transmitted to the First and Second Hungarian armies [118] were sabotaged by certain pro-German and pro-Arrow-Cross elements in the General Staff.[119] We had seen, however, that General Vörös and his aides had agreed, on a previous occasion, not to allow hostilities between German and Hungarian troops. The diary of General Vörös seems to indicate he made the changes in the orders on his own initiative, that in fact he prepared two directives explaining away the regent's proclamation to the troops (the first of these directives was held up for reasons Vörös does not state).[120] One must realize, on the other hand, that this entry in the diary may have been dictated by caution; General Vörös knew Horthy's regency was coming to an end and Hungary would be ruled, however briefly, by an Arrow-Cross government.[121]

Horthy's confidence in the loyalty of the Hungarian officer proved to be often misplaced. The regent believed, or at least pretended to believe, that Hungarian officers were not political beings or that,

116. Rahn, *Ruheloses Leben,* p. 266. This quid pro quo is not confirmed by Horthy (*Memoirs,* pp. 231–32).

117. Rozsnyói, "October Fifteenth, 1944," p. 98, and *A Szálasi puccs,* p. 80. See also June 2, 1961, Hungarian National Archives, Notes of General Lakatos.

118. The Third Hungarian Army was regarded as hopeless from the beginning inasmuch as it was commanded by General Heszlényi, whose pro-Nazi sympathies were well known. This Third Army, however, was still weak and incomplete.

119. Rozsnyói, "October Fifteenth, 1944," pp. 93–94, and *A Szálasi puccs,* pp. 89–91.

120. Oct. 15, Diary of Vörös.

121. A month or so later General Vörös went over to the Soviet forces and eventually became a member of the republican "Debrecen government," Hungary's first postwar government.

in a showdown, they would sacrifice their political beliefs and follow him, their "supreme warlord" (*Legfőbb Hadúr*).[122] Yet the higher posts in the army had been stacked, since the premiership of Gyula Gömbös, by ethnic German and pro-Nazi Hungarian officers, and these officers were not prepared to sacrifice their political sympathies.[123] The armistice proclaimed by the regent on October 15 had little influence on the attitude of the Hungarian military, and the advantage to the Soviet forces was almost negligible. The commander of the First Army, Gen. Béla Miklós, crossed the front line with a few of his aides shortly after the regent's proclamation (in the very motorcar he had recently received as a present from Gen. Heinz Guderian, noted the latter!).[124] The commander of the Second Army, Gen Lajos Dálnoki-Veress, who was preparing to line up his units for a similar move, was arrested by German officers. A few Hungarian units went over to the Russians or retreated without warning the neighboring German units and thus caused some disruption.[125] But not much; it was only in the following few months that the Hungarian units were overrun or surrendered, piecemeal, to the Red Army, and not as a result of the regent's proclamation but because of the prevailing military situation. At the moment the greatest disruption in the ranks of the Axis was caused by the withdrawal of two German armored divisions and one armored battalion whose task it was to support Szálasi's coup d'état in Budapest.[126]

By the evening of October 15 it became clear that the regent's armistice plans had failed; yet at that stage it seems Horthy was still considering resistance. But in the course of the night Horthy allowed himself to be persuaded into resigning and putting himself and his family under German "protection."[127]

The German troops stationed around Budapest captured the strategic points in the city without a struggle. The commander of

122. Miklós Horthy, Jr., explained to me that the regent's seemingly blind confidence in his soldiers' honor may have been, at times, a way of averting the face of reality.

123. Dezsényi, *Hősök és árulók*, passim.

124. Guderian, *Panzer Leader*, pp. 378–79.

125. Friessner, *Verratene Schlachten*, p. 147.

126. These were the Thirteenth Panzer Division, the Tenth Panzer Grenadier Division, and the First Panzer Grenadier Battalion of the Twentieth Panzer Division. The 109th and 1110th armored brigades were also stationed near Budapest (ibid., pp. 121, 133).

127. Ránki, "L'occupation de la Hongrie," p. 52.

the First Hungarian Army Corps in charge of the defense of the capital, Gen. Béla Aggteleki, seems to have issued orders to attack the Germans even before the regent's proclamation was read over the radio but was placed under arrest by his administrative aide before his orders could be carried out.[128] The airport and the railroad stations were occupied by German troops. The radio station was captured by an SS unit, one of whose members, who spoke Hungarian, read a proclamation prepared by Ferenc Szálasi.[129] In the meantime, Gen. Károly Lázár ordered the mining of the approaches to the Vár. And in the night and early morning hours of October 16, the German tanks, including some remote-controlled Goliath tanks, lined up for an attack on the Vár.[130] Colonel Skorzeny, in charge of the assault, does not indicate how many tanks there were. My father, whose hideout at the time was just beneath the Vár, was unable to count them either:

> The siege of the Vár began at dawn. The Germans lined up right here, underneath our windows, and marched up Tábor Street. We heard cannon shots, machine-gun fire, but only intermittently . . . The siege did not last long—at nine it was over. Did they capture Horthy, or did he suffer an even worse fate, I do not know. For a quarter of a century he held the fate of the country in his hands, he was the country's absolute master. And it was under him that the country sunk to such depths that it actually disintegrated; at the moment when he had finally reached a manly decision for which he accepted full responsibility, he could find not a single man who was willing to follow with conviction the cause for which the regent had exposed himself.[131]

128. It is to this person, Maj. Gen. Iván Hindy, that Macartney dedicated his magnum opus on Hungary, *October Fifteenth;* Macartney explained, in a subsequent edition, that Major General Hindy, although a soldier following orders (?), was condemned to death by a Hungarian people's tribunal for political reasons. See also Rozsnyói, "October Fifteenth, 1944," p. 95. Regarding the arrest of Aggteleki, read András Pogány, "What Really Happened on October Fifteenth, 1944, at the First Corps Headquarters in Budapest?"

129. Winkelmann report, 2574491. Imre Kovács wrote that he and his friends exchanged shots with the Germans who occupied the radio station (*D'une occupation à l'autre,* p. 59); Kern, however, indicates that the German fire was not returned (*Die letzte Schlacht,* p. 62).

130. Otto Skorzeny, *Skorzeny's Secret Missions,* p. 208.

131. Miksa Fenyö, *Az elsodort ország,* p. 416, entry for Oct. 16.

Actually, this statement may have been wishful thinking on my father's part. Rather than accepting full responsibility for his decision, the regent once again wavered. The concluding episodes of Horthy's abortive coup may serve to illustrate this aspect of his personality; but the events of the night of October 15 to 16, and of the day after, did not affect the fate of Germany, the fate of Hungary, or the outcome of World War II.

On the night of October 15–16 the regent found himself almost alone, and he was persuaded to surrender. During an interrogation in 1947, Horthy declared he had surrendered, and ordered the surrender of his bodyguard, to prevent a senseless bloodbath, as there were 600 German tanks in Budapest.[132] There could not have been that many tanks anywhere near Budapest (in fact, there were about 40 and about 25,000 troops), but doubtless armed resistance would have been futile because of the overwhelming German superiority in arms; yet part of Horthy's bodyguard (about 200 men, plus a regiment of about 160) fought a token battle against the assaulting German troops, partly because not all outposts had received word of the surrender and partly because some elements felt it incumbent upon themselves to save the country's honor.[133]

Historians do not blame the regent for not having insisted on a do-or-die last-minute effort, but historians have accused the regent of having given legal sanction to the take-over of the country by Ferenc Szálasi and his Arrow-Cross party.[134] During the early morning hours of October 16, Horthy was led into German custody, thanks to the intervention of his aide-to-camp, General Vattay, and of Prime Minister Lakatos.[135] The regent insists, in his *Memoirs,*

132. Affidavit by Horthy, May 27, 1947 (interrogations, NA Record Group 238, World War II War Crimes Records). Winkelmann's comment was: "Horthy hat diesen Befehl aber erst kurz vor seinem Übersiedeln zur Dienststelle des Befehlshabers der Waffen-SS gegeben. Daraus geht einwandrei hervor, dass seine Kapitulation aus einer hundsgemeinen persönlichen Angst entsprungen ist und nicht etwa aus Sorge, es konnte unter den ungarischen Truppen ein Blutvergiessen enstehen" (NA Microcopy T-175, roll 59, 2574492).

133. On the German side, there were 4 dead and 12 wounded. The Hungarians lost 3 dead and 15 wounded (Skorzeny, *Skorzeny's Secret Missions*, p. 215); see also Dezsényi, *Hősök és árulók*, p. 132.

134. For instance, Ránki, *Emlékiratok és valóság*, p. 301.

135. As a comment on Macartney's account of these events, to the effect that Horthy and Lakatos had placed themselves under German protection, Lakatos wrote: *"Not true!* I was arrested" (June 2, 1961, Hungarian National Archives, notes of General Lakatos). The idea of asking for German protection seems to have originated with Vattay, and Horthy later denied that he had ever agreed to Vattay's proposal

that despite Vattay's assertions, he had never intended to ask the Germans for protection or asylum: "I can explain his behavior only if I postulate that Vattay, who never failed in loyalty to me, took his otherwise inexplicable course of action in order to save my family." [136] At any rate, Lakatos made certain diplomatic requests from the German representatives in Hungary, including (a) asylum for Horthy, his family, and some companions; (b) no defamatory statements about the regent in the German press; (c) every effort on the part of German authorities to prevent an outbreak of civil war in Hungary. Hitler readily agreed to these requests when consulted by telephone.[137] It was perhaps as a counterpart to this agreement that Horthy gave out orders not to resist the Germans. But there were further German demands. While under German protection but still in the Vár, Horthy was visited three times by Veesenmayer and Lakatos demanding that he appoint Szálasi as Hungary's next prime minister (to replace Lakatos). On the third occasion Horthy signed the document announcing his own abdication and the appointment of Szálasi. Lakatos and Veesenmayer, as well as Rudolf Rahn, had pointed out to him, declared Horthy, that his failure to appoint Szálasi would mean the death of his son, who was a prisoner in some German concentration camp.[138] During an American interrogation somewhere in Bavaria, Horthy declared that Lakatos had come to him, on the third occasion, with a piece of paper:

> It was a dirty paper, written in German and Hungarian, that I nominate Salashi [*sic*] as Prime Minister, and I told him that he knew I refused yesterday twice and how could he come and ask me. And then he said that if I would sign it then my son would join in my train and come with me. And, of course, I trembled for the life of my only child. And I told him after the loss of every country [?], if I sign that is nothing after the law. But as you give me your word of honor that my son really joins us in the train, then I put my name here on this paper,

---

(Hennyey, "Ungarns Weg," pp. 712–13). Dezsényi, however, blames Lakatos (*Hősök és árulók,* pp. 135 ff.).

136. *Memoirs,* pp. 234–35.

137. Winkelmann report, 2574492; see also Rahn, *Ruheloses Leben,* pp. 269 ff.

138. *Memoirs,* p. 236; see also affidavit, May 27, 1947, interrogations, NA Record Group 238, World War II War Crimes Records.

not under the writing, but over it, saying that it is not of value, because I can only resign to my parliament, not to him, the German Minister, and not to these men with machine guns.[139]

In any case, it has been argued, the appointment was not valid, because orders signed by the regent have to be countersigned by the pertinent minister.[140] Yet Ferenc Szálasi was able to claim, at his first appearances in the Hungarian National Assembly and in the upper house, that he had been legally appointed by the regent; few people believed him.

Ferenc Szálasi took over, at least outwardly, the leadership of the part of Hungary still occupied by the Germans in the name of his "Hungarist" movement. It is possible, as has been claimed, that the basic purpose of the Arrow-Cross, or Hungarist movement was "to raise the social standard of non-Jewish proletarians." [141] In practice, however, the outstanding characteristic of this new regime was the resumption of terrorism directed against the Jewish population of Budapest and against surviving liberal or left-wing elements. The military situation did not permit the completion of the extermination process. Two months after taking power, Szálasi's cabinet fled to one of Hungary's westernmost cities, Sopron. The Red Army began the siege of Budapest in the early part of December, and the city was completely encircled by December 26.[142] The siege of Budapest lasted two months and constituted one of the major battles of the war. Budapest was completely in the hands of the Red Army by February 13. While German troops, assisted by a smattering of Hungarian units, held out in western Hungary until April 4, the date of February 13, 1945, may be taken as the date of Hungary's elimination from World War II.

The discussions of Allied leaders at Quebec and at Moscow in the fall of 1944 seldom focused on Hungary. It appears that the Soviet authorities failed to inform the American and British leaders of some details of the armistice negotiations with Hungary, but in any case, the Soviet occupation of Hungary was the natural out-

139. Interrogation of Horthy, Aug. 27, 1945, NA Record Group 238, World War II War Crimes Records.

140. According to the Constitution of 1920 (*Tanulmányok a Horthy-korszak*, p. 46).

141. Kutas, "Judaism, Zionism, and Anti-Semitism in Hungary," p. 385. That Szálasi's party was indeed radical and pro-proletarian, not only in its rhetoric, but also in its true objectives, is convincingly argued by Nicholas M. Nagy-Talavera in *The Green Shirts and the Others*, passim.

142. Peter Gosztony, *Der Kampf um Budapest, 1944–45*, p. 30.

come of the military position of the Allies. While Churchill had theoretically secured for Great Britain a share of influence in post-war Hungarian affairs, it is obvious the western Allies were not prepared to insist on their claims vis-à-vis the Soviet leaders and local Soviet authorities. The western leaders were simply unconcerned, despite the relative restraint exhibited by the Soviet Union, during three years, in sponsoring a socialist revolution: but I have no intention of broaching another chapter of Hungarian history.

12. Conclusion: The Impact of World War II on Hungary

> The dictatorship or the attempt at dictatorship of the excited and excitable masses in Hungary frightens me. I watched how easily these masses were swayed by the slogans of the Arrow-Cross or Swastika agitators; they may be equally swayed by slogans castigating "gentlemen" and priests, especially if the political circumstances promise them power in their stead. I cannot see who their leaders are, I don't know in what spirit they prepare for their work. Nor do I see those personalities who could bring about a bourgeois democracy in Hungary. The regime which now prevails, especially since March 19 [1944], destroyed whatever valuable organizations there remained in the country and handed the most valuable individuals over to the Gestapo. If the Germans flee from here tomorrow, as well as those "gentlemen" who have good reason to flee, will there remain anyone qualified to assume responsibility for the fate of this country?

Thus wrote my father on September 8, 1944, in his secret diary of the German occupation.[1] The loss in capable leadership, through emigration, through extermination, may have been the major impact of the war, a factor that cannot be accurately evaluated even today. But what were the more immediate effects of the war on Hungary?

In some respects Hungary's role in World War II was not different from that of Germany's other allies; in other respects it was unique. Hungary was both an ally of Germany and a country betrayed by Germany.

The allied Axis countries included Italy, Slovakia, Croatia, Bulgaria, Finland, and Romania. Inasmuch as Italy was a main Axis partner and also the first one to surrender, Hungary's position can hardly be compared to that of Italy. Slovakia and Croatia owed their existence as independent nations to National Socialist Ger-

Much of the material in this conclusion has been published in the *East European Quarterly* 3 (Summer 1969): 219–28, under the title, "Some Aspects of Hungarian History during the Second World War."

1. Miksa Fenyö, *Az elsodort ország,* p. 309.

many or to Italy; it is no wonder the leaders of these two states felt obligated to the leaders of the main Axis countries. While the government of Bulgaria professed friendship toward National Socialist Germany, the country never took part in the "crusade against bolshevism." The Finnish people and the Finnish government were willing to participate in the war against the Soviet Union, if only to recapture territories Finland had lost during the Winter War, but her geographical position sheltered her from effective pressure by the German government. Hungary's role most closely resembled that of Romania. Romania's economic significance for Germany lay in her vast oil resources, without which Germany would have been unable to wage war; during the war Hungarian oil production rose from practically zero to over 840,000 tons a year. While her production remained well below Romania's, Hungary was, nevertheless, the second most important source of oil within the German sphere of influence and about the only source after the Romanian about-face in August of 1944.[2]

Both Romania and Hungary were prompt to rally, in June of 1941, to the campaign against the Soviet Union, in the case of the Hungarian government perhaps because it had an exaggerated impression of the pressures exerted upon it by the German government. After the battle of Stalingrad the Hungarian government, like the Romanian, sought to make amends for its premature political and military commitments on behalf of the Axis; both governments tried to establish secret contacts with the Anglo-American Allies (but preferably not with the Soviet Union), envisaging an eventual surrender. These negotiations, the secret of which was not well kept, were one of the justifications for the German occupation of Hungary. While a large number of German troops were stationed in Romania, ostensibly in preparation for the offensive against the Soviet Union and later to protect Ploesti against Allied air raids, Romania was never actually occupied by Germany. Unlike the two Antonescus (Ion and Mihai), Miklós Kállay was unable to avoid a German occupation of Hungary, mainly because of a geopolitical factor: Hungary lies between Germany and Romania. After March 19, 1944, the date of the German occupation, the status of Hungary

---

2. Microcopy T-84, roll 135, 1438130–32. German statistics and other records pertaining to Hungarian economy during the war are reproduced among the Miscellaneous German Records Collection, NA Microcopy T-84, and the Records of the Headquarters, German Armed Forces High Command, NA Microcopy T-77.

was not very different from that of the Protectorate, of Serbia, or of certain occupied territories in the West.

Hungarian history in this period may be significant in other regards as well. The dissolution of the Hapsburg monarchy in 1918 resulted in a further "balkanization" of east-central Europe. A number of Hungarian politicians and scholars hoped, after the signature of the Treaty of Trianon in 1920, that a Danubian federation of some kind, comprising Austria, Czechoslovakia, Hungary, Yugoslavia, Romania, and Bulgaria, would come about. This hope was not selfless; such a federation might have numbed the pain caused Hungarians by the enormous losses in territory and population, at the same time leaving the door open for a renegotiation of the Treaty of Trianon directly with the "successor" states. Any such renegotiation, it was felt, could only have benefited Hungary. The other alternative, it seems, was not considered: friendship with the "successor" states, and perhaps a Danubian federation, could also have been achieved had Hungary publicly renounced her revisionist claims. The origins of World War II demonstrated, however, that a Danubian federation would have benefited not only Hungary but all the states concerned: the Anschluss, the dismemberment of Czechoslovakia, could hardly have taken place. The encouragement given by the British government to the Hungarian reoccupation of Ruthenia (Carpatho-Ukraine) on March 15, 1939, may have been a belated recognition of the desirability of a strong power in east-central Europe. By this aggressive move, Hungary gained a common border with Poland; Poland and Hungary have been friends throughout most of their history, and in 1939 their governments and social systems seemed alike conservative, even fascist, according to some historians. The Polish-Hungarian border did not and could not, of course, result in a power bloc potent enough to thwart the German *Drang nach Osten*. It only served as an escape route for tens of thousands of Poles fleeing the German attack and the German and Soviet occupations in the fall of 1939. The Hungarian government adopted a creditably neutral attitude during the Polish campaign.

The subsequent decisions of the Hungarian government appear less creditable, if I may be permitted to pronounce such a value judgment; in fact, the policies of the Hungarian government in 1940 and 1941 seem to lead logically to the war against the Soviet Union and even to the Arrow-Cross dictatorship of late 1944.

Even though, on the first occasion, the British and French governments had signified their disinterest and even though these revisions may have been justified from an ethnic point of view, it must have been clear to the Hungarian leaders that the new solutions of the territorial problems were less than ideal, especially since they were favored by the Italian Fascist state and the German National Socialist government. Not until 1941, however, did Hungary take an active part in the war. The Hungarian participation in the attack on Yugoslavia discredited the Hungarian government in the eyes of the western democracies; Great Britain, in fact, protested by withdrawing her diplomatic mission from Hungary. The suicide of the prime minister, Count Teleki, may have cleared his own reputation, but it did little good for Hungary. The count had warned that Hungary would be following a dishonorable policy by despoiling what after the German attack would essentially be the corpse of Yugoslavia; his warning went unheeded by the regent and the succeeding Hungarian cabinet.

Hungary's declaration of war against the Soviet Union on June 27, 1941, has become the subject of historiographical polemics. At first, Hungary did not figure at all in Hitler's plans for a campaign against the Soviet Union; in the later stages of the planning, however, Hungarian participation was regarded as at least a possibility. But the bombing of Kassa (Košice) on June 26 is still a question mark. The immediate official explanation was that the city had been bombed by Soviet aircraft, or by Soviet aircraft disguised as German aircraft. Since the revelation of Col. Ádám Krudy, a witness of the raid, has become public, most historians, with some notable exceptions, assert along with the colonel that the bombing was carried out by more or less disguised German airplanes. The notable exceptions include C. A. Macertney and certain authors with pro-German sympathies; they can justifiably point to the fact that so far no documents have come to light implicating either the German General Staff or the Hungarian General Staff, which is supposed to have collaborated with the Germans. But, in any case, the discussion is academic. The Bárdossy government, out of a desire to repay the Germans for past favors, out of a desire to obtain new favors, out of conviction, or simply out of weakness, seemed all too willing to declare war on the Soviet Union; Hungary would have drifted into the war sooner or later.

Prime Minister Miklós Kállay, who replaced Bárdossy in March

1942, faced the same three alternatives as the previous government: all-out cooperation with National Socialist Germany, unyielding resistance to National Socialist pressures or requests, and the policy actually adopted. Had the second of these alternatives been consistently pursued, National Socialist Germany would have had to occupy Hungary maybe as early as 1941 in order to secure its rear in the campaign against Yugoslavia and the Soviet Union and to insure the unhampered shipment of Romanian (and eventually also of Hungarian) oil. The German police or a Hungarian satellite government would have had plenty of time for the extermination of Hungary's Jews and anti-Nazi politicians. In the long run, a liberated Hungary might have received consideration during the postwar peace treaties, perhaps even territorial concessions; but at what price? The policy the Kállay government decided to follow was something short of full cooperation with National Socialist Germany. Upon the instance of Joachim von Ribbentrop and Marshal Wilhelm Keitel in the winter of 1941–42, Hungary agreed to send an entire army to the eastern front—still, less of a contribution than the two armies sent by Romania. Successive Hungarian governments had passed oppressive anti-Semitic laws; still, compared to Germany and other countries in eastern Europe, Hungary was often regarded as a refuge by the nearly one million Jews who existed there. It was only at the time of the battle of Stalingrad, and especially after the rout of the Second Hungarian Army around Voronezh, which began on January 14, 1943, that the Hungarian leaders realized an Axis victory was unlikely. Attempts were made to establish contact with the Anglo-American Allies, against whom the Hungarian government was also waging war. At the same time, Miklós Kállay was anxious to avoid provoking a German occupation. But Kállay's policy failed on all counts: the German occupation came on March 19, 1944, while the Anglo-American Allies, not to mention the Soviet Union, remained unconvinced of Hungary's good intention.

The German attack could well have redeemed Hungary in the eyes of the Allies; yet for several reasons, this did not turn out to be the case. For one thing, it took the German forces only one day to occupy most of Hungary. Having little trust in its largely pro-German officer corps, Miklós Kállay did not seriously attempt to rally the Hungarian army in defense of the country, let alone to spark spontaneous resistance; he sought refuge inside the Turkish legation in Budapest. The regent, who was almost as zealous an anti-

Nazi as he was anti-Communist, initially put up even less resistance to the German occupation. Lured out of the country, together with Hungary's two top military leaders, on March 18, he allowed himself to be persuaded or browbeaten by Hitler into permitting the German occupation, and he promised to remain at his post. A number of explanations have been offered for the regent's collapse on this occasion; what mattered to Hitler, however, was simply that the continued reign of the regent seemed to give legitimacy to his aggressive move.

The story of the German occupation of Hungary has been told often enough; and perhaps, as mentioned earlier, it is not essentially different from the story of other occupations—except in one respect. A number of articles have been published on the subject of resistance in Hungary; [3] actually, however, there was very little resistance. A few guerilla units operated in the Bácska and the Baranya and in the Carpatho-Ukraine; but these units seem to have been manned mostly by Serbs or Ukrainians. Furthermore, the new Hungarian government, led by Döme Sztójay, the former Hungarian minister in Berlin, cooperated with the German authorities in every regard. Although this government did not include members of the extreme right-wing and racist Arrow-Cross party, its activities resembled those of the Arrow-Cross government which exercised power briefly after October 15, 1944, over a portion of Hungary. Measures pertaining to the deportation of the Hungarian Jews or to the exploitation of Hungary's economy for the "common cause" were usually approved, or rubber-stamped by the government of Döme Sztójay.

How was this possible? How could a Hungarian government hand over Hungary's resources and Hungarian citizens to another country and enjoy the passive tolerance of the population? No doubt there was considerable sympathy toward Germany among segments of the Hungarian population. Germany and Hungary had lost World War I together. Pro-German and pro-Nazi sentiments were particularly strong among members of the German ethnic group in Hungary,

3. For example, Miklós Lackó, "L'antisoviétisme—l'entrave principale de la lutte contre le nazisme," pp. 146–56, and Ferenc Mucs, "Quelques aspects de la résistance armée en Hongrie contre le fascisme," pp. 155–69, both in *European Resistance Movements 1939–1945* (New York: Macmillan, 1964); István Pintér, "Adatok a magyar nemzeti felkelés felszabadító bizottságának történetéhez" [Contribution to the history of the liberation committee of the Hungarian national uprising], dealing with the activities of Endre Bajcsy-Zsilinszky; Sallai, "Die Befreiungskämpfe um Budapest," 3 : 148–57, and "Von der Teilnahme der Ungarn am europäischen Widerstandskampf," both in *Internationale Hefte der Widerstandsbewegung;* and others.

and a large percentage of the Hungarian generals, it seems, came from this ethnic group. Pro-German feelings were reinforced, after the advent of National Socialism in Germany, by anti-Semitism, which had become widespread in Hungary after the Communist regime of Béla Kun in 1919 during the White Terror. Anti-Communism also became a factor; as a Hungarian Marxist author and politician stated, the direction of the illegal Communist party in Hungary was able to maintain contact with only about a dozen members in 1942 and 1943.[4] It may seem inconceivable to those who lived on the Allied side during the war that the apparently crude methods of the German propaganda machine, which were imitated in Hungary, could have led part of the population to believe in the possibility of a German victory as late as November 1944 when the Red Army was at the gates of Budapest; but, even in 1944, many Hungarians felt that German victory was not only possible but likely. How? Thanks to the miracle weapons, perhaps. As for the so-called leaders, who may have been able to assess the military situation more accurately, it was simply a matter of a few more days of wilful power.

Perhaps the history of German-Hungarian relations in World War II provides no real lessons for us. For the romantically inclined (among which I must number myself), this history is another chapter in the vicissitudes of a nation which, like Poland, has been much overrun, much oppressed by foreign and sometimes native despots. Certainly this history may prove of interest to the citizens of other small nations that are the neighbors of great powers; although it may not provide them with exhilarating examples of heroic resistance to pressures exerted by a great power. This history may also serve to illuminate human nature through a study of diplomats, politicians, and their politics. For instance, Admiral Horthy may strike the reader as a man who, while lacking neither courage nor a sense of honor, was remarkable mostly for his hesitations, his indecisions: witness his orders regarding the First Cavalry Division of the Hungarian army, countermanded six times.[5] The most remarkable fact of recent Hungarian history may be that this somewhat dull personality was Hungary's leader for more than a score of years and was regarded by some outside observers, and by the victims of the conservative (and often reactionary) policies of the Hungarian government, as a strong man, and sometimes justifiably so.

4. Kállai, *A magyar függetlenségi mozgalom,* p. 113.
5. Diary of Vörös, passim.

Perhaps each student of history is driven, consciously or unconsciously, by an urge to become a moral judge, by the desire to ascribe to each actor, each participant in the historical drama, his just merits. Professors, in any case, have an inclination to hand out good grades or bad grades to their students; the historical personalities who are the objects of their investigations undergo similar treatment. Nor can it be said that grades are awarded or merits are ascribed according to strictly scientific criteria. But then the majority of personalities, in this study at least, are now dead, and the dead cannot appeal the verdict of the student of history.

Bibliography

Polemics regarding the role of Hungary in World War II have been waged from three vantage points. First appeared the writings of Hungarian politicians who, having been participants in the war, found refuge in western countries after the war, the most prominent and complete of these being, in the sequence of their publication, Antal Ullein-Reviczky's *Guerre allemande, paix rusee,* Miklós Horthy's *Ein Leben für Ungarn*—eventually translated into English under the title *Memoirs*—Miklós Kállay's *Hungarian Premier,* and Stephen D. Kertersz's *Diplomacy in a Whirlpool.* These writings share the common characteristic of memoirs: they are self-justificatory. Apart from enhancing the role of the author in the political life of Hungary, they also reflect favorably on the author by describing the political system in which he participated as most advantageous for the country. The admittedly polemical work of the Hungarian historian György Ránki, the title of which may be translated as "Memoirs and Facts Regarding Hungary's Role in World War II," analyzes mercilessly the mistakes or exaggerations resulting from this common human foible.

Many accounts written in Hungary since 1945 do not admit to being polemical; yet they are rather easy to characterize, all having a tendency to place the responsibility for most of the woes of the Hungarian people in the past and even in the future on the previous political regime, the regency of Admiral Horthy. The period between 1919 and 1944 is described as the Horthy-Fascist era, and Horthy is often credited with the invention of fascism. Besides, that period is also characterized as "feudal," while critics of the Horthy regime abroad often content themselves with the epithet "semi-feudal." In order to underscore the evil of Horthy's Fascist and feudal regime, many Hungarian historians found it necessary to stress the close relationship of the Hungarian governments and the Hungarian ruling class with the National Socialist regime in Germany. Sometimes the thesis went one step further: the authors purported to show that Hungarian foreign policy, both before and during the German occupation, was a deliberate effort to gain the friendship of the National Socialist leaders and by the same token a betrayal of the true interests of the Hungarian people. The more recent contributions of Hungarian historians, since about 1958, have been sophisticated and scholarly. The authors generally distinguish three or four groups of Hungarian politicians, even among members of the ruling class: thus, there were the pro-German and the pro-Anglo-American groups who shared power, the extreme right, and various shades of left. The conservative leaders of Hungary were no longer universally condemned. The recent works of Hungarian historians recognize that there were a number of elements among the Hungarian ruling class, including the regent, who sought ways and means to elude German demands and to curtail the nefarious activities of the homegrown National Socialists. One cannot neglect the recent contributions of Hungarian scholars on any aspect of Hungarian history.

The third vantage point, that of German generals, politicians, and historians, is the most difficult to characterize; in fact, perhaps no generalization applies to it. German politicians who wrote their memoirs shortly after the war, such as Franz von Papen and Erich von Kordt, have deprecated the foreign policy of the National Socialist leaders with regard to Hungary. This is still the attitude of the "liberal" generation of German historians, none of whom, however, seems to concern himself particularly with the countries of southeastern Europe. There is, on the other hand, a tendency toward revisionism. The retired officers who have written extensively about Hungary as a theater of military operations, in particular Generals Heinz Guderian and Hans Friessner, and Major Erich Kernmayr, write of Hungarian betrayal, as if loyalty to Hitler to the last, on the part of Hungarians as well as of Germans, had been the only honorable solution. Professor Andreas Hillgruber, the German scholar who has written more about the recent history of southeast Europe than any other, has a tendency to conceal or ignore certain aspects of Hungarian history which might reflect unfavorably on Germany (albeit National Socialist Germany): the economic exploitation of Hungary, the deportation of Jews. In these authors some Hungarian historians, especially before 1958, found an unexpected ally: in both cases the most significant underlying assumption is that National Socialist Germany exerted little if any pressure on Hungary, whether economic, military, or diplomatic; collaboration was on the initiative of the Hungarians themselves.

There is at least one serious historian dealing with Hungarian history whose vantage point is quite his own: Professor Carlyle

Aylmer Macartney. In fact, Professor Macartney's monograph, variously titled *October Fifteenth* and *A History of Hungary, 1929–1945,* is the only systematic survey of Hungarian history in this period and perhaps the only study which covers the same ground as mine and more. His work, as indeed all his works on Hungarian and east European history, is the result of a lifetime of studies and observation. Yet Macartney's work has curious oversights, partly due to the fact that he wrote his book too soon: it is based on interviews or correspondence with the surviving personalities of World War II politicians and on an examination of newspapers of the period. Macartney had apparently neglected to consult documents, apart from those in his personal possession. The German and Hungarian documents were still unprocessed or unavailable in 1959 when Macartney's monograph first appeared (see Miksa Fenyö, "C. A. Macartney magyar történelme" [The Hungarian history of C. A. Macartney]).

BIBLIOGRAPHIES

"Bibliographie d'oeuvres choisies de la science historique hongroise 1945–1959." *Etudes historiques* 2 : 487–756. Budapest: Académie hongroise des sciences, 1960.

Catalog of Records of the German Foreign Ministry Archives. Edited by George O. Kent. 3 vols. Stanford: Hoover Institute, 1962–67.

Guide to German Records Microfilmed at Alexandria, Virginia. 59 vols. to date. Washington: National Archives, 1958–.

Hillgruber, Andreas. *Südost-Europa im zweiten Weltkrieg: Literaturbericht und Bibliographie.* Frankfurt-am-Main: Bernard & Graefe, 1962.

Meyer, Klaus, *Bibliographie der Arbeiten zur Osteuropäischen Geschichte aus den deutschsprachigen Fachzeitschriften 1858–1964.* Berlin: Otto Harrassowitz, 1966.

Niederhauser, Emil. *Bibliographie d'oeuvres choisies de la science historique hongroise 1945–1959.* Budapest: Akadémiai Kiadó, 1960.

Schreiber, Thomas. "Historiographie hongroise de la deuxième guerre mondiale." *Revue d'histoire de la deuxième guerre mondiale* 11 (1961) : 31–56.

Südosteuropa-Bibliographie. Edited by Gertrud Krallert-Sattler. 3 vols. Munich: R. Oldenbourg, 1956.

Tihany, Leslie C. "Bibliography of Post-Armistice Hungarian Historiography." *The American Slavic and East European Review* 6 (1947): 158–78.

UNPUBLISHED DOCUMENTS

Documents of the German Foreign Ministry. Archiv des Auswärtiges Amtes. Bonn.

Documents of the German Foreign Ministry. National Archives Microcopy T-120. Washington, D.C.

Documents of the Hungarian Ministry of Foreign Affairs. Országos Levéltár [National Archives]. Budapest.

Documents of the Italian Ministries and the Duce's Office. National Archives Microcopy T-581. Washington, D.C.

General Records of the Department of State. National Archives Record Group 59. Washington, D.C.

Hungarian Collection. National Archives Microcopy T-973. Washington, D.C.

"Lisbon Papers." National Archives Microcopy T-816. Washington, D.C.

Miscellaneous German Records Collection. National Archives Microcopy T-84. Washington, D.C.

Notes of General Lakatos. Országos Levéltár [National Archives]. Budapest.

Papers of Herbert Pell. Franklin D. Roosevelt Library. Hyde Park, New York.

Papers of Cordell Hull, Library of Congress, Manuscript Division. Washington, D.C.

Records of Headquarters, German Armed Forces High Command. National Archives Microcopy T-77. Washington, D.C.

Records of the National Socialist German Labor Party. National Archives Microcopy T-81. Washington, D.C.

Records of the Office of Strategic Services. National Archives Record Group 220. Washington, D.C.

Records of the Reich Leader of the SS and Chief of the German Police. National Archives Microcopy T-175. Washington, D.C.

World War II War Crimes Records. National Archives Record Group 238. Washington, D.C.

BOOKS

Ádám, Magda; Kerekes, Lajos; and Juhász, Gyula, eds. *Allianz Hitler-Horthy-Mussolini*. Budapest: Akadémiai Kiadó, 1966.

Adonyi, Ferenc. *A magyar katona a második világháborúban, 1941/1945* [The Hungarian soldier in World War II]. Klagenfurt: F. Kleinmayr, 1954.

Andics, Erzsébet. *Fasizmus és reakció Magyarországon* [Fascism and reaction in Hungary]. Budapest: Szikra, 1945.

Anfuso, Filippo. *Du Palais de Venise au lac de Garde.* Paris: Calmann-Lévy, 1949.

Basch, Antonín. *The Danube Basin and the German Economic Sphere.* London: Kegan Paul, Trench, Trubner, 1944.

Bazna, Elyesa. *I Was Cicero.* Translated by Eric Mosbacher. London: André Deutsch, 1962.

Beck, Jozef. *Final Report.* New York: Robert Speller, 1957.

Bereczky, Albert. *A magyar protestantizmus a zsidóüldözés ellen* [Hungarian protestantism against the persecution of the Jews]. Budapest: Református Traktátus Vállalat, 1945.

Berend, Iván, and Ránki, György. *Magyarország a fasiszta Németország életterében 1933–1939* [Hungary in the *Lebensraum* of Fascist Germany]. Budapest: Közgazdasági és Jogi Könyvkiadó, 1960.

————. *Magyarország gyáripara a második világháború elött és a háború időszakában* [Hungary's manufacturing industry before World War II and during the war]. Budapest: Akadémiai Kiadó, 1958.

Biss, Andreas. *Der Stopp der Endlösung. Kampf gegen Himmler und Eichmann in Budapest.* Stuttgart: Seewald, 1966.

Boldizsár, Iván. *The Other Hungary.* Budapest: The New Hungary, 1946.

Borsody, Stephen. *The Triumph of Tyranny.* New York: Macmillan, 1960.

Buchinger, Manó. *Küzdelem a szocializmusért: emlékek és élmények* [Fight for socialism; experience and memories]. Budapest: Népszava, 1946–47.

Buzási, Jenő. *Az ujvidéki razzia* [The razzia at Novi Sad]. Budapest: Kossuth, 1963.

Caminada, Jerome. *My Purpose Holds.* London: Jonathan Cape, 1952.

Cavallero, Ugo. *Comando Supremo.* Rocca S. Carciano: Capelli, 1948.

Christopher, Felix. *A Short Course in the Secret War.* New York: E. P. Dutton, 1963.

Ciano, Count Galeazzo. *Diario 1939–1943.* 2 vols. Milan: Rizzoli, 1963.

The Confidential Papers of Nicholas Horthy. Edited by Miklós Szinai and László Szűcs. Budapest: Corvina Press, 1965. (Translation of *Horthy Miklós tiktos iratai.* Budapest: Kossuth, 1962.)

Csatári, Dániel. *Forgószélben (Magyar-román viszony 1940–1945)* [In the whirlwind (Hungarian-Romanian relations)]. Budapest: Akadémiai Kiadó, 1969.

Csécsy, Imre. *Ha Hitler győzött volna* [Had Hitler won]. Budapest: Vajna és Bokor, 1947.

Czebe, Jenő, and Pethö, Tibor. *Hungary in World War II: A Military History of the Years of War.* Budapest: New Hungary, 1946.

Darvas, József. *Város az ingoványon* [City on the swamp]. Budapest, 1945.

Deakin, F. W. *The Brutal Friendship*. New York: Harper & Row, 1962.

The Destruction of the Hungarian Jewry: A Documentary Account. Edited by Randolph L. Braham. 2 vols. New York: World Federation of Hungarian Jews, 1963.

Dezsényi, Miklós. *Hősök és árulók* [Heroes and traitors]. Budapest: Magyar Téka, 1948 [?].

Diplomáciai iratok Magyarország külpolitikájához, 1936–1945 [Diplomatic records pertaining to Hungarian foreign policy]. Edited by Magda Ádám, Gyula Juhász, and Zsigmond László. Budapest: Magyar Tudományos Akadémia, 1964.

The Documents on German Foreign Policy, 1918–1945. Series C and D, 15 vols. Washington: Department of State, 1949–62.

Eden, Anthony. *The Reckoning: The Memoirs of Anthony Eden.* London: *The Times,* 1965.

Eichmann in Hungary. Edited by Jenő Lévai. Budapest: Pannonia Press, 1961.

Farkas, Ferenc (Kisbarnaki). *Tatárhágó visszanéz* [The Tatar-pass looks back]. Buenos Aires: Kárpát, 1953.

Fenyö, Miksa. *Az elsodort ország* [A country adrift]. Budapest: Révai, 1946.

————. *Hitler.* Budapest: Nyugat, 1934.

Foreign Relations of the United States (1941–1944). Washington: Government Printing Office, 1958—.

Forst de Battaglia, Otto. *Zwischeneuropa.* Frankfurt-am-Main: Verlag der Frankfurter Hefte, 1954.

Friedman, Philip. *Their Brothers' Keepers.* New York: Crown, 1957.

Friessner, Hans. *Verratene Schlachten.* Hamburg: Holsten Verlag, 1956.

Fuller, J. F. C. *The Second World War, 1939–1945.* London: Eyre & Spottiswoode, 1962.

Galantai, Maria. *The Changing of the Guard: The Siege of Budapest, 1944–1945.* London: Pall Mall, 1961.

Geheime Reichssache: Papst Pius XII hat nicht geschwiegen. Edited by Jenő Lévai. Cologne: Wort und Werk, 1966.

Geleji, Dezső. *Magyarország 1944-ben* [Hungary in 1944]. Budapest: Gergely R., 1945.

The Goebbels Diaries, 1942–1943. Edited by Louis P. Lochner. Garden City, N.Y.: Doubleday, 1948.

Gosztonyi, Péter. *Der Kampf um Budapest, 1944–1945.* Munich: Schnell und Steiner, 1964.

Guderian, Heinz. *Panzer Leader.* Translated by Constantine Fitzgibbon. London: Michael Joseph, 1952.

Hagen, Walter [Wilhelm Hoettl]. *Die geheime Front.* Linz and Vienna: Nibelungen Verlag, 1950.

Halder, Franz. *Kriegstagebuch.* 3 vols. Stuttgart: W. Kohlhammer Verlag, 1963.

Hilberg, Raul. *The Destruction of the European Jews.* Chicago: Quadrangle Books, 1961.

Hillgruber, Andreas. *Hitler, König Carol und Marschall Antonescu.* Weisbaden: F. Steiner, 1954.

Himler, Márton. *Igy néztek ki a magyar nemzet sirásói* [The faces of the gravediggers of the Hungarian nation]. New York: St. Marks, 1958.

Hirschmann, Ira. *Caution to the Winds.* New York: David McKay, 1962.

Hitlers Lagebesprechungen. Edited by Helmut Heiber. Stuttgart: Deutsche Verlags Anstalt, 1962.

Höhne, Heinz, *The Order of the Death's Head.* New York: Coward-McCann, 1970.

Honti, François. *Le drame hongrois.* Paris: Editions du Troilet, 1949.

Horthy, Nicholas [Miklos]. *Memoirs.* New York: Robert Speller and Sons, 1957. (First published under the title *Ein Leben für Ungarn.* Bonn, 1953.)

Horváth, Jenő. *Az országgyarapitás története 1920–1941* [The history of the country's increase]. Budapest. Magyar Külügyi Társaság, 1941.

Horváth, Miklós. *A. 2. magyar hadsereg megsemmisülése a Donnál* [The annihilation of the Second Hungarian Army at the Don]. Budapest: Zrinyi, 1958.

Hull, Cordell. *The Memoirs of Cordell Hull.* New York: Macmillan, 1948.

Izsáky, Margit. *Ország a keresztfán* [A country crucified]. Budapest: Müller Károly, 1940.

Jócsik, Lajos. *German Economic Influence in the Danube Valley.* Budapest: New Hungary, 1946.

Juhász, Gyula. *Magyarország külpolitikája, 1919–1945* [Hungary's foreign policy]. Budapest: Kossuth, 1969.

Kádár, Iván. *A munkásosztály helyzete a Horthy-rendszer idején* [The conditions of the working class during the Horthy regime]. Budapest: Szikra, 1956.

Kállai, Gyula. *A magyar függetlenségi mozgalom, 1936–1945* [The Hungarian movement for independence]. Budapest: Szikra, 1948.

Kállay, Miklós. *Hungarian Premier.* New York: Columbia University Press, 1954.

Károlyi, Michael [Mihály Károlyi]. *Faith without Illusions.* New York: E. P. Dutton, 1957.

Karsai, Elek. *A budai Sándor palotában történt* [It happened in the Sándor palace in Buda]. Budapest, 1963.

Karsai, Elek. *A budai vártól a gyepüig, 1941–1945* [From the castle in Buda to the western frontier of Hungary]. Budapest: Táncsics, 1965.

———, ed. *"Fegyvertelen álltak az aknamezőkön"* [They stood in the minefields defenseless]. 2 vols. Budapest: A Magyar Izraeliták Országos Képviselete, 1958–67.

———, and Szinai, Miklós. *"Országgyarapítás"—Országvesztés* ["Increasing the country"—loosing the country]. Vol. 2. Budapest: Kossuth, 1961.

Kasztner, Rezso. *Der Bericht des jüdischen Rettungskomitees aus Budapest, 1942–1945.* N.p., 1946.

Keitel, Wilhelm. *The Memoirs of Field-Marshal Keitel.* New York: Stein and Day, 1966.

Kern, Erich [Kernmayr]. *Die letzte Schlacht; Ungarn 1944–1945.* Göttingen: K. W. Schultz, 1960.

Kertesz, Stephen D. *Diplomacy in a Whirlpool.* South Bend, Ind.: University of Notre Dame Press, 1953.

Kis, Aladár. *Magyarország külpolitikája a második világháború előestéjén* [Hungary's foreign policy on the eve of World War II]. Budapest: Kossuth, 1963.

Kissel, Hans. *Die Panzerschlachten in der Puszta in Oktober 1944.* Neckargemünd: Kurt Vowinckel, 1960.

Komlós, János. *Elárult ország* [A country betrayed]. Budapest, 1961.

Kordt, Erich. *Wahn und Wirklichkeit.* Stuttgart: Union Deutsche Verlagsgesellschaft, 1948.

Korom, Mihály. *A fasizmus bukása Magyarországon* [The fall of fascism in Hungary]. Budapest: Kossuth, 1961.

Kossa, István. *Dunától a Donig* [From the Danube to the Don]. Budapest: Szépirodalmi Könyvkiadó, 1960.

Kovács, Imre. *D'une occupation à l'autre: la tragédie hongroise.* Translated by René Jouan. Paris: Calmann-Lévy, 1949.

Kriegstabuch des Oberkommandos der Wehrmacht, 1940–1945. Edited by Helmuth Greiner, Andreas Hillgruber, and Percy Ernst Schramm. 4 vols. Frankfurt-am-Main: Bernard & Graefe, 1961–65.

Kun, Andor. *Berlinből jelentik* [Reporting from Berlin]. Budapest: Kossuth, 1965.

———. *Enyhitő körülmények Magyarország bűnperében* [Mitigating circumstances in the judicial trial of Hungary]. Budapest: Általános Nyomda, 1946 [?].

Lackó, Miklós. *Arrow-Cross Men, National Socialists, 1935–1944.* Budapest: Akadémiai Kiadó, 1969. (Slightly abridged version of *Nyilasok, nemzetiszocialisták.* Budapest: Kossuth, 1966).

Lányi, Mrs. Ernő, ed. *A szabadság hajnalán* [On the dawn of freedom]. Budapest: Kossuth, 1965.

Lévai, E. [Jenő Lévai] *Eichmann in Hungary.* Budapest, 1961.

Lévai, Jenő. *Black Book on the Martyrdom of the Hungarian Jewry.* Zürich: Central European Times, 1948.

————. *Horogkereszt, kaszáskereszt, nyilaskereszt* [The swastika, the hooked cross, and the arrow-cross]. Budapest: Müller Károly, 1945.

————. *Hungarian Jewry and the Papacy.* London: Sands, 1968.

————. *L'Eglise ne s'est pas tue: le dossier hongrois, 1940–1945.* Paris: Editions du Seuil, 1966.

————. *A Margitkörúti vészbírák* [The bloodthirsty judges on the Margit boulevard]. Budapest, 1945.

————. *Zsidósors Magyarországon* [The fate of the Jews in Hungary]. Budapest: Magyar Téka, 1948.

Leiss, Otto Rudolf, and Peschaut, Theodor. *Ungarn zwischen Ost und West.* Hannover: Berenber, 1963.

Listowel, Countess [Márffy-Mantuano]. *Crusader in the Secret War.* London: Christopher Johnson, 1952.

Lukacs, John A. *The Great Powers and Eastern Europe.* New York: American Book, 1953.

Macartney, Carlyle Aylmer. *October Fifteenth.* 2 vols. Edinburgh University Press, 1961. (Revised edition of *A History of Hungary, 1929–1945* 2 vols. New York: Praeger, 1956–57.)

Magyarország és a második világháború [Hungary and World War II]. Edited by Magda Ádám, Gyula Juhász, and Lajos Kerekes. 2d ed. Budapest: Kossuth, 1961.

Montgomery, John Flournoy. *Hungary, the Unwilling Satellite.* New York: Devin Adair, 1947.

Mosca, Rodolfo. *Le relazioni internazionali del regno d'Ungheria.* Budapest: Societá Mattia Corvino, 1943.

Moyzisch, L. *Operation Cicero.* New York, 1950.

Munkácsi, Ernő. *Hogyan történt* [How it happened]. Budapest: Renaissance, 1947.

Nadanyi, Paul. *Hungary at the Crossroads of Invasions.* New York: Amerikai Magyar Népszava, 1943.

Nagy-Talavera, Nicholas M. *The Green Shirts and the Others.* Stanford: Hoover Institute, 1970.

Nagy, Vilmos Nagybaczoni. *Végzetes esztendők, 1938–1945* [Fateful years]. Budapest: Körmendy, n.d.

Nazi Conspiracy and Aggression. Washington: Government Printing Office, 1946–48.

Nemes, Desző. *Magyarország felszabadulása* [The liberation of Hungary]. Budapest: Kossuth, 1960.

A németek magyarországi politikája tiktos német diplomáciai okmányokban (1937–1942) [The German's Hungarian policy as revealed in the secret German diplomatic records]. Edited by Elek Bolgár. Budapest: Szikra, 1947.

Neubacher, Hermann. *Sonderauftrag Südost, 1940–1945: Bericht eines Fliegenden Diplomaten.* Göttingen, 1957.

Office of Strategic Services. *The Hungarian Coup d'Etat of 15 October 1944.* Washington, 1944.

———. *Political Hesitation in Hungary.* Washington, 1944.

Pačlisanu, Zenobius. *The Hungarian Order in Central Europe.* Bucharest, 1944.

Paikert, Géza. *The Danube Swabians: German Populations in Hungary, Rumania, Yugoslavia, and Hitler's Impact on Their Patterns.* The Hague: Martinus Nijhoff, 1967.

Páloczi-Horváth, György. *In Darkest Hungary.* London: Victor Gollancz, 1944.

[Páloczi-Horváth, György]. *The Undefeated.* Boston: Little, Brown, 1959.

Papen, Franz von. *Memoirs.* New York: E. P. Dutton, 1953.

Parragi, György. *Mauthausen.* Budapest: Keresztes, 1945.

Paulus, Ernst Alexander. *Ich stehe hier auf Befehl!* Frankfurt-am-Main: Bernard & Graefe, 1960.

Pearlman, Moshe. *The Capture and Trial of Adolf Eichmann.* New York: Simon & Schuster, 1963.

Petur, Laszlo. *Egy ország eladó* [A country for sale]. Budapest: Minerva, 1961.

Petyke, Mihály. *A Gestapo foglya voltam* [I was a prisoner of the Gestapo]. Budapest, 1945.

Picker, Henry, ed. *Hitlers Tischgespräche im Führerhauptquartier, 1941–1942.* Stuttgart: Seewald Verlag, 1963.

Racz, Andras. *Les réfugiés polonais en Hongrie pendant la guerre.* Budapest, 1946.

Rahn, Rudolf. *Ruheloses Leben.* Düsseldorf: Diederichs Verlag, 1949.

Ránki, György. *Emlékiratok és valóság Magyarország második világháborús szerepéről* [Memoirs and facts regarding Hungary's role in World War II]. Budapest, 1964.

———. *1944 március 19.* Budapest: Kossuth, 1968.

———, and Berend, Iván. *The Development of Manufacturing Industry in Hungary, 1900–1944.* Budapest: Akadémiai Kiadó, 1960.

Refuge en Hongrie, 1941–1945. Paris: Éditions de la Calanque, 1946 [?].

Reitlinger, Gerald. *The Final Solution.* 2d ed. New York: Thomas Yoseloff, 1968.

———. *The SS: Alibi of a Nation.* Toronto: Heinemann, 1956.

Révész, Mihály. *Fél evszázad* [Half a century]. Budapest, 1947.

Rozsnyói, Ágnes. *A Szálasi puccs* [Szálasi's coup d'état]. Budapest: Kossuth, 1962.

Saly, Dezső. *Szigorúan bizalmas* [Strictly confidential]. Budapest: Anonymøus, 1945.

Scheibert, Horst. *Zwischen Don und Donez.* Stuttgart: Kurt Vowinckel, 1961.

Schmidt, Paul. *Hitler's Interpreter.* New York: Macmillan, 1951.

Seton-Watson, Hugh. *Eastern Europe between the Wars, 1918–1941.* Hamden, Conn.: Archon Books, 1962.

Sipos, Péter. *Imrédy Béla és a Magyar Megujulás Pártja* [Béla Imrédy and the Hungarian Renaissance party]. Budapest: Akadémiai Kiadó, 1970.

Skorzeny, Otto. *Skorzeny's Secret Missions.* New York: E. P. Dutton, 1950.

————. *Skorzeny's Special Missions.* London: Robert Hale, 1957.

Stalin, Joseph. *On the Great Patriotic War of the Soviet Union.* Moscow: Foreign Language Publishing House, 1944.

Sulyok, Dezső. *A magyar tragédia* [The Hungarian tragedy]. Newark, N.J.: Published by the author, 1954.

Szalai, Alexandre. *Jugements du peuple contre les criminels de guerre hongrois.* Budapest: Athenaeum, 1946.

Szűts, László. *Bori garnizon* [Garrison at Bor]. Budapest: Renaissance, 1945.

Tanulmányok a Horthy-korszak államáról és jogáról [Studies on the constitution and law of the state during the Horthy era]. Budapest: Közgazdasági és Jogi Könyvkiadó, 1958.

Telpuchowski. *Die Sowjetische Geschichte des grossen Vaterländischen Krieges.* Frankfurt-am-Main: Bernard & Graefe, 1961.

Tilkovszky, L. *Revizió és nemzetiségpolitika Magyarországon, 1938–1941* [Revisionism and nationalities policy in Hungary]. Budapest: Akadémiai Kiadó, 1967.

Trial of the Major War Criminals before the International Military Tribunals. 42 vols. Nuremberg, 1947–49.

Trials of War Criminals before the Nuernberg Military Tribunals. 15 vols. Washington: Government Printing Office, 1952.

Trevor-Roper, Hugh, ed. *Hitler's Secret Conversations, 1941–1944.* New York: Farrar, Straus, and Young, 1953.

Ullein-Reviczky, Antal. *Guerre allemande, paix russe.* Neuchâtel: Éditions de la Baconnière, 1947.

Vádirat a nácizmus ellen [Charge-sheet against Naziism]. 3 vols. Edited by Ilona Beneschofsky and Elek Karsai. Budapest: A Magyar Izraeliták Országos Képviselete, 1958–67.

Vambéry, Rustem. *The Hungarian Problem.* New York: *The Nation*, 1942.

————. *Hungary To Be or Not To Be.* New York: Frederick Ungar, 1946.

Vigh, Károly, ed. *Kortársak Bajcsy-Zsilinszky Endréről* [Contemporaries write about Endre Bajcsy-Zsilinszky]. Budapest: Magvető, 1971.

Vihar, Béla, ed. *Sárga könyv: adatok a magyar zsidóság háborús szenvedéseiből, 1941–1945* [Yellow book: data on the sufferings of the Hungarian Jewry during the war]. Budapest: Hechaluc, 1945.

Vipler, Vladimir. *Prispevok k dejinam okupovaneho uzemie juhovychodneho Slovenska* [A contribution to the history of the occupied territory of southeastern Slovakia]. Bratislava: Vydavatelstvo politickej literatury, 1963.

Warlimont, Walter. *Inside Hitler's Headquarters, 1939–1945.* Translated by R. H. Barry. London: Weidenfeld and Nicolson, 1964.

Weidlein, Johann. *Geschichte der Ungarndeutschen in Dokumenten, 1930–1950.* Schorndorf, 1959.

————. *Schicksalsjahre der Ungarndeutschen: die ungarische Wendung.* Würzburg: Holzner Verlag, 1957.

Weissberg, Alex. *Advocate for the Dead: The Story of Joël Brand.* London: André Deutsch, 1958.

Weizsäcker, Ernst Heinrich von. *Memoirs.* Translated by John Andrews. Chicago: Henry Régnery, 1951.

A Wilhelmstrasse és Magyarország [Wilhelmstrasse and Hungary]. Edited by György Ránki, Lóránt Tilkovszky, Erwin Pamlényi, and Gyula Juhász. Budapest: Kossuth, 1968.

Wulf, Josef. *Raoul Wallenberg.* Berlin: Colloquium Verlag, 1958.

ARTICLES

Ausch, Sándor. "A háború finanszirozása és az 1938–1944 évi infláció" [Financing the war and the inflation of the years 1938–1944]. *Közgazdasági szemle* [Review of economics], October 1955.

Baksay, Zoltán. "Adatak a Csepeli Vas és Fémművek munkásainak bérviszonyaihoz, 1931–1943" [Data concerning the wages of workers at the Csepel iron and metal works]. *Történelmi szemle* [Historical review] 3 (1960) : 510–24.

Balvanyi, D. A. von. "Der Untergang der 2. ungarischen Armee am Don, 1943." *Allgemeine Schweizerische Militärzeitschrift,* 1960, pp. 1054–67.

Bárány, George, and Ránki, György. "Hungary." In *Native Fascism in the Successor States, 1918–1945,* pp. 65–82. ABC-CLIO, 1971.

Berend, Iván, and Ránki, György. "Die deutsche wirtschaftliche Expansion und das ungarische Wirtschaftsleben zur Zeit des zweiten Weltkrieges." *Acta Historica* 5 (1958) : 313–59.

————. "Hadianyaggyártás Magyarországon a második világháború alatt" [Manufacture of war materials in Hungary during World War II]. *Századok* [Centuries] 91 (1957) : 696–715.

————. "Magyarország ipari színvonala az europai összehasonlitás tükrében a második világháború elött" [The level of Hungarian industry in relation to Europe before World War II]. *Közgazdasági szemle* [Review of economics] 8 (January 1961) : 59–73.

————. "Német gazdasági expanzió és a magyar gyáripar a szovjetellenes háború idején, 1941–1945" [German economic expansion and Hungarian industry at the time of the war against the Soviet Union]. *Századok* [Centuries] 89 (1955) : 634–60.

Bihl, Wolfdieter. "Zur nationalsozialistischen Ungarnpolitik 1940–1941." *Österreichische Osthefte* 11 (1969) : 21–26.

Boldirev, Zyrill. "Zwei Grosse aus der Welt von Gestern." *Osteuropa* 7 (1957) : 187–92.

Borbándi, Gyula. "A zólyomi tárgyalások" [The negotiations at Zvolen]. *Uj látóhatár* [New horizon] 13–21 (1970) : 135–56.

Borsány, Julián, "Kik bombázták 1941 junius 26. -án Kassát?" [Who bombed Kassa on June 26, 1944]. *Uj Pátóhatár* [New horizon] 5–6 (1970): 427–39, 555–66.

Broszat, Martin. "Deutschland-Ungarn-Rumänien: Entwicklung und Grundfaktoren nationalsozialistischer Hegemonial- und Bündnispolitik 1939 bis 1941." *Historische Zeitschrift* 206 (1968) : 45–96.

————. "Die jüdischen Arbeitskompanien in Ungarn." *Gutachten des Instituts für Zeitgeschichte.* Munich, 1958.

Csatári, Dániel. "A magyar-román ellenállási mozgalmak történetéből" [From the history of the Hungarian-Romanian resistance movements]. *Hadtörténelmi közlemények* [Bulletin of military history] 6 (1959) : 3–27.

Csima, János. "Adalékok a Horthy hadsereg szervezetének és háborús tevékenységének tanulmányozásához, 1938–1945" [Contributions to a study of the organization of the Horthy army and its activities in the war]. Publication of the Central Record Office of the Ministry of Defense. Budapest, 1961.

Dálnoki-Veress, Lajos. "Lehetőségek és mulasztások 1944-ben" [Possibilities and omissions in 1947]. *Uj látóhatár* [New horizon] 13–21 (1970) : 157–65.

————. "Miért nem sikerült a 'Kiugrás'? [Why did the "bailing out" not succeed?]. *Uj látóhatár* [New horizon] 13–21 (1970) : 157–65.

Dampierre, Robert, Comte de. "De l'Autriche impériale à la Hongrie nazie." *Revue d'histoire diplomatique* 67 (July–September 1953) : 217–26.

Deák, István. "Hungary." In *The European Right,* edited by Hans Rogger and Eugen Weber. Berkeley and Los Angeles: University of California Press, 1965.

"Eichmann in Hungary: A Documentation." *New Hungarian Quarterly* 2, no. 4 (October–December 1961) : 179–86.

Fenyo, Mario D. "The Allied Axis Armies at Stalingrad." *Military Affairs* 29 (Summer 1965) : 57–72

Fenyo, Mario D. "The Diary of the Chief of the Hungarian General Staff in 1944." *East European Quarterly* 2 (September 1968) : 315–31.

———. "Some Aspects of Hungarian History during the Second World War." *East European Quarterly* 3 (Summer 1969) : 219–28.

Fenyo, Miksa. "C. A. Macartney magyar történelme" [The Hungarian history of C. A. Macartney]. *Látóhatár* [Horizon] 9, no. 3 (1958) : 33–43.

Gesterding, Joachim Schwatlo. "Probleme der Naht." *Wehrwissenschaftlichen Rundschau*, Beiheft 10 (August 1959).

Giannini, Amedeo. "L'ammiraglio Horthy." *Rivista di studi politici internazionali* 24 (1957) : 312–15.

Gindert, Károly. "Az 1. páncélos hadosztály harcai a 2. magyar hadsereg doni hidfőcsatáiban, 1942, július–október" [The operations of the First Armored Division of the Second Hungarian Army at the Don bridgehead, July–October 1942]. *Hadtörténelmi közlemények* [Bulletin of military history] 8 : 457–503.

Gosztonyi, Péter. "A magyar-szovjet fegyverszüneti tárgyalások, 1944 október" [Hungarian-Soviet armistice negotiations]. *Uj látóhatár* [New horizon] 12 (1969) : 401–18.

———. "Lakatos Géza beszámolója miniszter-elnöki tevékenységéről" [The account of Géza Lakatos about his activities as prime minister]. *Uj látóhatár* [New horizon] 5 (1970): 440–58.

———. "Német katonai okmányok október 15 előtörténetéhez" [German military documents regarding the history of the events leading to October 15, 1944]. *Uj látóhatár* [New horizon] 12 (1969) : 515–23.

———. "A voronyezsi tragédia" [The tragedy of Voronezh]. *Látóhatár* [Horizon] 6 (May–June 1963) : 215–37.

Graham, R. "Pius XII's Mercy Saved Thousands of Hungarian Jews from Nazis." *Catholic Messenger* 82 (June 1964).

Hennyey, Gustav. "Hogyan akart Magyarország kiválni a második világháborúból [How Hungary wanted to extricate herself from World War II]. *Uj látóhatár* [New horizon] 8 (1964) : 427–42.

———. "Ungarns Weg aus dem Zweiten Weltkrieg." *Wehrwissenschaftliche Rundschau* 12 (1962) : 687–719.

Hillgruber, Andreas. "Das deutsch-ungarische Verhältnis im letzten Kriegsjahr." *Wehrwissenschaftliche Rundschau* 10 (February 1960) : 78–104.

———. "Deutschland und Ungarn, 1933–1944." *Wehrwissenschaftliche Rundschau* 9 (1959) : 651 ff.

———. "Der Einbau der verbündeten Armeen in die deutsche Ostfront, 1941–1944." *Wehrwissenschaftliche Rundschau* 10 (December 1960) : 659–82.

"Horthy's Secret Correspondence with Hitler." *New Hungarian Quarterly* 4 (July–September 1963) : 174–91.

"Hungary in the Second World War." *New Hungarian Quarterly* 1 (September 1960) : 193–201.

Juhász, Gyula. "Magyarország hadbalépése Nagy-Británnia és az Egyesült Államok ellen" [Hungary's entry into the war against Great Britain and the United States]. *Történelmi szemle* [Historical Review], no. 1 (1965).

Karsai, Elek. "Edmund Veesenmayer's Reports to Hitler on Hungary in 1943." *New Hungarian Quarterly* 5 (Autumn 1964) : 146–53.

———, and Szinai, Miklós. "A Weiss-Manfréd vagyon német kézbe kerülésének története" [The history of the German acquisition of the Manfred Weiss fortune]. *Századok* [Centuries] 95 (1961) : 680–719.

Kosa, John. "Hungarian Society in the Time of the Regency (1920–1944)." *Journal of Central European Affairs* 16 (1956–57) : 253–65.

Kovács, Imre. "Kiugrási kisérletek a második világháborúban" [Attempts at bailing out during World War II]. *Uj látóhatár* [New horizon] 6 (1963) : 93–110, 238–66.

———. "A megszállás anatomiája" [Anatomy of the occupation]. *Uj látóhatár* [New horizon] 12 (1969) : 369–73.

Kun, József. "Magyarország második világháborúba való belépésének katonapolitikai vonatkozásai" [Hungary's entry into World War II and her military policy]. *Hadtörténelmi közlemények* [Bulletin of military history] 9 (1962) : 3–39.

———. "Magyarország német katonai megszállásának előkészítése és lefolyása, 1943 szeptember–1944 március" [The preparation and execution of Hungary's military occupation by Germany]. *Hadtörténelmi közlemények* [Bulletin of military history] 10 (1963) : 37–84.

Kutas, E. R. "Judaism, Zionism, and Anti-Semitism in Hungary." *Journal of Central European Affairs* 8 (January 1949) : 377–89.

Lackó, Miklós. "L'antisoviétisme—l'entrave principale de la lutte contre le nazisme." In *European Resistance Movements, 1939–1945,* pp. 146–56. New York: Macmillan, 1964.

Lengyel, Klára. "Magyarország politikai viszonyai a második világháború időszakában" [Political conditions in Hungary at the time of World War II]. *Pártélet* [Party life] 5 (1960) : 640–74.

Macartney, Carlyle Aylmer. "Hungary's Declaration of War on the U.S.S.R. in 1941." In *Studies in Diplomatic History and Historiography,* edited by A. O. Sarkissian, pp. 153–65. New York: Barnes & Noble, 1961.

———. "Ungarns Weg aus dem Zweiten Weltkrieg." *Vierteljahreshefte für Zeitgeschichte* 14 (1966) : 79–105.

Major, Róbert. "The Churches and the Jews in Hungary." *Continuum* 4 (Autumn 1966) : 371–81.

———. "Hungarian Nazis Abroad." *Wiener Library Bulletin* 4 (September–November 1950) : 34.

Mourin, Maxime. "Les tentatives de décrochage de la Hongrie dans la deuxième guerre mondiale." *Revue de défense nationale,* n.s. 10 (1954) : 65–77.

Mucs, Sándor. "A magyar fegyveres ellenállási mozgalom megszervezése és szerepe Magyarország felszabaditásában" [The organization of the Hungarian armed resistance and its role in the liberation of Hungary]. *Hadtörténelmi közlemények* [Bulletin of military history] 4 (1957) : 32–54.

Nagy-Talavera, Nicholas M. "The Second World War as Mirrored in the Hungarian Fascist Press." *East European Quarterly* 4 (1970) : 179–208.

Ölvedi, Ignác. "Adalékok Horthy és a Lakatos-kormány katonapolitikájához" [Data regarding the military policy of Horthy and the Lakatos cabinet]. *Századok* [Centuries] 103 (1969) : 30–65.

Paikert, Géza. "Hungary's National Minority Policies, 1920–1945." *American Slavic and East European Review* 12 (April 1953) : 201–18.

Pelenyi, John [János Pelényi]. "The Secret Plan for a Hungarian Government in the West at the Outbreak of World War II." *Journal of Modern History* 26 (June 1964) : 170–77.

Pethö, Tibor. "Contradictory Trends in Policies of the Horthy Era." *New Hungarian Quarterly* 4 (1963) : 115–31.

Pintér, István. "Adatok a magyar nemzeti felkelés felszabaditó bizottságának történetéhez" [Contribution to the history of the liberation committee of the Hungarian national uprising]. *Hadtörténelmi közlemények* [Bulletin of Military history] 8 (1961) : 431–56.

———. "A Kállay kormány 'hintapolitikája' és az anti-fasiszta ellenállási mozgalom" [The "pendulum policy" of the Kállay ministry and the anti-Fascist resistance movement]. *Történelmi szemle* [Historical review] 5 (1962) : 470–96.

———. "A magyar ellenállás és 1944 Október 15-e" [Hungarian resistance and October 15, 1944]. *Századok* [Centuries] 104 (1970) : 35–69.

Pogány, András. "What Really Happened on October Fifteenth, 1944, at the First Corps Headquarters in Budapest?" *Hungarian Quarterly* 5 (1965) : 98–112.

Puskás, A. I. "Adatok Horthy-Magyarország külpolitikájához a második világháború éveiben" [Data pertaining to the foreign policy of Horthy-Hungary during World War II]. *Századok* [Centuries] 95 (1961).

Ránki, György. "A német-magyar viszony az utolsó háborús évben és az európai biztonság [German-Hungarian relations in the last year of the war and European security]. *Történelmi szemle* [Historical review] 4 (1961) : 373–77.

———. "L'occupation de la Hongrie par les allemands." *Revue de la deuxième guerre mondiale,* pp. 37–52.

————, and Berend, Iván. "The German Occupation of Hungary." *Acta Historica* 11 (1965) : 261–83.

————. "Hadianyaggyártás Magyarországon a második világháború alatt" [The manufacture of war materials in Hungary during World War II]. *Századok* [Centuries] 91 (1957) : 696–715.

————. "Magyarország belépése a második világháborúba" [Hungary's entry into World War II]. *Hadtörténelmi közlemények* [Bulletin of military history] 6 (1959) : 28–48.

————. "Das ungarische Wirtschaftsleben im Dienste der deutschen Kriegswirtschaft zur Zeit des zweiten Weltkrieges." In *Probleme der Geschichte des zweiten Weltkrieges,* pp. 238–59. Berlin: Akademie Verlag, 1958.

Rozsnyói, Ágnes. "1944 október 15. A Szálasi-puccs története" [History of the Szálasi coup d'état]. *Századok* [Centuries] 93 (1959) : 373–403, 871–92.

————. "October Fifteenth, 1944." *Acta Historica* 8 (1961) : 57–105.

Sabille, Jacques. "La tragique épopée de Raoul Wallenberg, héros suédois de la dernière guerre." *Le Figaro littéraire,* September 22, 1951.

St. Iványi, Alexander. "Our Man of Destiny in 1944." *Hungarian Digest* (April–June 1966), pp. 32–36.

Sallai, Elemer. "Die Befreiungskämpfe um Budapest." *Internationale Hefte der Widerstandsbewegung* 3 (1961) : 148–57.

Somogyi, Joseph de. "The Historical Development of the Danubian Problem to the Present." *Journal of Central European Affairs* 7 (April 1948) : 45–57.

Stern, Leo. "A második világháborúval foglalkozó reakciós történetirás föbb irányzatai" [The main trends of reactionary historical writing on World War II]. *Századok* [Centuries] 92 (1958) : 202–21

Thomas, Pierre. "Coup d'oeil sur la Hongrie en guerre." *Le mois suisse* 5 (March 1943) : 52–61.

Tilkovszky, L. "Volksdeutsche Bewegung und ungarische Nationalitäten-politik (1938–1941)." *Acta Historica* 12 : 59–110, 319–45.

Tóth, Sándor. "A Horthy-hadsereg helyzete a Szovjetunió elleni háborúba lépés idején" [The condition of the Horthy army at the time of the entry into the war against the Soviet Union]. *Hadtörténelmi közlemé-nyek* [Bulletin of military history] 8 (1961) : 500–43.

"Von der Teilnahme der Ungarn am europäischen Widerstandskampf." *Internationale Heft der Widerstandsbewegung* 2 (1960) : 94–103.

Weidlein, Johann. "Ungarns Frontwechsel im Kriege." *Zeitschrift für Geopolitik* 25 (1954) : 412–21.

Zsigmond, László. "Két dátum; Magyarország hadüzenetének (1941 június 27) és németek által való megszállásának (1944 március 19) előzmé-nyeihez" [Two dates; the circumstances of Hungary's declaration of war

on June 27, 1941, and of her occupation by the Germans on March 19,
1944]. *Történelmi szemle* [Historical review] 1 (1958) : 192–214.

————. "La politique extérieure de la Hongrie de 1933 à 1939." *Revue
d'histoire de la deuxième guerre mondiale* 62 (April 1966) : 8–21.

INDEX